HENRY ADAMS IN LOVE

The more you please others,
the more you delight me.

—Henry Adams to
Elizabeth Cameron, 1891

Elizabeth Cameron
portrait by Anders Zorn

HENRY ADAMS IN LOVE

The Pursuit of Elizabeth Sherman Cameron

Arline Boucher Tehan

UNIVERSE BOOKS
New York

Published in the United States of America in 1983
by Universe Books
381 Park Avenue South, New York, N.Y. 10016

83 84 85 86 87 / 10 9 8 7 6 5 4 3 2 1

Printed in the United States of America

Library of Congress Cataloging in Publication Data

Tehan, Arline Boucher.
    Henry Adams in love.

    Bibliography: p.
    Includes index.
    1. Cameron, Elizabeth, 1857-1944. 2. Adams, Henry,
1838-1918. 3. United States—Biography. 4. Historians
—United States—Biography. I. Title.
CT275.C268T43   1983   973'.072024 [B]   83-4991
ISBN 0-87663-427-7

FOR JOHN   IN MEMORIAM

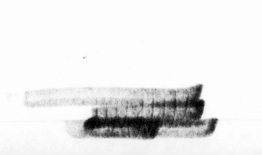

Contents

Illustrations

The author is grateful to the following persons and institutions for their courtesy in permitting the reproduction of illustrations in this book:

AAH — the late Abigail Adams Homans, Boston, Mass.

AJM — Arthur J. McDowell, Bethesda, Md.

CAC — City Art Commission, New York, N.Y.

ESH — Elizabeth Sherman Hughes, Cleveland, Ohio

HHA — Harvard Historical Archives, Cambridge, Mass.

JR — Julia Reber, Tyringham, Mass.

LC — The Library of Congress, Washington, D.C.

NMAA— National Museum of American Art, Smithsonian Institution, Washington, D.C.

NPS — National Park Service, Washington, D.C.

NYPL — Picture Collection, New York Public Library, New York, N.Y.

SH — Sean Haldane

SHO — Senate Historical Office, U.S. Senate, Washington, D.C.

SR — the late Samuel Reber, Princeton, N.J.

HENRY
ADAMS
IN LOVE

1

"My Reckless Wasted Life"

Under a steady downpour of lukewarm rain on an early December twilight in 1915, the streets of Paris were nearly deserted, the lights dimmed because of the danger of German bombing. It was almost a year and a half since the Great War had begun, and although the Kaiser's armies had not succeeded in taking Paris, the city's inhabitants—mostly women, old men, and children—were living under martial law. Most of the "fluffy, fuzzy people," in the words of Edith Wharton, had left the capital for the relative safety of the French Riviera. The war was expanding. In May, Italy had joined the Allies, while in October, Bulgaria had entered on the side of the Central Powers, overrunning the neighboring Balkan nation of Serbia.

A year earlier, Elizabeth Sherman Cameron had already been plagued by the horror of war. "What does it all mean?" she had written to her niece. "Is there some force in nature which prompts us at intervals to kill each other? I sometimes wonder if in this planetary system this little globe is the lunatic asylum?"

When the war came, Mrs. Cameron had closed her salon on the avenue du Bois de Boulogne (now avenue Foch), which is an easy walk from the place des Etats-Unis. On and off for more than a decade, with Henry Adams she had presided over her salon, that peculiarly French institution devoted to the art of conversation, which welcomed such literary and artistic lions as Henry James, Edith Wharton, John La Farge, and Auguste Rodin.

The people now thronging into Paris were refugees from the French countryside and from devastated Belgium—a ragged army of the dispossessed, stumbling on foot, jolting along in carts, dazed and fearful and hungry, seeking refuge in the French capital which most of them had never seen. In Paris, there were shops, such as the Grocery Depôt run by Elizabeth Cameron, that dispensed food stamps for refugees—*bons*, or tickets, allowing them a 50% saving on whatever food was still available. The newest contingent of refugees were old people and half-starved children fleeing occupied Serbia. Shepherded by a Russian mission of Red Cross nurses, they had made the terrible journey on foot, struggling for eleven days through snow-covered mountain passes, clad only in rags, many of them barefoot. In one group, a boy of five clung numbly to the hand of his mother as she struggled along. Since their flight had begun, the child had not spoken a word but had stared before him with vacant eyes.

These were the people who with their pitiful stories came into Mrs. Cameron's shop, the Grocery Depôt on the rue Pierre-Charon between the Champs-Elysees and the Seine. They were the people she described that winter in letters "after nine hours daily of hearing such tales of misery and seeing such livid faces." The elegant hostess of the Bois de Boulogne had now become "just Mrs. Cameron, an indefatigable war worker and an invaluable friend to the crowd of poor refugees who have made her acquaintance across the little table in the Grocery Depôt. There are generally plenty of children clustering like flies around the table where she sits, doing her accounts or knitting for the soldiers, with a tin of sweets beside her or perhaps a toy or two displayed in the window." Although neither the condition of the city nor the long, busy days allowed Elizabeth Cameron much attention to her surroundings, she could not sacrifice an effort on behalf of taste. "I have found the prettiest little shop," she wrote to her niece Cecilia Reber. "I don't like the French way of having dirt around. So I made it all green and white."

Since September 1914, she had worked with the rescue effort called Le Foyer aux Réfugiés, later known as the American Hostels. Edith Wharton had summoned her, and then had gone, exhausted, to the south of France. "I am doing Edith's work—badly—and my own as well," Mrs. Cameron wrote to Henry Adams. From her vacation home at Hyères, on the southern coast, Edith Wharton sent a grateful note from her rest-curing: "If it weren't for you I shouldn't have been able to begin my book" (apparently the eventual bestseller *Glimpses of the Moon*). Lizzie Cameron, besides doing her refugee work, had made all the arrangements for Mrs. Wharton's trip back to Hyères. Now she was persuading reluctant French officials to find empty buildings in which to house her refugees, convincing wholesale food dealers to give her a price on scarce foods, and extracting money and clothes from her rich American friends.

At the age of 58, Lizzie Cameron carried herself with the assurance of a woman who was still beautiful. Tall and graceful, with an infallible sense of style, she wore her dark hair piled high above a smooth forehead. Her features were clear-cut, her eyes blue or violet depending on the light. She was still mistress of the art of pleasing men—still, in the words of an envious British peeress, "a dangerously fascinating woman." Although she had never worked a day in her life, whether as a girl in Cleveland, a bride in Washington, or a mother educating her daughter in Europe, she had known what it meant to take care of someone, and she was versed in a kind of adroit diplomacy that produced results. What was new was her participation in the meanness of life and at the same time the divesting herself temporarily of nonessential matters. At times she loved it all. "As for Paris," she wrote to her niece, "I have never found it so agreeable. There is no social life—everybody works too hard." Later she added, "Nobody dresses, everybody is shabby and nobody cares. There are so few foreigners it is really a French town at last."

La Dona, as her intimates called her (besides a compliment, a pun on her husband's given name), had begun to make France virtually her home. She was separated from her husband, former Senator James Donald Cameron of Pennsylvania, 24 years her senior, who had left the U.S. Senate in 1897. Facing certain defeat, he had turned his efforts to railroads, mining ventures, and other enterprises that had already been occupying more time than a marriage and a political career could bear. La Dona, deprived of Washington society, had taken her only daughter, Martha, who was born in 1886, to Europe to acquire French and German and a familiarity with international society. The amount of time Mrs. Cameron spent on the Continent, apart from her husband, gradually lengthened; what had originally been a marriage of convenience was now a marriage in name only.

Before the turn of the century, Mrs. Cameron had belonged among the privileged group of traveling Americans (who would today be called the Beautiful People) who were frequently described in the newspapers, especially the Paris *Herald,* as spending part of every year in the French capital. One of these distinguished expatriates, "Pussy" Wharton, had admitted "Dearest Lizzie" into what Kenneth Clark later called her "social fortress of which the doors were occasionally opened for a second to admit newcomers." Lizzie's own fortress, now quiet, was an elegant three-story duplex apartment at 6 square du Bois de Boulogne, a tiny mews just off the avenue du Bois which was approached by a little gravel path bordered with ivy. Here she lived with one servant. The apartment had a large drawing room and a library with bookshelves reaching to the ceiling. The walls were covered with soft gray, and the chairs, which Henry Adams had helped her select, were Louis XV *fauteuils* in walnut, upholstered in faded silk damask.

In the letter that she wrote to Henry Adams on the evening of 7 December 1915, she described her return from the Grocery Depôt at six o'clock amid a downpour that had lasted for days. She had left for home on foot, having dismissed her carriage as an austerity measure. Although she complained, "I lose so much time walking," she chose this over the use of a horse cab, sometimes giving the money thus saved to her refugees. Edith Wharton, a month earlier, had chided her for her generosity—in this case, a gift of coal. "But you mustn't give to all my charities. *I* don't." On this evening, Lizzie clung to a large umbrella, which offered little protection against the driving rain, and she came in soaked to her cold house. (Coal cost $30 a ton, when it could be obtained, and even firewood had to be used sparingly.) No one was at home to greet her. Her daughter Martha, now 29, lived with her husband Ronald Lindsay, a junior officer in the British Foreign Service whose present tour of duty was in a place farther away than wretched Serbia—and given the precarious health of Martha Lindsay, only slightly safer: Cairo, Egypt.

Lizzie's maid was not there; she had left the mail on the escritoire as she always did. In the mail was something unusual—a letter from America. With German submarines operating unpredictably in the Atlantic, letters from home were sporadic, but today one had arrived. Elizabeth Cameron recognized the handwriting on the envelope as that of Henry Adams, from whom she had not heard since July.

The letter was dated Washington, 10 November. Opening it, she paused. "For a moment I could not read for the tears that would well up. A letter from you! In your own inimitable handwriting. . . . As a treasure it is almost too great. I must keep it in a bank vault." The familiar rounded script, which for some 30 years had carried his messages to her, was wavering a little; Adams, now 77, had suffered a stroke in 1912. But the manner of expression was characteristic. "Are you not surprised to see what looks like me?" he asked. "Really it is not exactly I, and you need not suppose I am writing news. As you know, the game came to its end for me some four years ago, and I have not moved a finger since, nor do I mean to begin again. Your letters still entertain and delight me, but I have nothing to say in reply." In the room in which she was reading, she and Adams had sat some 10 years before, in the Louis Quinze chairs before the fireplace. Then he had had much to say. He came in, frequently, to read aloud from his manuscript of *Mont-Saint-Michel and Chartres,* the book about medieval France that he addressed specifically to young women rather than to fellow historians. That had been followed almost immediately by a book about himself, or at least parts of himself, *The Education of Henry Adams.* Both books were issued privately, each with 100 copies for friends.

"He used to bring his chapters on *Mt-St-Michel* and *The Education* to me as they were finished," Mrs. Cameron later recalled. "When I asked him why he wrote them since he did not mean to publish them, he told me it was his way of mastering a subject. He was not sure of it until he wrote it."

She was in her forties when he read them to her, in the years from 1902 to 1906. In his *Education,* Adams, writing of himself in the third person, discussed the following proposition: "Adams owed more to the American woman than to all the American men he ever heard of." Although in his book he was characteristically silent on what he owed to Elizabeth Cameron, nevertheless in his letters and in his actions Adams acknowledged frequently the gift of her presence in times of severe deprivation and transition. When, in 1885, his wife, Marian, had committed suicide in Washington, Elizabeth Cameron was not only nearby on Lafayette Square but she was the one person sufficiently intimate with both the Adamses to penetrate his grief and minister to him with both tact and affection. When in November 1891 he ended his two-year pilgrimage around the world—which was both a search and a flight—she was in Paris to meet him. When his closest friend, Secretary of State John Hay, died in 1905, she pledged to take his place as best she could. "I cannot be what he was to you, but I can be less cranky than I am." Indeed, she even replaced his family. "My family never saw the *Chartres* or heard of La Vierge. I honestly think they never read a word of me either." When lurid international crises—the brush fires before the conflagration of the Great War—were observed by Adams on all horizons, it was to Mrs. Cameron that he wrote his most agonizing letters with their prophecies of the destruction of civilization. When he told her "Now I write *d'outre tombe*" (recalling the title of the memoirs of Count François René de Chateaubriand), which allowed him to continue his elaborate pose of leading a posthumous existence, it was Lizzie Cameron who challenged him: "You are *not* dead, but a living presence by my side."

On 7 December 1915, as she read on, Lizzie realized that this latest letter, unlike the hundreds of others he had written to her, had a special urgency. Her faithful "tame cat" (as he liked to call himself) was concerned about how Americans of the future would remember his Washington, not only its politics in all its theatricality and futile frenzy, but the few distinguished and colorful individuals who created for themselves lives of style amid the circus. She remembered the salon in Lafayette Square that Adams and his wife had established in the late 1870s. It had appeared in due time—not disguised to those who knew it—in Henry James's tale "Pandora." Mrs. Cameron had known all the people of that salon in the early 1880s before Marian Adams's suicide: Clarence King, geologist and raconteur; architect Henry Hobson Richardson, huge in physique and reputation, who was chosen by Adams to build his new house; artist John La Farge, for whom Adams openly expressed his admiration in *The Education*. But mainly there had been the members of the acknowledged ruling class whom Lizzie had known for decades: John Hay and his wife, Clara, from her own home city of Cleveland; Senator Henry Cabot Lodge, one of Adams's graduate students at Harvard, and his wife, Anna; President Theodore Roosevelt and his second wife, Edith.

To establish his own idiosyncratic version of the record, and to forestall biographers, whom he described as "murderers," Adams had written his *Education*. And just published in October were two volumes of the life and letters of John Hay, by William Roscoe Thayer. But neither of these books would preserve the story of Lafayette Square as he and Lizzie Cameron had known it—each from a different but complementary perspective. Of Thayer's efforts Adams seemed to approve, but only as a preview of a promising motion picture. He told Lizzie, "It does not matter whether you like it or not, as long as it helps to build the legend of our Square and to open the road to more and better." His appeal to Lizzie as a kind of master film-maker was unmistakable.

"You know that for ten years I have tried to drape myself and my friends neatly for their final tableau before the audience that is to take stalls in the movie-show when we go. [This was the year of the film *Birth of a Nation*.] The only chance now rests with you. As far as I know, you are the only letter-writer and letter-receiver living and if you have kept your letters, you must have tons which you can select to print together with your own. I have all your letters for thirty years in a box. You can easily choose volumes of them to be copied."

In his old teasing tone he continued. "Luckily you have never believed me or minded my works and had best not do so now for I am certainly an idiot whereas you may have happened once or twice in 36 years to have had traces of sense. Not that I remember, but then my memory is gone. . . . Of course, if you can't do it, say no more. You need not publish or print them unless you like. Just lock them up and name a literary executor."

Then Adams held up before her five people and a statue to symbolize the civilized society and the brief, bright hope of taste and creativity that they had shared during the rebirth of the nation in the Washington of his era. The statue was the hooded figure that Adams had erected in bronze over his wife's grave in Rock Creek Cemetery. Designed by his old friend Augustus Saint-Gaudens in a setting by Stanford White, it remains perhaps the most powerful work by America's finest sculptor of his time. (While the sculptor was working on it, Adams set sail for the South Seas, and at his request, Lizzie had kept watch, sending him news of it.) The five distinctive individuals were Marian "Clover" Adams and Henry Adams, John Hay, Anna Cabot Lodge, and Elizabeth Cameron. "I would like to feel you there," Adams wrote, "with Clover and me, and Nannie and Hay, till the Saint-Gaudens figure is forgotten or runs away." Wistfully, he added, "It is all I have left."

This plea for the youngest of the participants to serve now as publicist and perpetuator could not fail to move La Dona. For Henry Adams even to mention his dead wife was extraordinary. In her cold room, in the midst of a war that seemed likely to destroy Paris and the whole country that had so often been their refuge together, she replied:

> What you suggest has been in my mind for a long time. When Martha married and our home in Washington was lost, I destroyed my journals, gave [my nephew] Sherman Miles all my letters which I looked on as autographs and generally cleared out the house. But I kept every scrap you have ever written me, all John Hay's letters, all Springy's [those from Cecil Spring-Rice, the British diplomat] and certain others which seemed to touch us nearly. They are all in a chest in Stepleton. If the time ever comes when you can safely send me what papers you have, send them to Stepleton. I always meant some day to put them in some kind of sequence and order, but I was always staggered by the immensity of the work. I am now. I have no knowledge of metier, no literary training, no starting point even.

Lizzie was understandably staggered by the enormity of the task. There were, by actual count later, just over nine hundred letters from Adams alone. These and her responses documented life not only in Washington but literally around the globe. Although the Lafayette Square quintet lived in Washington, the film, through the far-flung scope of Adams's letters, would have scenes from all over Europe—Taormina, Trondheim, the Scottish Highlands—to say nothing of Cuba, Hawaii, Samoa, and the striking details of daily life in primitive Tahiti.

Emerging from the intact sequence of these letters is the extraordinary romance of Henry Adams and Elizabeth Cameron. No less a connoisseur of subtle human alliances than Henry James had described it, 14 years earlier, as "one of the longest and oddest American *liaisons* I've ever known. Women have been hanged for less—and yet men have been, too, I judge, rewarded with more." The first person eventually to see the letters, other than the two principals, would be a historian, Worthington Chauncey Ford, who lacked Henry James's vantage point of direct observer. Yet Ford, too, saw in them something extraordinary—nothing less than a drama of salvation.

> One cannot read the letters that passed between you [he wrote to Mrs. Cameron] without realizing that you were his preserver. With a leaning toward introspection that becomes dangerous when carried too far, he could easily have become intolerable, strong and self-centered as he was. But from the first you gave him something to think of outside himself and a sentence or a word in his letters shows how deep the feeling was. He was fortunate in this and so I can pay you the highest tribute a man can, without a trace of flattery. Having said so much, perhaps too much, I pass on. The *Education* needed a supplement not by other hands but by his own. . .the letters supply it.

In *The Education of Henry Adams,* the author sees America, as well as himself, as a failure. "The American man is a failure! You are all failures!" But especially on the failure of the American woman, whom he considered superior to the man, he was eloquent. "The cleverer the woman, the less she denied the failure. . . . She had even failed to hold the family together, and her children ran away like chickens with their first feathers; the family was extinct like chivalry." She failed to create, in the New World, a "new society" to replace Church or State. "She might have her own way, without restraint or limit, but she knew not what to do with herself when free. At 40 her task was over, and she was left with no stage except that of her old duties or of Washington society. . . "

Elizabeth Cameron had been just 40 when her husband left Washington, convinced that he could not be reelected to the Senate. With her "stage" gone and a half-grown daughter as her principal responsibility, she was far from free.

In the letter that she wrote to Adams on the rainy December evening in Paris, she seems to picture herself as the failed American woman of whom Adams had written:

> Do you remember the little dedication that John La Farge wrote in his letters from Japan? How like the little stream, through the meadow, giving life and color to the earth, was the influence of his Japanese friend [Okakura] coloring and irrigating every impression.
>
> I think of my reckless wasted life, with you as the only redeeming thing running through it, always giving me the sustaining power to keep going, always keeping me from withering up. Whatever I have or am is due to you, to that never-failing, never-ending, never-impatient nor exhausted friendship. I wish I were more credit to you.

Elizabeth Cameron wrote no autobiography or memoirs, and she destroyed her journal. She never edited the Lafayette Square letters. But in this letter, with its remarkably candid self-evaluation, she expressed, perhaps for the first time, her sense of the wasted years. At the age of 58, she forced herself to look back, dismayed at the years of restless wandering about the Continent, with no fixed center—except for "the sustaining power to keep going" that she had found in Adams's devotion. Now that for the first time in her life she was engaged in a needed and useful work, she recognized the self-indulgence of her fragmented life and all the lost opportunities that her talents and social position should have allowed. Despite the episodic excitement she had derived from the discreet but unmistakable adulation of her many admirers, she realized how little they weighed against the terrible lack of love that her life reflected—except for that one "never-failing friendship" which Henry Adams had offered and which had kept her from "withering up." In reviewing his "friendship" that had sustained her, she may have finally appreciated the treasure that he had patiently yet obliquely offered her and that she had so recklessly wasted.

It is a moving letter, and in expressing her sense of failure as an American woman, that failure which Adams had prefigured in his *Education,* she is perhaps too harsh in her judgment. According to Worthington Ford, Mrs. Cameron had been the savior of Henry Adams—and that was no mean feat. For Adams, the intellectually vain, self-pitying, tormented historian, was a great man certainly, but he was also a permanently flawed character. And she must have known that he was in love with her and that, had she wished it, she could have led him into a second marriage. But perhaps what she *had* offered him during these years—her presence, her sympathy, her concern— was ultimately more valuable to him than if she had made that total gift of self which is the essence of marriage. There was the likelihood of her doing him lasting harm if she had divorced her husband to marry Adams. For despite her capacity to inspire love, La Dona had shown herself unable or unwilling to make the kind of self-surrender that would have been necessary to assuage the tortured, self-regarding quality of Adams's love. The delightfully American Mrs. Cameron was very French in her handling of the role of *femme fatale*—as Elisina Tyler would observe of Lizzie, "Although she liked to flirt and tease, to kiss and cajole, she never went all the way." Accordingly, this emotional restraint gave her a self-mastery in matters of the heart that the more vulnerable Henry Adams lacked. It also enabled her to analyze their situation without illusion and to foresee the probable consequences of any lasting union. She cared enough for Henry Adams to spare him the devastation of a marriage that might have been even more tragic than his first.

And like a grateful student addressing a beloved teacher, she was sincere when she wrote, "Whatever I have or am is due to you . . . I wish I were more credit to you."

Yet in using the words "reckless" and "wasted," she may also have been recalling that fateful decision from which so much of this wasted loss derived—the decision, which was made for her nearly 40 years before, and which she had accepted with reluctance. It concerned her marriage, a marriage that had seemed to those proposing it a shrewd and promising alliance between two powerful families, a marriage in which she safeguarded herself by requiring a formal financial as well as legal contract. The only thing reckless was the absence of love. The year was 1878.

2

The Arranged Marriage

Washington in the winter of 1877-78 was gradually pulling itself out of the mud, literally and figuratively. The open sewers of Tiber Creek had been covered over, and new asphalt paving replaced the old wooden sidewalks, which in wet weather squelched with mud. In this capital city of 150,000 people, of whom one-third were freed slaves, the political climate was mild after turbulence. The new "reform" president, Rutherford B. Hayes, who had squeezed into the White House by one electoral vote, had replaced Ulysses S. Grant and his corrupt administration. Although Hayes's opponents mocked him as "His Accidency" or "His Fraudulency," one of his staunchest admirers was Oliver Wendell Holmes, Jr., who referred to him as "His Honesty." In an attempt to honor his campaign promises, Hayes was reforming the civil service and dismantling the spoils system, a move that offered the nation a season of hope.

Henry Adams, who had recently moved to Washington, explaining, "I gravitate to a capital by a primary law of nature," was regarding the social and political scene with uncharacteristic optimism. "One of these days," he told his British friend Charles Milnes Gaskell, "this will be a very great city if nothing happens to it. Even now it is a beautiful one and its situation is superb. As I belong to the class of people who have great faith in this country and who believe that in another century it will be saying the last word of civilization, I enjoy the expectation of the coming day."

For Henry Adams at the age of 40, hard at work on his biography of the statesman Albert Gallatin and seemingly happy in his marriage, it was indeed a season of expectation. The descendant of two presidents, he lived on Lafayette Square across from the White House, his ancestral home. He was the uxorious husband of lively Marian Hooper of Boston who adored him— "as well she might," declared Henry's brother Charles Francis Adams, "for his patience and gentleness seemed inexhaustible." Everyone called her Clover, and their old friend Henry James later said of Adams, "He was so proud of her that he let her shine as he sat back and enjoyed listening to what she said and what others let her say." Adams was absorbed in his career as historian and biographer, although he deplored the passage of time, complaining, "Life is slipping away so fast and I grudge every hour which does not show progress in my work."

The aristocratic historian, who remembered his grandfather John Quincy Adams from his childhood and who had heard the family legends about his great-grandfather John Adams, had watched grimly as the office of the presidency declined under Grant. In 1870, he had made the dire prediction, "In 100 years the United States will be more corrupt than Rome under Caligula or the Church under Leo X." Adams would continue his scathing criticism of society in general and government in particular for the next 40 years, successfully silencing most of his hearers because they were seldom remotely capable of answering him.

Adams was short, trim, and going bald. He dressed fastidiously, spoke with a slight British accent, and carried himself with the erect dignity of his grandfather John Quincy. Although he was fundamentally reserved, he was nevertheless fascinated by the intricacies of human behavior. One observer who had watched him for a long time remarked, "His eyes took in everything in a flash, usually watching without being caught. Yet all his guest could see was a profile." Now after a brief stint as an assistant professor of medieval history at Harvard College, his alma mater, he had returned to Washington, his natural home, where he could follow the unfolding of the political comedy with ironic detachment but without feeling the need to play a role in it himself.

Clover Adams was a sprightly and caustic New Englander whose lineage, including the Hooper and Sturgis families, was as old as his own. Clover held strong views on every subject, especially on who should be received in their drawing room on Lafayette Square. In the 1870s and 1880s, Washington society was divided between the Cave Dwellers—those 80 or so families who could trace their residence in the capital back for at least two generations— and the New-comers—the ever-shifting mob of office-holders and politicians who arrived, shone briefly, and departed. Married to an Adams, who was indisputably a Cave Dweller, Clover could dictate her guest list as she pleased, according to her prejudices. She could ignore whom she chose, declining most invitations, and calling this "a process like picking off burrs." She was pleased to note, however, that admission to her home was eagerly sought.

Not far from the Adams residence was the four-story brick home of John Sherman, the secretary of the treasury in Hayes's cabinet. Just arrived for a visit with her Uncle John was radiant young Elizabeth Sherman of Cleveland, the daughter of his brother Charles, a United States judge for the District Court of Northern Ohio. This was Lizzie Sherman's last unmarried winter. A match had been arranged by her uncle "Long John" Sherman, and with his wife Cecilia he had summoned her to the house at 1323 K Street. She arrived early in January 1878, followed by her friend Julia Parsons, whose father was the publisher of the Cleveland *Herald*. Although the two girls appeared bent on romantic conquest, the capital's insiders whispered that Lizzie's fate was already sealed. During her visit to Washington the previous winter, a husband had been selected for her. To the Sherman household the two young ladies from Cleveland were warmly welcomed by Lizzie's quiet, diffident Uncle John and her Aunt Cecilia. Secretary Sherman had the clear-cut features and penetrating blue eyes that persist today among Sherman descendants. He tended, the caustic Clover Adams once remarked, "to swallow his sentences, perhaps fearing no one else will." His stately wife dressed severely, wearing her tawny hair drawn back and gathered in a Greek coil without ornament. The couple had one adopted daughter, Mamie, aged nine.

The Washington *Critic* greeted the girls' arrival with redundant rapture. "Mrs. Sherman has beautified her home this winter with two unusually beautiful girls from Cleveland." The paper described Julia "as fresh and sweet as a June rosebud." Not overlooking Lizzie, her uncle General William Tecumseh Sherman, who had been impatiently awaiting her arrival, wrote to his wife, "Lizzie is here and she is as fresh and beautiful as ever." Despite the newspaper rave, Julia Parsons was quite plain. But she noted without envy that her friend Elizabeth became an immediate favorite. "The men all rave about her."

Small wonder. For Lizzie, who had just turned 20 in November 1877, was tall and slender and had an enchanting smile. She also had a virginal quality that proved irresistible to men, and she carried herself with the mysterious authority of beauty. Occasionally, when her animated face was in repose, a look of sadness crossed it which seemed inappropriate in one so young and lovely. Her mother had always insisted that Lizzie's oldest sister Mary, now married to Colonel Nelson Miles, was the family beauty and that Lizzie was merely pretty. Yet "pretty" was inadequate to describe her. A period photograph shows her with lifted head and searching gaze under level brows. She has the sloping shoulders that Victorians regarded as a mark of beauty and a hint of voluptuous curves beneath the confining costume of the day. She wears a sheathlike bodice, which is lengthened to a point in front, lying close to the hips with the fullness gathered to the back and flowing into a short train. Her cheeks are girlishly round, her nose is short and straight, and her coiffure is fashionably coquettish. A closer scrutiny of the photo reveals a marked firmness of chin. Poised and ambitious, she knows her own mind and is aware of her power over men.

Both Sherman uncles—John the politician and Cump the four-star general—were relieved that Lizzie had actually arrived in Washington. Their plans for her future required her presence, and recent reports from Cleveland had not been reassuring. For Lizzie, according to her mother's letters, had fallen deeply in love at 19 with a man whom her family considered wholly unsuitable—Joseph Russell, a handsome young lawyer from New York. Tremulously, Lizzie had confided in her oldest brother Henry, who was also a lawyer. She felt closer to him than to her father, the studious but ineffectual Judge Sherman, who was by now 66, or to her mother, the melancholy but ambitious Eliza Williams Sherman. To her dismay, Lizzie learned that her family were united in opposition to Joe. Rumor had reached them that he was a heavy drinker, and, without confirming this, they concluded that he would never amount to anything. Besides, his family connections did not impress Mrs. Sherman. Despite Lizzie's infatuation, family opposition was too strong. In vain she struggled against the objections of her mother and her brother and her ailing father's silent acquiescence. Henry Sherman, prodded by his mother, urged Lizzie to reject Joe Russell, dwelling on the horrors of his alleged drinking. Mrs. Sherman pointed out that Lizzie could "do better" and reminded her that her sister Mary was married to a distinguished Army colonel who was on his way to becoming a general. Eventually Lizzie succumbed and like a dutiful Victorian daughter sent her suitor away.

This abortive love affair would have disastrous consequences for her future. At 19 the enchantment of first love was overwhelming. To deny it, under family pressure, and to agree to a pragmatic marriage in which love was not a consideration, had the effect of chilling the spontaneity of her affections and of introducing an element of calculation into any love affairs she might engage in. At the same time, she could not forget her early love for Joe. It rankled like a broken promise, as her nephew Hal would discover years later. As a teen-ager, in the presence of his Aunt Lizzie and his mother, Hal would mention Joe Russell's name and watch his aunt lose her self-possession and, "white and trembling, she seemed about to faint." Ironically, her family's estimate of Joe Russell proved wrong, for he never became a drunkard but did have a successful law practice and enjoyed a comfortable marriage.

Like that of many of her contemporaries, Lizzie's future was determined by her family. And the family into which she was born in Mansfield, Ohio, on 10 November 1857 was a distinguished one. Her father, Judge Charles Taylor Sherman, was the fourth in a line of New England jurists. His father, grandfather, and great-grandfather had all been respected lawyers. When Charles Taylor Sherman was an infant, his father Charles Robert Sherman and his mother Mary Hoyt Sherman decided to move from Norwalk, Connecticut, to Ohio to settle in the "firelands" of the Western Reserve which the state of Connecticut had awarded to families whose lands had been pillaged by Benedict Arnold during the American Revolution. In 1811, the young parents set out on horseback, the mother holding her infant wrapped in a shawl and resting on a pillow in front of her saddle, journeying the 640 miles to Lancaster, Ohio. Charles Robert Sherman set up a law practice and became a justice of the Ohio Supreme Court as well as the father of thirteen sons and one daughter. When he died at age 41, his son Charles Taylor Sherman was only 18 and a sophomore at Ohio University in Athens. Aided by a friend of his father's, he was enabled to finish college. He read law in Dayton and was admitted to the Ohio bar at age 22. Moving to Mansfield, he soon began to help his widowed mother and her enormous family, and he did not marry until he was 30. In 1867, President Andrew Johnson appointed him a judge of the United States District Court of Northern Ohio. With his family he moved to Cleveland when Lizzie, his youngest child, was 10 years old.

Eliza Jane Williams Sherman, who was 11 years younger than her husband, was born in Dayton, Ohio. Her family owned a plantation in South Carolina, but since her mother died at Eliza's birth, her upbringing was handed over to her Stoddard aunts in Dayton. At 19 she was married to the 30-year-old Charles Taylor Sherman in Mansfield, and she bore him seven children of whom one died in infancy. Eliza was an ambitious, worry-ridden woman who soon discovered that her studious, kindly husband was lacking in the aggressiveness necessary to make money. Hence she constantly struggled to maintain the standards of gentility to which she was accustomed while meeting the demands of a family of six children. After years of scrimping, she was determined to spare this youngest daughter, who was her namesake and her favorite, a similar fate.

Lizzie's childhood was happy. As a baby, she was petted by everyone, especially by her 47-year-old father and her brother Henry, who was 13 years older than she. Toward the end of the Civil War, when she was seven years old, she and her sister Mary were visiting in Raleigh, North Carolina, where Mary was courted by Nelson Miles, a handsome young officer who would soon win the Congressional Medal of Honor. Lizzie later told Miles, whom she nicknamed "Nekkon," "It was my first memory—of the big soldier in uniform who was engaged to my beautiful sister Mary. I used to recite 'Captain Jinks of the Horse Marines' for you in my panties. [This popular music-hall ballad later gave its name to a play in which Ethel Barrymore made her debut.] My vivid recollection is of my first sense of beauty. It was Mary seated on her horse, slender, willowy, with auburn hair glinting in the sun and her blue eyes shining. It is as clear in my mind as if that mind were a photographic plate. And I remember too the adoring love I gave to my big brother. You were so good to me!"

As a child, Lizzie was taken to visit the great Stoddard house in Dayton where her mother had grown up. She peered curiously at the tall Negro footmen who wore white gloves while performing their duties. When she visited the Williams family plantation in South Carolina, she remembered especially that the kitchens were housed in a separate building from the big house and that outside the kitchen doors stood large barrels filled with wood ash, fat, and water, an appalling mess which, she was told, would be made into soft soap. In the big wooden barn she glimpsed heavy bags hanging from the beams which she found contained coffee, each bag dated and waiting to mature.

In the 1870s, the nation was expanding with unprecedented energy as the railroads pushed westward and eager settlers, some still traveling in covered wagons, trekked toward a new promised land. As a girl, Lizzie was a good horsewoman and did not flinch at the rigors of camping in the wilderness. In her teens, she was invited by Uncle Cump to accompany him on an inspection tour as far as the Yellowstone River in Montana. Their journey began by train, but when they reached the railhead, they were furnished with two sturdy horses, and, accompanied by guides, rode for 28 miles to the nearest camp, where they spent the night. Next morning, they remounted their horses for a westward journey that would last for four months. When they regained the camp where they had stayed earlier, Lizzie was astonished to see that it had grown into a town with 3,000 inhabitants. And everywhere ranches were springing up along the trail where on their way out west they had seen only wilderness. On the train, Lizzie heard passengers boast that they had been shooting buffaloes from the train for sport.

Lizzie was a light-hearted girl who had acquired a deep love of reading from her father. She loved to curl up in his library, where she could devour a volume on history or even a novel. They held long discussions in the evening about her reading, and he allowed her the freedom of his extensive collection. In school, she showed a quick and inquiring mind and developed fluency in the French language. When Lizzie was nearly 16, her mother decided that she needed training in the demanding code of the social arts, so she was sent to a ladies' finishing school on Mount Vernon Street in Boston overlooking Louisburg Square. This was not far from the home of Charles Francis Adams, the father of Henry Adams, whom she would not meet for another eight years. She quickly became the belle of the Boston teen-age set, attending numerous chaperoned dances and social events in Cambridge, where the brothers of two of her schoolmates were students at Harvard College.

When Lizzie's education was "finished," she returned to Cleveland, where Mrs. Sherman began her campaign to obtain a brilliant match for her youngest daughter. She had married off Mary to Colonel Nelson Miles and Lida to Colgate Hoyt, the scion of a wealthy Long Island family. (Of her second son, Jack, an amiable young man who drank, very little was expected.) But for Lizzie she was counting on the influence of John and William Sherman to obtain a "good catch." Now that the negotiations for the match were completed, it was up to Lizzie to confirm it.

The previous summer, in order to distract Lizzie from the loss of Joe Russell, her sister Mary, while visiting in Cleveland, had invited Lizzie to return with her to Fort Keogh. There, Lizzie would await the arrival of Uncle Cump, who had written to her, "I have a present for you which is too valuable to risk. I will count on your being at the post when I get there."

The Army post that Nelson Miles commanded was located at the junction of the Tongue and Yellowstone rivers in the wilds of Montana. Here, the handsome Nelson, whom the family called "Gen" although he had not yet officially gained that rank, was leading his troops against the lightning raids of Chief Sitting Bull and his Sioux warriors. As Mrs. Sherman loyally declared, "I hope Gen will not be called out again to fight that savage and hostile tribe. The whole country is not worth the risk that Gen runs in fighting them." The trip to Fort Keogh, upriver by steamship from Fort Leavenworth, was an arduous one for Lizzie and Mary, who were accompanied by the latter's seven-year-old daughter Cecilia, who was always Lizzie's favorite niece. With the wives of several Army officers, the ladies boarded the steamship *Don Cameron*. When the boat was 40 miles below Sioux City, it hit a snag in the river and sank quickly. Fortunately, the ship was escorted by another steamboat, *General William T. Sherman,* so the crew of the latter rescued all the passengers, but their luggage was lost, leaving the ladies and children only the clothes they were wearing. If Lizzie Sherman had been superstitious, this strange mischance of nearly drowning on the *Don Cameron*, only to be rescued by the *General Sherman,* might have given her pause and even have changed her destiny. As it was, the ladies arrived bedraggled at Miles's headquarters, which General Sherman would describe as "a good log house, with flat tin roof, really mostly comfortable, considering the surroundings." At Fort Keogh, they learned that Miles was many leagues distant, scouting for Sitting Bull. Nearby was an Indian encampment where hundreds of Sioux braves were waiting for the U.S. government to decide where they were to be settled permanently. They held nightly powwows, which were enlivened by occasional fights. When Nelson Miles returned to the cantonment, resembling "an ebullient giant hard as a Sioux brave after months of campaigning," he was accompanied by General Sherman, his uncle-in-law and military superior, who was making an inspection tour of the Northwest Territory. The two military men wanted to show the ladies all the natural wonders of the wilderness. Accompanied by an armed escort, they rode out on camping expeditions into country no white woman had ever seen. Bands of friendly Crow Indians followed them, "just to see what sort of creatures Mary and Lizzie were."

On one trip, a breathless scout galloped up to tell Colonel Miles that a band of hostile Sioux warriors, stragglers from Sitting Bull's army, were camped just ahead. The women rushed back to the cantonment, and a column of troops was sent out, with Miles leading the chase against the disgruntled Sioux. A sharp skirmish ensued, with one or two soldiers and several Indians killed. "Afterwards Miles rode back to camp to resume his vacation with his family as unconcerned, it seemed to Mary, as if he had been rabbit shooting."

At headquarters, Mary and Lizzie set out to entertain their distinguished uncle, and Lizzie organized some impromptu balls and "kettle drums" which the sociable general enjoyed. Reveling in the adventurous life of the wilderness, Lizzie tried to postpone her return to Cleveland and the events to follow. And after she was back home, Miles visited the Shermans before Christmas and urged her to pay them a return visit. Regretfully, she declined, telling Mary, "Gen says he will take me back to his post at Tongue River. To tell you the truth, I am crazy to go. But, of course, it is impossible. Uncle John and Aunt Cecilia have asked me to go to Washington. I would so much rather go with Gen."

Although she knew well enough the purpose of her proposed visit, Lizzie never mentioned the name of her intended husband, preferring to thrust it from her consciousness. When she was ready for her departure, her mother wept. "I hate to see you go—it will be so lonely." Her father, old and tired and ill, said nothing.

But Lizzie was naturally buoyant. Washington was vastly more exciting than the industrial backwater of Cleveland. Turning her back on the memory of Joe Russell, she arrived at Uncle John's K Street home and soon wrote to her mother, "I've never had such a good time in my life."

Washington in the winter of 1878 was outgrowing its earlier informality as a sleepy southern town. To the young ladies from Cleveland its sophistication was dazzling. They soon learned that Washington society was governed by a rigid protocol. The rules were codified in handbooks of etiquette that were intended for the uninitiated. But the rules themselves were already engraved in the hearts of the country's leading hostesses. As the arbiters of mid-Victorian society agreed, "Etiquette is a protection against the impertinent and vulgar. It is indispensable to the welfare of society." The aim of the elaborate code was to keep in their place all those who were below one on the slippery ladder of social importance, while clinging ferociously to one's own rung and inching upward to the next.

During the Season, which stretched from New Year's Day until Ash Wednesday, ladies followed a rigid course of paying and receiving calls. The six weeks of Lent were regarded as a penitential season during which social life was suspended. After Easter, the Season resumed until the beginning of hot weather.

The paying of calls was governed by iron-clad rules. Any lady who was or wanted to be in society must first leave her printed calling card before making a visit. Her footman presented it to the servant of the house, and if the corner was turned down it signified that the lady had come in person. The lady for whom she left the card must, within seven to ten days, leave her card in return. This ritual use of the engraved bits of pasteboard was a means of testing the social temperature before entering the water. Next came the exchange of formal calls. One etiquette writer declared, "You cannot invite people to your house (however often you may have met them elsewhere) until you first call on them in a formal manner and they return your visit. It is a safeguard against undesirable acquaintances. If you don't wish to continue the friendship, you discontinue to call and no further advances are made. But it is bad manners not to return a call in the first instance."

Newcomers to Washington were expected to pay the first call, then wait for a return call. In theory, "Any well-mannered white who could afford servants" could join the game. But every card was subject to the penetrating scrutiny of the leaders of this ritualistic society. As someone remarked of Washington society, "No one was ever missed and no one was ever forgotten." The reigning queen was Mrs. Hamilton Fish, whose husband had been President Grant's secretary of state. Like Caesar's wife, Mrs. Fish was above suspicion. Impeccable in lineage, authoritative in manner, she wore stiff white side curls and had a determined chin. Whenever a tricky social question arose, the response was "What would Mrs. Hamilton Fish say?"

The paying of calls was especially demanding on the wives of congressmen and cabinet officers. One weary young senator's wife, conscientiously returning calls paid on her by the wives of three congressmen, stopped her carriage before the boarding house where they were staying and ordered her footman to ring and present her cards. A black manservant appeared at the door, took the cards, and went back inside. After a long wait, he reappeared, carrying a paper from which he solemnly read, "Mrs. S. is out. Mrs. B. is taking a bath. And Mrs. D. is dead."

Everyone who was anyone had an "at home" day prescribed by rule. Monday was for the wives of Supreme Court justices, Tuesday for senators', Wednesday for the wives of cabinet members. Cecilia Sherman invariably received on Wednesday, presiding in a neat black dress and white lace cap that gave her the look of a Quaker matron as she towered over her shorter sisters. Over the red carpet stretching from the door of her house to the curb, her visitors trooped. Flanked by the two young ladies from Cleveland, Mrs. Sherman greeted "all persons of respectable character and becoming dress" who appeared at her door from 3 to 5 P.M. Since all ladies in society must call on cabinet wives and their calls must be returned within three days, Cecilia's visiting list might easily number several thousand. A hostess was required to be at home only on her special day. On other days she was herself paying calls. Fastened to her door was a neat basket for cards, each of which must be promptly acknowledged in order to prevent "any coolness in social relations."

Such formalized behavior, hostesses insisted, was necessary in a society where the "lower instincts" of men must be controlled. Left to themselves, the women believed, all men would revert to barbarism. Many congressmen, unable to afford the expense of housing their families in the capital, lived in rented quarters in Wormley's Hotel or in boardinghouses run by the needy widows of generals or admirals. Here, freed of the civilizing influence of wives and daughters, they quickly descended to their natural state, which led, in the House of Representatives, to their lounging with feet on desks, openly chewing tobacco, and, as often as not, missing when they spat into the pink and gold cuspidors set by each chair. Across the street from the Treasury Building where John Sherman presided, government clerks lunched on sandwiches and drank their coffee from shaving mugs, taking their sugar from holy water fonts chained to the wall, and sprawling in their wicker chairs. Under such conditions, only rigid restraints could prevent social chaos.

Into this controlled society Lizzie Sherman plunged like a mermaid into her native element. Since she was the niece of a cabinet officer and a general, all circles were open to her. Aunt Cecilia rejoiced in her niece's success. "She is the greatest of belles. I have never known anyone so universally admired. I wonder she is not as vain as a peacock." But Lizzie was never vain. She accepted men's adulation as she accepted the air she breathed. It was there—it was necessary—and it would never run out. This being her last winter of freedom, she was determined to capture as many hearts as possible, since her own heart was no longer vulnerable. She told her mother that Julia was "hoping to find a political husband" but predicted that she would not succeed because "the political men are rather wary."

The popular dance that season was the Bachelor's German—an elaborate cotillion in which first the men, then the ladies, chose partners for the next dance, presenting their choice with a favor. Lizzie easily won the most favors and was partnered by a Mr. Wetmore, "one of the best dancers in Washington whom I met here last winter. He has improved—he is now so handsome I am proud to take him around." Little gasps of envy greeted his announcement that he must catch the 1:30 A.M. train to New York since on the following day he had "a luncheon engagement at Mrs. Astor's." In this relatively small, tightly structured society fanning out from the White House and Lafayette Square, the same crowd attended the luncheons, dinners, teas, balls, and receptions that made up the Season. One evening the girls attended a reception by the venerable historian George Bancroft. Julia wrote, "The crème de la crème was there." Lizzie's escort was Mr. Brautigan, and "We were greeted by Mr. Bancroft himself, with his long white beard which looked like a neckpiece of silk lace." As their host turned to greet the next guests, a new admirer sprang forward to claim Lizzie, who gaily tossed her bouquet to her escort Brautigan and sailed off, leaving Julia to console the young man, who clung limply to the flowers as he gazed after her. Later Julia remarked, "When he cannot have her, he falls back on me."

A rising star in Washington that winter was John Hay from Cleveland, who was accompanied by his portly wife, the heiress Clara Stone Hay. A former secretary to President Lincoln, Hay was writing with John Nicolay a biography of the murdered president. John Sherman was mildly impressed by Hay, calling him "that clever little gentleman." Both girls remembered Hay from Cleveland. Lizzie was inclined to accept him, remarking, "Last night at dinner Colonel Hay was present but Clara was sick and couldn't go. That threw the table out but it gave me a double allowance of men so I don't mind. I sat between three men and talked to all three at once."

But Julia was more critical of Hay, remarking at another dinner how he played the role of ladies' man while his wife smiled serenely. Julia objected to his "tiresome flattery which takes you so unflatteringly for granted and which he thinks is so successful—but which I can see straight through. His wife Clara has a beautiful face although her figure is too stout. Last week she looked very handsome in a dark brown costume." Bitingly, she added, "She didn't give her husband the mental stimulus he didn't need. But she did give him the devotion and security of a woman of integrity and practical sagacity."

Too busy amid social engagements for the reading that she loved, Lizzie accepted from a young major a copy of his new book on military tactics, then wrote urgently to her sister Mary, "Although I won't understand a word of it I'm going to go into rhapsodies. Please tell me all about it when you write."

Lizzie found the pace exhilarating. "Last evening there were four parties. I only went to three, then rushed to my room to dress for dinner. After, we went to Mrs. Swayne's until twelve. A lovely evening—so many men."

Naturally the girls visited the White House, where they stayed until 1 A.M., "when the general rabble was about to be received." Before the reception they were ushered into the family room and descended the private staircase to the East Room, where, beneath the crystal chandeliers, President and Mrs. Hayes presided. Julia commented, "You would not notice the President anywhere—although Uncle John has the highest opinion of him. But the First Lady is strikingly good-looking with a very attractive face from which her hair is tightly pulled back. She wore a gown of rich material, very simply cut. She has a lovely smile without being beautiful. Outside the White House her very cordial manner would be charming but it is a little too familiar here and not dignified enough for the Mistress of the White House. A French diplomat called her '*Pas grande dame mais tout bonne mere*' [not a great lady but an excellent mother]—a fitting tribute to a woman who had borne eight children."

The Arranged Marriage

On fine days the girls rode horseback along the bridle paths of wooded Rock Creek Park, dressed in snugly fitting riding habits and black velvet, visored caps. Lizzie begged her mother to overlook her occasional lapses from her promise to write her daily. "Do not think me dreadfully undutiful. But we *must* go to all these receptions—Uncle John says it is expected of his family."

The girls encountered the world of the art collector when, shepherded by Uncle Cump, they visited the Baltimore mansion of William W. Walters, the railroad magnate who had amassed a collection of paintings and *objets d'art* from around the world. Lizzie was impressed. "Mr. Walters' house is so gorgeous. The bedroom is an exact copy of Marie Antoinette's which he has spent 20 years in furnishing. His picture gallery is the best collection of paintings in America—and they are all originals! They say the paintings are worth $400,000." The long gallery containing the paintings was covered with a Russian carpet, and double divans were placed down the center of the room to enable visitors to study the paintings in comfort. Later, the philanthropist's son would present the collection to the city of Baltimore where today it is known as the Walters Gallery.

The party dined in the formal dining room, with its walls of carved wood and panels of stained glass reaching almost to the ceiling. On the walls hung paintings of live game, "because," Lizzie explained, "Mr. Walters considers paintings of dead game revolting in a dining room—and I agree." Already Lizzie had learned to flatter an older man by listening to him in rapturous agreement.

At one of Cecilia Sherman's "at homes," the girls were presented to Helena Modjeska, the Polish actress who was appearing on the Washington stage. They sat at her feet, and next day Lizzie proudly announced, "We are going to see Mme. Modjeska in 'Camille'—she says it's her favorite role." The Dumas play about a Parisian prostitute struck Uncle John as "too racy" for them, but Uncle Cump laughingly volunteered to escort them.

The Civil War hero, with his infectious laugh and fiery temper, was "a great drawing card," Julia noted. "He is a character. No wonder everyone loves him. He absorbs everything and unlike Uncle John he wants to be in the swim. 'What? What's that?' he inquires and then is off on some story of his own. He is the most inexhaustible talker. He and his brother are devoted to each other but when Gen. Sherman gets off a joke on the Secretary, it is funny to see the Honorable Gentleman who does not have his older brother's irresistible sense of humor. But the General can take fire on an instant and I can fancy him rather terrible when angry, although he is the tenderest-hearted man and would be over it immediately." According to his enlisted men, General Sherman's disposition compared unfavorably with that of a snapping turtle.

As Julia wearied of the social round, Lizzie remained tireless. Aunt Cecilia looked longingly toward Lent. "Thank God this will soon be over." To insure an immediate respite, she imposed a curfew of 1 A.M., so Lizzie was forced to "tear herself away" from her admirers. Thursdays, after the ordeal of greeting several hundred callers on "at home" day, the girls slept until noon, then were whirled off in the evening for a late supper at Welcher's, equally famous for its oyster pie and for the discretion of its owner. Artlessly, Lizzie wrote, "Addie and I are great belles. Count Bluhdorn, the Austrian nobleman told us, 'Mein Gott! One must walk over corpses to see you!' "

Suddenly, below the rhapsodic treble of Lizzie's delight, an ominous bass note sounded. Just outside the circle of eager young men surrounding her loomed the large, silent figure of "Mr. Cameron," whom she mentioned in her letters with growing frequency but small enthusiasm. "Mr. Cameron had a small party for us . . ." "Mr. Cameron took me to 'Trovatore'. . . Mr. Cameron and I saw Sothern in 'David Garrick. . . Mr. Cameron said . . ."

Mr. Cameron was the tall, lanky, scowling Senator James Donald Cameron, with drooping moustache and forbidding air. The taciturn boss of Pennsylvania politics, he had not been reappointed as secretary of war in Hayes's cabinet. So his father Simon Cameron had offered his own resignation as U.S. senator from Pennsylvania in order that Don could be elected to his senatorial seat in what critics labeled "The Cameron Transfer Company." Don Cameron was a 45-year-old widower, the father of five growing daughters and one son. Reputedly worth $3,000,000, he was 24 years older than Lizzie Sherman, who was the same age as his oldest daughter.

Don was the son and political heir of old Simon Cameron, "the tall Sycamore by the Winnebago," but he lacked his father's genial personality. As Emily Briggs, the Washington columnist for the Philadelphia *Press*, wrote, "The iron crown which Don Cameron inherited from his old Highland father seemed too heavy for his tender temples and weaker brain. He looks pale and extremely nervous." Simon Cameron was a canny, self-made millionaire who controlled all of Pennsylvania politics and was nicknamed "Corruption Cameron." As a boy, he had once taken a trip to Philadelphia with the aging Lorenzo da Ponte, the librettist for Mozart's operas *Le nozze di Figaro, Don Giovanni,* and *Così fan tutte.* His guiding principle, as both secretary of war and senator, had been simple—"An honest politician is one who when bought stays bought." In 1863, President Abraham Lincoln had eased Simon Cameron out of his cabinet by sending him as U.S. minister to Russia. Henry Adams, who was then in London, wrote to his brother Charles Francis that he hoped that the "whited sepulcher" would "disappear into Russia to wander for eternity!"

A widower for the past four years, Don Cameron was rumored to be almost as successful with the ladies as his notoriously gallant progenitor. Gossips had been whispering about Don's covert romance with the daughter of Justice Jeremiah S. Black. But then Don caught sight of Lizzie and, with the cooperation of her two uncles, the deal had been arranged. As Lizzie once remarked, "He buys his way through everything with utmost patience." To many in Washington, it seemed an unnatural alliance. Lizzie's uncles had been foes of Clan Cameron. During the Civil War, when Lizzie was not yet in school, General Sherman and Simon Cameron, then secretary of war, had collided bitterly when Simon publicly humiliated Sherman by referring to him as "the mad General." The press, which Uncle Cump always distrusted, picked up the epithet and headlined it across the country. Only a personal appeal to President Lincoln by Sherman's wife, Ellen Ewing Sherman, had calmed the storm. Yet now both General Sherman and his brother John were promoting this union between their young niece and the graceless son of a ruthless father.

Washington society watched the courtship with mild incredulity. Even in an age when an advantageous marriage was the goal of most girls, this alliance between Lizzie Sherman and "Old Man Cameron" was suspect. One gossip writer called them "Beauty and the Beast," noting that "Miss Sherman is as graceful in her every motion as the Senator is clumsy."

Julia Parsons assessed Senator Cameron thoughtfully. "The Senator is a remarkable man in some respects, set in his own will but with no imagination and with his feet solidly on the ground." She had overheard Cameron discussing the forthcoming presidential election with John Hay, and heard the senator declare, "It is not a personal matter with me. I am sincerely patriotic but I am for the man who can win."

With an astuteness beyond her years, Julia Parsons prophesied, "Much as I like Senator Cameron, I think the odds are against Elizabeth in this marriage. I don't think she appreciates him and he is too old for her. She had better marry a young man." (Perhaps she was thinking of Lizzie's unfinished romance with Joe Russell.)

Watching the couple as they appeared together, Julia noticed that "Elizabeth never looked lovelier and Mr. Cameron just beamed. My lady keeps him in order, but, an I mistake not, there is a canny Scotch will of his own hidden somewhere about this young-elderly lover. So have a care, Elizabeth," she warned.

But Lizzie was too confident of her powers to be concerned.

The experienced Cameron knew how to overcome Julia's objections. With Scottish tenacity, he laid siege to her, sending her flowers, escorting her to dinners and receptions, listening to her opinions, standing stolidly by her side as they both watched Lizzie adding to her conquests. Finally Julia exclaimed, "Lizzie's friend—or rather her fiancé (but of course it is not yet announced) is the nicest man here."

In mid-January, Lizzie wrote to her mother.

> I promised to write you as soon as my little affair was definitely settled so now prepare yourself to hear what of course you have been expecting for some time. Mr. Cameron and myself had a long talk yesterday, the result of which was that I promised to marry him, at some day, to be appointed by myself, without any coercion from him.
>
> This last I had him put down in writing, knowing how most men are rich in promises but poor in fulfillment. [Was she perhaps recalling the promises of Joe Russell, who had nevertheless accepted her dismissal without any heroic attempt to change the verdict?]
>
> This is to be absolutely and entirely secret as long as I choose it to be, for I intend to have a good time this winter and am by no means ready to give up my attention. And he is perfectly willing I shall flirt as much as I want to.
>
> Auntie and Uncle know of this and I shall tell each and all of my

own family but I shall expect them to be ready to swear it is not true if any occasion occurs. The fibs I will carry on my own conscience so they need not trouble you. Caution Father more particularly. Being a man, his tongue sometimes carries him away. If Jack is at home, you can tell him. If not, do not mention it in your letters. Hattie will be surprised as I refused him while she was here but I found I couldn't stand it so when he wanted to come around again I said he might. The arrangements so far are perfectly satisfactory and I think they will continue to be so.

My dearest Mother, do not cry or weep over this. It is not to be for a long, long time so I shall be with you for many months and remember that you are first to me always and ever. No one can step in between us, not even the best man in the world. I love you best of the family now and everyday. I love you so much I have not room for anyone else above you. And if I had to leave you soon, I would fling everything to the winds, but I shall be your baby a long time yet.

He is very nice about it all and keeps away from me except when I tell him he can come—and that is only once or twice a week. Today he sent me a magnificent basket of buds, but this is the only demonstration he has made. Do not be blue over the news but write and tell me you are not sorry and don't for the world let it slip out.

This extraordinary letter from a girl of 20 to the mother who was engineerng her marriage is remarkable for its restraint. Lizzie shows no resentment at being propelled into a loveless marriage but asserts, "No man can step between us" and "you are first to me always and ever." Undoubtedly she is a little timorous at the prospect of marrying this unromantic stranger, and she longs to remain in the shelter of her mother's affection "for a long time yet." There is pathos in the plight of Lizzie, deprived of her first love, facing a marriage without love, yet clinging to the love of the mother who is willing to sell her daughter.

If Senator Cameron had seen the letter, he could hardly have been reassured by her boast that he "keeps away from me except when I tell him he can come—and that is only once or twice a week."

To this fiat a remarkable parallel occurs. Lizzie Sherman, the delicately nurtured daughter of an Ohio judge of New England ancestry, coolly sets out the terms of her relationship with the powerful Senator Cameron in almost the same words that the French novelist Emile Zola would put, two years later, into the mouth of Nana, the heroine of his sensational novel about a Parisian prostitute. For Nana outlined her demands to the importunate comte de Muffat in almost identical terms. Zola writes: "At the start, Nana put the count on a proper footing and closely mapped out the conditions of their relationship. She insisted on being treated with consideration, on enjoying complete liberty and on having her every wish respected. For instance, she was to receive everyone she chose on her day and the count only at stated times. This was to suffice him."

Lizzie's reasons for accepting the senator as her husband puzzled not only her contemporaries but her descendants. Was it, as Sherman family legend suggests, a business deal between Uncle John and Senator Cameron in settlement of a bad debt of Judge Sherman's? Or was it, as a Cameron descendant insists, a pay-off after Lizzie's father was rescued by Don Cameron from "certain difficulties he had gotten into"? Was it the lure of Cameron's wealth, which she felt would provide her with lasting security? According to custom, Lizzie signed a prenuptial agreement by which the senator turned over to her the income from $160,000 worth of securities, which would have been substantial in 1878.

The Shermans were intelligent and ambitious, well bred and patriotic—many of them becoming statesmen, judges, and military leaders. They were noted for their integrity and courage, but they seldom set out to amass a fortune. In contrast, the Camerons, father and son, were successful politicians, pragmatic, aggressive, often unscrupulous. Like his father, Don wielded immense power. Having tripled the inheritance of his first wife, Mary McCormick, with investments in railroads, banking, and publishing, he had become a very rich man. Judge Sherman lived modestly in Cleveland—not poor, but certainly not in any way equaling the Camerons in worldly possessions.

Was Lizzie perhaps dazzled by Cameron's political power? Simon had boasted of Don's key role in the recent disputed presidential election, declaring, "The campaign of '76 cost my son Don a pile of money. Hayes was whining for pocket money so Don gave him $5000 out of his own wallet. Who says Hayes is reforming anything?"

But political influence was hardly a novelty to Lizzie. Uncle John was in the president's cabinet and was being talked of as a presidential candidate. Uncle Cump was still a popular war hero. More likely, because she was forced to give up the man she loved, she had decided to abandon all thought of romance. Instead, she would leap from the social stagnation and genteel poverty of Cleveland to the assured foothold of a senator's wife in the nation's capital, whose society seemed very dazzling to her 20-year-old gaze. She would marry this man who, in material terms, could give her everything she wanted and whom, with youthful optimism, she hoped to hold at arm's length.

Perhaps, too, Lizzie had an unconscious leaning—which she would show again and again—toward an older, more experienced man. This particular man may have appealed to a hidden quality of ruthlessness in her that would make her attempt to bend his will to her own.

Temperamentally the two were wholly unsuited. Lizzie was vivacious, imaginative, and pleasure loving. Eager to please, she was also eager to rule and quick to learn. Clearly her heart was not involved—her ambitions were. She had a sensibility that made her responsive to the pleasures of art, music, and literature. But for these pleasures the blunt Cameron cared nothing. His only reading was the daily newspaper, his only friends politicians. He was pragmatic, unimaginative, unsociable. His chief interests were outwitting his foes, playing poker, eating heartily, drinking excessively.

This was the man whom Lizzie had agreed to marry and must love, honor, and obey. Right now she wanted only to play. Still young enough to enjoy a romp with Julia, she left one of the fashionable receptions and hurried off to an old-fashioned taffy pull. Lizzie wrote, "I had the jolliest time—I haven't laughed so hard for a long time."

Despite his social limitations, the experienced Cameron knew how to please his fiancée and arouse the envy of his colleagues by showing off Lizzie at the theater, the opera, dinners, and balls where he could watch her dazzle every man she met. Don took her to the Spanish Ball, which was held in honor of the impending marriage of Prince Alfonso and Princess Mercedes. In Wormley's Hotel, the residence of the Spanish minister, the long parlors were massed with orange trees, magnolias, and banks of flowers that completely covered several of the doors. "Even the chandeliers were a mass of flowers," Lizzie wrote to her mother. "And Mme. Mantilla was blazing. She wore a white silk gown covered with a network of seed pearls. Her magnificent arms and shoulders were bare and covered with diamonds. Her crown was made of old Mantilla family jewels, an immense tiara of dead gold, studded with diamonds nearly as large as your thumbnail. I never saw a more stunningly beautiful woman."

Although Lizzie had insisted on keeping her engagement secret, rumors quickly surfaced. She greeted them with a bland smile, admitting and denying nothing. Senator James Blaine, the perennial presidential aspirant who never reached the White House, considered himself a professional charmer. During one whole evening he promenaded with Lizzie, trying to get at the truth. But the "Plumed Knight" was unsuccessful even here. Lizzie laughingly evaded his questions and wrote to her mother, "If I can just keep the news secret until the Season ends, I won't mind if it gets out."

To announce Lizzie's engagement, Aunt Cecilia planned a formal luncheon in her home. Distinguished guests included the opulent Mme. Mantilla, hung with her jewels, and the stately widow of President Tyler in her Mary Stuart cap. But despite all Cecilia Sherman's precautions, the news was leaked by the wife of Senator Eugene Hale, a friend of the Sherman and Cameron families. Before the luncheon was underway, she whispered the sensational tidbit to Mrs. Blaine, and immediately, as Cecilia noted with dismay, "Everybody knew it." The news spread through the room and throughout the city with a speed that rivaled electricity—that amazing new form of energy that was beginning to replace gaslight in Washington and that caused the lights to flicker and splutter "like untamed tigers in captivity."

Leaving their food untasted, the luncheon guests crowded around the blushing Lizzie to offer felicitations. The hostess was understandably vexed. "I felt very much annoyed at Mrs. Hale for announcing it so publicly at my own luncheon." All through the evening, at every dinner and reception and ball and even in the gentlemen's clubs, it was the only subject of conversation. A cluster of ladies cornered Cecilia Sherman, slyly congratulating her, "as if," she complained, "they thought it was the result of my successful management." This she tried to deny, but one persistent dowager artfully inquired, "Are you going to marry off your other niece, Mrs. Sherman?" While trying to parry this question, Mrs. Sherman was confronted with the grim daughter of a senator—the lady was still unmarried after three seasons. Acidly, the lady remarked, "Why, Mrs. Sherman, you are the champion matchmaker. All the young ladies will be desirous of visiting you." Vainly Cecilia disclaimed "all ability in this line."

Lizzie's news met a varied reception from her family. Her mother, not trying to hide her satisfaction, wrote to Mary Miles, "You have doubtless heard of Lizzie's engagement to Mr. Cameron. I suppose it did not surprise you as Gen must have prepared you for it. Now we feel that Lizzie has gone into this with her eyes open, with nothing from the family to encourage and none to really oppose. I think we *all* as a family, since Lizzie has written us her reasons for accepting him—we all feel glad."

This was scarcely true. Lizzie's father, sick and unhappy, said nothing. Her brother Henry, his mother reported, was "displeased." Perhaps he was also horrified at how Lizzie had followed his advice—even Joe Russell might have been better than this. "At first," Mrs. Sherman noted, "Henry rather threw cold water on it." But she brought certain pressures to bear on him, and finally he conceded that "if Lizzie really prefers the Senator to all others and has that esteem and respect for him that she proposes to have, then I suppose she may be happy with him."

Of course, Mrs. Sherman could not altogether overlook the reaction of Senator Cameron's children. The oldest, Eliza, was outraged at being supplanted as her father's hostess. Her sisters and brother agreed with her. But Mrs. Sherman minimized this, writing, "My only objection is his family. But the strangest thing is, I hear that his daughter Eliza appears quite pleased." This rumor proved to be as false as the one about Joe Russell. "Anyway," the bride's mother concluded, "if anyone can get along with them, Lizzie can, I imagine." She expressed her approval at Lizzie's handling of her intended. "I think the way Sen. Cameron has been behaving this winter—the consideration he shows toward her, giving her such scope and allowing her such a nice time without annoying her with his attentions, convinces me he is not a jealous disposition and will always be kind and considerate."

Everyone concerned with the match mustered optimism. Aunt Cecilia wrote to Lizzie's mother, "I suppose there are some who will think the disparity in their age and his family are objections. But all, with one vote, pronounce him a charming man and express their faith in his qualities as a husband. Several who knew his wife say he was a very tender, kind husband always." That he had also been a heavy drinker and a ladies' man she chose to pass over.

As a successful matchmaker who dreaded to see her work undone, Cecilia Sherman added a pious warning that she had already voiced to her niece—namely that Lizzie did not properly appreciate her good fortune.

> Often [she wrote] we have felt she did not treat him with the respect his character and position deserved even while he is her suitor. Hereafter she may not show him as much as now. I think she has a sincere regard for him, but it is her manner. He is devotedly at-

tached to her and she is conscious of her power over him. She is envied by all the other girls—although they all seem to like her. She is certainly the luckiest girl in the world. I do hope she will prove worthy of all the blessings a kind Providence sends upon her. She has capacities which if rightly developed will make her a noble and useful woman. I would hate to see her be merely a reigning queen over society like Mrs. Kate Sprague.

Then she added the astonishing postscript: "We all feel that *he* is running a greater risk of future happiness than Lizzie is." To buttress her arguments Cecilia added, "Aunt Ellen [General Sherman's wife] says she believes that if Lizzie is a good wife she will be very happy. If not it will be her own fault!"

As Lizzie, a little grimly now, pursued the social round, the family began to exert pressure on her to set an early date for the wedding. There should be no long engagement—the Shermans were agreed on that. Late in February, Senator Cameron indicated that he was "very anxious" to be married in April or May, Aunt Cecilia reported. "His reasons are such as should be considered. Mr. Sherman [this was her husband] thinks she ought not to insist on having her own way in everything." Cameron's reasons for wanting an early wedding were clear enough—there would be a political convention in Harrisburg in mid-May. With the wedding out of the way, he could bring his bride back there in time for the event over which he intended to preside.

But Lizzie still evaded the very thought of the wedding, wistfully hoping it would not be "for a long time yet." Senator Cameron thought otherwise.

With feminine practicality, Aunt Cecilia suggested holding the wedding in Washington, because of Judge Sherman's poor health. "I don't see how she can be married in Cleveland without great inconvenience. I think if you [Mrs. Sherman] and the Judge assent to an early date that Lizzie may yield to the united wishes of all."

Prodded by Lizzie's mother, the family began to make the necessary gestures. Her sister Lida Hoyt and her husband Colgate wrote their congratulations to Senator Cameron, which "pleased" him, Lizzie said. Finally, her reluctant father wrote to him, and Lizzie gushed in reply, "Mr. Cameron says he is going to write you. Oh Mother, he is so good to me. I am sure you will all love him."

Ellen Sherman showed a grim Victorian optimism when she wrote to Lizzie's mother, "I think Lizzie has made her choice wisely. She will always have the respect and affectionate devotion of her husband. Mr. Cameron has such good government in his own family and withal is so kind and fond a father that there cannot be any want of harmony or any interruption to perfect domestic happiness. He is an excellent man and she must be able to love him as devotedly as I am sure he now loves her. He is prepossessing, too, and his children are very attractive and good."

Strangely silent among this chorus of praise was Uncle Cump. Although he had agreed to this match and had helped it along, the red-haired general, who was now 58 years old, was still ambivalent at the prospect of his favorite niece's marrying a man aged 45 whose father had once publicly humiliated

John Sherman

William Tecumseh Sherman

Simon Cameron

J. Donald Cameron

him. But he still held the "valuable present" that Don Cameron had asked him to deliver to Lizzie, when he had been secretary of war and as such General Sherman's superior. At a reception in Decatur House, General Sherman had approached Lizzie, who was radiant in her white satin gown with its modest décolletée ("I hate to go low-neck," Lizzie said). She was surrounded by a circle of young men offering their envious felicitations. Up strode Uncle Cump, in full military dress, his eyes flashing. Greeting Lizzie abruptly, he extended his hand and in a voice hardly controlling his fury, declared "Madame, the secretary of war presents his compliments and has asked me to give you this ring." Then he added in a loud voice, "Permit me to say, Madame, that I wholly disapprove." Turning on his heel, he strode away.

General Sherman's behavior on that occasion had been strangely at variance with his later actions.

When Lizzie and Julia were ready to return to Cleveland, Senator Cameron offered to send them in his private railroad car. But Uncle John objected that it would look "too conspicuous and ostentatious." So they traveled as ordinary passengers.

Lizzie now showed ingenuity in her attempts to postpone the wedding date, indulging in a favorite disability of the day—a sprained ankle. This did not for a moment deceive her family. Of course, no one mentioned it, but there was the remote possibility that the lusty senator, who was bent on matrimony, might, if kept dangling too long, actually get away. Someone recalled the story that while he was married to his first wife he had paid clandestine court to the wife of Senator Edward Wolcott of Colorado. Although she was no charmer, Don Cameron sought her company. Departing from his home in the morning, ostensibly to go bicycling in Rock Creek Park, he would turn in at Mrs. Wolcott's residence while her husband was occupied in the Senate. The crafty Don would carry his bicycle, which was equipped with a mileage meter, into her drawing room, and while he flirted with the lady, he would spin the wheel of the cycle to add up the mileage and thus bolster his story of bicycling in Rock Creek Park.

Such a man would not be put off by maidenly reluctance. But since Lizzie would not decide, the impatient bridegroom turned to General Sherman for assistance. Uncle Cump was a doer. On 1 April he wrote to Lizzie, "You know how much I admire and love you and pray for your happiness. I dined last night with Mr. Cameron. Late in the evening he invited me into his private office where he told me he is very uneasy and unhappy by the terms of the letter he received from you. He said that your foot continued to pain and distress you and that you had named May 14th for your wedding." But this date did not please the senator at all because, as Uncle Cump pointed out, "It happens that the convention which he is so interested in will meet in Harrisburg on May 15. He said he has asked you to name an earlier date and that your reply was actually cold and intimated a postponement till fall."

This last show of spirit by Lizzie, which her family interpreted as dallying, would not do—the family was agreed on that. So the general, who, although no diplomat, could be very persuasive, was given the task of inducing Lizzie to make up her mind—soon. "This I do now," Uncle Cump wrote to her, "with my normal bluntness and awkwardness. Now you know that Mr. Cameron, not unlike yourself, is of a most sanguine if not imperious nature and thinks and feels faster than most. So he infers that either you were in pain from your sprained ankle or that, like most women, you thought the Pennsylvania convention a small matter compared to the wedding. He asked me to write to you."

Of course, Sherman insisted, he knew she was fully competent to make all decisions for herself. "But once you are engaged, I advise an early and speedy fulfillment—the sooner the better. So I ask you for an earlier date. Time is short and no one but yourself can act. You should study the problem of life so as to act positively and with every possible deference to the interest, pride, feeling and position of the man you have agreed to marry." Then, turning more practical, he said he must know the date so his wife Ellen in St. Louis could plan her dress.

Lizzie was weakening. A few days later General Sherman wrote to her again. "Ellen asks about the dresses needed for the wedding. Mr. Cameron will be with you on Monday—I hope you have made up for the consequences of his haste at which you should be flattered."

At last, the reluctant Lizzie set 9 May as the date of the wedding in Cleveland. The prominence of the two families and the discrepancy in age between the two principals interested the newspapers. Reporters from Cleveland, Philadelphia, and New York competed with Washington journalists for details of the approaching nuptials. When they lacked factual details they resorted to speculation. A reporter from the New York *Herald* confided to his colleagues that he was careful to select for his interview with Miss Sherman "an hour when no male member of the family was present to kick me downstairs." A young reporter from the Philadelphia *Bulletin* obtained an interview with her and wrote rapturously, "She is a blonde, with blue eyes, a delicate complexion, a tall graceful figure that would delight a painter, with a small, well-shaped head, a wealth of brown hair and a facial expression unusually refined and attractive. She is in the full bloom of youth, health and beauty." Apparently the reporter was too dazzled to decide whether Lizzie was a blonde or a brunette.

Out of loyalty to the senator from Pennsylvania, the Philadelphia *Bulletin* criticized "those papers which were making such an ado about the marriage of Senator Cameron with their many columns of vulgar and silly twaddle. The editors are doing their best to educate the public to gloat over all kinds of indecencies concerning the performance of what is usually considered a sacred rite. These same papers are all edited by great Reformers, who strive to reform manners and morals by making the most serious event of a man or a woman's life the subject of indecorous comment side by side with divorce cases and scandals of even a worse character."

To purchase her trousseau Lizzie planned a few days' visit to New York. In a spirit of senatorial camaraderie, the U.S. Senate adjourned from Thursday until Monday "to give Senator Cameron a chance to go to New York to see his girl."

Before the adjournment, however, a familiar figure was seen on the Senate floor. Simon Cameron, a lusty 79 years old, was visiting his former colleagues. Still tall and straight, with a mane of white hair and piercing eyes, he towered over his former colleagues. One senator asked him, "What do you think about Don's marriage?" The canny Simon replied, "It will be a very good thing for the young man." Another asked, "How is he doing in the Senate?" To which Simon retorted, "Pretty well, but he ought to learn to improve his manners." Old Simon roared with laughter when his friends teased him about the widow Mary Oliver, who, the previous winter, had brought suit against him for $50,000 for his failure to keep his promise to marry her. The pretty widow had delivered a baby out of wedlock whose paternity she attributed to Simon Cameron. She had even threatened to bring the child onto the Senate floor. Although the furor had subsided, it had not been forgotten. Senator John Percival jested with Simon Cameron: "Bless you, my boy. It isn't every man who has $50,000 worth of affection at the age of 79!"

At last Judge and Mrs. Sherman sent out a thousand invitations to their daughter's wedding, which would take place at 8 P.M. on 9 May in St. Paul's New Episcopal Cathedral in Cleveland with Bishop Bedell officiating. Since their modest home was too small for the reception, they planned to hold it in the Cleveland home of Lida and Colgate Hoyt. As the notable guests began to arrive in Cleveland, they established themselves in Kennard House, where seven suites of rooms were reserved for Senator Donald Cameron and party.

Distinguished by his absence, Simon Cameron was reported to "fear a railway accident"—an excuse that nobody believed. A more likely explanation was his political antipathy to John Sherman, whose cabinet appointment he had opposed.

The night before the wedding, General Sherman was honored by a huge reception at Kennard House. Tramping to the blare of a marching band, many of Sherman's old soldiers arrived, and behaved like excited children. The "old war horse" and his stern-faced brother John stood at the head of the curving staircase in Kennard House, shaking hands with the mob who pushed and jostled to greet him. Many of them stared at him to see if he resembled his photographs in the newspapers. Ebullient Uncle Cump soon tired of what he called "the bore of American society" and skipping up to his room left Long John Sherman to continue glumly shaking hands.

The bride had decided on a tropical effect for the interior of St. Paul's Cathedral. Senator Cameron ordered the florist to spare no expense. After every flower and shrub in Cleveland greenhouses had been gathered, the florist sent to New York for additional plants. Under the senator's close scrutiny, the florist and his crew worked for hours to transform the church into a bower. Both sides of the chancel were filled with three tiers of palms, evergreens, roses, camellias, begonias, and lilies. Before the altar stood a huge arch of roses and lilies entwined with greens, beneath which the couple would stand.

Elizabeth Sherman as a bride, 1878

Back at the Sherman home, amid the confusion of wedding preparations, one upstairs door was closed. Standing outside, 9-year-old Mamie Sherman, the adopted daughter of John and Cecilia, listened, her eyes round in fascination. Inside she heard a storm of weeping, then the voice of her cousin Lizzie sobbing, "I won't—I will not—marry him—I cannot." She heard the plaintive tones of Aunt Eliza, Lizzie's mother, then the firm low tones of Cecilia Sherman saying, "Now, Lizzie, you must go through with it. You cannot refuse, you have promised..." Silence prevailed, and the child hastily tiptoed downstairs.

As 8 P.M. approached, contingents of Cleveland police held back the crowd surging outside St. Paul's Cathedral and cleared a path as the wedding party approached. Promptly at 8 P.M., General Sherman, in full uniform, marched up the aisle, escorting Eliza Cameron, the senator's oldest daughter, who was dressed in cream silk. The young lady was ostentatiously brushing away her tears as she walked. The distinguished guests followed, escorted to their seats by six ushers. One was Tom Sherman, the general's son, who would shortly create a family uproar. Then came six bridesmaids, two by two, gowned in sheer white Swiss over satin slips.

Finally, the groom appeared in somber black, escorting the mother of the bride. She was in mourning for a relative and wore a black silk gown trimmed with jet and Chantilly lace. The Cleveland *Leader* reported, "For an ex-Cabinet officer and the father of an interesting family Sen. Cameron was remarkably youthful in appearance."

As the organ played the Coronation March from *The Prophet* by Meyerbeer, the bride appeared on the arm of her brother Henry. Lizzie wore a gown of white grosgrain, princess style, fashioned with a low waist and short sleeves, trimmed with Duchess and point Venice lace. Her white tulle veil, short in front, was held by orange blossoms and lilies and floated the full length of her long train.

While the guests watched the slight, graceful figure approaching the altar, some of the women's eyes were wet. Older guests recalled the senator's first wedding. The jewel-decked Mme. Mantilla whispered to her neighbor, "The bride—she is so beautiful—all the men are in love with her."

Before the Episcopal bishop of Cleveland, G. T. Bedell, Lizzie and Senator Cameron exchanged their vows in tones audible throughout the church. The New York *Herald* noted, "Neither the bride nor the groom displayed any embarrassment throughout the ceremony. Both carried themselves in a stately fashion as they left the church."

Standing on the top step of the church, with his bride on his arm. Senator Cameron called imperiously, "Order Mrs. Cameron's carriage at once!" As they awaited its arrival, Julia Parsons noted that the bride looked pale.

The reception at the Hoyt home was noisy and jubilant. Long after, Julia recalled, "Elizabeth was so beautiful. I can see her now, standing between tall General Sherman and short General Philip Sheridan as she cut the wedding cake. Eliza Cameron, the senator's daughter, looked on with haughty mien, the only one of that brilliant company to have no smile for her young stepmother."

The guests were suitably impressed with the lavishness of the wedding gifts that were on display—a profusion of bronze figurines, solid silver tea services, Dresden china shepherdesses, and gold plate—reputedly worth $100,000.

At half past nine, the senator and his bride departed unaccompanied for the depot, where they entered the palace car Ohio of the Lake Shore and Michigan Southern Railroad. On her wedding night, amid the anonymous sheets and pillows of a private railroad car, Lizzie yielded to the demands of her lusty middle-aged husband. Years later she confided to a friend in England that this first encounter with sex was virtually a rape.

But in Lafayette Square, Henry Adams, who had been married to Clover for six years, was musing, "The only thing worth having in life is the first five or ten years of a happy marriage."

3

The Meeting

The Cameron honeymoon lasted less than a week. Scarcely had Lizzie unpacked the five trunks containing her trousseau than the couple were back in Harrisburg in mid-May as her husband had planned. Brushing aside romance, Don Cameron plunged at once into the management of the state political campaign of 1878, guided by his wily old father. Meanwhile, the bride was left to face a hostile circle of Don's children — Eliza, the eldest, whose tears were scarcely dried after the wedding, and her adolescent sisters and brother — Margaretta, Virginia, James, Mary, and Rachel.

Lizzie, not yet 21, was now a stepmother. She had been the youngest, in the Sherman family, of four sisters and two brothers with whom she had grown up in a warm, loving relationship. She always got on well with children, but as she faced these six silent, accusing teen-agers whose mother had died four years earlier, she saw that to them she was an intruder. Her first move was a tactical necessity but one that they would never forgive. As the new wife of Senator Cameron, she was also his hostess — whether they were living in Washington or in Harrisburg. Eliza, who was her own age, had recently graduated from Miss Porter's School in Farmington, Connecticut, and for the past few months had proudly played the role of hostess for her father. The new Mrs. Cameron, realizing that no kingdom, however small, can support two reigning queens, found it necessary to banish the children to the nursery and take over the reins of the big household herself. With the servants there was no trouble. But with Eliza this indignity caused a rift that would never be healed. (Eliza always referred to Lizzie as "that woman" and would not allow her grandson, Montgomery S. Bradley, to visit her. Even today, more than one hundred years later, the family bitterness survives. As Eliza's step-great-grandson J. Gardner Bradley, Jr., declares, "Mrs. Cameron left our family only a legacy of hatred.")

Yet Lizzie tried, against all odds, to play the difficult role of stepmother, while her husband sided with his own children against his bride. Lizzie proved to be a natural hostess, remarking, "I have a faculty of liking people on the surface while despising them underneath — a sort of paper currency which you seldom care to have redeemed in gold. But it is convenient in the small exchanges of life." This social grace, which worked brilliantly in the drawing room and the ballroom, made no impression at all on the teen-aged Camerons.

Lizzie discovered that she had married a man of property, for Don had taken over from his father Lochiel, the three farms 30 miles southeast of Harrisburg, overlooking the Susquehanna River, which he used as a summer residence. The red brick farmstead was a showplace of 50 rooms, set on a knob of the South Mountains, with a Southern-style veranda that commanded a broad view. Simon Cameron also owned an estate in Lancaster County named Donegal Spring, which contained 1,200 acres of rich farmland and yielded 35,000 pounds of tobacco in 1880. This residence, as well as the Cameron Victorian mansion in Harrisburg, would pass to Don on Simon's death.

After the excitement of the wedding and her "last unmarried winter" in Washington, Lizzie found Harrisburg duller than she had imagined. Once the political convention was over, the couple, followed by Don's older children, returned to the senator's home on K Street in Washington, not far from Uncle John Sherman's residence. Don's massive house was suited for entertaining, with a big oak-paneled drawing room which in winter was warmed with a blazing wood fire. In the adjoining billiard room, Don and his cronies gathered every night to play poker for what were rumored to be the highest stakes in town. As lucky at cards as he was in his numerous investments, Don liked to boast, "Everything I touch turns to gold."

To her dismay, Lizzie learned that her husband was a heavy drinker. She must have recalled with irony that because of this alleged weakness she had been forced to turn down Joe Russell, only to marry a man who bragged that he consumed a bottle of bourbon a day. Although he boasted that he could hold his liquor, he found it necessary, when threatened with delirium tremens on occasion, to "take the cure." Lizzie tried to introduce him to champagne in the wistful hope that the pleasant giddiness which that drink induces might improve his disposition and make him more amenable to her wishes. But his disposition only worsened and her wishes were ignored.

The senator had few intimates, but he had one admirer—his father's political crony Benjamin Brewster who had been Grant's attorney general. Owing Simon many political favors, he managed to see only the best in Don. "I cultivate Don," he wrote to Simon, "as I would a younger brother. . . . I have never met a man of his own age with more firmness of purpose, more clearness of view, a warm, generous and impulsive nature with great energy and power of execution. He is open to conviction, has no stubborn nonsense about him and is loyal to the backbone." This was, however, a minority opinion.

But despite Don's unpopularity, Lizzie had achieved an assured role in society which she undertook with grace and purpose and which helped to neutralize his critics. Although Simon Cameron had boycotted her wedding out of antipathy to the Shermans, she quickly won him over. Soon Simon was writing her, "I am proud to call you daughter."

Historic Decatur House on Lafayette Square was owned by General Edward F. Beale, who loved to indulge the eccentricities of his willful daughter Emily, who paraded around the square with a giant staghound on a leash. Young and frivilous, Emily quickly allied herself with Mrs. Don.

At a reception in the great ballroom of Decatur House, Senator Cameron's new bride stood encircled by male admirers, while a shy young woman, Anna Farwell, looked on. Years later, as the wife of the musician Reginald de Koven, she wrote, "My most vivid memory of Mrs. Cameron is of her standing in the ballroom. From a dress of black velvet adorned with a cluster of yellow jonquils, her exquisite Clytie's head and shoulders emerged. [Clytie, according to legend, was a beautiful ocean nymph who fell in love with the sun god Apollo and was turned into a sunflower in order to follow him always with her gaze.] With a perfection of grace and manner, Mrs. Cameron seemed to me a picture of accomplished seduction of which her able and ambitious mind was in no way unconscious."

Less than a month after Lizzie's wedding, disgrace overtook Uncle Cump and his family. The general's adored older son Tom, who had been studying law in St. Louis, suddenly announced to his father that he intended to become a Jesuit. General Sherman was outraged, writing to Nelson Miles, "If I had seen him shot dead at my feet, the news would not have been more cruel. I wrote to Tom, imploring, begging, commanding him to change his purpose. . . ." But Tom was adamant and departed to begin his studies at the Jesuit Seminary in Roehampton, England.

Lizzie Cameron did not share her uncle's anger. She felt only a secret admiration for her cousin Tom and rejoiced that he, at least, had the courage to defy his family. Although Uncle Cump decreed that no one in the family should mention Tom's name, Lizzie was not intimidated. She wrote comfortingly to him and later spent time with him when he returned home for a visit.

Near Decatur House, at 1501 H Street, the historian Henry Adams and his wife Marian, whom Lizzie had not yet met, were preparing to go abroad now that he had finished his political novel *Democracy*, a clever satire on Washington politics. (The following winter, Adams published this *roman à clef* in strict anonymity, owing partly to his sense of irony and partly to the fact that as a serious historian he was reluctant to appear as a novelist, at least until he learned how the book would be received.) During his European travels, Adams intended to begin the research for his monumental *History of the United States during the Administrations of Jefferson and Madison*. He planned to consult the national archives of London, Paris, and Madrid. While abroad, he and his wife would also shop for paintings and *objets d'art* with which to adorn their Washington home. Before deciding to go, the Adamses had turned down an invitation from Nelson Miles, Lizzie's brother-in-law, to visit him at his post at Fort Keogh because Mrs. Adams's father, Dr. Robert W. Hooper, feared that the trip would overtax her limited strength.

Outwardly Henry and Clover Adams were well matched. Both were short—Henry was five feet four, Clover was two inches shorter. Both were well proportioned and carried themselves with grace. Henry was physically strong, possessing great powers of endurance that Clover could not match. In time, he would develop a slight strut to compensate for his small stature, and he would grow in distinction. Impeccably attired, sporting a trim Van Dyke beard and modifying his piercing gaze with a frequent twinkle, he would become known as "the Sage of Lafayette Square."

But in temperament, Henry and Clover Adams were very different. Henry had an inbred poise that derived from his being an Adams. Behind his façade of watchful reserve he was wholly self-possessed. His depths of feeling were revealed only to his intimates. His mind was unquestionably the most brilliant and probing of his generation—and he knew it. A scholar who was gifted with the imagination of an artist, he easily inhabited both worlds. Beneath his pose of cynicism lay an emotional steadiness that would carry him through disappointment and tragedy. And despite his pessimistic motto *"Rien ne vaut beaucoup"* (Nothing matters much), Henry Adams's philosophy was essentially life affirming, as the body of his work shows. Throughout a lifetime of unremitting study and discovery, his skeptical mind was locked in a constant struggle with his will to believe. Although the skeptic ultimately triumphed, Adams never yielded to despair.

Clover Adams was more volatile. She was high strung and restless in temperament. Acute in perception, unrestrained in speech, she never seemed wholly at ease. Left motherless at the age of five, she grew up with a strong emotional dependence on her father that did not lessen after her marriage. She always preferred men's company to women's. Her temperament demanded excitement and constant activity, yet she tired easily. Frequently she insisted on a "curfew" of 10:30 P.M., when Henry was just getting under way. Clover was impulsive and generous with those whom she liked. But her likes were limited and her dislikes intense.

Clover was undoubtedly conscious of the well-known hereditary instability in her mother's family. When Henry's brother Charles Francis had learned of his impending marriage to Marian Hooper, he had blurted out, "Heavens no! The Hoopers are all crazy as coots. She will kill herself just like her aunt." The unfortunate Charles never forgot his dire prophesy.

Clover's wit was flashing and cut like a diamond. In its exercise she had been indulged by her father and later by her husband, who enjoyed showing her off to their guests at Lafayette Square. Quick and graceful in movement, she could be charming when she chose. She could also be haughty and imperious. Even Henry James, who had known her for years, was impressed by Clover's intellect and once called her "a perfect Voltaire in petticoats." But out of a need to startle her hearers and live up to her reputation for sarcasm, she could be caustic, even cruel. Her withering comments on Boston society had antagonized her in-laws, and Charles Francis, Sr. summed up the reaction to her. "I pity rather than dislike his wife...I must regard her only as a marplot and a subject of commiseration." An equally unfavorable opinion was voiced by Henry Adams's friend William Walter Phelps, a congressman from New Jersey. "The reason for Mrs. Adams's bitterness," he said, "is that there are refined circles in Washington into which she cannot gain admittance."

Scornful of religious observance, Clover flouted the convention that prohibited social activity during Lent by holding specially lively dinners during that period, explaining with a shrug, "The principles of agnostics are not respected." She smiled condescendingly as devout churchgoers passed her window each Sunday on their way to St. John's Church. Clover was proud to be considered a snob. "I avoid resident bores by having no 'days,' " she wrote. But above all, she was undeniably homely. Even her adoring Henry, in announcing his engagement to Charles Milnes Gaskell, wrote, "I think you will like her, not for her beauty, for she is certainly not beautiful and her features are much too prominent, but for her intelligence and sympathy which are what hold me." Aware of her plainness, Clover refused to be photographed. Once, when she could not avoid it, she managed to have her face partly hidden by a hat as she sat on her horse. She described herself ironically as having "a most queenly presence, an aquiline nose rendered less prominent by full cheeks and a wealth of chin." Versed in Latin, Greek, and the classics, she was undoubtedly a bluestocking. Her mental agility and her acid wit enabled her to keep pace, but just barely, with her husband. But it was at a price, for she seemed always to be standing intellectually on tiptoe.

Clover easily dominated Henry in practical matters, and he enjoyed "handing over the reins" to her. In her fierce independence she differed from the more conventional wives of his brothers. But the Henry Adamses differed from his two older brothers and their wives in another way—they were childless. For him, who adored children and longed to continue the Adams line, it was difficult enough. But for her, sensing his disappointment and perhaps blaming herself, it must have been harder. Whether the problem was due to his impotence or her infertility is not known. But Adams had investigated the condition, for his library contained a book on sterility by Dr. J. A. Sims. The Adamses endured their plight with slightly forced gaiety, and Henry remarked, "One consequence of having no children is that husband and wife become very dependent on each other and live very much together. This is our case but we both like society and try to conciliate it." But his real anguish over their childlessness is glimpsed when he has the heroine of his novel *Democracy* cry, "Was the family all that life had to offer?"

In May 1879, Henry and Clover Adams left their wistaria-covered house, which they rented from the philanthropist and art patron W. W. Corcoran, for their first trip to London and Paris since their honeymoon six years earlier. During their nine days' crossing of the Atlantic, Adams suffered from his usual seasickness. Weary and bedraggled, the couple arrived in London and settled into rooms in Half Moon Street, two blocks away from their friend Henry James. The expatriate novelist greeted them with pleasure, noting that "Adams is very sensible, though a trifle dry." But to Henry James, Clover seemed "toned down and bedimmed from her ancient brilliance." The novelist dropped in on them regularly and accompanied them to dinners, receptions, and exhibits.

During the fall of 1879, the art world in Europe was in ferment. Impressionism, that unprecedented explosion of light and color, had erupted in France, while in London the Pre-Raphaelites were opposing the conservatism of the Salon. James McNeill Whistler, the monocled American artist who "strutted like a bantam cock in dapper frock-coat and polished dancing-pumps," was involved in a libel suit against the English critic John Ruskin. On viewing Whistler's *Nocturne,* Ruskin had thundered, "Whistler has flung his paint pot in the face of the public!" The sensational case was dividing the art establishment in England.

Tingling with curiosity, Clover Adams attended a showing by the Pre-Raphaelites in the Grosvenor Gallery. Slowly pacing the long rooms, which were paneled in crimson brocade, Clover peered at the paintings, exclaiming at the "many shocking daubs." When the elegant Mr. Whistler was presented to her, Clover reacted typically, later reporting to her father, "Whistler is even more mad away from his paint pots than near them. His etchings are so charming that it is a pity he should leave them to woo a muse he cannot win."

Standing near Clover in the Grosvenor Gallery as she examined the paintings was Mrs. Jack Gardner, the spirited art patron who was their summer neighbor at Beverly Farms in Massachusetts. As the two ladies were preparing to depart, there was a delay in the arrival of their respective broughams, so they stood chatting side by side for 20 minutes, "smiling pityingly," as Clover reported, "on the Britons and sympathizing over the awful gowns." Clover's scorn for British fashion was withering. She dismissed the women as "fat fugues in pea green, lean symphonies in chewing-gum color and all in a rusty minor key."

It was easy for the Adamses to meet everyone who counted. Henry had spent several years in London during the Civil War, as secretary to his father, who had been the U.S. minister to the Court of St. James's, so they were entertained everywhere. In addition, Clover played hostess at formal dinners for eight at which, as U.S. Minister William J. Hoppin noted, "The talk was very good." She responded with pleasure, as when she was seated at dinner next to the French humanist philosopher Ernest Renan, whom she described as "sympathetic and big as a whale," or the positivist philosopher Herbert Spencer, whose "assumption of omniscience in manner" she found "reassuring in this age of unbelief." Yet she concluded that only one dinner in six was worth going to. "The other five are Sloughs of Despond."

Clover uttered her judgments with her customary asperity. Prime Minister Benjamin Disraeli she dismissed as "That Jew bagman with his quack medicines." Robert Browning, she noted, had a voice "like steel—loud and harsh and incessant.... People say he can talk well. I've never heard him. His face has the intellectual apathy of a chronic diner-out." She liked Matthew Arnold a little better but thought "he has a tendency to slop over."

That fall the Adamses were shocked to hear that the American artist

William Morris Hunt, who had painted a portrait of Henry's father in London, was dead by drowning—reportedly a suicide off the Isles of Shoals. Clover, with her horror of lingering illness, remarked, "He has put an end to his wild, restless, unhappy life. Perhaps it has saved him years of insanity which his temperament pointed to."

Next the Adamses crossed the Channel to settle in Paris, where Henry could continue his research in the national archives. Their apartment had two windows overlooking the Tuileries Gardens. When they attended the Comédie Française to see Sarah Bernhardt starring in Victor Hugo's *Ruy Blas*, Clover could not conceal her Bostonian revulsion against the French actress who was the toast of Europe. "We detest her voice, looks, posing and all," she pronounced. Defensively she added, "Coquelin, a member of the same company, is a most charming actor. He hates her too. He says she is *'Pas serieuse ni comme femme ni comme artiste'* [not serious either as a woman or as an artist]." Bernhardt was conducting a long-standing feud with Coquelin over the management of her company. "But," Clover concluded regretfully, "she is chic and the rage."

A little hesitantly, the Adamses attended the Parisian "Varieties," a kind of French burlesque which was worlds removed from Boston theater. "The Varieties were very broad and very long," Clover confided to her father. "In defiance of all sense of decorum, we laughed to a shocking extent."

Before her marriage, Clover had shown little interest in fashion. But Henry had explained to her, "People who study Greek must take pains with their dress." So she decided to spend her father's Christmas check in Paris on "a velvet gown the color of fresh Jacqueminot roses with a kind of farthingale at the hips and two side flaps a shade deeper, like a curling leaf." With typical generosity, she ordered gowns for three of the motherless daughters of her brother Ned Hooper but warned her father that the dresses were to be a surprise for Thanksgiving dinner and "on no account to tell the infants."

Now that they were settled in the fashion capital of the world, Clover allowed Henry to "bully" her into visiting the designer Charles Worth. Mrs. Jack Gardner was a longtime customer of the famous British-born couturier who catered to empresses, countesses, and society leaders, so she brought her friend Clover, accompanied by Henry, to Worth's salon at 7 rue de la Paix, where, as a writer observed, "The stairs are like Jacob's ladder with an angel on every step." Clover approached Mr. Worth with caution, for she had heard a rumor that he drank. But she was pleasantly surprised, noting, "I found him respectful and sympathetic. . . . His manner was always calm—but his glance was Napoleonic." He opposed the growing fad for gowns with extremely low necks, declaring, "I dress ladies—let the demi-monde go elsewhere."

Clover was delighted with the atmosphere of elegance—the gowns, the designer, the salon, and the spaniels. She ordered eight gowns "like a serious peacock." When she came back for a fitting on her 37th birthday, she was flattered when the designer set aside Mrs. Astor and Mrs. Vanderbilt to devote himself to her.

In more serious vein, her husband was musing on Albert Gallatin, the subject of his recent biography. "The inevitable isolation and disillusionment of a really strong mind—one that combines force with elevation—is to me the romance and tragedy of statesmanship." Adams had recently been introduced to the British historian John Richard Green, who was vastly impressed, remarking, "Henry Adams is one of the three people in the world to whom history has any meaning."

The winter in Paris was frigid. "Paris is like St. Petersburg," Henry complained. Both he and Clover were growing restless for home, with Clover exclaiming, "Paris is nothing but a huge shop and a restaurant." Henry declared with characteristic exaggeration, "At the best of times Paris is to me a fraud and a snare but in December and January it is frankly impossible." Nevertheless, he continued to work steadily every day from 10 A.M. until 4 P.M. in the archives, while Clover peered out the windows at the Tuileries Gardens. "The atmosphere is like gray pea soup—we've had no sunlight for eight days. It is often hard to read at noon." Henry, always conscientious, insisted, "I must do my work thoroughly as I don't mean to come to Europe again if I can help it."

Finally, they returned to London and further research in the British Museum. Henry James reappeared, relishing the chance "to have in London a couple of good American confidants." Adams reported with satisfaction, "Henry James is standing on the hearthrug with his hands under his coattails talking with my wife until midnight as if we were in Marlborough Street." Clover was in her element as she joined in the inspired gossip. "He comes in every day," she told her father, "sits chatting by our fire, but he is a frivolous being, dining out. Tomorrow is an off night so he has invited himself to dine with us." One memorable evening, James brought along his brother William the philosopher, and Clover wrote, "The three men are busy with cigars in the billiard room."

While Henry and Clover were wintering in Europe, Lizzie Cameron in Washington decided to have her portrait painted by the American artist George P. A. Healy. His portraits of famous Americans—Lincoln, Andrew Jackson, and President Grant—as well as Pope Pius IX and Franz Liszt, had been shown in Paris and New York. Healy's vogue was widespread, and one critic praised "his rugged and forcible characteristic portraits, when the subject is favorable and the artist is in earnest. He has facility and enterprise, though the likeness often wants delicacy."

Urged on by her family, Lizzie had set her mind on this portrait. Married less than two years, she did not approach her husband with this request, but instead she turned to Uncle Cump to persuade the senator. General Sherman, who had himself been painted by Healy, was visiting in Washington, and he wrote to Lizzie in Cleveland, "I am just back from the Senate where I saw Mr. Cameron who seemed *perfectly willing* for Mr. Healy to paint your portrait." Uncle Cump then praised Healy as "one of the best portraitists living, with fame at home and abroad. And you," he told Lizzie, "are a splendid subject, but in order to catch the play of your features, he must see more of you. For your expression changes often and rapidly."

Uncle Cump, who was always a manipulator, advised Lizzie to approach the artist obliquely, "Do not tell him your purpose at first but discuss his work, giving him your honest opinion." Then the general advised his niece to get into a discussion with Healy and "if you can, in the discussion get a little angry and spirited, so much the better. For you are better looking when 'moved' than in repose. Let Healy have the sittings, three-quarter face, with your hair a little disheveled and an earnest expression, as though you were looking for somebody you wanted to meet." Healy, he added, "has no imagination but paints and paints well what he sees. You ought to make a beautiful picture. Try to make your sittings suit his convenience. He will paint a portrait of you that all will admire."

Almost as an afterthought, General Sherman added, "Mr. Cameron said his consent to you would involve a similar consent to Eliza and Virginia [his two eldest daughters]. So much the better for Healy to support his family in Paris. He has appointments in New York and Paris and is disposed to hurry. But I don't want him to 'hurry' yours. I will write a note you can deliver to him."

Uncle Cump believed in leaving nothing to chance. As if he were planning a military campaign, he mapped out for the artist the steps to take in painting Lizzie's portrait. In the note to Healy that he gave Lizzie, he ordered "A portrait of the size and style of that of Mary Anderson [a beautiful American actress] and for the same price of $450. Should you succeed," he continued, "Mr. Cameron wants others of his two grown daughters. So it is in your interest to paint Lizzie in your best style, idealized somewhat but nevertheless a strong likeness." Lest Healy have any remaining doubts as to how he was to carry out this commission, General Sherman continued, "We think Lizzie very beautiful, not only in features but in character but, like all the Shermans, passing rapidly from great animation to a state of repose that is almost gloomy. If you can catch the animation you will give satisfaction to a large circle. Let her face be as perfect as you can make it, leaving the hair free and even disheveled."

The artist's reaction to this presumptuous advice is not recorded. Indeed the portrait itself has vanished, although many of Healy's works may still be found in the Boston Museum of Fine Arts and the Metropolitan Museum in New York.

In the fall of 1880, Lizzie Cameron was called upon to handle the arrangements for the wedding of Eliza Cameron to William Bradley of Newark, son of U.S. Supreme Court Justice Joseph P. Bradley. The lavish affair went smoothly except for two unexpected setbacks. The bride, who was still implacably opposed to this stepmother of her own age, was mortified to notice what the reporter for the Philadelphia *Times* perceived, that "It was the stunning figure of Mrs. J. Donald Cameron, attired in a white corded silk gown with diamonds which stole the show." All of the Camerons were disappointed at the absence of former President U.S. Grant, the crony of Simon and Don Cameron, who had accepted an invitation to the wedding. Grant later wrote to apologize — he had planned to come but he "forgot."

That same autumn, Henry Adams was nearing the end of his European research. "My material is enormous and I now fear the task of compression will be painful. If it proves a dull story I will condense, but it is wildly interesting at least to me." Clover was weary of their traveling, but she wrote dutifully, "Of course we were homesick and were before we started. But that's no reason for going home until Henry finishes his work." In late September, they bade good-bye to Henry James, who watched their departure with regret. "In England they appear to have suffered more than they enjoyed. But they are rather too critical and invidious. I shall miss them much, though—we have had such inveterate discussions and comparing of notes. They have been much liked here."

Returning to America in October 1880, Henry and Clover Adams put up temporarily at the popular Wormley's Hotel, where they had to wait for two months while their new residence was being renovated. This was W. W. Corcoran's "Little White House," a three-story residence at 1607 H Street, facing the White House across Lafayette Square. The house had six bedrooms, two baths, and an annex with quarters for their four servants, for which they would pay a rent of $200 a month.

The Adamses were delighted to be back, especially Clover, who had once called traveling "quite perfect if one could only go home at night." Clover admitted that they were very particular about any house they lived in. "Mr. Corcoran didn't realize when he undertook to put the house in order that he would have two driving New Englanders at his heels."

The problem of settling into the house caused Clover great irritation. The sewer was blocked, they found, and the new ceiling fell because the roof was not tight. Through it all Henry remained "patient and amiable in these crises." Their moving involved receiving and arranging 15 wagonloads of their furniture which had been in storage in Boston, besides the paintings and *objets d'art* they had purchased in London. Clover also found it "a horrid bore, on top of all the hard work, to scuffle with raw servants untrained to my ways."

While Clover fretted, Henry tried to comfort her. He was feeling satisfaction at the progress of his work, and he declared comfortably, "I look forward to recurring winters and summers in Washington and Beverly until a cheery tomb shall provide us with a permanent abode for all seasons."

In mid-October, Sarah Bernhardt arrived for a triumphal American tour. The strait-laced citizens of Boston, New York, and Washington raised a protest that provoked columnist Gail Hamilton to write in the New York *Tribune*, "It is the superb actress that people go to see, not the bad woman." With her golden voice, the divine Sarah could move her audience to tears, yet such was her emotional control that during a death scene she could turn aside her tear-stained face to wink at a stagehand.

Just as in Paris, Clover was outraged. But she attended the matinée performance of *Camille*, then commented, "To us she says nothing. She is startlingly like Emily Beale though without her snap." Sternly she ordered her father, "See to it that Boston snubs her off the stage. It's so nice that Bernhardt is being socially tabooed on this side. Our English cousins make such asses of themselves." But Bernhardt was hardly tabooed in America. Instead, she enjoyed a triumphal tour of the leading cities throughout the 1880s and 1890s, starring in *Camille, Tosca,* and *Cleopatra.*

Lizzie Cameron also watched Bernhardt in *Cleopatra* and observed, "It is the dullest, most wretched play but she carried off even that!" Later, Lizzie was candid about the actress's appearance. "She has grown fat in front and has the funniest figure." But the French star was undeniably fascinating, and Lizzie and her party went backstage to meet her. The close-up view was disappointing. "She is a much dyed, painted, smallish woman, very French, very vivacious and very common. Her eyes are handsome. She did not impress me at all." But Lizzie impressed Madame Bernhardt. Word reached her that the great actress asked her stage manager every night if Madame Cameron was present and where she was sitting. At this news Lizzie was unashamedly flattered.

The craze for décolletage, which the designer Worth had opposed, was sweeping Washington. "Dresses are low enough," wrote the columnist Carp, "to sprout the seeds of consumption in many a fair woman's chest. Only a strap over the shoulder holds up the low-cut bodice. Yet during the day the same belles wear flannel underclothes, heavy gowns and sealskin wraps. At night they might as well be attired in the summer costume of an Indian squaw. At one reception the Korean minister stared in bewilderment at the ladies' low cut gowns, then asked his host 'Does it not seem to you that these ladies are very much above their clothes?' "

In this Washington version of Vanity Fair, Henry and Clover Adams inhabited their own little kingdom, which they ruled with a high-handed but sure touch. They enjoyed the best of two worlds—riding each morning, he on the mare Daisy, she on the stallion Prince, through the winding trails of Rock Creek Park. Dogs were a passion with them both. They sported with their two Skye terriors Boojum and Possum, paid no ritual calls, and entertained at tea or dinner only those whom they wished to see.

They saw themselves as "two happy refugees from Boston who strut around as if we were millionaires." "This part of life, from 40 to 50, would be all I want," Henry remarked in deep contentment. "There is a summer-like repose, a self-centered, irresponsible, devil-may-care indifference to the future."

But Clover was not so content. Living largely in bursts of nervous energy and lacking Henry's physical stamina, she was often moody. Illness and the death of friends disturbed her. "Fate has a strange way of dealing," she mused. "Poor A—who has and gives no pleasure to anyone may live to bury all her contemporaries. And others are called from a full feast. The moral," she decided, "is to take all you can from life and live it to your fingertips." Her preoccupation with death was heightened as she looked out her window at the frequent funeral processions approaching St. John's Church. Mockingly, she described the hearses of white and gold as "bon bons on wheels."

The Meeting

In January 1881, Clara and John Hay held a reception which Clover and Henry Adams graciously consented to attend. Adams and Hay would shortly become inseparable, and Clover and Clara Hay were sympathetic. In the Hay drawing room, standing beside his petite Clover, Henry Adams first met the tall and radiant Elizabeth Cameron.

Afterward Clover noted indulgently, "Mrs. Don Cameron asked if she might come to tea and declined to wait until I called her first." By thus lightly flouting one of society's rigid rules, Lizzie showed herself above the law. And Clover, who could be merciless when she disapproved, accepted her. "Mrs. Cameron," Clover wrote her father, "is very young, pretty and I fear, bored with her middle-aged husband who is fighting a boss-fight in Harrisburg."

Adams did not record their meeting. But later he wrote of her, "Here comes Mrs. Cameron, as ambitious as Eve herself, and in the full consciousness of all her powers as a mischief-maker in politics—the most amusing of all feminine ambitions."

Perhaps in this first encounter with Lizzie, the articulate scholar may have caught the sound of a language that needs no words.

4

The Education Of Elizabeth Cameron

So Mrs. Don came on Friday and wailed about Harrisburg and was quite frank in her remarks about men and things," Clover wrote to her father. "Poor Don will think she has fallen among thieves when he comes back." Clover Adams's sympathy for the senator's young wife and her unexpected mildness toward Cameron himself were observed with curiosity by one writer. "Mrs. Adams is a bit exacting, pouring out the vials of her wrath on nearly everyone, with the egregious Don Cameron one of the rare exceptions."

For both Henry and Clover Adams, their new visitor had an immediate appeal. Henry, with the eye of a connoisseur, was alert to her beauty, while her intellectual curiosity drew an immediate response from this former Harvard professor. Clover, with her instinct for penetrating all pretense, was captivated by Lizzie's spontaneity and innocence. She seemed to them so young — Mrs. Don always subtracted two years from her age, so now she passed for 21 years although she was in fact 23. After less than three years of a marriage in which she was still untouched by passion, she retained that virginal quality that inevitably attracted men.

With no child of their own, the aristocratic Henry Adamses were drawn to Mrs. Don. She seemed to them "little more than a baby from Cleveland" who had fallen, if not among thieves, then among the relentless climbers in a society that they knew from the inside. In her turn, Lizzie, who was bored with her husband's politicking and unoccupied while he was on his frequent forays, was delighted to become a member of the Adamses' Lafayette Square household and to mingle with their sophisticated guests. Although Clover had boasted that she barricaded their doors until sunset to prevent any interruption to Henry's writing, that did not prevent Mrs. Don from getting in. Accompanied by Emily Beale, she stood on tiptoe outside Adams's study, and together the two ladies rapped on his window with their dainty parasols. "Of course they got in," Clover reported. She and Henry listened indulgently as the irrepressible Emily explained, "This is better than ringing, because you can't say you're engaged." With piteous expressions, they begged their hosts "for some good tea — we've just come from a house where the tea was bad and the sugar impossible." Accepting this transparent excuse, Clover welcomed them to her tea table, where each afternoon "this hostess of liberal proclivities" presided over tea and gossip. Her husband often joined them, sometimes listening with a glint in his eye, sometimes dominating the conversation. They were a merry foursome, as Clover wrote her father. "Mrs. Don and Emily Beale come to tea every day—it is great fun." (Emily was no favorite of Clover's, but she realized that Mrs. Don could hardly travel about alone, and she saw that the youthful Lizzie enjoyed Emily's audacity. So Emily was tolerated.) To reassure her father concerning Mrs. Don's social credentials, Clover added, "She is a sister of General Miles's wife and a niece of General Sherman."

So the education of Elizabeth Cameron began under the expert tutelage of Henry Adams and his wife. The responsive young woman from Cleveland — who had actually been born in Mansfield, Ohio, a fact she generally managed to conceal — was the perfect foil for the sophisticated historian. As a pupil, she was bright and intuitive, quick to respond, eager to follow. Adams was, above all, a teacher who understood the responsibilities of his profession. "A parent," he once wrote, "gives life, but as a parent, he gives no more. A murderer takes life but his deed stops there. A teacher affects eternity. He can never tell where his influence stops." His influence on Elizabeth Cameron would be incalculable. From the beginning, their minds reacted on each other in a creative exchange — her readiness to follow his lead caused him to surpass himself. He guided her intellect, taught her to question, to explore, to judge. At the same time, her responsiveness engaged him so wholly that he found himself, whenever they were apart, writing to her, and receiving her answers, in a continuing dialogue that resulted in the most masterly letters among the thousands he wrote during his long lifetime.

But although Henry Adams was the principal teacher in matters of intellect and taste, Clover, being of a more practical turn of mind, instructed her in social matters with such effectiveness the Lizzie was able to lure into her employ the cook at the British Legation, a decided coup in a society devoted to elaborate dining.

The society in which Lizzie was being instructed was described by Henry Adams with characteristic exaggeration as one in which "Money plays no part whatever." Adams could coolly dismiss the importance of wealth as long as his and Clover's joint income amounted to $25,000 a year, which would equal perhaps $250,000 today. "But cleverness," he added "counts for a great deal and social capacity for more." These were attributes that could be acquired from an experienced teacher.

Adams had been fascinated with the world of diplomacy since his days as secretary to his father at the Court of St. James's. In 1881, Queen Victoria was represented in Washington by Sir Lionel (later Lord) Sackville-West, a member of the British nobility who was the owner of Knole Castle in Kent. Sackville-West had held an earlier diplomatic post in Madrid, where he had enjoyed a long liaison with the Spanish dancer Pepita, who had borne him seven children. Sir Lionel had brought with him to Washington his 18-year-old eldest daughter Victoria, undeterred by the fact that the girl was illegitimate. This defiance of convention the Henry Adamses decided to overlook, when they invited the Sackville-Wests, father and daughter, to their drawing room. Henry found young Victoria "a sweet girl, just out of a French convent, talking very broken English in a delightful accent. She is the ideal ingénue of a French comedy. I have never met one before in real life. The poor child is illegitimate, we are told, and of course there is a disposition to receive her kindly. Her father is a dull little man but he has 5000 pounds a year and is thought a great swell. I've no doubt she will be happy here if none of her relatives come over. It is a kind society and covers all the sins it can."

This lordly willingness to disregard the irregular birth of the daughter of a wealthy British title was not lost on Lizzie Cameron. She saw that young Victoria, slim and white as a lily in her brown convent dress, seemed at first shy and inarticulate but that underneath she possessed an unshakable self-confidence. She would grow up to marry a cousin of the same surname, acquire the family title, and become the mother of Vita Sackville-West, the poet and novelist. She and Lizzie, who was five years older than Victoria, became fast friends, and 30 years later, Lizzie would be among the witnesses for her defense in the legal battle known as the Romance of the Sackville Peerage in the High Court of Justice in London.

Nor did it escape Mrs. Don's notice that the Cave Dwellers in Washington showed a very different face toward another untitled visitor from England. Preceded by a drumbeat of publicity, the Irish-born writer Oscar Fingal O'Flahertie Wills Wilde descended on New York and Washington for a nationwide lecture tour. At age 28, Wilde had not yet written his great plays or achieved notoriety as the lover of Lord Alfred Douglas. But as the preposterously affected leader of the new "Art for art's sake" movement, Oscar Wilde had already created an international furore. His wicked epigrams were quoted everywhere. In a period when men were sober in manner and somber in dress, Wilde wore a velvet coat with silver buttons, knee breeches, white stockings, and buckled shoes and carried a sunflower.

Clover Adams caught her first glimpse of him when she was on a visit to New York, and she alerted her followers, "Last week on Park Avenue I met a tall slender man, café au lait in the face, long hair, dressed in stockings and tights, a brown plush tunic, a big yellow sunflower pinned above his heart and a queer cap on his head." As the apparition passed, she turned around to look, while acknowledging to herself that such behavior was "very vulgar." To her astonishment, she saw a large card on his back reading "Oscar on a wild toot."

Henry James was also visiting the country of his birth, trying to escape the attention of the press by using a pseudonym. He eyed Washington condescendingly as "A Negro village liberally sprinkled with whites." As a rising American novelist whose home was London, James knew it was expected of him to acknowledge the visiting celebrity. Gravely he greeted the irrepressible Oscar, remarking that he was "very homesick" for London. Wilde's eyes widened in mock astonishment. "Really?" he replied. "You care for *places*? The world is my home."

The Education of Elizabeth Cameron

The British Legation sponsored a Bachelor's German in honor of Wilde to which Lord George Montague, third secretary, issued a formal invitation to the Adamses. But Clover, "in elegant language," declined, pleading a previous dinner engagement. When pressed to meet Wilde at a dinner at the Lorings', she exclaimed, "Fools don't amuse me."

Although Henry James was publicly genial to Wilde, he confided to the Adamses, "He is a fatuous fool and a tenth-rate cad." Naturally, Clover repeated this remark to her intimates, and Lizzie had another lesson in social behavior. But however Henry James might behave toward Wilde, Clover Adams intended to offer him no recognition — public or private. He was, after all, not a member of the nobility, and his flamboyant manners scandalized her. So she instructed Henry James, "Don't bring your friend Oscar when he comes. I must keep out thieves and noodles."

But Clover's disapproval had no effect on Wilde's visit. Official Washington welcomed him. As the Washington *Star* reported, "The Bachelor's German was attended by the best element of society. Mr. Oscar Wilde arrived at 11 P.M. with Congressman and Mrs. Robeson. Dancing was suspended for the reception. He was pleasant, affable and created a favorable impression." Wilde was always unpredictable — just when he was expected to act most outrageously, he behaved in a wholly acceptable manner.

Lizzie Cameron may have been amused at this extraordinary prudishness among the Cave Dwellers. In Cleveland it was to be expected. Her own family were staunch upholders of mid-Victorian proprieties. (Her sister Mary Miles objected to Tolstoy's recent novel *Anna Karenina,* calling it "the most pernicious book on the market. It should never be put into the hands of any young man or woman." Of course Lizzie had managed to read it.) But in Washington she may have hoped for more tolerance and sophistication than she was witnessing. The self-righteousness of the "cream" of society was not reflected in the attitude of the masses who greeted with enthusiastic curiosity such colorful foreign visitors as Wilde and Bernhardt. This American condemnation of any behavior that disregarded Puritan conventions astonished many Europeans, who saw in it a ridiculous dichotomy. Oscar Wilde summed it up after his visit when he wrote, "America is a land of unmatched vitality and vulgarity, a people who care not at all about values other than their own and who love and hate you with a frighteningly passionate zeal."

Later that year, Lillie Langtry arrived in New York to tour the country in her newly adopted role as an actress. The Jersey Lily was more famous for her beauty that for her dramatic ability, and everyone was rhapsodizing about her looks. Even the artist Whistler was captivated and exclaimed, "To look at Lillie is to imagine one is dreaming. She is so extraordinary that not even I can do her justice in a painting." Mrs. Langtry was four years older than Lizzie Cameron, but she had crowded the experience of several lifetimes into her less than 30 years. The daughter of an Anglican clergyman from the Channel Isle of Jersey, she caught the eye of Edward, prince of Wales. She became his mistress, was courted by the nobility, then overstepped the social boundaries and suffered ostracism in England.

Oscar Wilde, who had always admired her, greeted her extravagantly. "I would rather have discovered Mrs. Langtry than to have discovered America. She is the most beautiful woman in the world and will be a beauty still at 85."

When Lillie Langtry reached Washington, Mrs. Don heard Henry Adams grumble, "The estimable Mrs. Langtry is here. I dare not hint a doubt of her virtue for fear of getting myself into trouble. I expect to see her dined by the President and embraced by every staid matron in Washington. It is revolting."

But as in the case of Oscar Wilde, the moral outrage expressed by the Cave Dwellers had small effect on their intended victim. Lillie Langtry enjoyed a triumphal tour of the major American cities. Public discussion of her morals only increased her box office sales. In New York, tickets for first-night performances at the Park Theater were auctioned off at a top price of $345 for a front box. The lively Lillie was equal to any occasion. When the haughty New York social leader Mrs. Paran Stevens refused to call on Lillie, the actress, who knew that Mrs. Stevens was the daughter of a wealthy grocer and had married a hotel magnate, shrugged and dismissed her as "only a cook."

Although Lizzie Cameron had not yet met Henry James, his presence pervaded the Adamses' drawing room as Clover excitedly received a copy of his latest novel *Portrait of a Lady*. This was the story of an arranged marriage, a subject with which Mrs. Don was familiar. Clover was fond of Henry James, but she was characteristically critical of him. "The young emigrant has much to learn. He may in turn get into the swim [here] but I doubt it. I think the real, live, vulgar, quick-paced world in America will fret him and he prefers a quiet corner with a pen where he can create men and women who say neat things and aren't nasal or eccentric."

Clover's daily tea parties were the setting for another Adams exclusive—the Five of Hearts. This tiny club of intimates included three gentlemen—Adams, John Hay, and Clarence King, a trio whom the publisher Henry Holt once described as "three little chaps." It also included two wives—petite Clover and portly Clara Stone Hay, who was the only sizable figure in the group. The talented Clarence King, who became the first director of the U.S. Geological Survey, was a raconteur and dandy who was presumed to be a bachelor. Both Adams and Hay showed such intense admiration of King that Clover remarked pettishly, "I never knew such frantic adoration could exist in this practical age." Adams in *The Education* would explain this "adoration." "Women were jealous of the power he had over men, but women were many and Kings were one. The men worshipped not so much their friend as the ideal American they all wanted to be. The women were jealous because at heart, King had no faith in the American woman; he loved types more robust." A strange, brilliant bird of passage, King was apt to arrive unexpectedly in Washington, descend on the Adamses, then vanish just as suddenly. This was a trait that irritated Lizzie, who once exclaimed to Adams, "If he were my friend, I should hate him. I almost do for your sake as it is." For

Henry Adams in 1885

Clarence King

Clara Stone Hay

John Hay

years, no one in Washington guessed his secret—that the high-spirited King, who admired women "of chocolate hue," had a common-law wife, the black nursemaid Ada Todd, with whom he set up a household in Brooklyn and by whom he had five children. With all these dependents, the brilliant mining engineer and geologist (who was nicknamed "King of Diamonds") was chronically short of money, although he engaged in numerous speculations which failed. As John Hay observed, "A touch of avarice would have made him another Vanderbilt."

Although Lizzie Cameron did not belong to the Five of Hearts, she was aware, as an intimate of the Adams household, of the subjects they discussed and the reputations they dissected. She even added her own observation, which Clover picked up, "Senator Eugene Hale is a brute." Everything about the Hearts piqued the curiosity of Washington society—its exclusiveness, its secrecy, its symbols. The club had its own tea set and its stationery—five tiny hearts engraved on heavy white note paper.

Enlivening the tea-table gossip at the Hearts and throughout Washington's drawing rooms was the question, "Who wrote the new novel *Democracy?*" The book that Adams had published in deep secrecy in 1879 was now selling briskly in the United States, and in England and France as well. The British public greeted the author as "a new Disraeli," while French critics compared him to Alphonse Daudet. American readers were indulging in some wild guesses—John Hay, Senator Blaine, Clarence King, or even Clover Adams. Henry Adams adored the general bafflement, especially when his brother Charles Francis unsuspectingly wrote a letter to *The Nation*: "The work is crude, with a half-educated touch which is always provokingly near being very good." He suggested that the author must have worked on a newspaper and knew nothing of business, but added, "Who he is I have not the remotest idea." Emily Beale declared, "It's a horrid, nasty, vulgar book written by a newspaperman who is not in good society." Only the British novelist Mrs. Humphrey Ward guessed correctly.

A brilliant satire of the corruption and hypocrisy of Washington politics, *Democracy* reflects Adams's disillusionment with government and social pretensions and his amusement at the attempt of a naive young woman to penetrate politics. His heroine, Madeleine Lee, an attractive young widow, arrives in the capital eager to understand politics and encounters the rascally Senator Ratcliffe, aged 50, "a great ponderous man, over six feet high, very senatorial and dignified," who wishes to marry her.

Whether Lizzie Cameron suspected that Adams was the author of *Democracy*, she certainly read the book—all of Washington society was devouring it. It became a vital part of her education, for Adams pointed out so many truths that she was experiencing, such as the "historical fact that elderly senators have had a curious fascination for young and handsome women." Adams was not kind in his assessment of senators, whose common characteristic, he wrote, was "a boundless and guileless thirst for flattery." And the Bulgarian minister Baron Jacobi describes an American senator as "the type which, to his bleared European eyes, combined the utmost pragmatical self-assurance and overbearing temper with the narrowest education and the meanest personal experience."

As a senator's wife, Lizzie could appreciate Adams's description of Ratcliffe's career. "He had not fought his own way in life for nothing.... The weak side of the senator lay in his blind ignorance of morals.... The beauty of his work consisted in the skill with which he evaded questions of principle." Perhaps Lizzie had once felt a twinge of compassion for the senator "who really loved her as earnestly as it was in his nature to love anything." But she recognized that his temperament was "naturally dictatorial and violent, only long training and severe experience had taught him self control and when he gave way to passions his bursts of fury were still tremendous." At first, deciding that "men were valuable only in proportion to their strength and appreciation of women," Madeleine toys with the senator's affections and is accused of being "a cold-blooded, heartless, unfeminine cat." Disillusioned when she discovers his corruption, she rejects him and decides to flee to Egypt because "Democracy has shaken my nerves to pieces."

A second milestone in Lizzie's education was the novel *Esther,* which Adams was now writing and would publish under the pen name Frances Snow Compton, insisting that the publisher do no advertising at all. A fictional struggle between love and religious doubt, it is also a *roman à clef,* with all the characters drawn from life. Esther is, of course, Clover. The artist Wharton is John La Farge; the Reverend Mr. Hazard is the Bostonian clergyman Wendell Phillips. Adams himself is Strong—"his forehead was so bald as to give his face a look of strong character which a dark beard rather helped to increase." Esther is a skeptical and spirited young woman in 19th-century New York whom the author compares to "a lightly sparred yacht in mid-ocean.... She sails gaily along though there is no land in sight and plenty of rough weather coming." The only child of a widowed father, she had all her life been used "to act for herself and to order others." Esther, Adams observed, "like most women, was timid and wanted to be told when she could be bold with perfect safety. She had the instinct of power but not the love of responsibility. To be steadily strong was not in her nature. She was audacious only by starts and recoiled from her own audacity."

In *Esther* Adams mirrors his wife and strikes an ominous note in his forecast of "plenty of rough weather coming." The story opens in the new Church of St. John on Fifth Avenue, which is nearing completion. Esther, an aspiring painter, is helping to decorate the interior. Its rector, the Reverend Mr. Hazard, encourages her, although the artist Wharton evaluates her as only "a second-rate amateur who had studied under good masters." From faraway Colorado comes 21-year-old Catherine Brooke (who is Lizzie), "as fresh as a summer's breeze with a complexion like the petals of a sweetbriar rose." Esther asks her to sit as a model for her portrait of St. Cecilia, but she is surprised to find "what a difficult model she was, with liquid reflections of eyes, hair and skin that would have puzzled Correggio. Do what she would,

Catherine's features defied modeling and made the artificial colors seem hard and coarse."

The "new Madonna of the prairie" captivates everyone. Displaying an inherent coquetry, she was "ready enough to try her youthful powers on most men...Soon she became a favorite. No one could resist her hazel eyes and the curve of her neck or her pure complexion which had the transparency of a Colorado sunrise." With the transposition of the word "Ohio" for "Colorado," the description mirrors Henry Adam's perception of Lizzie Cameron.

As the story unfolds, Esther is torn between her religious skepticism and her love for the minister Hazard. Sadly she acknowledges the truth of her cousin George's words,"Faith is a state of mind like love or jealousy. You never can reason yourself into it. Faith means submission. Submit." But she cannot.

Meanwhile, the artist, who is saddled with a disastrous wife, is enchanted by Catherine. He instructs her, and she proves an apt pupil. Adams writes, with unconscious chauvinism, "She listened to all the discussions and picked up the meaning of his orders and criticisms. In a short time she began to maintain opinions of her own. A quick girl soon picks up ideas when she hears clever men talking about matters which they understand."

Representing the voice of 19th-century experience, Esther's aunt observes, "Girls must have an education and the only way they can get a good one is from clever men. As for falling in love, they will always do that, whether the men are clever or not."

The story proceeds inexorably to its unhappy ending. Desolate at her father's death, Esther cannot resolve her religious doubts, so she dismisses her uncomprehending suitor. Like the 19th-century hero, in fact and in fiction, he cannot credit his senses that she is actually rejecting him. Esther's aunt remarks, "If things go wrong, she will rebel and a woman who rebels is lost."

The fate of Catherine Brooke and of Wharton is not disclosed.

Tragic in tone, closely paralleling the events of his marriage, the book meant everything to Henry Adams, who once wrote, "I care more for one chapter or for any dozen pages of 'Esther' than for the whole History. The public could never understand that such a book might be written in one's heart's blood." Of the 1,000 copies published, only 500 were sold.

Mrs. Cameron read *Esther* and enjoyed it. She may have recognized herself in the character of Catherine, but she did not say. A few years later, after she had learned the author's identity, she wrote to Adams, "You are a poet of a very high order and 'Esther' if not my own sonnets have convinced me."

While Adams was absorbed in writing his novel, Clover was greedily devouring *L'Histoire de ma vie*, the autobiography of George Sand, who had recently died in Nohant. Clover enlivened the conversation at the tea table with her reactions to it. To her father Dr. Robert W. Hooper in Boston, who was also reading it, she exclaimed, "I'm in the 15th Volume — I'm sorry it ends with Volume 20." Dr. Hooper, a retired oculist, had studied medicine in Paris in the 1830s, and Clover pointed out excitedly, "George Sand must have jostled you daily in the Latin Quarter dressed in men's clothes and dining in cheap restaurants."

At dinner, Clover sat next to the scholarly Dr. Bessels of the Smithsonian Institution and heard him describe his meeting with the French author in 1867. "He dined with Mme. Sand and Dumas Fils in Paris," she wrote to her father, "and later visited her for two days at her chateau at Nohant." Dr. Bessels described the charming countryside and the dining room whose folded doors "opened onto a large terrace where Chopin once dragged his piano and played to the stars. Mme. Sand looked like a sheep and had no conversation, but watched the others."

These glimpses, once removed, of George Sand and the artist's life in Paris stirred the imagination of Elizabeth Cameron, especially since Don was planning a trip to Europe for them both. The Camerons at this time had moved into a large new house on Scott Circle, and Don was rapidly acquiring new real estate.

Coached by the socially experienced Clover, Mrs. Don was developing her natural talents as a hostess. After former Attorney General Benjamin Brewster met Lizzie, he wrote excitedly to Simon Cameron, "Be sure to bring that angelic Mrs. Cameron. She has left an impression that time will never efface. Such women were created to smile on men and make them happy." Dinners at the Cameron home were often enlivened by the hearty laugh and expert story-telling of Uncle Cump. Once when Clover found herself seated next to a dull New Yorker, she leaned across the table to catch the merry blue eyes of General Sherman. All that he needed was one question about his military career and General Sherman became "very lively over his March to the Sea, repeating it with knives and forks on the tablecloth. Finally he swept the rebel army off the tablecloth with a pudding knife to the amusement of his audience."

But Washington social life was not all dinners and receptions. The theater and the opera were equally popular. Lizzie loved music and responded to it with the same rapturous intensity with which she listened to Henry Adams's discourses. Of course Don Cameron did not share this interest. His excursions to the opera had ended with his marriage. When the diva Adelina Patti was singing in Washington, Clover wrote, "We have taken seats for a full week with Mrs. Don. Her Senator is 'ill' so his substitute is General Miles."

During Lent, Mrs. Don was away, visiting relatives in New York. Clover scoffed, "Here comes Easter Sunday when the spirits rise of our good Catholic and Episcopal friends. For forty days and nights they have rather slowed up—only operas, dinners, poker parties and such penitential rites." Shortly after Easter, Clover exclaimed, "Mrs. Don returned yesterday from six weeks' illness in New York. I'm going to see the poor little woman now. She has drawn a blank, I fear, in Don, for all his money and fine houses and she's not over 23, a mere baby." (Actually Lizzie was 25.)

Before he returned to London, Henry James was introduced to Mrs. Don, and Clover Adams reported, "He was charmed." But Lizzie witnessed Clover's indignation at James's farewell letter to her in which he called her "the incarnation of your native land." She retorted, "Am I then vulgar, dreary, impossible to live with?" It required all of Henry Adams's affectionate diplomacy to soothe her.

By now, Henry and Clover realized that the Cameron marriage was only a façade. Lizzie's occasional bouts of illness were attributed to "nerves," but in reality they were the result of her unhappiness. The unromantic Don Cameron was lacking in tenderness, while his wife was thirsting for affection. "I soak it up like a sponge," she confessed. In this marriage of convenience, Senator Cameron had triumphed. He had acquired a captivating hostess, as well as a chaperone for his unmarried daughters. Lizzie had gained very little — a certain status but small freedom. The wealthy senator whom she had married held firmly to the purse strings and controlled her activities. He made all the decisions — where they would live, where they would travel, whom they would entertain. Although she was ripe for love, Lizzie was deprived even of affection.

Moved by pity, Henry Adams and his wife cultivated Elizabeth Cameron. This necessarily meant including her husband. With growing frequency, Clover mentioned them. "The great Don came to tea and admired Possum," or "The Camerons are coming to tea and Mrs. Don is much amused that her husband proposed coming," or "We enjoyed a dinner party and reception at the Camerons'. Our host's downfall in Pennsylvania has sobered if not saddened him." This was a jab at Don Cameron's drinking, which Lizzie had not succeeded in curbing.

Cameron was involved in a boss-machine war in Pennsylvania whose principal insurgent was his brother-in-law Wayne MacVeagh, a former attorney general and an advocate of civil service reform. Their viewpoints were invariably opposed. When Clover encountered Mrs. MacVeagh, who was Don's sister Virginia, she inquired, "Where are you staying in Washington?" The tall, witty female replica of old Simon Cameron replied with grim humor, "We are staying with my brother Don. We hear so much about you from them that we thought if you associate with them that we can."

At dinner, Clover Adams sat next to Senator Cameron and spoke warmly of Wayne MacVeagh. Glumly, her host replied, "His politics are peculiar." To which Clover retorted, "I wish yours were peculiar in the same direction." Writing to her father, she declared, "If Senator Cameron doesn't watch out, the reform movement will sweep over his state and beach him high and dry in Harrisburg."

Fortunately for Lizzie, this prediction did not come true. Surfeited with politics, but dreading her husband's retirement, Lizzie complained to her mother, "I would about die if Don had to leave Washington and we had to live all year round in Harrisburg."

By now, Lizzie had made a staunch ally of Simon Cameron, who still controlled his son's political career. When Simon's daughter Margaret made an unfortunate marriage, Lizzie's sympathetic letter to Simon pleased him mightily. "Your kind words about Maggie," he wrote to Lizzie, "must remain to your credit as long as I live and are a proof to me that you are a true-hearted good woman." Later, he urged his daughter-in-law to invite Maggie and her children for a visit. "Donald must make the invitation or you must insist on it. They won't stay long but it will make all of them happy. I am very old now and have done many disinterested acts but sometimes, when least expected, they have paid more than compound interest."

News of Don's political downfall, however ardently desired by his enemies, proved premature. Simon Cameron's power, which he wielded through his son, was still operative. To Simon in his Lancaster County summer home at Donegal Spring, his political crony Benjamin Brewster wrote, "Don, with whom I dined last night, suggested that we offer to Alexander Cassatt the mission to Italy which is now vacant. [Cassatt was the president of the Pennsylvania Railroad and the brother of the Philadelphia artist Mary Cassatt, whose growing fame as an Impressionist painter in France was reaching her native land.] The appointment of Cassatt would strengthen us with the railroad interests and would gratify him. He would make a fine, showy, useful minister, he would not hold it for long and he would be of great service to us. I suggested to Don that you come here and say a word with the President." Although the Cassatt appointment was not forthcoming, Brewster's letter underlined Simon's continuing influence on his son's political career.

Senator J. Donald Cameron the practical politician was a strange companion for Henry Adams the political philosopher. As the two couples spent more time together, Adams remarked with a trace of malice, "You should see Don Cameron's smile—he loves us like a father. Don is behaving himself again this winter and entertains. We were asked to a charming dinner and I am now a tame cat around the house. Don and I stroll around with our arms around each other's necks." (This was plainly impossible, for Don Cameron was eight inches taller than Adams.) Then Adams added facetiously, "I should prefer to accompany Mrs. Don in that attitude but he insists on loving me for his own sake."

Two more polar opposites could hardly be found in 19th-century Washington. Don Cameron was a shrewd businessman, an audacious politician, a canny manipulator of men. As a senator he devoted most of his energies to getting reelected. During his 20 years in the Senate, he introduced only eight minor bills and none of these became law. Don was blunt, unimaginative, coarse-grained, and inarticulate, and he served as a hardworking operator of the Pennsylvania political machine. He was a bourbon-drinking, tobacco-chewing, poker-playing "pol." While his wife was entertaining prospects for him in the drawing room, Don was often playing poker in the billiard room for the highest stakes in Washington.

In contrast, Henry Adams was a brilliant scholar of political science who understood the realities of power politics as thoroughly as Talleyrand, a knowledge which may have been transmitted through Adams's genes. As someone remarked, "Adams was not much in politics but politics was much in him." But since he was never offered a chance at public office, he continued his aristocratic scrutiny of politics, constantly prophesying disaster while holding aloof from the sordid details. Adams's sophisticated palate savored vintage champagne, while Cameron slaked his thirst with Kentucky bourbon. Like the senator, Adams was a prodigious worker, but in a realm that Don Cameron never entered. Adams had a mind of infinite subtlety—probing, analytical, sardonic. His complex mental processes once caused his friend John La Farge to exclaim in exasperation, "Adams, you reason too much."

But of Senator Cameron, Adams would observe, "As minds go, his was not complex. It reasoned little and never talked, but in practical matters it was the steadiest of all American types, perhaps the most efficient and certainly the safest."

Don Cameron was the archetype of the successful politician who had emerged during Grant's administration. Henry Adams, who was now accepted as a member of the senator's household, had ample opportunity to study him. Later in *The Education of Henry Adams* he would write a brilliant description of Cameron which still serves as a portrait of a certain kind of American politician.

> Months of close contact teach character if character has interest [wrote Adams], and to Adams the Cameron type had been interesting ever since it had shipwrecked his career in the person of President Grant. There is a narrowness to the Pennsylvania mind, as narrow as the kirk, as shy of other people's narrowness as a Yankee's; as self-limited as a Puritan farmer's. To him none but Pennsylvanians were white—Chinaman, Negro, Italian, Englishman, Yankee—all was one in the depth of the Pennsylvania consciousness. The mental machine could only run on what it took for American lines.
>
> However [Adams conceded], the machine worked, by coarse means on coarse interests, but its practical success had been the most curious study in American history. Practically the Pennsylvania politician forgot his prejudices when he allied his interests. He then became supple in action and large in motive, whatever he thought of his colleagues. When he happened to be right, which was, of course, whenever one agreed with him—he was the strongest American in America. As an ally he was worth all the rest because he understood his own class which was always a majority and knew how to deal with it as no New Englander could. If one wanted work done in Congress one did wisely to avoid asking a New Englander to do it. The Pennsylvanian could not only do it, but he did it willingly, practically, intelligently.

For years, this oddly assorted pair—Adams and Cameron—conducted an alliance that could have passed for friendship except that Henry Adams knew and expressed what Cameron wordlessly understood—that there was not and could not be any real reciprocity between them. As Adams noted, "Never in the realm of human possibilities had a Cameron believed in an Adams—or an Adams in a Cameron but they had, curiously enough, always worked together. The Camerons had what the Adamses thought the political vice of reaching their objectives without much regard to their methods." While Adams studied this "perfect and favorable specimen of the American type which had so persistently suppressed his own," he could detect "no trace of any influence which he exerted on Cameron. Not an opinion or view of Adams on any subject was ever reflected back on him from Cameron's mind, not even an expression or a fact. Yet the difference in age [five years] was trifling and in education slight [Harvard vs. Princeton]."

Although Don Cameron offered no opinion of Henry Adams; it is likely that he knew he was hopelessly outclassed by him in intellect and in expression. A better listener than speaker, Cameron often sat glumly in the background while Adams held his listeners spellbound with his witty and provocative comments. When Adams's speculative imagination took wing, Senator Cameron's scowl showed that he "profoundly mistrusted Uncle Henry's whimsical philosophical musings," but he could think of no way to answer them. Although suspicious of "literary fellows," he had sense enough to recognize Adams's gifts and did not hesitate to call upon him for help in preparing speeches. Don was highly flattered at the courtly attention that Adams and his distinguished circle were paying to his wife. On the whole, the relationship ran smoothly under Adams's subtle management. A student of human behavior, Adams sensed that Don Cameron could be a dangerous enemy although he was a generous host. A kind of quid-pro-quo relationship could be sustained, with Cameron acting as the complaisant husband and Adams taking charge of the social formation of his wife.

During the early months of 1883, Cameron was not well. His drinking was worse — a gossip writer told of his being drunk for 10 days in February and "approaching the d.t.'s". Also, as Brewster wrote to Simon, "Don's old malady frets and worries him. He is a terrible sufferer. He fears this terrible operation may be necessary." It was, and during March the senator underwent minor surgery, from which he was soon recuperating. But his ineptitude in the Senate was apparent even to him, and he threatened to give up his seat. To this course, Simon was firmly opposed. "It won't do," he wrote to Brewster, who replied, "It's a pity if he wants to leave that he cannot. However, in a short time he can go abroad as you suggest."

Clearly Simon was still in charge. The sycophantic Brewster assured him, "Don fairly worships you. He is a fine fellow, with a warm, bold nature and a long head under that red topknot. The older he gets, the more he assimilates you and he has a positive submissiveness to your wisdom and experience which I like to see in a youngster." (Don was then 50 years old.)

Simon's and Brewster's insistence on a European trip for Don indicated that, partly due to his drinking, his career was in a shambles, and only if he were removed from the scene could the two old pros mend his shattered fences. Brewster argued, "A foreign journey would do him a great deal of good, give him time to meditate and contemplate things from a distance, give him a new field for thought. It would furnish him with new and lighter amusements than we get here, relax the severity of his constant anxieties and bring him home better equipped for his duties." Obviously the two old trainers wanted their fighter out of the ring for a time. Brewster concluded, "It would be a wise step, a happy finish and polish to his career just at mid-life as he is reaching the summit. It would assure his position again with greater comfort to himself and greater discomfort to his and your enemies."

Simon Cameron set up the itinerary for his son's junket, which included England, Ireland, Scotland, France, Germany, and Belgium. He wrote to Don urgently, "You must see Ireland and look into the political and domestic conditions. Few of our diplomatic men know anything of that unfortunate country and you can distinguish yourself by knowing it thoroughly. I hope you will see every old cathedral and abbey in Ireland, old castles and ancestral estates in Scotland and also go to Liverpool."

Meanwhile, Mrs. Don was packing, bubbling with excitement about the forthcoming trip, recalling all she had heard about Paris and London during the past two years in the Adams ménage.

Although Henry Adams possessed social contacts in London that would assure the Cameron party entrée into the best circles, he was unwilling to furnish them with letters of introduction, explaining to John Hay in London, "I would like to give her letters but I cannot swindle my friends with Don." In a burst of feeling, he added, "I adore her and respect the way she has kept herself out of scandal and mud and done her duty by the lump of clay she promised to love and respect." Then, in a characteristic compromise, he told Hay, "Please say to Ambassador Lowell that we expect him to take *her* under his special charge. Tell Sir John Clarke to make her acquaintance but warn him against Don. I will in no way be responsible for Don in England but if you can tell our friends to show her kindness, pray do so. She will carry plenty of letters but none from us."

Adams also wrote to his British friend Charles Milnes Gaskell: "Should you come across my dear little friend Mrs. Don in England, you should make her acquaintance and tell her I introduced her. I could not do as much for her husband who, though a Senator of the United States, is not my ideal companion for a cottage."

The Camerons planned to sail for Europe on 19 May 1883. The evening before their departure, Clover and Henry entertained them at a small farewell tea for 16. The menu was topped off with ice cream and strawberries and a bon voyage toast in champagne. Lizzie was radiant with excitement and, as Uncle Cump had noticed, "better looking when moved than when in repose." As she made her farewells, she caught a look of sadness on the faces of her hosts as she heard Clover murmur, "We shall miss you much. . . ."

The Camerons left Washington by private railroad car for their embarkation from New York. The Adamses did not see them off, but later that day Henry Adams wrote to Elizabeth Cameron. It was the first letter in a correspondence that would last for 35 years. With an exaggerated pose of grief which only partly concealed his longing, he wrote,

> We did not come to see you off at the station. Our feelings overcame us. The dogs wept all morning. The puppy positively screamed and has not stopped yet. The town is desolate without you. . . . My wife and I ride by your house and wonder where you

are, in Italy perhaps or in Asia, for you have been away a year or two and we hear nothing from you. I see no good in such long absences. Your friends grow old and you forget them. Aristarchi Bey [the Turkish minister to the U.S.] follows you on the 23rd. You will see him in London. . . . I have half a mind to run over for the pleasure of getting up a picnic for you at Penshurst or Cambridge. . . . Goodbye. If you were going to Baltimore or Harrisburg we would be hopeless. As it is only Europe, *à bientôt.*

A few days later, Adams wrote to his old friend James Russell Lowell, who was U.S. minister to the Court of St. James's. Although Adams had refused to write the Camerons an official letter of introduction, nevertheless he wanted to make certain that Mrs. Don was taken care of on her first visit to London.

"Both my wife and I are very fond of Mrs. Don," he wrote. "Don has some good qualities and some pretty poor ones and does not shine in society. But he is a good deal better than he seems. . . . For our sakes be kind, if you have a chance, to all the Camerons and especially take Mrs. Don to some big entertainment and point out to her the people she wants to see or know."

He added, "You will fall in love with her as I have . . ."

5

Prince Orloff

new phase of Lizzie Cameron's education began with her first trip abroad in 1883. The Camerons' first stop was London, where the senator's young wife enjoyed a dazzling social success. U.S. Minister James Russell Lowell (having received Henry Adams's letter with its limited endorsement of Lizzie but not of her husband) hastened to advise her. "I think *Mr.* Cameron, as well as yourself, should be presented to H.R.H. *Your* social salvation depends on it." This court presentation to Queen Victoria, which was the seal of acceptance into London's *beau monde*, was duly arranged, and instead of risking social damnation, the Camerons found themselves taken up by British society. In addition, Senator Cameron could make use of his father's long-established connections in the Scottish Highlands.

Lizzie's first triumph occurred at an evening reception given by Prime Minister Gladstone. Every man in the room was aware of the American senator's bewitching wife, whose fair complextion was set off by her long black velvet gown. Her entrance caught the eye of Minister Lowell, but he was not quick enough. Next day he wrote her a wistful note: "I had a glimpse of you last night at Gladstone's but ere I could get at you, you had vanished like a beautiful dream."

Shortly afterward, Andrew Carnegie, a longtime friend of Simon Cameron's, held a dinner in their honor at the Grand Hotel, where Lizzie captivated both her host and his guests. One of these was Matthew Arnold, who later confided to Adams, "She is lovely if she is the Mrs. Cameron I sat next to in London."

During her triumphal progress through London at dinners and balls, musicals and receptions, Lizzie was radiantly responsive to the well-bred adulation of her frock-coated cavaliers and blithely unaware of the disapproving glances of their wives or the dour silence of her husband.

As the Season waned, Lizzie found time to write to Henry and Clover Adams at Beverly Farms. Adams's response was immediate. "Your letter gave us a genuine surprise and excitement. A month's retreat in the country has already reduced me to barking like Boojum and Marquis. We are all barking wildly on hearing of your news." He reported that Clover was busy with her new hobby of photography, while he was correcting the proof-sheets of his

Prince Orloff

History. Noting a recent newspaper report that the Camerons were planning to spend two years in Europe, Adams sighed. "We must resign ourselves. What is more you must make a thorough campaign if you mean to get pleasure out of it. I suppose you have already conquered England. Should you meet my old and dear friends Milnes Gaskell and Robert Cunliffe, be as kind to them as you can. There are bears in England but Ralph and Robert are lovable. I suppose by this time the season is over and you are fleeing."

The same mail brought Lizzie a letter from Clover, explaining, "Henry had been grumbling at your not answering his note but as I never write letters I expected none to begin where we left off." Clover described the recent photographs she had taken of Henry with their two dogs, sitting at the window of the small playhouse in the Beverly woods which she had had built for her small Hooper nieces. "Henry has his typewriter there and works a great deal. Henry James had been staying near us. He inquired tenderly for you."

At Clover's next request, Lizzie must have paused thoughtfully. "When you are in Paris, will you go to the Louvre for me? In the middle of the Long Gallery, find the portrait of a lady in black with a young child, standing, by Van Dyck and tell her that she haunts me." Lizzie may have felt a surge of sympathy at this glimpse of the childless Clover Adams confessing she felt "haunted" by this Dutch painting of maternity.

During a brief visit to the Scottish Highlands, which Simon Cameron had insisted on in devising their itinerary, Don Cameron professed himself contented. As the Philadelphia *Press* noted with sarcasm, "Sen. Don Cameron writes from Scotland that he has forgotten all about politics. Happy man! Lucky politics!"

Next the Camerons proceeded to Paris, where they established themselves in a Right Bank hotel. Paris in the 1880s was still a walled city of two million inhabitants and one of the loveliest in Europe. On its spacious tree-lined boulevards laid out by Baron Haussmann, the curious visitor could watch the unending pageant of carriages, Victorias, barouches, coach and fours and the bright mosaic of leisurely pedestrians—a mingling of the fashionable and the famous, artists and statesmen and tourists as well as the middle-class Frenchmen and women to whom this city was home. On the winding Seine, spanned by a dozen stone bridges, ancient and new, the visitor could glimpse, amid the launches and sailboats and barges, the humble *bateaux-lavoirs* from which French washerwomen did their laundry.

Bounteous and beautiful, Paris was the art center of the western world. In the late 19th century the capital was enjoying a Renaissance in art, music, literature, and theater, one of those explosions of creative energy that occasionally illuminate human history. After years of public rejection, the Impressionists—Manet, Pissaro, Degas, Monet, Renoir—were finally gaining acceptance, and their paintings would soon transform the face of art with their new understanding of light and color.

At the Comédie-Française, audiences were applauding the plays of Edmond Rostand and Alexandre Dumas *fils*, in which Sarah Bernhardt and Coquelin starred. To the ornate Opéra, audiences thronged to hear the music of Charles Gounod and Jules Massenet. Emile Zola's naturalistic novels, Guy de Maupassant's stories, and the avant-garde poetry of Charles Baudelaire and Stéphane Mallarmé were refashioning literature. Paris in the 1880s was a dream of beatitude for lovers of the arts.

Like many Americans in Paris at the time, Senator Cameron was inescapably provincial. Wearing the prescribed top hat and puffing on a cigar, the Pennsylvania politician strode along the boulevard de l'Opéra or up the Champs-Elysées, listening to the clatter of the horse-drawn traffic and exclaiming, "The constant whip-cracking of the Paris cabmen makes me feel like a perpetual Fourth of July celebration." The senator's chauvinism was equally evident when he visited the German capital and observed, "Berlin has more the appearance of an American city than any in Europe." But Lizzie was more responsive than her husband to the uniqueness of her surroundings. She had easily made the cultural leap from the Cuyahoga River to the Seine, and now as she breathed the air of Paris she felt a *frisson* of pleasure as she realized that this incomparable city was designed for all manner of adventures.

Her husband's adventures were largely gustatory. A hearty trencherman, Senator Cameron savored the French cuisine, of which he could never get enough. He wrote to his father, "My complete contentment here is due to the excellent food." He did not reveal whether he was obeying his doctor's orders to give up drinking. And as he usual he did not mention Lizzie.

In order for the Camerons to have a proper tour of Paris, Don's old Philadelphia friend Clement A. Griscom, the president of the American Steamship Line who was now living in Belgium, came over from Antwerp. After Don was ceremoniously presented to the prime minister of Belgium, the American senator showed an unexpected trace of humor in a letter to Simon. "I met the P.M. But as he don't speak English and my French isn't exactly the kind used in polite society, our conversation was limited. But the bows which passed between us were very elaborate."

During the 1880s the cosmopolitan society of the French capital included many titled Russians—grand dukes, princes, Imperial Army officers, and boyars. Their exotic tastes were catered to by the leading hostelries and purveyors of all types of entertainment—partly for money and partly out of fear. On their appearance in public the cry would go up, "Here come the Cossacks!" In exchange for Russian sables and matched pearls, the sprightliest demimondaines dispensed their favors. Once the Grand Duke Serge presented a courtesan with a pearl necklace valued at 20,000,000 francs on a platter. Meanwhile, "proper" ladies gossiped in well-bred horror about the amorous escapades of the Russian nobility with the *"grandes horizontales."*

An ancient palace on the rue Saint-Dominique housed the Russian Embassy, whose secretary was the legendary Prince Nikolay Alekseyevich Orloff. A towering Cossack who had lost an eye in the Crimean War, years before Elizabeth Cameron was born, he boasted an ancestry that was as formidable as his appearance. He was descended from a notorious family—in particular, from Gregory Orloff, who in 1762 had persuaded his brother Alexis to murder Tsar Peter III in order to put Catherine II on the throne of Russia. Until he was supplanted by Gregory Potemkin, Gregory Orloff had been the tsarina's lover. This grandfather of Prince Nikolay Orfloff had sired four illegitimate sons, of whom Alexis, the father of Nikolay, had served as head of the Russian secret police in 1844 and been ennobled by Tsar Alexander II in 1865, thus establishing the title. Although the present Prince Orloff had been decorated for bravery on the battlefield, he had recently been summarily dismissed from the Imperial Army because of a disgraceful episode that almost cost him his life.

After quarreling with a German officer, Orloff had challenged him to a duel, not with swords or pistols, but with glasses of Cointreau. His German adversary had toppled over unconscious after the eightieth round, but the indomitable Orloff continued to drink, stonily downing his liqueur until he reached his one hundred and twelfth glass. Rising unsteadily, he managed to leave the room erect. But the next day he suffered a nearly fatal liver attack. For this indiscretion he was "exiled" to the Russian Embassy in Paris. Here his undemanding duties as secretary, enlivened with a succession of flagrant love affairs, made his exile tolerable.

At a ball at the embassy, the host was Prince Orloff, who was still wearing his Imperial Army uniform, encrusted with medals and gold braid. Despite the black patch he wore over his ruined eye, he could still note with appreciation the young wife of the senator from Pennsylvania, glimmering in an ivory satin gown with a short train. Neither Lizzie nor Prince Nikolay had ever met anyone quite like the other. Lizzie looked up coquettishly at this noble savage, thirty years her senior, and greeted him in reasonably fluent French.

The story of the Prince Orloff affair, which Lizzie closely guarded, was told in a letter written forty years later by Elisina Palamadessi di Castelvecchio Tyler, the Italian countess who was married to William Royall Tyler, Sr., a close friend of Edith Wharton's. Mrs. Tyler met Lizzie Cameron during World War I, when both of them worked with the novelist in her Foyer aux Réfugiés in Paris. Elisina Tyler, who had a gift for friendship and an ear for gossip, managed to uncover the details.

"Very soon after their meeting," Mrs. Tyler recalled, "Prince Orloff became the most enamoured of Lizzie's beaux."

Confronted with this aging but formidable Russian prince, who was accustomed to conquering on the battlefield and in the boudoir, Lizzie felt a fascination tinged with terror. Nothing in her experience in Washington or in Cleveland had prepared her for this. With practiced coquetry, she led him on. As Mrs. Tyler remembered, "Prince Orloff gave her sables and all sorts of lovely presents as he sank deeper in subjection to her."

But Lizzie never forgot her Ohio upbringing, based on the stern New England code of the Sherman family. One day Prince Orloff drew up in his carriage outside the Camerons' hotel. Leaping out impetuously, he fell and broke his leg. Although youthful Madame Cameron fluttered about in horror at the sight of the prostrate prince, she did not lose her head. Firmly she rejected a suggestion that he should be carried into her suite, explaining, "It would compromise me." Even though she lamented the Russian's plight, she could not take him in; instead, she arranged for him to be carried away to hospital and "made him bear the pain of the journey without even a splint."

Such treatment was a novelty to the amorous Russian, and it only heightened his ardor. Soon he was convalescent and showing himself remarkably agile for a one-eyed man whose leg was in a cast. He invited Madame Cameron to dine with him in a *cabinet particulière*, an elegantly appointed room hidden away over a fashionable restaurant at a discreet address, where a titled man could entertain a lady in perfect privacy. It was whispered that these rooms were sometimes the locale for sadistic orgies — at any rate, they held all the piquancy of the forbidden. Lizzie, who was naturally curious to see such a trysting place, agreed to meet the prince there. Clad in the Russian sables that he had given her, she was ushered into a candlelit room that was furnished with a small circular dining table, plush divans, and, half-hidden in the shadows, a canopied bed. When the maître d'hôtel bowed himself out, pulling the velvet portieres across the door, Lizzie found herself alone with the heavy-breathing hero of the Crimea.

"He urged his suit again," Elisina Tyler recalled. "But Lizzie was adamant. Although she liked to flirt and tease, to kiss and cajole, she never went all the way." Suddenly, the Russian prince realized that the wife of the American senator was trifling with him. Outraged, "he rose in his Russian wrath," wrote Mrs. Tyler. "And he stripped all her clothes from her. Then he beat her very hard indeed and left her to find her way home as she could."

The picture of Lizzie, cowering under the Russian's blows, then, sobbing, bruised, and disheveled, creeping back to her hotel, has all the aspects of Victorian melodrama. The lasting effect on her of such barbarous behavior can only be surmised. Whether or not she may have unwittingly invited the savagery of Orloff, she certainly did not expect it. Her actual experience with men had not been extensive — even the embraces of her unromantic, often alcoholic husband did not include physical cruelty. The psychological damage must have been profound for this gently reared lady whose disappointment in first love had been followed by the disillusion of a marriage of convenience. Youthful and coquettish, she had been searching in Paris for a harmless romantic adventure, like her many earlier ones, to overcome the boredom of her marriage to a husband who appreciated only politics and whiskey. Instead, she had encountered attempted seduction and physical abuse. This debacle must have confirmed her distrust of men at which she had hinted five years earlier in her letter to her mother announcing her engagement. It may also have increased her yearning for a tenderness that she had not yet experienced.

Elisina Tyler, who was the only historian of this unhappy episode, recalled it years later, when Lizzie was in her seventies, and remarked, "No wonder that poor Lizzie had her ups and downs of kindness and spite, after such a *partie fine* as that!"

The inglorious Orloff died a few years later at his chateau in Fontainebleau, and Lizzie never mentioned his name. But his fame is perpetuated in the dish Salle de Veau Orloff (Saddle of Veal Orloff) which was created to honor him at Maxim's in Paris and is still served in three-star restaurants. A rich and savory mixture of veal, cooked with shallots, in white wine and port, with a purée of mushrooms, truffles, and sauce Mornay, it is a fitting tribute to a man of appetite.

Lizzie was not sorry when Don decided that they would move on. During that gray November, Paris had lost its luster for her, and she went willingly with him to Dresden. Here the senator wrote to his father on 11 November: "For the birthday of Martin Luther the town will have a torchlight procession. The Germans don't care so much about Luther per se, but they think it annoys the Catholics and they have such a holy hatred of them that they take particular delight in making all the demonstrations possible." For the first time Don mentioned his wife. "I have a severe cold today and am feeling very unsociable and uncomfortable as Lizzie has been sick ever since she came here. I have determined to return to Paris and to take my trip from there to Vienna. Joe Mason [a general factotum whom Simon had sent along to make their trip easier] does everything to make our trip agreeable and promises to come back to Paris with us. I will try to write when I get rid of this cold and don't have Joe Mason buzzing in my ear."

Their next stop was Berlin, where Senator Cameron was eager to meet Chancellor Otto von Bismarck, whom he regarded as the "foremost man in Europe." Unfortunately, the Iron Chancellor was away from the capital, so the Camerons departed for Antwerp.

Throughout their trip, Don Cameron kept harking back to the perfections of Paris. "The cooking here is not so good as in Paris," or "I like Dresden though it differs from Paris — the houses are in better condition and there is not so much noise and rattle in the streets."

Lizzie found it difficult to share her husband's enthusiasms.

Shortly after Christmas she received a letter from Adams lamenting her absence; "We miss you more than ever and until you come back we shall never be quite content. Last night Mrs. Bonaparte gave a little dance and I looked earnestly about for someone to fill your place. No one was there. Come back to us before another winter has given your future rival a chance . . ."

Adams confided the momentous news that he and John Hay were buying adjoining lots on the corner of 16th and H Streets, facing Lafayette Square, on which they planned to build two connecting houses designed by Henry Hobson Richardson. "What we paid no mortal shall ever know. I am ruined by it. We are going to get Richardson to put up a shanty."

Lizzie had heard of Richardson. A Harvard classmate of Henry Adams's, he was the leading architect of his day. When he had built Trinity Church in Boston, his genius was at once evident. Richardson had succeeded in adapting the massive Romanesque style to public buildings and later to private residences in America. At once picturesque and powerful, monumental and humane, his architectural style dominated the 1880s and was known as "Richardson's Romanesque."

A Rabelaisian figure, Richardson weighed 345 pounds and dressed flamboyantly, frequently encircling his enormous girth in a bright yellow waistcoat. Clover had dubbed him "man-mountain Richardson," yet both she and Henry were fond of the architect, who was afflicted with a stammer that made him speak in a series of explosions.

For Henry Adams, whose intention was "to help make Washington handsome," the choice of Richardson as the designer of his new home on Lafayette Square was appropriate. Together, Adams and Clover and Richardson bent over the blueprints for what would one day be called "the first house in Washington, a dream of comfort and charm." This massive house, built like a medieval fortress, in which Clover would never live, would become a frequent refuge for Lizzie Cameron.

About a fortnight later, while Lizzie and Don were in Italy, Lizzie received an extraordinary letter from Clover. During Lizzie's absence, Clover's habitual restlessness had grown much worse. Despite her interest in photography, her devotion to Henry, her expertise in collecting and dispensing gossip — the latest tidbit was the discovery of "the shady priest Msgr. Capel at whose flowing robes half the women in town are tagging" — despite all these interests, Clover was chronically uneasy, absent-minded, often melancholy. At times she seemed as taut as a violin whose strings are tuned too tightly and which the lightest touch might break. Quickly irritated, then as quickly repentant, she showed flashes of anger followed by moods of depression that her husband was powerless to understand or change. Her letters to Lizzie showed her rapid fluctuations of mood. She began by addressing Lizzie as "Perdita to sight, to memory carissima," then explained with forced gaiety, "This Tuscan dialect is in case you are in the land of macaroni so that you may be able to read my note." Suddenly she broke out with an anguished cry, "We miss you — miss you — miss you." Abruptly she turned to the current gossip about Perry Belmont. "Left on the wharf as they say. I'm sorry for him but I fancy it's better for both. Marriage as an *egoisme à deux* is very hell but as an *egoisme à un* not so gay. Henry and I wonder how any man or woman dares to take the plunge."

From these dark musings she darted to the subject of their new house. "We've drawn our own plan for the inside of the house. No stained glass, no nothing, a library the size of the one on the South and no parlor because I can sit all day in the library and study next it, the dining room opening on a balcony overlooking the garden. I who have always been utterly opposed to building am the one who plunged first. I like to change my mind all of a sudden . . ."

Again she sounded melancholy. "We are not so happy as we once were. We have 15 cousins in town and another unborn due this month. We do not love any of them passionately and wish they were in Boston. I shall send you a new basket of home-made photographs. *Come home.*"

Somewhat later, Henry Adams was writing to a friend, "My wife and I are rather more solitary than at any other season," while Clover was explaining to her father, "I wouldn't go to hear Gabriel perform a solo on his trumpet." Yet amid her seclusion Clover still relished the gossip of Washington. "All the better class of Catholics are in a rage with Monsignor Capel, the

Henry Hobson Richardson

The Adams House at 1603 H Street designed by Richardson

scandalous priest. The wife of the Russian minister Mme. de Streve says he asked her for a rendezvous and she told him 'I will meet you in Hell.' "

Of the society "rabble" Clover was inexpressibly weary. "It is nauseating. The only way of existing at all is to keep out of it. The watering-place part of this life is getting intolerable and the pushing people who almost force themselves into your home—no one is admitted by my majestic butler if they ask 'if I receive.' So only those who walk in without asking come at all."

The Adamses refused an invitation to a White House reception, preferring to attend a violin recital in the lively company of Emily Beale. Clover, with her new mournful awareness of death, reflected on Theodore Roosevelt's double tragedy—both his wife and his mother had died on the same day. Sadly she recalled meeting the youthful Roosevelts, Theodore and Alice, in Cairo while the Adamses were honeymooning. "They were young, gay, rich, full of life and overwhelmingly hospitable to us in New York."

Late in February 1884, Clover was momentarily cheered when Richardson sent them the plans for the new house. "It will be a great interest. We adore building and can watch every brick and plank from next door."

She was also pleasantly diverted when asked to photograph the two Bonaparte children. They were the grandchildren of Prince Jerome Bonaparte, Napoleon's brother, who had undertaken a morganatic marriage with Betsy Patterson of Baltimore that the emperor had never recognized. Madame Bonaparte brought the little boy and girl to the Adams house, and Clover exclaimed, "So I took Jerome Bonapare astride a chair, blaring his trumpet—a pretty little brown-eyed Italian-looking boy of six, suggesting his ancestors in Corsica of 100 years ago. Also the same boy driving his small sister with a shawl strap for harness."

But this was only a momentary lightening of mood. She wrote to her father, "Why do the Episcopalians pray not to have sudden death? My silent prayer is for heart disease or lightning when my time comes." A few days later she wrote, "What pleases Henry and me most is that when one is 40 and on the home stretch it's consoling to find it suits one better to look ahead than behind."

Lizzie's return to Washington in May was greeted with enthusiasm by her mother, who wrote to her daughter Mary Miles in a shower of clichés: "Lizzie is back and she never looked handsomer except when she was married. She is thin as a rail in figure and she is as straight as an arrow and very stylish with some exquisite Parisian dresses trimmed with quantities of lace. She said it was cheap compared with what you got in this country. She brought me some kid gloves."

Mrs. Sherman, who was what late Victorians called "a crepe hanger," worried now about Lizzie's future. "Lizzie says that Mr. Cameron would not remain in Washington if he were out of politics—this she found out when they were abroad. Lizzie says she would *about die* if they had to live the year through in Harrisburg. Much as she dreads it in the summer she would be quite reconciled to stay through the summer if Mr. Cameron *can only be kept in politics*. She is going to stay in Washington while Congress is in session, so I will probably be kept here until June. But how little I see of her," Mrs. Sherman complained, "for she is surrounded by her friends and is dining and lunching out every day."

Clearly Lizzie's travels in Europe, by expanding her intellectual and social horizons, had unfitted her for life in Harrisburg and had added a new dimension to the education begun by Henry Adams.

When Mary Miles, now living at Fort Leavenworth, Kansas, asked her sister for advice about schooling for her adolescent daughter Cecilia, Lizzie's reply was a remarkably modern statement on women's education:

> I am so disappointed about Cecil. I have not much faith in her doing much studying in a garrison and in fact the child don't know how. She has never learned how to study and it is for that reason I have advocated a boarding school. I would be more than glad to share the expense of two or three years at a good New England school or at Farmington [a reference to Miss Porter's School from which Eliza Cameron had graduated].
>
> *The chances are always against a woman's happiness in this world.* If she marries happily and her husband is not learned or ambitious it won't matter. If he is cultivated and pushing he will be mortified at her inability to cope with him. If she is unhappy, the one thing which can sustain her and enable her to rise above it is a thorough education and a habit of application. I love the child dearly. No other niece or nephew can ever take her place in my heart. Therefore you must not be offended at my making an appeal for the one good gift that parents can give a child. Money may go, health may go, happiness slip by, disappointments come on every side. But a sound education and a cultivated mind always remain. The requirements of education are now far higher than when you and I went to school. Yet we are far better educated than Cecil now is. I don't mean education in the sense of having "been through" as children say, certain books, but the education of having a disciplined mind and habits of concentration and application.
>
> Of course, having passed the age at which that work is usually done, it will come harder to her but indeed she ought to have the chance. So I risk offending you by interfering with your affairs because I want to make this last appeal.
>
> You know the ups and downs of American life. It is impossible to tell what the future will call upon her to do. But it is only fair to put in her hands the weapons to fight the battle of life. It is like a man learning to swim—he may never get into deep water but if he does the knowledge will save his life. So if you love your child, give her, at whatever sacrifice, the weapons to enable her to fight the battle on equal terms with her adversaries. Day school won't do. She needs the discipline and routine of a boarding school with nothing outside to distract her mind. Choose a good New England school. Talk it over with Gen and let me take her East and go halves with you on the expense.

6

"Poor Clover's Self-Destruction"

For a while after La Dona's return to Washington in 1884, amid the blossoming of May, all seemed well with the Adamses. Both Henry and Clover shook off their winter gloom now that their "Perdita" was recovered. Over Clover's tea table, Lizzie regaled them with her spirited accounts of her adventures abroad (prudently omitting the Orloff incident).

But La Dona noticed that Clover's old gaiety seemed forced, that her attention wandered. Henry's wife, once so animated and self-confident, was beginning to show signs of that morbid introspection that had afflicted so many members of her family. As Charles Francis Adams later wrote in his reminiscences, "Henry's wife inherited a latent tendency to suicidal mania. It was in the Sturgis blood. Shortly after the birth of her son Sturgis Bigelow, Clover's maternal aunt, a Sturgis, one day, without the slightest cause, killed herself. Clover, who was a mere child at the time and rather a favorite niece, was with her aunt when she took the fatal dose of arsenic. The thing made a dangerous impression on her mind for she was old enough to have some idea of what it all meant." Of course, this tragedy was well known to the Adams family as well as to Boston society. But Henry Adams, like any lover on the brink of marriage, had been confident that his love and care would protect Clover from the deadly legacy. "I know better than anyone the risks I run," he wrote to his brother Brooks. "But I have weighed them carefully and accept them." Despite a frightening episode of severe depression that Clover had experienced during their honeymoon in Egypt, she managed to keep her precarious balance. But throughout the 13 years of their marriage, as Charles later learned, "Any period of excitement and unnatural action in Clover's case, was sure to be followed by a corresponding period of depression and morbid reaction and then her whole thought ran on self-destruction. Presently when the general health of her system was restored, the morbid tendency passed away. During her married life she passed through three of these periods which, though he never spoke of them, must to Henry have been periods of Hell."

While Clover was suffering these agonizing passages, Henry managed to conceal them, even from his family and from Lizzie. Constantly watchful over his wife's moods, Henry stood guard. Now that Mrs. Don was back, he rejoiced, not only for himself but for Clover's delight in her return.

Yet Clover's feelings were ambivalent. Despite her pleasure in Lizzie's company, she could hardly miss the contrast between them. Although she displayed no tinge of jealousy toward the younger woman, she could not fail to see how eagerly all the gentlemen, including her own Henry, responded to this incarnation of spring.

The contrast was marked. Clover Adams had always relied on her caustic wit to dominate any gathering of Henry's friends. Her brittle epigrams provoked explosions of laughter, but they often left her hearers with the uneasy fear of becoming her next victim. In the same gathering. Lizzie Cameron had only to smile on men and they became her captives. Clover liked to match wits with the statesmen and writers, artists and scientists who frequented the Adamses' salon while Henry looked on indulgently, not wishing to outshine her by unleashing his more deadly satire.

Mrs. Don, who was too intelligent to upstage a man in public, merely listened rapturously to whichever partner her hostess had assigned to her, posing an occasional question which would loose a torrent of masculine oratory that left the speaker feeling remarkably satisfied with both himself and his dinner partner. By her gift of paying attention, she attracted attention.

Clover was a stimulating but exhausting hostess. With her constant witticisms, her scathing judgments, and her unconcealed prejudices, she created an atmosphere of intellectual ferment. Yet physically she was not strong, and she tired easily. Lizzie, however, was inexhaustible, as the Washington *Critic* observed. "Mrs. Cameron is the most beautiful person in society. Although she is the stepmother of six children she still presents a brow unlined by care and a voice and manner as gay as possible. Constant late hours and the wear and tear attendant upon the onerous task of continued entertaining which her husband's position exacts has not told upon her at all."

The contrast between the two hostesses was not lost on Washington society. Despite his anxiety, it was not lost on Henry Adams.

The ambitious Clover was a driving force who could not resist pushing her husband, while he was engaged in writing his monumental *History*. She reminded him of how many candles old George Bancroft (the American historian who was also a cousin of Clover's) had burned before breakfast while he was writing *his* history. Yet Henry needed no prodding. He was a prodigious worker whose output was systematic and prolific.

Lizzie Cameron, as the youngest in a large family that included an ambitious mother, a passive father, three sisters, and two brothers, had learned the folly of nagging any man. Instead, she cajoled and flattered men and ultimately got her own way. Even while Clover was prodding Henry Adams about his work, Lizzie was offering him her wordless admiration, which caused Adams to put aside briefly his prodigious labors to write her playfully: "I shall have you carved over my stone doorway. I shall publish your volume of extracts with your portrait on the title page. I am miserable thinking that none of these methods can express the extent to which I am yours."

Before the Adamses departed in June for their summer home in Beverly Farms, they extracted a promise from Lizzie to visit them. Adams, gnawed by anxiety, was hoping that the wooded retreat on the North Shore which Clover loved, the solitude, and the familiar faces of their Beverly Farms neighbors, might restore his wife to her earlier high spirits.

But the experiment failed. A few weeks later he was writing to John Hay, "My wife and I are growing green with mold, bored to death with ourselves and see no one. At times we chirp feebly to each other, then sleep and dream sad dreams." As this was quite unlike their usual behavior, he warned Hay, "Don't quote me on this."

Lizzie, meanwhile, had gone with her mother to visit Don's summer place, Lochiel, not far from Harrisburg. On the Southern-style veranda that commanded a broad view of the South Mountains, she and Mrs. Sherman enjoyed a rest until, two days before they were scheduled to return to Washington, Senator Cameron arrived. Brightly Mrs. Sherman wrote to her daughter Mary, "Mr. Cameron was apparently glad to see us and made it very pleasant for us. He is his old self and *I think* has given up all kinds of stimulants."

Meanwhile, from Beverly Farms, a disappointed Clover was writing to Lizzie, "We have been hoping all season you'd come as you promised. Are you well and happy?"

Lizzie was well but scarcely happy. Life in remote and drafty Lochiel, surrounded by a brace of stepchildren, her worry-ridden mother, and her unwelcome husband was far from stimulating. She was delighted when it was time to return to Washington. Soon the Adamses also were back, and in the fall of 1884 Lizzie joined them in the vigil of watching their new house as it was being built under Richardson's dilatory direction. Clover was calling his massive Romanesque style of architecture "Neo-Agnostic," while Henry was noting, "Mrs. Don is here every day."

Although Adams was a tireless worker who was able to write under nearly all conditions, now he found concentration difficult. To John Hay, whose new house, also designed by Richardson, adjoined his own, he wrote, "Ten times a day I drop work and rush out to see the men lay the bricks and stone in your house." Hay's house, which was connected with Adams's but was located at right angles to it, would face on 16th Street, while Adams's fronted H Street on Lafayette Square.

As colder weather set in, the inevitable delays that accompany the building of almost any house, compounded by Richardson's procrastination, disturbed Clover more than Henry, who wrote philosophically, "Richardson came in as earnest as ever. He says the house is done—a Rabelaisian jest."

Late in November, Adams photographed Hay's half-finished house in order to show him the big arch hanging in midair. But Clover, who had her own darkroom for developing her photographs, was "unable, on account of weather and other impediments," to print it. "Meanwhile the arch is no longer in midair but solidly in place," By midwinter Adams wrote, "We are about a month behind my hopes and likely to be more. Nevertheless we try to be happy."

"Poor Clover's Self-Destruction"

But Clover, despite all of Henry's efforts and her own, had lost the secret of being happy. She seldon smiled, and her animation was gone. She complained of fatigue and suffered from nameless agonizing fears. No longer could she enjoy the social life that had previously absorbed her, although their guests were as entertaining as ever — John La Farge, Henry Richardson, and lively Mrs. Jack Gardner. One evening Richardson, La Farge, and Clover's brother Ned Hooper arrived and "talked much art and nothing else," while Clover remained inscrutably silent. She seemed unable to concentrate and from time to time would put her hand plaintively to her forehead, rubbing it back and forth in a bewildered way.

One of her few remaining pleasures was the Sunday news-letter, which she never failed to write to her father Dr. Hooper. On 5 March 1885, Grover Cleveland was inaugurated as president, and Clover roused herself to join Henry on horseback after three weeks out of the saddle. To her father, she wrote, "Grover Cleveland was safely installed across the way. The city looks like a gigantic tulip bed. We breakfasted at 1 and rode..." Astride their mounts she and Henry watched the inaugural parade, with thirty thousand infantry horses trotting along Constitution Avenue for hours. Added Clover, "I expected to come home on a stretcher."

Two days later, Clover learned that her father was seriously ill. Dr. Hooper, who was now 74, had for some time been suffering from angina pectoris. Now he was worse and was confined to his bed. Tight-lipped and fearful, Clover set our for Cambridge to nurse him, leaving Henry to follow.

In his letters to his wife, Henry Adams told her that Senator Cameron was stricken with tuberculosis and that his doctors were ordering him to Los Angeles for five months in the open air. But Lizzie Cameron, not wholly believing the doctor's diagnosis, did not wish to accompany him. Adams went to call on Cameron, whom he found sitting with Lizzie on a sofa.

> I greeted him with affection and said I was very glad to see him before he went off. His reply was characteristic. "Are you truly?" he asked. "Yes," I said, "truly." The poor fellow seemed really pleased at this and for the first time became open and companionable.... [Adams noted that the cordiality of his greeting] had broken down the crust in which his queer self-distrust wraps him. "I am hit here," he said, putting his hand on his lungs. "Harder than I supposed; I am badly hit; I'm not in the least frightened, but I am going to cure it if I can." He thought himself not frightened, but he is scared to pieces and shows it in excitement.... The drollest thing was that he invited us out to stay with him. "I mean it" he said, "I am in earnest." Then Mrs. Don broke in to say she was going out in the summer and begged us to go with her.

Don departed for California while Mrs. Cameron stayed behind.

It was the conviction of Lizzie's mother, echoed by her daughter, that Don was something of a hypochondriac.

For six weeks in the spring of 1885, Clover Adams and her sister Ellen Gurney hovered by their father's bedside in Cambridge, watching him endure the acute spasms of angina, which the doctors could do little to alleviate. With uncanny precision, Adams in his novel *Esther,* which he once said was "written in my heart's blood," had prefigured the scene in the sickroom: "She knew that there was no hope and that her father himself was only anxious for the end, yet to see him suffer and slowly fade out was terrible. . . . Esther had been told that she must not give way to agitation, under the risk of killing her father, who lay dozing, half-conscious, with his face turned towards her. Whenever his eyes opened they rested on hers."

This long death-watch was particluarly agonizing for Clover. Ever since she had been left motherless as a small child, she had turned to her father for the love and acceptance that a daughter usually receives from both parents. As a result, she had grown emotionally dependent upon him. Despite her devoted love for Henry, she now watched helplessly as the pillar of her emotional life collapsed. On 13 April, Dr. Hooper died.

During the simple funeral service in Cambridge, Henry Adams stood protectively by his stricken Clover. Afterward Adams wrote of Dr. Hooper, "Our relations were most friendly. I like the quiet and general respect which the society of Boston and Cambridge showed at his funeral. He made me and [Ephraim] Gurney [another Hooper son-in-law] executors and trustees with his son." (Adams, with his knowledge of finance, had been chosen by his late father-in-law to aid in the settlement of the half-million-dollar estate.)

The Adamses returned to Washington, and Clover rallied briefly. Henry noted, "My wife has come back in better condition than I feared." Clover described with tenderness her father's death in a letter to the Hays: "His humor and courage lasted until unconsciousness came on the ninth and on the thirteenth he went to sleep like a tired traveler. I used to think in those sad weeks how you and Mrs. Hay had gone over the same road — but without the comfort and even gayety with which my father walked to his grave." (Mrs. Hay's father, the wealthy Cleveland builder Amasa Stone, had recently committed suicide.)

As another May arrived in Washington, Henry, who was increasingly solicitous of Clover, decided that they should not return this summer to Beverly Farms. The association would be too painful for Clover, since her father had also had a summer home nearby. Adams considered their taking a six-week pack-trip to the Yellowstone country. But when it was evident that Clover had neither the strength nor the interest for such a trip, they decided to visit a quiet mountain retreat at Old Sweet Springs, West Virginia. While they were packing, they heard the news that Senator Cameron had prevailed on Lizzie to accompany him to the West Coast. Don, whose real estate deals were legendary, had just sold his house at Scott Circle. The details of this latest coup spread through Lafayette Square, and Adams commented enviously, "Think of $95,000 for that house! Don certainly has abilities. My own opinion is that this house [W. W. Corcoran's "little White House," which the Adamses were renting from him and which was next door to their new house] is better suited to Mrs. Don. I will let Don have a lot of furniture if he will only be my dearest friend."

But acquiring new furniture was the last thing the Camerons wished. Instead, Lizzie was performing the laborious task of "breaking up housekeeping." They were allowing the greater part of the standing furniture to go with the house. But Lizzie packed away her pictures, bric-a-brac, handsome writing desk, her best china, a hall settee that her mother had given her, and a standing clock. The latter two items, as well as all of her books and an Egyptian statue, she left with her mother, who wrote, "My house now looks grand with so many additions."

The Camerons were planning a long trip—first to Cleveland for a family wedding, then on to Chicago to visit Don's sister Mrs. Wayne MacVeagh and to attend the college commencement of Jim Cameron, the senator's only son. From there they would proceed to California.

Lizzie was ordinarily in robust health, but this long train trip to the Pacific Coast in summer heat seemed to undermine her health. She complained of exhaustion, causing her mother to blame her indisposition on her inconsiderate husband. To Mary Miles, Mrs. Sherman wrote, "I feel more and more as if I could never forgive Mr. Cameron for that piece of selfishness—the most nonsensical, the most inhumane thing I have ever known a husband to do—to allow her to take such a journey in the hottest month of the year—and taking her to such a climate."

What her mother did not realize was that, after seven years of marriage, Lizzie Cameron, age 28, was newly pregnant and was expecting the birth of her first child in May or June of 1886. Whether the pregnancy was deliberately planned Lizzie did not reveal. But the queasiness that often accompanies the first trimester of pregnancy, complicated by the oppressive heat of the trip, incapacitated her.

The fact that La Dona was absent from Washington from May until November and that Henry Adams was first in West Virginia, then in Beverly Farms during the crucial months of August and September, completely invalidates the later rumor that Henry Adams was the father of her child. Clearly Senator Cameron's delight in a prospective heir was tempered by no doubts as to its paternity.

The Adamses' stay in Old Sweet Springs sounded idyllic. Henry wrote of their living "in a little wooden cottage, quite alone. We go to the hotel for our meals. We swim, ride and write. A vast oak shades our porch." But the solitude and relaxation failed. Clover was still no better. In August, Adams wrote sadly, "Various domestic necessities forced us to abandon our Yellowstone venture. We spent a month rambling through the Virginia mountains, then rushed to Quincy and are now in Beverly."

Their retreat to Beverly was an admission that Clover's condition was worse. Her apathy and fatigue alternated with hectic bouts of agitation, in which she suffered from nameless fears and complained of feelings of unworthiness. With characteristic restraint, which did not conceal his anxiety, Adams wrote to Hay, "My wife has been out of sorts for some time. Until she gets well we can do nothing. The seaside offers no excitement to us who live here. We go every week to Quincy to see my parents. The rest of the time is spent on history or on horseback..."

"On history or on horseback" is the plaintive cry of a historian who still hopes, against all reason, that his wife's interest in history, plus their mutual love of riding, will somehow rescue her from the shadows closing in on her.

They saw only their family and closest friends, all of whom shared Henry's anxiety. With her biting wit gone, Clover seemed very small and forlorn. Unable to concentrate, she rubbed her forehead back and forth as if trying to understand. A Beverly neighbor, Mrs. James Eliot Cabot, later wondered "how Henry endured it."

By mid-October, they returned to Washington and went into seclusion at once. Adams wrote to Hay, "We lead a quiet and very reserved life at present as my wife goes nowhere." On 22 November he wrote to him, "I see no reason why you may not by New Year's move into your house if only to stop the mouths of fools who say you cannot. I am in no hurry and may wait still longer, but my house is really finished except for paving."

In the same letter, Adams reported, "Mrs. Don came back terribly used up and takes a house on 19th Street." Lizzie was put to bed, while her mother hovered over her, complaining to Mary, "How sick and weak Lizzie is—she is confined to bed and improvement is so slow. I cannot think of Mr. Cameron with any patience. I must not elaborate..."

While Lizzie was lying abed in an interesting condition, fussed over by her mother, across from Lafayette Square Henry Adams helplessly watched his wife descending into madness. Apparently he made no attempt to obtain psychiatric help for her, although both he and Clover had entertained the eminent neurologist Dr. S. Weir Mitchell of Philadelphia who was successfully treating cases that showed the same symptoms as Clover's. Three years earlier, Dr. Mitchell had published his *Lectures on Diseases of the Nervous System Especially in Women*, and he was regarded as the country's leading specialist in cases of "nervous prostration."

Adams's inability to act decisively in the face of Clover's impending madness was a mark of his emotional entanglement with his wife. Although his was the stronger, more decisive nature, he had yielded, throughout their marriage, to her intense practicality. Like many a Victorian wife she had shielded him from the ordinary details of life—running their household, arranging their social life, even rescuing the dogs when they strayed.

Also the seldom-discussed fact of Clover's childlessness was a major factor in his dependence and in her depression. Her friend Mrs. Alexander Whiteside would later remark, "How often we spoke of Clover having all she wanted, all that the world could give except children—and not having any was a greater grief to Mr. Adams than to her." This may have seemed true to an observer, yet for a mind as analytical as Clover's and a temperament as intense, her disappointment may have been even sharper. If it were true, as rumor later suggested, that her husband suffered form impotence, then Clover could hardly have blamed herself. Yet this secret must have weighed as heavily on her as on him, for as a loving wife it was her responsibility to buttress his sense of masculinity, even while she attempted to conceal her own sense of loss. But if, instead, she knew that the childlessness was due to her own deficiency, this could have produced a sense of guilt, which would only strengthen her feelings of unworthiness. In either case, Clover, now in her 42d year, was tormented by her childlessness and by a growing sense of unreality. All during that anguished last summer, Ellen Gurney later recalled, Clover would turn to her and cry piteously, "I am not real — Oh make me real — you are all of you real!"

Her childlessness and Henry's overprotectiveness created an unhealthy mutual dependence. Now that Clover, in her severe depression, could no longer control her own life, her husband, who had boasted of his willingness to let a woman "take the reins," found that he could no longer seize the slackened reins from her. He could only retreat with her into their silent house. Here they would await the fate designed by the gods — gods in whom Clover did not believe.

Katherine Simonds, a writer who was a friend of both Henry and Clover, watched their plight with sympathy and later wrote, "Their very closeness could have aggravated for each, particularly for her (for his was the stronger, more egotistical mind) their fears and doubts of the world. Like two people in a lonely house, they added to each other's terror and terror drove them nearer together. They were devoured by the same torment, yet dealt with it differently."

Part of Clover's problem, her friends believed, was her ingrained agnosticism. In an age that was ruled by convention and that gave lip service to the practice of Christianity, Clover, like her prototype Esther, found herself unable to believe in God. In her unflinching honesty she could not pretend a belief that she did not hold. But her skepticism went further — for she reveled in a witty defiance of everything pertaining to religion. And now that she was beset by mental anguish, she found that her militant agnosticism was useless to comfort her.

Since her husband did not share her mocking attitude toward religion, it only widened the gulf between them. Clover could not believe — but Henry's case was more complicated. A descendant of New England Calvinists, he had rejected any formal practice of religion. But he was haunted by a need to believe. As Miss Simonds observed,

> The anguish which impelled Henry Adams to write "Esther" remained with him for the rest of his life. His inability to believe or to cease longing to believe is written into his worship of the Virgin, his yearning after the ages of faith which was the preoccupation of his last years. "Esther" is the spiritual biography of Henry and Clover Adams....
>
> It was necessary for an Adams to be great. This had come to him with a double force for physically he was small. All the chairs in his house were made to fit himself so that it was the visitor who was uncomfortable. His wife was more sensitive and insecure, because she was more terrified. He saw but he could not help.

Henry's brother Charles Francis, who was always blunt, glimpsed her on the train early in December and later expressed his horror at her condition. "I went to where they were sitting and tried to talk with her. It was painful to the last degree. She sat there, pale and care-worn, never smiling, hardly making an effort to answer me, the very picture of physical weakness and mental depression. As she was then she had been for a long time. Her mind dwelt on nothing but self-destruction. She was engaged the whole time in introspection and self-accusation."

Rebecca Rae, a faithful friend, called every day to cheer her. After one visit, as Henry was showing her out, he thanked her. "For what?" she asked. "Because you made Clover smile," he replied.

Although she seldom went out any more, Clover roused herself to show her concern for her neighbor Lizzie. Mrs. Sherman, in constant attendance at her daughter's bedside, wrote to Mary Miles: "Mrs. Adams and her husband called frequently for Lizzie. Once Mr. Adams came alone and sat for an hour, telling us about his wife's nervous prostration—after nursing her father who died in the spring. Mr. Adams had just waited for his wife to get stronger to get into their new home."

On Friday evening, 4 December, Clover Adams visited Lizzie. She had sent her "A gorgeous bouquet of Maréchal Niel roses" which were set in a vase by Lizzie's bed. This was a poignant meeting for the two women—wan, distracted Clover facing her young protégée who, despite Mrs. Sherman's gloomy reports, was looking surprisingly well. In La Dona's approaching maternity, Clover could glimpse the bleak contrast between Lizzie's future and her own. The knowledge that Lizzie would soon be a radiant young mother while she would never have a child of her own was shattering. Her crippling sense of her unworthiness was heightened by the unconcealed self-satisfaction shown by Don Cameron and the realization that her own husband would not become a father. This critical encounter could have been the final blow to her self-esteem.

On Sunday morning, Henry Adams, who was plagued with a toothache, set out to visit his dentist. After he had left, Clover sat down at the desk on which she had written so many Sunday letters to her father. To her sister Ellen Gurney, she wrote, "If I had a single point of character or goodness I would stand on that and grow back to life. Henry is more patient and loving than words can express—God might envy him." (In this desperate moment the agnostic Clover could compare her husband favorably with the God in whom she did not believe.) She continued, "he fears and hopes and despairs hour after hour—Henry is beyond all words tenderer and better than all of you even."

Clover laid the letter, still unsigned, on her desk.

Then she went into her darkroom and took from the cabinet a bottle of potassium cyanide that she used in developing her photographic prints. She mixed the colorless salts with water in a vial and went back into her room. Standing before the fireplace, she drank the poison.

In less than an hour, Adams returned. Hurrying up the stairs, he entered her sitting room, where he found the contorted body of his wife, still warm, lying on a rug before the fire. Beside her lay the empty vial with the odor of bitter almonds still clinging to the glass.

"Poor Clover's Self-Destruction"

When Senator Cameron brought the dreadful news to Lizzie, her mother noted, "The roses that Mrs. Adams had sent her were still on her bedside table."

At first the news was reported as a simple death. The Washington *Critic* announced the death of Mrs. Adams from "heart paralysis." The *Washington Post* reported that "Mrs. Adams had been an invalid for several months but had been quite rapidly recovering. Indeed yesterday morning she told her husband in reply to questions concerning her health that she was better than she had been for a long time. The unexpected suddenness of her death made the blow the more severe."

On 9 December, Clover Adams was buried in Rock Creek Cemetery, following a ceremony conducted by the Reverend Mr. E. C. Hull, who had come from Cambridge to officiate. The same day, the news of the cause of her death was out. Under the headline "Was it Suicide?" the Washington *Critic* reported: "The certificate of Coroner Patterson and Dr. Charles E. Hagner, In the case of Mrs. Henry Adams, who died suddenly in this city on Sunday is to the effect that she came to her death through an overdose of potassium cyanide administered by herself." A correspondent for the New York *Sun* wrote: "There is no doubt that she intended to take her own life. She was just recovering from a long illness and had been suffering from mental depression."

Among the flood of condolences that poured into Adams's Lafayette Square home was one from Senator Cameron, who was not usually known for his eloquence. Yet the note, which has been lost, touched Adams as did few other tributes. One of his first replies was written on 10 December 1885, four days after Clover's death, to Mrs. Cameron:

> Nothing in the course of my troubles has touched me more than your husband's note and your own illness. To have been able to ask for help would have been a pleasure but there are moments in life when one is beyond all help; and I was almost relieved to know you were not in a condition to think of doing anything for me or my poor wife. All I can now ask is that you will take care of yourself and get well. All of Clover's friends have now infinite value for me. I have got to live henceforward on what I can save of the wreck of her life and it is lucky for me that she has no friends but the best and truest.
>
> Please tell your husband that I love him. I am not given to making such declarations but a note like his deserves it. This note is confidential. Please keep it to yourself or show it to no one but Mr. Cameron.

From London, Henry James wrote of "the sad rumors of poor Clover's self-destruction. The event had everything that could make it bitter for poor Henry. She succumbed to hereditary melancholia. What an end to that intensely lively Washington salon."

In the bleak days following Clover's death, Henry Adams confided in his brother Charles Francis — "talking freely and so finding relief he told me the whole story — and sad enough it was. Henry maintained confidently in his talks with me that the physical change [for the better] had even then taken place in her and that, could he have saved her then, she would have come through and again been well. How this may have been I do not know, his theory was certainly specious." With a hint of contrition, Charles Francis concluded, "Me she never liked; nor can I blame her much for that — I trod all over her, offending her in every way."

At Christmas, Henry Adams sent Mrs. Cameron a piece of his wife's jewelry with the note, "This litle trinket which I send you was a favorite of my wife's. Will you keep it and sometime wear it to remind you of her?"

On 30 December 1885, Ellen Gurney wrote to a friend: "I hear from Henry constantly — far better news on the house than he or Clover could have dared hope. I trust he will be in his new house tonight. The associations of the old were too intense to be safely borne. Henry rides . . . moves his books, looks out of the window, is like a small child. He reads Shakespeare aloud evenings . . . has several familiar friends, mostly Mrs. John Field and women just now."

It is significant that the women in Clover's and Henry's families, all of whom regarded themselves as his nieces in fact or in wish, could never bring themselves to mention the name of Mrs. Cameron. At no time was she ever regarded as a "niece" — in fact, it was always silently understood by them that she "came first."

7

Madonna – La Dona

Stunned by the tragedy of Clover's suicide, of which he wrote, "I admit that fate at last has smashed the life out of me, but for twelve years I had everything I most wanted on earth," Henry Adams was determined to go on. "My only chance of saving what is left of my life can consist in going straight ahead without looking behind. I feel like a volunteer in his first battle. If I don't run ahead at full speed, I shall run away."

Not far away, in her rented home on 19th Street, La Dona, three months pregnant and still exhausted from her Western trip, was confined mostly to bed, except for a short drive every day, when she was carried to her carriage and surrounded by pillows. In the evenings, she was assisted downstairs to recline on the overstuffed lounge in the parlor. Although Dr. Wales pronounced her much better, her mother was unconvinced, complaining, "She is so thoroughly used up that I have never felt anything like the fatigue and anxiety. Her improvement is so slow." She had learned from Lizzie's physician that he had advised Senator Cameron not to take his wife on the long trip, and this disregard of his medical advice horrified Mrs. Sherman. "I cannot think of him with any patience. I must stop now."

A chronic worrier, Mrs. Sherman now mentioned a new anxiety. "The Cameron children," she wrote, "are at home now and I tremble lest Lizzie will be the worse for it. I can only pray she may not." The six grown children, still antagonistic toward their stepmother, were far from pleased that she was going to have a child who would be a new claimant to their father's fortune. However, they could hardly fail to be pleased with his new house—the elegant Ogle Tayloe mansion that Senator Cameron had bought for a reputed $60,000 and into which they planned to move late in June 1886, when their present lease expired. "The house," Mrs. Sherman noted, "is quite old-fashioned, but very, very nice. I think Mr. Cameron bought it for a home and partly as an investment, the ground being very valuable."

The house was a gracious, three-story cream-colored brick residence of the Federal Period, which retains its original façade, although it is no longer a private home but is used mostly for entertaining by members of the United States Judiciary. Built in 1828 by the architect WIlliam Thornton, the house was first owned by Benjamin Ogle Tayloe, son of the John Tayloe who built the Octagon House farther downtown in Washington.

Don Cameron was undeniably proud to be the owner of this historic showplace. After he took possession, he remodeled it somewhat but left the original façade unchanged. On the third story above the bay are three Palladian windows. To the right of the entrance, at the second-floor level, a wrought iron balcony runs across the house, from which trailed wistaria vines in profusion. *The Washington Post* described it as "a well-nigh perfect expression of latter-day comfort and elegance."

During the late winter and spring of 1886, La Dona awaited the birth of her baby, while Adams was driving himself to complete the first draft of his *History* before departing on a voyage to Japan with John La Farge. He wanted to be off, but "I can't go to Europe," he wrote. "It is full of ghosts."

As she whiled away the months of waiting, La Dona became the center of a little court of gallants in a 19th-century version of a medieval court of love. Diplomats and statesmen vied with each other in paying her extravagant literary tributes, despite her interesting condition, which they professed not to notice. Among the regulars were Adams and John Hay, as well as a recently arrived young British diplomat, Cecil Spring-Rice, who had a long thin face, an aquiline nose, and almond-shaped eyes. He spoke with a slight lisp in a low-pitched Eton voice and was usually untidy in his dress. From his post as third secretary at the British Legation at Connecticut Avenue and N Street, he sent her a stream of ardent sonnets and witty notes and insisted to the other members of their circle, "Mrs. Cameron is more beautiful than ever which is superfluous." John Hay, whom Julia Parsons had spotted earlier as "a ladies' man," was not to be outdone in literary outpourings. But he recognized that Lizzie was not taken in altogether by flattery when he observed, "She endures society like the cynical saint she is."

The final weeks of her pregnancy dragged on, and the expected date of her confinement in May passed. For five weeks more, with remarkable cheerfulness, she endured the humidity of a Washington summer, as well as the discomforts of a late pregnancy, while supervising the planning of their move to 21 Lafayette Square after the baby's arrival.

Finally, on 25 June 1886 a daughter was born to Lizzie Cameron, aged 28, and her husband Don, aged 53. Lizzie wrote to Mrs. Hay (in a letter which Hay enclosed with his own to Adams) that they had wanted to call the baby Marian, "but Mr. Adams was so far away there was no means of knowing whether he would like it or not and I dared not give her the name without permission. So Mr. Cameron, to gratify his father, gave her the old-fashioned name of his grandmother — Martha Cameron — which I like very well, but which had no association as the other would have had."

The delight of the Cameron family in the new baby was genuine if short-lived. Mrs. Sherman proudly noted, "Mr. Cameron's affection to the child is perfect idolatry. This dear baby that to the Cameron children was so unwelcome has made them new people." Piously she quoted, " 'and a little child shall lead them.' So many people say that Lizzie's influence over that family—who you know are high-steppers—has been lovely." Of course, Simon Cameron was pleased and wrote Lizzie, "You have gratified me much by giving my mother's name to your baby. May it live long and be as great a blessing to its mother as my mother was to me is the sincere wish of your Father, Simon Cameron."

Amid the congratulations that reached the Cameron household there was no word from Henry Adams, who was now en route to Japan but would certainly have received the news from the Hays.

Secretary of the Navy William Whitney, whose wife had recently given birth to a daughter, wrote to Lizzie, "Our two girls will boss this town as their mothers have." From Uncle Cump came word, "This is an event that will form a new era in your life and I hope a happy one. I hope to see you and the baby next winter."

The Washington summer was especially hot and humid. Lizzie's sister Mary Miles planned to visit her, but her mother wrote, "You are wise not to start in this hot weather. It has been so hot and Old Probabilities [the popular nickname for the U.S. Weather Bureau] says there will be a change within 36 hours. I go down to see Lizzie every evening. Last evening she was feeling very nicely but I do not approve of her seeing any but the immediate family. I know she will feel it later. Already her milk is going. She has no idea if she will have any when she gets about." Getting about for new mothers was a slow process in the 1880s. They were expected to spend two weeks in bed, two on the bed and two near it, wrapped tightly from bosom to hips in tough muslin bandages a yard wide, pinned tightly to the body, and producing a mummy effect.

Radiant in her new motherhood Lizzie was, as one of her courtiers had foreseen, "healthier, happier, and prettier." All was harmony in the Cameron household as Don proudly handed out cigars to his political cronies and the Cameron children took turns holding and admiring the infant Martha. These six young adults, who until now had seen nothing admirable in their father's young wife, had to acknowledge that she made a perfect picture of motherhood, and they even grudgingly recognized her loyal efforts on behalf of her family's interests.

As the youngest Sherman daughter who had made the "best" marriage, Lizzie had worried over the situation of her widowed mother, who was living precariously in a rented home in Washington. She persuaded Don to buy her mother a house on 18th Street and to furnish it. For this generous gift, Mrs. Sherman was effusively grateful, writing to Lizzie, "How much, my dear unselfish child, I have to thank you for. I feel overwhelmed with all your goodness to me and feel I am unworthy of such self-denial." To Mary Miles, Mrs. Sherman reported, "I believe she takes more interest in fixing up my house than her own. She gives me an allowance and $300 beside. She denies herself to do it and it troubles me to take it."

Lizzie also undertook to advance the career of her brother-in-law Nelson Miles, who was an excellent soldier but a difficult person. Despite his success in destroying the power of Chief Crazy Horse and in driving the defeated Chief Sitting Bull into Canada, and although he had won a Congressional Medal of Honor on the battlefield, Miles was still passed over for promotion to the rank of full general. Even his military superior, General Sherman, who was also his uncle-in-law, had not arranged for this promotion. So Lizzie took things in her own hands and persuaded her husband (who had formerly been secretary of war) to make a personal plea to President Cleveland. To her sister, Lizzie wrote of Nelson Miles's disappointment when a colleague was chosen and he was not, "Terry's appointment came like a thunderclap upon us, as Gen seemed to think both appointments would be made together. No one seems to be 'in' with the President, even his own Cabinet. Mr. Adams said today he had never known a more 'one-man' administration. Donald goes tomorrow to have a personal interview with the President and give his reasons for thinking Gen is the best man. You can rest assured that Donald will do all he can to help. I have never seen him more interested." Despite Senator Cameron's earnest efforts, the appointment was not forthcoming for a long time.

Far away in Japan, Henry Adams and John La Farge were leading an idyllic existence, with the artist instructing the historian in the technique of watercolor painting. Adams used his portable writing desk to record his daily impressions of the Orient in a continuing letter-diary, which, taken together, makes some of the best travel writing in American literature.

Although Adams was undoubtedly pursued by the bittersweet memories of his marriage and its terrible ending, he never wrote or spoke of Clover, preferring to bury her image in inscrutable silence. Of his grief he never spoke, nor of the sense of guilt that must have afflicted him at times. By the middle of August, he had begun writing to Lizzie, but made no mention of her baby. "Thank you for your kind little note. In six weeks we start for home. Shall I bring you an embroidered kimono for dressing gown or would you rather have a piece of lacquer? Or a sword? I am puzzled to know what to bring home to please myself. If I knew what would please you I would load a steamer with it. Remember me to Mr. Cameron." On 16 September 1886, he wrote to his secretary Theodore Dwight, who was "keeping an eye" on Mrs. Cameron, "I am starting home and will go directly to Washington to set the house going. Many thanks for your care of Mrs. Don."

Late in October, Adams reached San Francisco, then entrained for Washington. Although he did not record his first meeting with Lizzie and her infant Martha, it must have been a poignant encounter. He had not seen La Dona for a year and a half, and now on Lafayette Square he met her again holding her new baby. In this vision of the mother and child he found the symbol that would haunt his imagination and absorb his study for the rest of his life, leading him to make the pronouncement "Women are naturally neither daughters, sisters, lovers, nor wives, but mothers."

Martha Cameron was not christened until she was ten months old. Lizzie invited Adams to attend the ceremony on 24 April 1887, and he wrote, "I shall certainly come. Though not a promising figure for a fairy Godfather I shall not be the one who staid away." The actual godfather was Senator Benjamin Butler, a crony of Don's, and the godmother was Mrs. Wayne MacVeagh, Don's sister, with Mrs. Eliza Sherman acting as proxy.

Years later, when Martha was nearly grown, Adams wrote to Lizzie of their first meeting (slightly altered as to date), "Sixteen years ago I met a baby wagon in the Square with a six-months' infant who managed, with her mother's help, to get and help some friends. Her mother had a social instinct and charm to an extent which I have never known in any other woman." It was this charm that had captivated Adams from their first meeting. After enduring the long ordeal of Clover's madness, after listening all those years to her caustic witticisms, after parrying her New England prejudices, after living with a woman who was a mistress of epigram, an efficient mistress of his household, but who somehow lacked that elusive quality that would make her the mistress of a man's heart — after all this, he found himself drawn to the disarmingly feminine Mrs. Cameron. During those years in which he had instructed her in the ways of worldliness, he had noted with approval how readily she had responded to his teaching. With her education completed, she had become a formidable figure in society and the central figure in his emotional life. From now on their roles would be reversed — in the sphere of human relations she would instruct him.

Managing the senator's household and participating in Washington social life with a grace that many a capital hostess envied, Lizzie was more than just a leading hostess. Living in a political climate, she had develped a political instinct that enabled her to further her own ends through the indirect use of power, which was the only means open to women in the late 19th century.

When young Lloyd Griscom, whose father was a friend of Don's, visited the Cameron household in Washington, he was just out of the University of Pennsylvania with a degree in political science and a yearning to become a diplomat. Lizzie decided to take immediate action. "Why don't we make Lloyd's dream come true?" she exclaimed. "I know the American Minister to London, Thomas Bayard [who in 1893 would be elevated to the rank of the first U.S. ambassador to Great Britain], who is now packing to go to England." Within a few hours, through Lizzie's intervention, Lloyd Griscom's diplomatic career was launched.

This political finesse of Lizzie's was noted by Abigail Adams Homans, one of Adams's nieces, who remarked, "You must think of her as a brilliant and capable woman — and you must not diminish her stature by calling her 'a society leader' or 'a gracious hostess'. She was more. She was a political power and her salon was primarily a political one."

This political power Lizzie always wielded subtly behind the scenes. To influence legislation that she considered important she called not only on her husband, but on influential men in government, most of whom, when she appealed to them, became her willing accomplices.

It was inevitable that Henry Adams should be drawn to Elizabeth Cameron. And it was equally inevitable that she should respond. They were driven by a deep mutual need. Adams, who had recently been tragically widowed, had lost his emotional center. Lizzie, who had been unhappily mar-

The Ogle-Tayloe House
Jackson Place
Lafayette Square

ried for seven years, had never found hers. Adams, who had lost his first love
through Clover's suicide, saw in this youthful madonna the vision of a love
more profoundly romantic than any he had known. Before her he felt a sense
of mystery, and yet there was also a trace of anguish as he wrote, "One may be
innocent as the angels, yet unhappy as the wicked and I, who would lie down
and die rather than give you a day's pain am going to pain you the more, the
more I love you."

Lizzie Cameron, who was essentially a realist, had also lost her first love
and was enduring a marriage without love. In Adams she saw the promise of a
tenderness that she had never experienced and a sturdy devotion that would
undoubtedly offer more than it would demand. Both of them, battered by the
cruel circumstances of life, were seeking the harbor of a shared love. Their
ritual courtship began.

Shortly after Adams's return to Washington, Lizzie regretfully turned
down an invitation to dinner at his new home on Lafayette Square. He replied,

> I am pleased you should be troubled by so delightful a cause as not
> dining with me. You have discovered a new way of giving pleasure
> by your absence. Some people can give it only in that way but on
> you it is a tour de force that I admire and wonder at. . . . You should
> reprove me whenever you please if only you will come to dinner to
> do it.

---8---

"Like A Sad Slave"

Now that Henry Adams was back from Japan to take up his "posthumous existence" in the handsome new house in which Clover never lived, he set up a social life that only an Adams could have contrived. In the midst of a society based on an elaborate system of etiquette, he ignored all the rules of etiquette, accepting no invitations, leaving no cards, paying no calls. It was his stated purpose to be regarded as no longer among the living. Yet with his intense curiosity about life and his need for intellectual and social stimulation, he soon drew around him a select circle who were admitted, not invited, to his elegant noon-day breakfasts. Visiting dignitaries, who had been meticulously screened, were allowed to come—as well as the "regulars," who included John Hay, Henry Cabot Lodge, Clarence King, Cecil Spring-Rice, and John La Farge.

Then there were his nieces "in fact and in wish" who surrounded Uncle Henry with their flattering attentions and whom he counseled and guided and admired:

> I am uncle to all the girls in the Atlantic Coast states [he remarked].
> They are as tame as mice and come in and out without a flutter and
> breakfast and dine with me as though they had never heard of a
> chaperone. They coo to me their little love affairs and their little
> troubles and even their little poetry, as sweetly as wood pigeons.
> They cause me terrors unspeakable, for I never know what they
> may do. They are jealous as tigers and their little feuds are savage.
> They are handsome and clever and well-educated and well-
> dressed and I can't provide husbands for all of them and I can't
> manage their mothers and I dislike their brothers and loathe their
> fathers as a rule. To keep out of their quarrels is the ambition of a
> lifetime.

The jealousy of the nieces was often focused on Mrs. Cameron. Since she never aspired to be a niece and, when she was in their company, reminded her great nephew Sam Reber of "a Bird of Paradise among wrens," she naturally ruffled their feathers. Aileen Tone, who would later become Adams's inseparable companion, recognized Lizzie's unique place in Uncle Henry's life "with a touch of jealousy." Mary Ogden Abbott eyed Lizzie warily, noting that "she thought little of women." And Margaret Terry Chanler, one of Adams's most adoring "nieces in wish," disapproved of her as "worldly." Yet Adams managed to contain their rivalries as they vied with each other for preference. And in his ostentatious withdrawal from society he managed to enjoy society on his own terms.

Although he never spoke of Clover — and no one dared to mention her name — it was clear that he still mourned her loss. He often visited her grave at Rock Creek Cemetery, sitting on the stone bench facing the bronze Saint-Gaudens figure.

Adams suffered frequent attacks of the hereditary melancholy that had afflicted generations of the Adams family. During these bouts of gloom and ennui, he would exclaim, "I'm bored. I'm mouldy. The world has lived too long. So have I. One of us has got to go. For the public good it had better be the world for at least I am harmless." Clover, who had grown accustomed to these black moods, had known how to bully him out of them before her own harsher melancholy deepened into madness.

In his ennui, Adams found himself turning with increasing interest to La Dona. Across the Square in the Cameron household, the curse of accidie — or world-weariness — was unknown. All was excitement and bustle at 21 Lafayette Square, and Adams observed with wonder the effortless way in which Lizzie managed the care of her rosy-cheeked infant Martha, the comings and goings of the Cameron teen-agers, and the social activities of a senator's wife, as well as responding to the gallantries of the mostly middle-aged courtiers who surounded her. For a time, Adams was content to be numbered among them and to play his part in their elaborate game of courtly love. He counted on Lizzie's influence more than he realized, for once when she asked if a thoughtless remark of hers had offended him, he solemnly replied, "You never said or did anything to give me a twinge. How can you imagine such an outrageous fiction? If it weren't for you I would have no spirits at all. If I'm low in mind, it is because I don't see you to keep me up. You have enough to worry about without more. Don't class me among your burdens."

By now Lizzie Cameron had won her place among the P. B.'s. The Professional Beauties were the newest vogue among the social leaders of the late 1880s. Likenesses of Lillie Langtry, Lillian Russell, and other notable beauties were publicly displayed by commercial photographers and eagerly bought and traded by collectors. Frances Cleveland, the young wife of the President, wrote to Lizzie from the White House, "I am grasping, I know, but may I have one of them?" She had seen a photograph of Lizzie Cameron, taken by a New York photographer, in the home of Mary Leiter, another P.B., who would later marry George Nathaniel Curzon (who became viceroy of India). Lizzie sent the First Lady a photograph of herself with Martha, and soon the two ladies were comparing notes on the progress of their respective daughters who were the same age.

Suddenly Adams, who liked to declare "I always expect the worst and it's always worse than I expected," found himself confronting the "worst." The news that dismayed all of Lafayette Square was that Lizzie Cameron was stricken with typhoid fever. Only two years earlier, as Adams remembered, Theodore Roosevelt's 49-year-old mother had died of that disease. For ten days, Lizzie was very sick and, like many victims of typhoid, she lost most of her hair. But her naturally robust constitution prevailed, and within a fortnight she was over the worst. As her mother Mrs. Sherman wrote to daughter Mary Miles, "Lizzie is much better. She hopes to get up the last of the week. How becoming her short hair is, coming in all thick and curly. She doesn't took a day over 16."

Soon Lizzie was back in the midst of her lively world, and her mother wrote, "Lizzie never looked handsomer except when she was married. She is thin as a rail in figure but full in face with a fine color. She and Lida [Lizzie's sister Mrs. Colgate Hoyt] were a picture of beauty as they drove off." Lizzie had loaned Lida one of her dresses and matching hats which she had purchases in Paris. Lizzie herself was "all in white lace with a magnificent sash of blue satin."

Like her mother, baby Martha became the center of a court of masculine admirers of whom none was more doting than Henry Adams. The childless historian was captivated, and he turned his study into a nursery for her, stocking it with dolls and toys, ginger snaps and chocolate drops. Ruefully noting that "Mrs. Cameron is more winning than ever," Adams turned his attention to winning her daughter. "I made love to Martha," he wrote, "and by dint ot incessant bribing won her attachment. She will come to me from anyone. She adores Del Hay's pigeons and she shows a fearful joy at visiting Daisy [Adams's mare] in my stable, then goes to her drawer of chocolate drops and ginger snaps." To further beguile her, he installed an elaborate doll house behind a sliding panel in his library.

But the baby's father was not to be outdone. Senator Cameron sent to England for three small ponies for Martha, and he also presented her with a $25 gold piece, which her mother prudently invested in stock. Even the Cameron children were won over. As Mrs. Sherman reported with approval, "I often see Mary and Margaretta with Martha in their arms. They appear devoted to her and she to them. Jim makes quite a fuss over her and Martha calls him 'Bozzer' [for Brother]. You would not know they were the same family. You can't please Mr. Cameron more than to expatiate on Martha's brightness. He is devoted to her."

The fond grandmother added her own praise: "Martha looks so much like her mother and is a perfect parrot. She says and repeats everything and trots about everywhere. She loves to come to "Bama's Ouse" as she calls my house. She is very English in leaving off the H. Such a good child and very devoted to Bridget, who is a good nurse with judgment and sense, so Lizzie is relieved of responsibility. At times, I see Martha so strongly in her mother — just as happy and sunny in disposition. She has her mother's eyes — otherwise she looks like her father. She is fascinating and has completely won everyone over."

A tireless observer of social behavior, Mrs. Sherman noted that "Mr. Henry Adams is perfectly devoted to Martha who is now 18 months. He says she has all the accomplishments of a fashionable belle. And the child is devoted to him—she calls him "Dobbitt" and often worries to see him. Whenever Martha goes there, Mr. Adams takes her all over the house and goes down on all fours with her and this pleases her immensely."

After Martha was able to walk, Adams told Lizzie, "I see Martha with a huge banana wandering away with her two nephews to the Bradley mansion." The nephews were the two baby sons of Eliza Cameron Bradley, who had so bitterly resented Lizzie's marriage to her father. Adams noticed that although Martha "smiled graciously on me, she prefers the society of younger men. Hay and I bow meekly to her will as we do to that of her mother. After all, the relation is not so very different. Martha's flirtation with baby Hay [John Hay's grandson] is leaving him quite broken up and desperate."

In June 1887, Senator Cameron decided to take his family to Lochiel, the Cameron farm in Pennsylvania. Adams admitted that their departure "cost me another day of low spirits," and in a week he followed for a short visit and found Lizzie and Martha awaiting him at the Harrisburg station. He spent only 24 hours at Lochiel, disapproving of "the foundries, railroads, and factories at their door. I cared not at all for the place but I enjoyed Martha and her mother." Then he headed back to Quincy to help in caring for his aging and crippled mother, who was losing her sight and her hearing and "horribly disgusted with her 80 years." To his friend Charles Milnes Gaskell he wrote, "Four months in Quincy are to me what four months of solitary prison in Ireland are to you." He looked on sadly at his mother's inexorable decline and mused, "I would be willing to go with her." Since he had no wish to return to Beverly Farms, he urged La Dona to spend the remainder of the summer with Martha in his summer home. It was agreed that mother and child would spend August, September, and October there. This was the first of many summers during which Lizzie and Martha would inhabit the Beverly retreat, to Adams's immense satisfaction. When Lizzie tried to discuss "business matters" with him, he replied with spirit, "I'm glad you've found Beverly tolerable. If you take care of it many years you won't part with it. You have no business matters to arrange with me. How many times must I tell you the house is yours and one does not pay rent to oneself for one's own house? If you say more about it I shall be angry and when angry I am quite terrible."

In August, Lizzie and Martha arrived in Beverly, and Adams in Quincy was alarmed to learn that the baby was ill, "knocked up by the journey." Anxiously he wrote to Lizzie, "I'm sorry not to be nearer when I might see to things, run a few errands. Today is gloomy. I feel you must be as low as the weather. I am the last person you need for encouraging you. I wish you were able, some fine day, to go down to North Easton with me to see La Farge's windows and Richardson's building." Learning later that day that Martha was better, he wrote of his relief, then suggested that when she was well, Lizzie and he might go to Cambridge to visit the Hooper children, the motherless nieces of Clover Adams. After she came, a fortnight later, Adams wrote to La Dona, "I enjoyed my rainy Monday more than anything in many moons. You were archangelic to come up and amuse those infants and me. I wonder if I could set up as a five-year-old and have a nursery to receive lady visitors?"

Since he could not leave his mother unattended—the nurse who cared for Mrs. Adams was on vacation—he urged Lizzie repeatedly to pay them a visit in Quincy. "I am tied here like a lamb...and my mother is not a good subject for masculine care." Yet during the following winter, when Lizzie paid his mother a surprise visit and Adams was no longer there, she was told by a uniformed servant that Mrs. Adams was not receiving visitors. Adams was horrified. "Mother is 'in pieces' to learn that the servant turned you away," he wrote to La Dona. "The old lady is particularly curious to inspect you, having heard your name recur so often of late. But she forgot to give special orders for your admission. Hence the explosion. I know how busy you are. I comfort her by replying that it was probably clear gain for you."

In the fall, Adams, returning to Washington after a brief trip to New York, just missed seeing Mrs. Don. Ruefully, he wrote, "I arrived as you were leaving. The New York Owl train was blocked for several hours. I wanted you to give me aid and counsel in New York on shopping and to see La Farge for dinner. These are might-have-beens which make life an incessant delusion." His old melancholy reasserted itself as he wondered why he had returned. "The first days of December here are always hard for me. I shall hardly see you before December and unless you want an escort to the World's end—to the White House, I can be of no use. I am sorry time does not seem to clear away the wreckage of life."

The heat in Washington was prolonged that fall of 1887, and Adams warned Lizzie to stay on in Beverly. "Washington is too warm for Martha—at 83 degrees her roses would fade, to say nothing of your own which are worth preserving for your many adorers. Springy spent last evening with me and was chanting your praises. He is better worth having in your train than most of us others."

Adams was always entirely correct in his behavior toward La Dona—only in his letters did he make an occasional show of daring as when, at Simon Cameron's death in 1889, Lizzie went into the customary deep mourning and Adams sent her a pair of black silk stockings that he had purchased in Japan. "I regret there is no garter à la King Edward."

Having completed the long labor of the third volume of his *History*, Adams celebrated the occasion by strolling in his garden and musing on the recollections of Edward Gibbon after he had completed *The Decline and Fall of the Roman Empire*. Like any author, he yearned for a favorable reception for his new work, and he observed, "I am beginning to suspect that women are the only readers—five to one, and one's audience must be created among them." Complaining that he was "homesick" for Lizzie, he longed to have her back as his attentive audience of one, while he waited through the warm October days. One rainy autumn evening he noticed that the windows of 21 Lafayette Square were open. Followed by his terrier, Adams hurried across the park only to learn that "Mrs. Cameron will not be back until the end of this week or next." Beneath the wisteria-covered balcony, Henry Adams stood, a small disconsolate figure with his little dog huddled beside him. Back in his study he wrote, "I am as solitary and melancholy as Possum, drenched with rain and disappointment."

When Lizzie's return was certain, Adams wrote eagerly, "Will you come to dine with the Chinese minister? He has some rare porcelain and I want to divide it between us. I shall try to survive until you come." Now that she was back, Adams fell into the habit of sending his servant several times a day across the Square, carrying notes, invitations, flowers, gifts, and poems to La Dona. Eager to serve her, he thought up errands he could run for her, even telling her, "My mother sent me to Europe to get maids, servants and clothes for her. Why don't you utilize me in the same professional manner?" One day he sent her a sonnet sequence with the deprecatory introduction, "The poetry won't give you the fame of Laura or of Shakespeare's Mr. W.H." But among the carefully constructed efforts of 14 lines each that praised her beauty, one line stood out:

Spring in her eyes and summer in her smile

As a more enduring tribute to her beauty, Adams turned to his friend John La Farge, asking him to paint a portrait of La Dona. However, the artist was unwilling to undertake the commision, although he was chronically in need of money for the support of his large family and would, in the ordinary course of things, have done anything for his old friend and traveling companion. The two men had a strong mutual regard, and Adams would write of him, "A most extraordinary man, his faculty for wasting time and energy is a downright fraud on me because it ends in his doing more work in a year than I ever did in a lifetime. He is the biggest miracle the Virgin ever struck. I thought him quite superior to any other artist I've met." After delaying over the request for some time, La Farge wrote to Adams on 20 November 1887, explaining that he had avoided painting portraits because "I am too sensitive to my sitter's influence. I am not incapable of making a likeness—every painter can do that—but everything affects me to the extent of a paralyzing result." This equivocation may have surprised Adams, who had seen some of La Farge's portraits—his *Woman Reading* (Mrs. La Farge), his striking *Self-Portrait*, his portraits of Bishop John Hughes of New York and of Father Augustine Hecker, the founder of the Paulist society, as well as his *Boy Reading*, a portrait of Garth Wilkinson James, the brother of William and Henry James. As the artist continued his explanation, the reason became clearer. Like other artists, La Farge found Lizzie baffling as a subject for painting. "A face like Mrs. Cameron's has all sorts of difficulties. There is a distinct interior which contradicts the exterior at moments—or rather there are changes which make one wonder whether they are not really most important. All this is stupid as an explanation—but I wish I were a portrait painter who learns to be very cool as he is most interested." La Farge never painted Lizzie, and her official portrait by Anders Zorn failed to please her.

The traffic in hand-carried notes across the Square continued. To

"Like a Sad Slave"

Lizzie's request that he dine with her, Adams replied, "Your invitation is seductive to a rootless wanderer. We are delighted to accept any invitation you send — dinner, breakfast, luncheon or supper in the parlor or the nursery. I am at your orders." In the steady flow of letters that he addressed to the baby Martha, which only her mother could read, Adams wrote in words that he dared not address directly to Lizzie, "I love you very much and I think of you a great deal, and want you all the time. I should have run away from here, and looked for you all over the world, long ago, only I've grown too stout for the beautiful clothes I used to wear when I was a young prince. So I can't come after you, and feel very sad about it."

Chronically restless, Adams took a three-month jaunt to Florida and Cuba. In Havana he reluctantly attended a bull fight. On his return, he was delighted to be met at the railway station by Lizzie and Martha. Presenting La Dona with an exotic fan, he apologized, "The only trouble is to find anything good enough for you to carry." Later he wrote sadly, "I asked myself if I wanted to return. My only instinct is to run away. If it were not for Mrs. Cameron and Hay I should run . . ." When Lizzie was away for three weeks and he had no word from her, he panicked, complaining of "nightmares of imagining." He would always suffer these attacks of unreasonable anxiety when for any reason he failed to hear regularly from her.

Wistfully he wrote to Lizzie, quoting three lines from Shakespeare's Sonnet 57 which begins

Being your slave, what should I do but tend

From this sonnet he adapted lines 9-11

Nor dare I question with my jealous thought
Where you and Martha may be, or your affairs suppose,
But, like a sad slave, stay and think of nought

He did not copy out the last three lines:

Save, where you are how happy you make those.
So true a fool is love that in your will,
Though you do any thing, he thinks no ill.

By sending her this fragment from the Elizabethan poet, Adams was obliquely, as always, revealing his own heart. Like Shakespeare's patron the earl of Southampton, Lizzie Cameron was busy with a thousand concerns and had only brief snatches of time for him. Hence it was the fate of her sad slave to wait, like Shakespeare himself.

What should I do but tend
Upon the hours and times of your desire?
I have no precious time at all to spend
Nor services to do till you require.

Surrounded by her courtly flatterers (as was the earl of Southampton), who plied her with extravagent praise, and subjected to the demands of her unpoetical husband, La Dona failed to notice that the sophisticated Adams, who habitually wore the mask of misanthrope before the world, was now in deadly earnest. For him this was no longer a courtly ritual in which he competed with rivals for her smile — for Henry Adams, the verses that he wrote her and the Shakespearean lines that he quoted were the outpourings of a vanquished heart. But since she gave no sign of recognizing this, he had to content himself with his role of her protector who was also her slave.

Lizzie's plans were frequently changed at the last moment because of some sudden whim of her husband's. In the summer of 1888, instead of going with Martha to Beverly, she went to Newport, at the senator's insistence, then took a cottage at Lenox in the Berkshire foothills. Adams did not follow her but sent his secretary Theodore Dwight "to help her from her carriage." The conscientious Dwight reported to Adams that he found Mrs. Cameron very much "reduced," just as she had been the previous spring when she was recovering from typhoid. Dwight reported, "She is still very plucky and proposes to dance a German next week. Yet she walks with difficulty and the physicians say she shouldn't leave her bed." Clearly Dwight was no match for Mrs. Cameron's willfulness. "I tried to enforce discipline," he lamented. But *what is a fellow to do?* Newport seems to be the cause although she attributes it to Lochiel and to the Senator's perversity in refusing her Beverly. She is very wishful to see you. Martha is superb, spends much time writing letters to you and calling 'Dobbitt come here.' Mrs. Cameron gave me the same message." Then the conscientious Dwight concluded, "I fancy she would think me rather disloyal if she knew I wrote of her state to you so frankly."

By the rules of the game they were playing, Adams could only express his concern for La Dona through his letters to two-year-old Martha, to whom he wrote, "Take good care of Mama. She does not know how to take care of herself and needs you to look after her and keep her out of mischief. I know she was in some mischief as she has not written for months. I sent Mr. Dwight to Lenox to look after you."

When Lizzie sprained her ankle (as she had done long ago when she tried to delay her wedding date), Adams wrote, "You have a genius for accidents." When in September the ankle was improved, he suggested half seriously that she and Martha take a trip with him to Mexico in October, in a party that would also include Clarence King, John Hay, and Sir Robert Cunliffe. He added "I would have all my little world together. We needn't come back…"

The expedition that Adams fancifully proposed never took place. Certainly Lizzie would have objected to traveling in the company of King, toward whom she had always felt dislike tinged with suspicion. With her keenly developed feminine intuition, she may have suspected King's hidden alliance with Ada Todd long before his friends learned of it. And King, in his turn, scarcely bothered to conceal his scorn for the influence he saw Lizzie exerting over Adams. She once suggested with delicate sarcasm that he should marry his cook. To this he gave an equally cutting reply, "Why this had never occurred to me I cannot conceive, but thank you fervently for the suggestion."

9

"*It Isn't Life Without You*"

y the spring of 1890, Elizabeth Cameron was beginning to perceive the unmistakable truth. Henry Adams, the patrician 52-year-old historian whose behavior toward her was always scrupulously correct, had nevertheless fallen in love with her. Although he consistently followed the dictates of Victorian social behavior, always addressing her as "Mrs. Don" or "La Dona," or even "my dear *proprietaire*," never compromising her by spending time alone with her, continually concealing his intensity of feeling beneath the carefully crafted lines of his sonnets or his letters — La Dona saw that his attentions were clearly different in kind from the extravagant flattery of her other admirers. Her husband, who was preoccupied with the rough and tumble of partisan politics, was generally complaisant toward her followers, flattered that they were so distinguished. Although he paid little attention to the constant presence of Henry Adams, the Cameron children, ever ready to find fault with Lizzie, were more observant, as were the ubiquitous gossips in the capital who were always on the scent of scandal. Lizzie remembered hearing Clover Adams exclaim years before, "What a whispering gallery Washington is!"

As an experienced hostess, Elizabeth Cameron knew the danger of giving even the appearance of scandal. She was a Sherman, after all, and she had observed from the careers of her two famous uncles that personal probity does not always protect against calumny. As the wife of a wealthy senator and the mother of a young daughter, she realized that her position in society was impregnable — unless, by carelessness, her reputation became the subject of clacking tongues.

Besides, she recognized her own vulnerability regarding Adams. Unlike him, she was not sure of her feelings. But she knew that their mutual need was too profound to be indefinitely denied. Adams, solitary after 13 years of marriage and four years as a widower, and possessing a temperamental dependence on women that no army of nieces could satisfy, was beginning to show the desperation of a loneliness that only La Dona could assuage. And Elizabeth Cameron, bored and unfulfilled after 12 years of marriage, found herself, at age 33, yearning for the tenderness she perceived that Adams alone could offer her. They were like two exhausted swimmers, tempted to cling to each other for support, yet fearing their urgency might drown them both.

So they decided on the well-tested device of temporary banishment. It would be an experiment in which they would learn what their real feelings were. Adams therefore invited John La Farge, with whom he had earlier voyaged to Japan, to sail with him on a round-the-world trip that would take them to Honolulu, Samoa, Tahiti, the Fiji Islands, Australia, and Europe. In turn, Lizzie would go with Martha to Beverly Farms, then to Cleveland and Lochiel, and finally to Europe.

By April Adams was writing to Gaskell, "I have fitted myself out for two years in the South Seas. I may return in two months or I may be gone for 20 years. My disease is ennui."

The news of their separate departures from Washington spread dismay among their friends. John Hay, whose adjoining home made him a constant presence in Adams's household, grumbled, "That pleasant gang which made all the joy in life easy, irresponsible Washington will fall to pieces in your absence." Hay also lamented to Adams the loss of "the goddess of your breakfast table." Among the frequent visitors to their Lafayette Square household who would also miss her was Theodore Roosevelt, now a rising star in Republican politics in New York City. He wrote to Lizzie in June, "You cast a gloom over us by your dreadful threat that as you had been good this winter you intended to be bad next winter. On behalf of the family, I protest."

But Lizzie was determined on a separation from Adams—for both their sakes she was sending him away. While he was out of the city in July making final plans for his voyage, and while her husband was off politicking in Pennsylvania, Lizzie enjoyed an unaccustomed few days of being alone with Martha in Lafayette Square. She described "the bliss of never having a caller until after nine at night, long days of reading and loafing, then short moonlit evenings on the balcony with iced watermelon, peaches and mint julep. I want to write an article on 'Washington as a Summer Resort' but am afraid of making it too popular and so losing my quiet."

Now that Adams had finished reading proof on the last three volumes of his *History*, he was psychologically ready for the trip. With the exhausted relief of an author who has completed a major work, he wrote to his publishers, "With the year 1890 I shall retire from authorship," estimating wryly that his writing had cost him $100,000 over the past 20 years.

While he was waiting for John La Farge, with whom he planned to sail from San Francisco in late August, Adams paid a two-day visit to Lizzie and Martha, who were "nesting in a summer hotel" on the Blue Mountain near Hagerstown, Maryland. The holiday proved unsatisfactory, and Adams wrote, "We have all grown thin. Martha lost four pounds. I lost 14. Mrs. Cameron too shows the effects of wilting."

On the day he was to leave Nahant for the train that would take him to New York on the first leg of his journey, he hurried to the railroad station in the early morning, carrying a farewell telegram to La Dona, in the faint hope that she, who was staying in nearby Manchester, Massachusetts, might be there.

She was not, and he wrote, "The mere hope of seeing you again made me try the experiment but it was foolish, for the disappointment is worse than the regret." Recalling Faust's famous pact with the devil, he added, "I feel the devil has got me for I have said to the passing moment 'Stay' but the devil paid a splendid price for a very poor article." Adams entrained for New York, where he stayed at the Knickerbocker Club. With his passion for order, he finished his packing, paid for his train tickets and his stateroom on the *Zealandia*, bought his "last little pair of shoes" (of which he already had a dozen), and then had nothing more to do but look after La Farge. This was itself a major responsibility, for at 9 A.M. on the day they were to leave New York, the artist informed Adams that he still had three pictures to paint, two windows to lead, and his packing to do. But he promised to be ready at four. While awaiting La Farge, Adams wrote to Lizzie, "I have never before felt the sensation of hurrying about with 100 things on my mind and only one thing in it. I have also been a stranger of late years to the choking sense of departure. Life has become a series of farewells..."

Their parting was far more painful to Adams than to Lizzie, who was now en route to Beverly by boat. From shipboard she sent him a note, which he greeted with delight. "It seemed to tell more than a volume on land. I hope you and Martha are now on the beach at Beverly. I would desperately love to be with you."

When Adams and La Farge reached the Palace Hotel in San Francisco and Adams realized the imminence of their separation, he panicked. "I am tired," he wrote her, "I am homesick. A sudden spasm overcame me at the foot of the hotel stairs that I *must* see Martha. I got over this with the help of a bottle of champagne and a marvelous dinner at the Club...I dare not let myself think."

Once the two travelers were afloat on the Pacific, Adams succumbed to his usual violent attack of seasickness. The first day out, a letter from La Dona was brought to his cabin. All night long he lay, face down on his bunk, fully dressed, groaning as he clasped her unopened letter in his hands. Only after 24 hours did he recover enough to read it. In reply, he wrote, "I feel quite proud to have really got so far. But in the long watches of the night, as the ship flops slowly from side to side, I think — and think — and go on thinking, and for the life of me I see no way out of it." Throughout his journey he kept a daily travel journal for Lizzie, and she in turn wrote to him weekly about her daily life as she moved from Washington to Beverly, Cleveland, Lochiel, and later London. Since their letters took three weeks to reach each other, it was important for them to write regularly and often.

In her first letter from Beverly, La Dona thanked him for the batch of sonnets he had sent, exclaiming, "You are a poet of a very high order. It makes me doubt I shall ever find your limitations. After you left, the skies were dull." She described a visit she had paid to Henry's cantankerous brother Brooks and his new wife Daisy, who were summering nearby. "He growled at me for an hour, principally about you and was too tiresome for words. And his wife really seems to like him. She echoes his opinions til I hated him and her and their very atmosphere. So I left." Although Henry Adams once told Lizzie that Brooks was just "an exaggerated version of me, another edition of a book you've read," the difference between the two was far more profound. In a biography of Brooks Adams by Arthur Beringause this distinction is pointed out: "Brooks and Henry were like a surgeon and a geriatrician. Brooks wanted to stab deeply with a sharp bayonet into the world's sores. Henry preferred to let civilization decline into a senility and death of its own making. There was no means of compromise and each brother went his own way."

La Dona settled into Adams's Beverly Farms house and was immediately content. "In 24 hours I felt I had never been away or like a tired traveler who had come home. I know now why this has from the first been home to me, the place where I belong. It has the atmosphere of *you* about it which I have always felt but never recognized before." Such spontaneous delight in the gift of his summer home could hardly fail to touch Adams. Lizzie told him that Spring-Rice, who was awaiting word of his next diplomatic assignment turned up, "so frankly delighted to see me it quite warmed me up. I am like a sponge and like to absorb all the affection I can get." Then she lamented, "Picture what this winter must be to poor me. The only two people I really saw anything of were you and Springy and who is to fill the blank? I become quite mushy with self-pity when I think of it. And books are not much of a resource unless I can talk them over with you."

The Pacific travelers reached Honolulu on 31 August, and Adams, in the tropical land and primitive culture so far removed from Washington, found himself a month later writing to Lizzie with a sense of discovery.

> Life is not worth living unless you are attached to someone . . . Now I find what I expected when I came away—that you are the only strong tie to what I suppose I ought to call home. If you should go back on me I should wholly disappear. I am glad to be dead to the old existence which was a torture and to forget it in a change as complete as that of another planet. You are the only remaining tie but I still cling to you although I shall be wholly white-haired when you next see me. If you throw me over I shall not struggle. Your letters are so much to me that I cannot help dreading lest you should think they are less than they are . . . So you think me a *poet?*

Lizzie replied with spirit, "You say I am the only tie binding you to the old life which you hate. Sometimes I think you would rather not have even that one? As for throwing you over, how could I? You are bound to me in no way. You went your way, free as air and I have no claim on you but the claim of the weak on the strong. It is for you to throw me over, not I you. The dependence is wholly one-sided and proved by your going away."

During these 14 months of separation, their letters present a curious counterpoint—Adams writing of a world of new sensations as he encountered an ancient culture, and Lizzie reporting the daily domestic details of the Cameron household and her problems with her perverse husband, her precocious child, and her ever-present admirers.

In October, Senator Cameron, who often acted on impulse, decided that Lizzie and Martha should leave Beverly Farms, which they loved and go at once to Lochiel, which they hated. Lizzie wrote to Adams "There [Beverly] I neither work nor keep house but there isn't a footpath where Martha's tired little legs have not explored nor a nook in the neighborhood where we have not perched with a stolen apple for refreshment or a picnic feast of barberries and wintergreen. The result is two fat rolling brown balls of human flesh. I gained 12 pounds and Martha eight. What if you should find me fat and greasy on your return?"

Senator Cameron was still convinced that there was something wrong with his lungs (perhaps as a result of his constant cigar smoking), and he was going, on doctor's orders, to "some place near Los Angeles where he can live out in the sun." Of course he expected Lizzie to accompany him, but as Mrs. Sherman reported worriedly, "Lizzie is not at all well and is unable to go. Mr. Cameron is quite blue about this but he has Liddell and Mary so he ought to feel happy." The disapproving mother-in-law added, "I do not believe there is much wrong with his lungs. But to me, from the peculiar whims he has and his morbidness and irritableness, I should not wonder if his case were similar to Will Cromwell of Cleveland [a former neighbor of hers who was discovered to be mentally ill]. I cannot believe a man in his right mind would have such peculiar whims." These whims included ordering Lizzie to visit relatives, who had not invited her, then insisting that she return at once. Mrs. Sherman, who was always impatient with the senator's behavior, advised Lizzie, "Look after yourself for a time to try to get your nerves quiet." To her daughter Mary, Mrs. Sherman complained, "Poor Lizzie is always the third fiddle. She is not strong and she is going into the Lochiel house which is without fires. Mr. Cameron even begged me to go with him today. He promised me everything nice. Of course I could not go at this late date."

But Lizzie's nerves were quickly restored after the senator's departure, and she was cheered by another visit from Spring-Rice. She described his visit to Adams: "he called it our honeymoon. He is ordered to Japan and leaves next month. One more gone." She told Adams that as she and Spring-Rice and Martha strolled through the Pennsylvania countryside on a warm autumn day, a swarm of bees attacked both mother and child. The restrained young Englishman, who had always been ill at ease with children, seized the screaming child and ran all the way up a steep hill, "holding Martha out at arms' length, too frightened to touch her closer. I laughed all the way up in spite of the stings. Martha yelled like a Comanche. I didn't know she had such lungs." Spring-Rice invited Lizzie to ride horseback with him, but she declined, "because I've neither horse nor saddle but drive the same little pair I had in Washington and also Martha's ponies."

By the age of four, Martha Cameron was proving precocious and consequently difficult to handle, Lizzie told Adams, "She made friends with one dog and whipped another for chasing a chicken, so she is contented and feels her own importance. Yesterday she was dismissed in tears from the table because she was offered half a cake instead of a whole one. She is in retirement in her room. She's better than in the hot weather but she still has occasional tantrums, poor baby, when she wishes she had a 'good mother' and speaks with increasing pathos that she is 'a poor little girl.' " Lizzie dressed up Martha and her little cousin Tommy in sailor suits and noted approvingly, "They look such ducks. She is now alternatively Martha in skirts and Tommy in trousers. She makes a handsomer boy than a girl too."

By mid-October, Adams and La Farge had reached Samoa. From there they obtained a little cutter manned by six native sailors, who were, Adams noted sarcastically, "as little fluent in English as though they had studied at Harvard." The two companions landed on the tiny island of Anua, and here in the hut of the local chieftain they were allowed, after it was established that they were not missionary spies, to observe the "siva," the native dance, which was forbidden by the Christian church. Out of his New England sense of propriety, Adams described the dance in detail to John Hay, instead of Lizzie, although he knew that Hay would undoubtedly share his letter with La Dona. Sitting on mats in the hut, lit with the flickering light of a kerosene lamp, the two Americans watched five native girls of varying hue, naked to the waist, their rich skins glistening with coconut oil, sitting cross-legged on the floor, swaying and singing through the undulating rhythms of the siva. Garlands of leaves encircled their heads and necks, and from waist to knee they were covered with lavalavas, or leaf clothes. Adams reported, "The whole scene gave so much freshness to our fancy that no future experience, short of being eaten, will ever make us feel so new again. La Farge's spectacles quivered with emotion and he gasped for sheer inability to take everything in at once." John Hay, of course, read this letter to his ladies of the breakfast table, then reported to Adams that Mrs. Cameron and Mrs. Lodge thought the old-gold girls "horrid" and Mrs. Cameron was "beautifully scornful."

La Dona, who could handle almost any man with ease, was finding her daughter harder to deal with. She wrote to Adams, "I am going to Cleveland with Martha—at least I say I am but Martha says she won't go and I'm afraid she means it." Clearly the four-year-old, who had been the center of so much attention since she was born, was beginning to display the Cameron willfulness. Lizzie finally carried her rebellious daughter aboard the railroad train, then sat at the desk in her drawing room to write wistfully to Adams, "Do you remember our journey down from Boston last year? And Martha [then aged 3] who said she did not like my manners? It was such a lovely journey—I thought so much of it in the train this time." En route to Cleveland, the train became derailed. No one was hurt, and "Martha bore it beautifully and wasn't at all cross but slept 12 hours without moving." During their visit, the child, for whom Lizzie had engaged a new Scottish governess, visited the local kindergarten with her cousin and loved it. Their visit with Lizzie's family was interrupted by a summons from Don bidding them to go to Lochiel, where they would remain until after the Pennsylvania state election. "It will be cold in this old rat-trap," Lizzie grumbled. Apparently the senator's lungs were sufficiently restored to render him impervious to the chill of the old Cameron house. "But I have no longing to go to Washington," Lizzie wrote. "Besides the sweet singing birds have gone..."

Drifting in Pacific waters in a canoe, clad in native costume, Adams waited eagerly for the boat bringing mail to the islands. When Lizzie's letters arrived, he would pore over them, gazing at the enclosed photographs of her and Martha, for hours. When she asked if he thought her running commentary on domestic affairs was "trash — just my old habit of chattering to you," his reply was prompt and emphatic. "Your letters are so much to me that I cannot help dreading lest you think them less than they are." Always on receiving his latest letter, Lizzie would become impatient. "Now I am wondering — already—when your next letter can come. I cannot see from your letters that you are more diverted than you used to be in Washington. But I told you that travel would change nothing unless you could leave yourself at home." But Henry Adams *had* left something of himself at home, and the farther he traveled from her, the more he suffered from a divided mind.

> My diary is all about myself when I want to write only about you. The rest you must fill in, you cannot make it too strong. As winter approaches, I think more and more about you and Martha and long more to see you. The constrast between my actual life and my thoughts is fantastic. The double life is almost like one's ideas of the next world. I dare not think of next summer if you go to Europe. I can't foresee when it will be possible for me to get there. Perhaps it is better not to go. Please tell me what to think *for I am distracted in mind* and being naturally as near a fool as is manufactured, I feel too much or too little when I ought to see as a matter of course what is correct. Anyway, remember that I belong to you and am *ever* yours.

Lizzie was pleased to receive from Scribner's two volumes of Adams's *History* that he had ordered sent to her. "So I shall have something of yours to read. Thank you for thinking of it. They seem more deliberately critical [than the first volumes]. Did you mean them to be?" As 10 November, her 34th birthday, approached, she lamented to him, "I feel a thousand years old. I am growing gray and wrinkled and my hands look old. So we will be just of an age when you return." Adams must have smiled wryly at such a false self-portrait, especially when, as the "fatal day" arrived, Lizzie's spirits soared. "It was so like old times that I forgot to feel old and depressed." When she came downstairs, she found the breakfast table covered with flowers and gifts, "and I had such shouts and huggings as I've not seen and felt since I left home. My brother Henry gives me the *Encyclopaedia Britannica*, his wife all of Parkman's books. So you see how rich I am. They were bought as presents for Martha to give and she is so proud. 'Wasn't I good to give you a birthday present?' she asks a dozen times a night. I feel as pleased as a child and a good deal more appreciative. Now I begin to remember and think of last year when you were with me. How long, I wonder?"

Throughout November they stayed at Lochiel, with Senator Cameron entertaining new members of Congress "assiduously," wrote Lizzie, "and we are likely to remain here until January first." The prospect appalled her, as did the social life to which she was subjected. "I spend my time smiling into the faces of Doodleburger, Sourbier, Heidlebridler and Dunkelburger. I'd take advantage of it to change my name. Isn't it awful to be called Sourbier?" Another of her responsibilities was entertaining Martha, which meant spending the mornings pushing her on the see-saw or playing Indians down on the bank of the creek, until pangs of hunger induced the child to return to the house. "I think between nursing and sawing wood I'd rather saw wood," Lizzie commented.

As Thanksgiving approached, Lizzie planned a hasty retreat to Washington, explaining, "I can't face a family feast here." She had sent her housekeeper Mrs. Churchill on ahead, so for a change she was keeping house herself, "and I love it. Don't laugh. I really believe I can. We leave tomorrow, the whole caravan and the head of it most vehemently." She confessed to Adams, "I gambled a little, the lottery now being shut up in Louisiana. So far I am much ahead. I'll buy a saddle horse against your return." With some perplexity, Lizzie confided to Adams, "Martha is much worried about dying. Someone told her she would die some day and she says she doesn't want to. She objects much to the orthodox picture of Heaven and wonders 'if you and me and God can play house together' . . . "

Once they were back in Lafayette Square, La Dona was plagued with memories of Adams and realized that she missed him even more at home. "I find the old associations crowding around. John Hay sent me this morning a box of dear beautiful camellias and they only gave me a pain." Adams had often presented her with these exquisite blossoms.

As 6 December, the fifth anniversary of Clover's death, approached, Adams's old melancholy came surging back. During a sleepless November night he wrote her a poem about death:

> Death is not hard when once you feel its measure
> One learns to know that Paradise is gain.
> One bids farewell to all that gave one pleasure,
> One bids farewell to all that gave one pain.

Finally his black mood passed, and he wrote, "I am not positively hilarious but if five years can pass I suppose I can stand ten." He was moved when he learned that on 6 December Lizzie had visited Clover's grave, in company with Theodore Dwight, Adams's secretary, who was in charge of his Washington household during his absence. Of the bronze memorial that Augustus Saint-Gaudens had been commissioned by Adams to build, Lizzie wrote, "The work is again delayed. They now promise it for January. It is most annoying for you, I know. I am so sorry. Mr. Dwight gave me two dear little pictures of you which I prize infinitely." LIzzie continued to check on the progress of the work for Adams and in March 1891 reported to him, "The work at Rock Creek is now finished. I will try to photograph it for you." During her hours of idleness, Lizzie had taken up photography as Clover had, and Adams even invited her to use the latter's photographic studio for developing pictures. Both Lizzie and Dwight photographed the Saint-Gaudens memorial, which Lizzie described as "inexpressibly noble and beautiful. The figure is beautiful, life-size, bronze, a beautiful color." The majestic, hooded bronze figure of indeterminate sex had not pleased Adams's hypercritical brother Charles Francis, who said sneeringly, "It looks like a mendicant in a horse-blanket." But Adams disregarded this opinion because he was used to Charles's Swiftian outpourings. To Lizzie he exclaimed, "If the statue is half

The Adams Memorial
Rock Creek Cemetery
sculpted by Augustus Saint-Gaudens

what you describe I shall be content to lie down under it and sleep peacefully." In an effort to be helpful, Dwight had mailed photographs of the memorial to Adams in Tahiti. On learning of this, the sculptor was enraged, as Charles later recalled in his *Memorabilia*. Saint-Gaudens was furious with Dwight for having sent the photographs of it to Adams, thus spoiling the first impression. " 'I would like to have broken Dwight's head for those photos' he told me." Then with the benefit of hindsight, Charles reversed his earlier scathing judgment of the statue. "With wonderful skill and in a most subtle way Saint-Gaudens has now worked the whole sad story into a memorial."

Meanwhile, Adams was learning to paint in watercolor under the expert tutelage of La Farge. Although the historian dismissed his own work as "gentlemanly though reflective dabbling," he made numerous sketches of the lush tropical scenery which he sent only to Lizzie. One of these she had framed to hang in her bedroom. But Adams could not resist describing his ineptness to John Hay. "I spread my net with infinite labor and catch only my fingers in the net." Eventually he abandoned painting but regarded the experience as one more aspect of the education of Henry Adams. "I learned to look at painting from the inside and to see a good many things about a picture that I only felt before."

As the months passed, their prolonged separation was oppressing them both. Lizzie wrote mournfully, "Last night I tried to catch Martha's toes on the staircase and she began to cry, 'I want Dobbitt,' which plunged me deep into gloom. How does all this seem to you out there in infinity? Are big matters trivial or are trivial matters important? As a child I used to wonder—when the Prince came to the end of the world and went down on the other side what did he find there? Are you really out of the world? And what do you find there? And is there such a place?" Adams told her he had read every book, and there were no more to read "except your letters which I know by heart already. The horrors of thinking are intolerable. I feel at times as though I must just run home to have an hour's conversation with you and that without it the world would run off the trestle."

By the middle of December 1890, Lizzie was regretting her banishment of her faithful gallant. "If you knew how I miss you here. I hate to think of you being in the South Seas for Christmas. It is sometimes dreary at home but it is infinitely more dreary abroad. And you of all men should not be a wanderer unless I wander with you. I have not been to your house—I cannot go yet. I do not feel very Christmasy when you who make all my holidays are away."

Such unrestrained longing was bound to elicit a prompt reply. Adams wrote back, "My only hope is to keep knocking about beyond endurance. Perhaps you may cure me after all and I shall come back contented and in repose of mind to be your tame cat after the manner of Chateaubriand." (Adams's reference was to the early 19th-century Romantic French writer Comte François René de Chateaubriand—nicknamed "Le Chat"—who enjoyed a long, probably platonic liaison with Madame Juliette Recamier, who teasingly referred to the Frenchman as "my tame cat.")

Lizzie told him, "Your letters are dear, but too sad. You are not dead but very much alive—a living presence by my side in many long hours and I think, I *have* to think, that you will come back. How I wish it might be soon. I come back again to the verses which I love. I always think each one you send me is the best. Is there anything you cannot do? I am so proud of you!" Then she added briskly that her husband had just been renominated for the Senate and his election was virtually assured. "Six more years of that life. I cannot feel very elated."

Noting that Martha "is growing very big and old but I think she is gooder," Lizzie described taking her daughter to the Senate dining room with Don, where the child ate a pint of ice cream "and a couple of yards of Italian bread. Yet I complain of her lack of appetite!" She concluded with the hope that her letter would reach him by his birthday on 16 February, "for which I send all love and greetings. I haven't a single adorer, not one," she added. Yet her husband apparently thought otherwise, for he showed a sudden streak of jealousy toward a Mr. Towza whom they had just met at a dinner party at the Lodges'. "Donald kept his eyes well on me," she reported, "and after dinner he sat on the nape of his neck in a corner and sulked until Towza came up to speak to me again. Then he insisted on going home at once. He was awfully cross!" But the spirited Mrs. Cameron would not tolerate such behavior and quickly put her husband in his place, "intimating that he must not make me pay for his jealousies and that I must talk with whomever I pleased whenever I pleased. Then the skies cleared." To Adams, who had endured his own pangs of jealousy concerning her, she added lightly, "I know how you sympathize with him so I tell you this. He was only funny and it amused instead of annoying me."

In February 1891, Lizzie was distressed to learn that Uncle Cump was dying at his home in Washington. "He has been my father for so long that I feel I am losing him all over again. Still I hope. He is 70 but his vitality is great—he may pull through." She described the public reaction, with bulletins published in all the papers and posted hourly on public buildings, where crowds gathered to read them. Telegrams from the sickroom arrived every hour at Lafayette Square. "The latest is more encouraging—he is conscious and has taken nourishment." A few days later the general's condition was still unchanged, but on 14 February General Sherman died, surrounded by all his family save Tom, who was hastening home from the Jesuit seminary on the Isle of Jersey but did not arrive in time.

When she heard the news, Lizzie exclaimed, "I can't believe he is dead. Death and he had nothing in common. He is the last of the heroes, very lovable, even his weaknesses were endearing ones."

The two leading American sculptors Saint-Gaudens and Daniel Chester French were called in to make the death mask, and Saint-Gaudens, a longtime friend of the general's, broke into tears while making the impression. At the last moment before burial, the young Jesuit Father Tom Sherman arrived and read the funeral service, although, according to Lizzie, "the Archbishop," who was also Baltimore's James Cardinal Gibbons, "forbade the slightest appearance of Catholicism in the funeral service." Later, Father Sherman celebrated a Requiem Mass for his father's soul in the Church of St. Francis Xavier on 16th Street.

"It is all wonderful to see," Lizzie reported tearfully to Adams. "There are black cloths and bells tolling and cannons firing and all the clap-trap paraphernalia of woe of a military funeral and a burial in St. Louis. You watch strong men weeping like children and the streets for five miles are lined with a silent sympathetic crowd and little children are held up to see the caisson passing." Among the crowds of mourners were hundreds of Sherman's men, who tried to cheer each other with stories of their idolized leader. One story revealed the general's long-standing distrust of the press. Early on the day of the Battle of Vicksburg someone reported to General Sherman that three newspaper correspondents had been killed. "Good," exclaimed the general. "Now we'll have news of hell before breakfast!"

After the funeral Lizzie was despondent and lonelier than ever for Adams. "I dared not write you yesterday," she wrote, "one of those days I felt you *must* come back. I could stand it no longer. If I had written I would have said 'Come'. Martha felt it in sympathy, talked of you all day and at tea wanted you 'so bad'. I do miss you more and more and have a horrible revolt when I think the days are passing and our lives are drawing nearer their ends and all these months are wasted loss. It isn't life without you!"

To which Adams responded in anguished simplicity, "How can I come back? I wish you would tell me how I can come home and be contented there. I get no sort of satisfaction from the consciousness that you are better off to be rid of me." Urgently she replied, "Not for the world would I bid you return if it must be to restlessness and unhappiness. I simply cannot bear to see you as I have sometimes. These last days' revolt have been made worse by your last letters—restless, unhappy, dissatisfied. If I could feel you were happy over there, I could be happy here or at least—but I must not write this way, I know. I thought there was no danger when I began. If you let me unsettle you, I shall never forgive myself. This final note goes now. I wish it could carry me with it—it does take my very soul."

Naturally, these cries of yearning from La Dona could not fail to move Henry Adams. He wrote, "If you think I ought to come home, I am willing to accept you as judge. I will agree to come. Can I say more?" Her cry was piteous: "Everything reminds me of you but it is like the little pointed medallions that ardent Catholics wear on their breasts, getting a sort of savage pleasure from their pain."

Adams was equally distraught, writing, "There is no one else in the world to whom I would dream of making such an ass of myself." Their long-distance courtship was more agonizing to Adams than to La Dona. In the familiar surroundings of Lafayette Square, she was, as always, surrounded by admirers, pressured by the affection and demands of a large family. Adams, homesick in the Pacific, was alone, except for La Farge, to whom he never revealed his inmost feelings.

He tried to soothe her by describing how her accounts of her everyday life in Washington, which he had formerly shared with her, affected him.

> You can't imagine that emotion I feel at having you take me by the
> hand and carry me with you in your daily life until I feel I've been
> with you all month. This sort of flattery is even more seductive than
> what you say of myself for though I suck in with the delight of a
> famished castaway, the flattery which you and Hay are alone in
> feeding me, I know myself and my work too well to be changed in
> an estimate of either. But the other sort of flattery raised my love
> both for myself and for you. . . . When you say you wish I would
> come back, I want to break in with observations that would soon tire
> you out. You will say I am not contented here. True. But I am not in
> mischief. I am not doing harm to anyone. What is the use? How
> can I come back?

In a lighter mood, he requested of her that if she should visit New York,
she ought to stop in at La Farge's studio on 10th Street and look at the
sketches of their South Sea travels that he had sent home. Adams was seldom
wholly approving of anyone—except La Farge. After months of the enforced
intimacy of travel, he could observe, "La Farge is a charming companion who
never complains or loses his temper or makes a foolish remark, but in the
despair of seasickness and cold and wet is just what he is at dinner table." So
he urged Lizzie to inspect La Farge's sketches. "They would certainly amuse
you. . . . He has the wonderful faculty of getting light into his color. I study in
vain to see how he does it, though I see all his process. My results are feeble
and timid, his always suggest the emotion of the moment."

Adams expressed his anxiety about Lizzie's report that Martha had
recently suffered from malaria. He had been observing the Polynesian witch
doctors and now he observed, "It is one of my fads to disbelieve in malaria in
winter and to distrust any doctor who covers his ignorance or incompetence
by that sort of medicine which is a cant as futile as the Polynesian incantation. I
wish the idea of malaria would go into the pigs and quit the devils of doctors.
We might then be seriously diagnosed."

Now that it was April, Don Cameron told his wife that she must make
her summer plans at once. Since the Cameron children would be summering
at Lochiel, he suggested that Lizzie and Martha could go to Europe as long as
they took along his daughter Rachel.

At the same time, Adams, torn by Lizzie's pleas for him to return and his
own desire to do so, wrote to her from Tahiti, delivering an ultimatum. "You
have three months to consider. In September you should be prepared to write
me in Paris or London your matured views as to what I had best do. I will
come home if you want. But shall I come home to stay or shall I come home
for no other object than to get myself miserable again and be forced to come
back here because I cannot make life suit?"

Lizzie was wavering. Of course she wanted him to return, for Washington was "most awfully dull" without him. She described a dinner she had
attended at Vice President Morton's with "the President and Donald representing the elderly respectable element. I am quite weighed down by the
depression of it." But, on the other hand, she was not quite sure how much
Adams would demand on his return. "What is it you want, I wonder?" she

asked. She reminded him of "the night that Nannie Lodge and I lay in the mint bed and you came down the dark avenue to find us and bring us home. What a delicious June it was. And the moonlight at Blue Mountain. Remember?"

Knowing of his curiosity about life in Washington, she told him of her recent encounter with Theodore Roosevelt, of whom Margaret Chanler once said, "Life to him is the unpacking of an endless Christmas stocking." The ebullient Roosevelt, sitting beside Lizzie at a dinner at the home of the Winthrop Chanlers', "bore me off to their library and declaimed ballads. He has just discovered that Lyall wrote better Indian verses than Kipling. He feels prouder than Columbus."

Although La Dona did not hesitate to pour out her loneliness to Adams, she was more stoical in enduring physical ills. In the spring, while the Camerons were entertaining house guests, the entire household, except for Martha, was stricken with influenza. Senator Cameron, the two guests, and three servants were all in bed, some for almost a month. Lizzie's mother, a connoisseur of horrors, reported: "The house was a perfect hospital. Lizzie took care of them all and at last she succumbed and was in bed until she was ready to start [her trip to Europe]." Lizzie had booked passage with Martha and Rachel on the *Teutonic* in early May, and they would spend the rest of the Season in London. Of course, Mrs. Sherman was apprehensive. "Lizzie was very weak and it seemed to me very risky in starting but she said it would only take two or three days of ocean air to restore her. . . . I was glad to get her away although we felt badly to part with her." The responsibility of chaperoning Rachel would fall to Lizzie, but as Mrs. Sherman observed, "I think she may enjoy it."

The gala social life of London was perfectly to Lizzie's liking. She was entertained at a dinner and ball given by Whitelaw Reid, later to be the U.S. ambassador to Great Britain and long ago the object of Clover Adams's scorn when she called him "a scheming tramp from Ohio, sold to Blaine body and soul."

Meanwhile, Adams and La Farge were enjoying a momentous visit to the island home in Tahiti of Tati Salmon, the 38-year-old ruling head of the Teva clan who was half-Jewish and half-Polynesian. To their host the travelers brought a letter of introduction from Robert Louis Stevenson, whom they had visited in Samoa. As a signal honor, the Teva clan adopted the American writer and artist, bestowing on each of them a native Teva name. Adams's name meant "Bird Perch of God," and La Farge's meant "Prince of the Deep." Among the numerous sisters of Tati Salmon was the divorced Queen Marau, a handsome woman in her thirties, who related to Adams the ancient tribal legends that pricked his historian's interest. With a trace of masculine boasting, Adams asked Lizzie, "Do you think it dangerous for me to get into such relations with a young divorced Tahitian queen? I should rather like to think myself in danger but whether I'm not in my twenties any more or am naturally clammy or am the property of some other woman—I am so indifferent to archaic woman with all her physical magnificence. I am afraid you will forget me and will not blame you if you do. Tell Martha when I come home I shall eat her à la Polynesienne."

"When I come home . . ." Adams had already made his decision to return. The lure of travel had faded—he wanted only to see Lizzie again. He wrote to her in London that he expected to meet her in Paris in the fall and to help her select her clothes at Worth's. "I could get a month to be with you at least. After that—*nous verrons.*" Then he added jubilantly, "My only source of energy is that I am actually starting on a ten thousand mile journey to you!"

In Washington, Clarence King listened to John Hay reading Adams's letters on their encounters with the "old-gold girls" of Polynesia. King was scornful of his friend's cerebral approach to the natural beauties of the islands. He was also resentful of the lasting influence that Mrs. Cameron exerted over Adams, informing John Hay, "I can see in my mind's eye the Dona making Henry kneel and unfasten the latchet of her shoe and the old-gold savage falling on his well-bred neck and getting no post-tiniest response." King might have been more generous to his friend's emotional enslavement since he himself once confessed his servitude to his common-law wife Ada when he wrote, "Certain women place men under their spell without leaving them the melancholy satisfaction of understanding how the thing was done. They may have absolutely repulsive features and a pretty permanent absence of mind—yet they manage to assume command." But King was also irritated that Adams, who was enjoying a Polynesian visit that would have enraptured King but that he could not afford, was, in his view, missing the essential point. So he grumbled, "What delighted Adams really were the things he could be sure the Dona would appreciate and enjoy, in short, the primitive culture."

Of course, Lizzie, disporting in London, was unaware of this Polynesian by-play. She knew only that Adams had made his fateful decision to return and was already started on his homecoming journey. Suddenly she must have sensed that her footloose freedom was slipping away. Having escaped for the moment the domination of her husband, she saw that she would soon be face to face with the importunate demands of the lovesick Henry Adams. So she slipped away on 17 May 1891, for a fortnight's holiday in Paris—leaving behind Martha and Rachel and their friend Hatty, under the firm supervision of her housekeeper Mrs. Ferguson and the Scotch governess Macintosh. Between them they could control the three girls while Lizzie was away. And as always when she was off on adventure, her letters to Adams ceased, although he continued to write his daily reports.

Paris in 1891 was the home of dozens of popular portrait painters, of whom one of the most promising was Paul César Helleu, a 32-year-old painter of French society women. Tall and cadaverous, with raven-blue hair, mobile features, and a pointed black beard, and dressed always in black, he looked, said one envious critic, "like an invitation to a funeral taking a holiday at the seaside." Helleu had a 19th-century artist's mystique, which proved irresistible to aristocratic Parisiennes into whose company he had been introduced by Comte Robert de Montesquiou. The count was the satanic friend of novelist Marcel Proust who would one day become the model for Proust's fictional hero the baron de Charlus in À *la recherche du temps perdu,* just as Paul Helleu himself would become the model for the artist M. Elstir in the same work. At the death of Proust in 1922, Helleu would be called on to produce a drypoint of Proust lying on his deathbed. An imaginative artist in pastel, Helleu had both technical virtuosity and a touch of genius.

Thanks to Montesquiou, Helleu was now launched on a career of depicting society ladies as alluring examples of feminine beauty. Sometimes his etchings proved more seductive than their subjects, so naturally the well-born ladies flocked in increasing numbers to his 18th-century studio at 15 rue Émile Menier. Helleu had developed a technique—or "trick," as his critics called it—in which he concentrated on a lady's hair and her headdress, with its monumental proportions—feathers, flowers, artificial birds—while leaving her features idealized but understated. In a typical etching by Helleu, a delicate white face peered out from under a mass of dark hair surmounted by a huge brimmed hat which grew larger and more elaborate as the Edwardian Age advanced. His subject was, in effect, a kind of frenchified Gibson Girl. When Helleu painted or etched the figure as well, he depicted a full-bosomed, wasp-waisted beauty who leaned forward with one slender hand resting languidly on a long-stemmed parasol. Because of his delicate flattery, French ladies, and later Americans, chose to be immortalized by him. From 1890 and through the whole Edwardian era, Helleu became the arbiter of feminine elegance, and designers from the leading Parisian courturiers—Worth, Doucet, and Felix—consulted him before creating their new designs.

Consuelo Vanderbilt Balsan, the American heiress who gained international notoriety because of her marital difficulties, wrote of Helleu: "He was a nervous, sensitive man with a capacity for the intense suffering that artistic temperaments are prone to. He thought himself something of a Don Juan and with his black beard, mobile lips and sad eyes he had the requisite looks but he was too sensitive for the role." Also he had neither the time nor the opportunity, for he was a busy artist married to a lovely young French girl, Alice Guérin, who was his frequent model and the mistress of his household. On what occasion Lizzie had met Helleu in the early days of his meteoric career is not certain. But the seductive young wife of an American senator, who was only two years his senior, was precisely the type of model whom Helleu cultivated. And her wealth and social influence were not overlooked. But for La Dona, this holiday in Paris would be entirely different from her earlier Parisian escapade with Prince Orloff. No longer the romantic young American on her first visit to Paris, Lizzie was now the poised mistress of herself. She was ambitious to widen her circle of conquests, and Helleu was ambitious to widen his circle of sitters. So they understood each other. They met frequently in his studio at rue Émile Menier or in the elegant restaurant Le Lion d'Or to which the artist introduced her. Helleu was a passionate admirer of the 18th century, and his apartment and studio were furnished entirely in white—18th-century chairs and sofa in white satin, walls and carpets in gray or white—a startling contrast with the prevailing decor of overstuffed furniture and plush hangings.

Elizabeth and Martha Cameron

Martha Cameron as a young girl

Elizabeth Cameron in the 1890s

Elizabeth Cameron sketch by Paul Helleu

On his mantelpiece was a porcelain bowl molded, he maintained, from the breast of one of the court favorites of Louis XV, perhaps Madame Du Barry.

When Marcel Proust visited Helleu's studio, he found it nestled high up in an apartment building whose windows overlooked the gardens of the Thiers Foundation as well as a vast expanse of sky. The artist worked in a room bathed in light, decorated wtih empty frames carved in the 18th-century style and placed along the white wainscoting. Canvases were stacked one behind another facing the wall.

Despite his leanings toward an earlier style, Helleu was decidedly ahead of his time in artistic perception. One of the first painters to recognize the significance of the Impressionist movement, he declared, "I was the only one who liked Monet and Manet until 60 of my friends followed in my footsteps."

Such was Lizzie's latest conquest. Theirs was a delightful game, toying over their aperitifs at Le Lion d'Or, but playing their cards with such skill that hearts were never involved. This was, of course, a conquest that Lizzie did not care to reveal to Henry Adams, who was now hastening back across the expanse of ocean to be with her. "I am on thorns for fear I won't reach England in time to find you there," he wrote. "I swear violently in advance."

But she did leave a memento of this romantic interlude, which was found among her papers after her death. It is a charming little poem written in French in her handwriting, 15 lines in length, which sums up her pleasure and her longing and shows a certain skill in portraying the atmosphere of romantic nostalgia that was her substitute for passion.

1891	Le 25 Mai	1892

Au Lion d'Or, ce soir de mai	At the Golden Lion, this eve in May
Qu'il faisait bon, bien attablée	How fine it is, seated at table,
Vous ci, moi la, et tout ennui	You here, me there, and all ennui
Jete au loin avec l'oubli	Cast away with forgetfulness
Qu'il fut demain un jour si gai—	And may tomorrow be so happy a day.
Et puis—Adieu! Et je m'en vais	And then—adieu! And I must go
Au loin, au loin—et plus jamais	Far, far away—and nevermore
On ne refait si belle nuit	Will we see again so beautiful a night
Au Lion d'Or	At the Golden Lion.
À mon corsage bleu, je mets	In my blue bodice I place
Ce souvenir d'un soir aimé	This souvenir of a beloved evening
Déja si loin, si loin—merci!	Already so distant, distant—thanks!
Car je ne retrouve aujourd'hui	For I will not find today again
Au soir d'antan, au mois de mai	In that long ago evening, in the month of May
Au Lion d'Or.	At the Golden Lion.

La Dona returned to London without regrets. Later, Helleu would beg her to sit for him. "Do you want me to make a drawing? In that case, you can pose Saturday at 2 o'clock in your blue bodice. Can you come tomorrow with your little girl?" Lizzie Cameron, who had perfected the art of managing her relationships with men, would later become the godmother of Helleu's daughter Paulette and a welcome visitor to the Helleu ménage.

Meanwhile, she returned to England to await—and manage—the arrival of Henry Adams.

Early in June 1981, Adams and La Farge left Tahiti. "Nothing short of necessity will prevent my seeing you in October," Adams wrote to Lizzie. "We can have some pleasant weeks in Paris and London and you shall dispose of my future movements. If you say so, I will return to Washington to try my old experiment of living; if you say not, I will return to finish in the East my interrupted wanderings. If you say nothing at all—well, I shall be no worse off.

Because the schedules of Pacific steamers were erratic and Adams was now "on thorns" in his impatience to be off, he decided to charter his own ship for $2,500 for the return voyage. In their "wretched little steamer," they ploughed through Pacific waters for ten days until they reached the Fiji Islands, on the first lap of their homeward journey. Anxiously, Adams wrote to La Dona, "I want to know where and how you are. My heart is come upon with doubtings as to the steamers that may sail in the future and I much fear that God troubles himself little about their schedules. . . . So we had better buy you pearls in London or in Paris. There is nothing worth buying for you here."

Adams had already traveled four thousand miles and still had thirteen thousand miles to go. "I have a desperate fear," he wrote to her, "of arriving too late. I don't want to go to Paris for nothing. There is much to consult you about. Even a few hours' talk would do everything. Give me all the margin you can." The travelers were now heading for Australia, where they arrived on 31 July. Since La Farge was unaware of the reason for his urgency and since Adams was determined to keep it secret, he chafed silently at every moment of delay, writing to Lizzie, "I have to be regulated by La Farge who knows nothing of my motives and is not easily hurried." Always circumspect about his affairs, Adams urged Lizzie to use discretion in discussing his plans. "Tell my friends as little as you think best. You are the only one who fully knows them and you take the risk and responsibility for me and for Martha and other like personal property of your own. Whatever you say or do is right." Since she had written nothing about her stay in Paris, he referred to her last account of her social triumphs in London, "I'm glad you liked London. I wish I could give you a lttle slice of the delight you have given me. Some day you will tell me all your visits and your conquests in worlds which I shall never enter and therefore want more to be enlightened on. As for your thinking of me through all your social whirl, I am more than touched."

From Sydney, Australia, he wrote, "I am as grateful as a ten-year-old boy whom you had smiled on and put in rapture at being noticed. The more you please others, the more you delight me. All the way out here, under your feet, my solitude in this howling Australian kangaroo of a city is made brilliant by the thought that you are enjoying all sorts of social electrification and still remember me. . . . Fascinate John Hay by all means."

Revealing the depths of his subjection, he told her simply, "If I come back it will be solely because you have said 'Come'. I can't give that reason to anyone but you and any other would be a lie. As you know, I ask nothing even from those I love most."

In mid-August, Lizzie wrote excitedly, "Dearest Mr. Adams! We ought to reach Paris in early October. I shall see you—shall take you home. I walk on air in consequence. I am waiting for you!"

Still oppressed by the fear of missing her on his return, Adams had La Farge wire his agent at rue Vaugirard in Paris to take rooms there "so I could, if necessary, leave John La Farge and hurry over to England immediately. If you don't sail before Oct. 25 I hope for at least a few hours with you."

Adams marveled continually at the social instinct that never deserted Lizzie. "What a comfort to think you have a genius for entertaining people so I can get, second-hand, through you, the amusement of society without its ennui. This alone makes my return to Washington seem possible. I've thought about it much in the long watches of the night of the last three months and in the pangs of sea-sickness. I can't face the idea of a return without your help." Then, in a sardonic mood, he bet her "a cartload of bric-a-brac versus a pair of your old gloves that you will break down and have to send me away to give you a change. A journey of 17,000 miles is no trifle. Hold on for three weeks more if only you can!"

With mounting excitement, as his journey accelerated, Adams wrote to La Dona, "In a week, look out! I am nearly there. In another week or ten days, if you have kept your plans exactly as I have, you may expect to see me walk into your parlor. If you fail me, I shall fly to Brahmin. Just now I am pretty miserable." He was suffering from a cough and a cold, and his dreaded sea-sickness returned as they sailed through the stifling humidity of the Indian Ocean.

On reaching Ceylon, Adams again revealed his uncertainty about the future. "The pleasure of seeing you once more overbalances everything else." Yet he could not repress his fear that "Mrs. Cameron will not care to see one so intolerably dead as I am. The more you see of such a being the more sorry you will be that you ever tried to bring him back to life. You are the best judge and you can always send me back to the East again by a word." Still anxious about his reception, he continued, "Yet how can I manage not to bore you? If only I knew that, I should feel quite a master of the world. A year of vegetation has unfitted me for Paris or London. Poor La Farge is my only victim and on his sufferings I could look with sardonic amusement but I could not bear yours. La Farge says I am always trying to attain Nirvana and never get near it. I don't know. Sometimes I think that intellectually I am pretty close to it. But even under Buddha's most sacred tree I thought less of him than of you."

On 2 October, Lizzie, accompanied by Martha and Rachel, arrived in Paris, where they settled into rooms at 12 rue Bassano, off the Champs-Élysées. Awaiting their reunion, Lizzie exclaimed, "Fourteen months! It's almost a life!"

Eight days later, after enduring a delay at the Suez Canal, Henry Adams arrived in Paris at midnight. Since he could hardly approach Mrs. Cameron at that hour, he waited in the Grand Hotel du Louvre until the following morning, then sent a messenger with the note, "Arrived at midnight, and wait only to know at what hour one may convenablement pay one's respects to you. The bearer waits an answer."

Finally, in her sitting room at the rue Bassano, on an October afternoon, they met. For Henry Adams their reunion was a bitter disappointment. Seduced by the cries of loneliness that had filled Lizzie's letters to him, he had set out on his "wild, tearing jaunt" across the Pacific to reach her side, sustained by hopes that he could hardly acknowledge to himself. Now, jolted back to reality by her elusive presence, he was beginning to recognize the futility of his fantasies and find the confirmation of his lifelong habit of pessimism.

For Lizzie Cameron the reunion held all the sadness of anticlimax. Faced with the actual presence of this importunate suitor, she recognized that the drama of their enforced separation, with its conflict between Adams's desire and her reluctance, heightened by his heroic journey of seventeen thousand miles in order to rejoin her—that this drama held far more of the romance that her nature craved than the reappearance of Henry Adams in the flesh. It was the confrontation between reality and romance, and the resulting mood for both of them was melancholy.

That she could not accept the reality of their encounter was not surprising. Having learned to endure the daily distress of living with a husband whom she could not abide and six stepchildren who regarded her as an interloper, Lizzie had been forced to invent another level of existence. With the instinct of a survivor, she had succeeded in covering the stark anatomy of her daily life with the cloak of romance—this she received in plenty from the insistent but harmless flattery of her admirers. As long as she could dangle them and juggle them and distance them with practiced skill, everyone was reasonably content. It was a delightful game, and if there were no winners there were no real losers.

But now she was confronted with the unmistakable face of naked longing in the features of Henry Adams. For him she had become the focus of all the mounting desire that his letters had revealed during those 14 months that she had lightly called "almost a life." Before his urgency she could only retreat. For two weeks she arranged it so that they were seldom alone. Bewildered, uncomprehending, he found that Martha and Rachel were constantly underfoot, despite the presence in the Cameron ménage of a governess, a housekeeper, and a maid. Adams complained, "I see much more of the two Miss Camerons than of Mrs. Cameron." During the three weeks of their reunion, he found that La Dona seemed to be constantly in demand and was seldom able to concentrate her full attention upon him. Unable to conceal his chagrin, he wrote to Rebecca Rae, an old friend of Clover's, declaring, "Mrs. Cameron is no good. She has too much to do and lets everybody make use of her, which pleases no one, because of course each person objects to the other person having rights that deserve respect. As long as she lives it will always be so and she will be everybody's slave and get no thanks."

Adams recognized his own state of slavery and its thanklessness. He continued, "If it greatly amused her or if she did it on calculation and for the return it brings in social popularity, I should think it all right. But of all the mysteries of life that have perplexed my life and driven me to absinthe, the greatest and most hopeless mystery has been my friends."

After the two-week visit in Paris that pleased no one, Mrs. Cameron prepared to depart. Accompanied by Martha and Rachel and followed by Henry Adams, she planned to cross the Channel for an overnight stop in London before sailing for home. Still clinging to his wilted hopes, Adams paid her a final visit in her London rooms at 5A Cork Street. But their good-bye was abrupt and perfunctory, and as he later wrote her, "It was all of a piece with my whole visit—fragmented, interrupted, unsatisfactory."

Yet he decided he must have one last glimpse of her. So he rose early in the morning, dressed with his habitual care, and went to stand silently by in the dimly lighted courtyard while Lizzie and the two girls climbed into the hansom cab that would drive them to the dock. In the pre-dawn darkness of Half Moon Street, he saw Mrs. Cameron lean through the window of the cab and gently inform him that their "Paris experiment" had not been so successful as they had hoped. With this statement Adams could hardly disagree. In the November gloom he stood staring after her retreating carriage, a small desolate figure in top hat and gloves, who at the moment of parting could find, amid his store of eloquence, no words at all to speak. Yet later he wrote her with unerring insight, "You being a woman and quick to see everything that men hide, probably knew my thoughts better than I do myself."

From London Adams abruptly left for the home of his old friend Charles Milnes Gaskell in Shropshire. Here, from his room in the mansion's Norman wing, he could gaze mournfully at the broken walls and crumbling arches of what had once been a great medieval abbey. Soon he received a short note from Elizabeth Cameron, written aboard the ship bound for New York. "Goodbye. Thank you a thousand times for everything. Write me what you do—*all* that you do." Clearly her relief at having escaped was greater than any lingering regrets.

Adams's reply, which he began writing on 5 November and continued for a week, is one of the most candid letters he ever wrote. All of his usual tricks of style—the elaborate self-concealment, the ironic self-deprecation—are absent. Here, amid his ruined hopes, in the eloquence of despair, he bared his heart.

He described the landscape at Wenlock Abbey.

> A long, lowering, melancholy November day, the clouds hanging low on Wenlock Edge and stretching off to the westward where you are steaming along the Irish coast and out to sea. As fate does sometimes temper its sternness with pity, the day, sad as it was, has been calm, as though the storm and strain were over. I was glad for your sake and a little on my own account for, as usual, I have passed a bad *quart d'heure* since bidding you goodbye. Perhaps I should have done better not to try the Paris experiment, for the

result of my six months' desperate chase to obey your bidding has not been wholly happy.

Recalling that as a Harvard collegian he used to read the poetry of Elizabeth Barrett Browning, he added, "You do not read her. No one does now. But two lines have stuck:

> Know you what it is when Anguish, with apocalyptic Never
> To a Pythian height dilates you and Despair sublimes to Power?

> The verse [Adams continued] is charmingly preposterous and feminine for a woman never recognizes an impossibility. But an elderly man, when hit over the head with an apocalyptic Never, does not sublime to Power, but curls up like Abner Dean of Angel's [a reference to a poem by Bret Harte] and for a time does not even squirm. Then he tumbles about for a while, seeing the Apocalypse all around him; then he bolts and runs like a mad dog any-where—to Samoa, to Tahiti, to Fiji, then he dashes straight around the world hoping to get to Paris ahead of the Apocalypse, but hardly has he walked down the Rue Bassano when he sees the Apocalyptic Never written up like a hotel sign at Number Twelve. And when he at last leaves London and his cab crosses the end of Cork Street, his last glimpse of Number Five A shows the Apocalyptic Never over the front door.

This image of a mad dog frantically but unsuccessfully trying to outrun the Apocalypse was consonant with Adams's lifelong habit of cynicism. But it was a cynicism tempered with a sense of realism as he showed when he wrote more soberly, "More than once today I have reflected seriously whether I ought not to turn round and go back to Ceylon. As I am much older and presumably the one of us two who is responsible for whatever mischief can happen, I feel as though I had led you into the mistake of bringing me here and am about to lead you into the worse mistake of bringing me home."

Then he touched the heart of the dilemma—should he attempt to resume their affair? "Not that I take a French view of the matter or imagine you to be in the least peril of falling into the conventional dilemma of French heroines; but because no matter how much I may efface myself or how little I may ask, I must always make more demand on you than you can gratify and you must always have the consciousness that whatever I profess I want more than I can have. Sooner or later the end of such a situation is estrangement."

Sadly he advised her, "I am not old enough to be a tame cat and you are too old to accept me in any other character." Adams reverted to his favorite image of the aging Chateaubriand playing the role of tame cat to the youthful Juliette Récamier. "You were right last year in sending me away. If I had the strength of mind of an average monkey and valued your regard at anything near its true price I should guard myself well from running so fatal a risk as that of losing it by returning to take a position which cannot fail to tire out your patience and end in your sending me off again in kindness or irritation."

Laying aside his dreams, he resumed his old habit of analyzing the situation with his peculiar realism.

But I cannot sublime to power and as I have learned to follow fate with a docility surprising to myself, I shall come back gaily with a heart as sick as ever a man who knew that he should lose the only object he loved because he loved too much. I am quite prepared to have you laugh at all this and think it is one of my morbid ideas. So it is, all my ideas are morbid and that is going to be your worst trouble as I have always told you. [In a burst of lover's generosity, he exclaimed,] I would gladly give you as many opals and diamonds as Mr. Cameron would let you wear if I could only for once look clear down to the bottom of your mind and understand the whole of it. I lie for hours, wondering whether you, on the dark ocean, sometimes think of me and divine or suspect that you have undertaken a task too hard for you—whether you feel that last month proved not wholly a success or that the fault is mine for wanting more than I have a right to expect.

With gallantry, he accepted the blame for the failure of their Paris experiment. "The fault is mine, for you are gentle, obliging and thoughtful as ever—nothing remains but to be sorry."

As he concluded his week-long letter, Adams, whose lifelong study of women had led him to a conviction of their natural superiority, discovered that he had failed to understand the one woman on whom his heart was set. In an outburst of longing, he exclaimed, "Yet I wish—I wish—I wish that I could see clear through your mind. You have a nature like an opal, with the softest, loveliest, purest lights which one worships and which baffles one's worship."

With his habitual sense of impending doom, he continued.

My long tearing wild jaunt of the last five months ends here, in a sense of ended worlds and burned-out universes. Progress has much to answer for in depriving weary and broken men and women of their natural end and happiness; but even now I can fancy myself contented in the cloister and happy in the daily round of duties if only I still knew a God to pray to, or better yet a Goddess; for as I grow older I see that all the human interest and power that religion ever had was in the mother and child and I would have nothing to do with a church that did not offer both. There you are again! You see how the thought always turns back to you.

Adams was seldom given to self-flagellation. But now he threw himself in metaphorical abasement at the feet of La Dona.

I try to be civil because you tell me I'm rude and I want to please you. In secret, I dread returning to the solitude of hotels and the weariness of self-self-self and the temptation to commit any folly that would give amusement or change. Always when I reach the desperate stage you say or do something that makes me feel unreasonable and brutal and ashamed of everything but loving you. [With a rhetorical flourish he added,] Why do I send this letter? It cannot give you pleasure, it is very likely to give you pain. Yet it is all me and the pain is actually mine; your position is right enough and easily held; mine is wrong and impossible. You are Beauty; I am Beast and until I turn into somebody else I cannot with propriety live a life fit for you to associate with. I must be a nuisance to you and to myself like Hamlet or Prince Bulbo [a ridiculous character in Thackeray's fairy tale].

Adams turned for a moment to the subject of John La Farge, who had recently left, after sharing his adventures in the South Seas, and spoke of their remarkable rapport. "We have never had a quarrel or a disagreement which proves he must have a wonderfully sweet disposition. He is the only man of genius I now know living and though he had seven devils, I would be his friend for that. If I could only give him a big window to do, like the Church of the Ascension.... So I am now alone for the first time—you gone, he gone, myself the gonest of the lot."

Sobered by his new sense of solitude, Adams was beginning to accept the inevitable. It was becoming clear to him at last that the elusive Mrs. Cameron would not return his passion; indeed, she probably could not really understand it. Charming and warm-hearted though she was toward men, basking in their adulation, she lacked the capacity for real commitment, for the kind of intense and whole-hearted devotion that Adams could offer her. It was scarcely her fault—ever since the abrupt ending of her girlhood romance with Joe Russell, Lizzie had developed a cool detachment toward men, a detachment that her insensitive husband did nothing to remove. Despite her 13 years of marriage and the birth of her child, she still retained the virginal quality that was her greatest attraction for men—each admirer, on meeting her, was certain that he could awaken the sleeping goddess in which the 19th-century masculine mind believed. From the time of Martha's birth in 1886, Lizzie had begun to focus the concentrated love that no man had yet awakened onto the developing child. Soon she became, in fact as well as image, the prototype of the madonna and child.

Never again would Adams write in so self-revealing a fashion. Never again would he express so openly the intensity and self-abasement of his love for Lizzie Cameron. Since he recognized that he would never possess La Dona, and since she would always haunt his imagination, he would gradually learn to sublimate his passion for her into the literary worship of the Virgin who dominated the Middle Ages, and this would in turn lead him to write his *Mont-Saint-Michel and Chartres*. But since he also knew that "life is not worth living unless you are attached to someone," he would force himself to be content with the only role that she would allow him—that of faithful protector and tame cat.

As for Lizzie, once the crisis was past and she was safely back in Lafayette Square, she continued to write to him, even mildly reproaching him for leaving her adrift. But his reply was spirited: "You at least have Martha. I have nothing. You can get on. I can't. The world amuses you, it bores me beyond surgery."

When Adams did not immediately return to Washington, she wrote, "Everyone is furious at you for not coming back and you quite deserve it." Soon he informed her to expect him back by February 1892 at the latest, but he cautioned, "Do not betray me. Keep it quite to yourself." He told her he had chosen a watercolor by the painter Turner as a gift for her. But to silence the tongues of gossips, he offered to send it "directly to you, not as a birthday present, but as if bought on your order or commission and you could send me a check. Suit yourself." He had also bought her a star sapphire ring in a new setting "which I think will please you. I will send it through the Legation with a little baby-pin for Martha."

Adams had learned that his friends the Cabot Lodges were devastated over the approaching marriage of their daughter Constance Lodge to Augustus Gardner. To comfort Mrs. Lodge he wrote, out of his hard-earned wisdom, "In all the real trials of love nothing can be said to any good purpose. One must bear or break and the marriage of a daughter even as young as Constance has got to be borne."

Having set out for a brief stay in Paris, he wrote to Lizzie, "I wish you were with me. We would take a bit of supper afterwards at La Maison d'Or." Then he described in detail how on receiving her latest letter, he had tucked it unopened into his pocket, "with as much care as with a big diamond for my white necktie." Feeling his treasure next to his heart, he had strolled in leisurely fashion along the rue de la Paix and up the boulevard des Capucines until he reached the Passage des Princes, "a bijou restaurant." Seating himself in a secluded corner of the elegant dining place, upon a blue velvet sofa, he dined regally on bouillabaisse, partridge, and Bordeaux wine. All during the dinner he speculated on what her letter might contain, secretly enjoying "its charming company." After slowly sipping his demitasse and smoking a favorite cigar, he opened and read it.

In her letter Lizzie expressed her delight at the gift of the star sapphire. Adams was pleased in turn. "You like the ring? Truly? The setting was my own, after an old pattern. I thought the stone became quite tender and moony under the influence of pearls. I read your letter again, then I smiled all by myself." His smile was tinged with irony. For in her letter Lizzie was advising him, as some of his close friends were doing, to marry again. "You know better," he protested to her. "You are only making a little fun of my sentimentality. I am past marriage—more's the pity," he insisted. "I would not marry now—no! Not even you—if I could. Is that a fair return for your scratch? I mean that life has for me no more interest or meaning and never had any except in marriage." In his emphatic pronouncement, there was just an element of protesting too much, which Lizzie must have sensed.

Adams finished his cigar, reread her letter, then strolled along the boulevard to attend a new play by Guy de Maupassant, "Mon Oncle B—a droll commentary on marriage," Adams noted. "Like you," he told Lizzie, "the French *fin de siècle* can't get on with it or without it." On Sunday he attended a concert, and he told her, "I sat near where we sat together two months ago. I heard Beethoven's Ninth as we then heard his First."

A few days later, Adams returned to the subject of marriage that Lizzie had raised. "You talk of marriage with a bitterness which I never use about anything. I am not bitter, only bruised and scarred till I don't dare lift my head. Then you say I ought to marry to take the bitterness out of my veins when for years I have defended marriage vehemently against your denunciations, a true feminine inversion of rules. How I pity at times that imaginary lady, my possible wife. How quickly and comfortably I would suck the blood out of her. . . an innocent victim to my ennui."

La Dona's reply was prompt and vehement. "And it is I who say it to you. Women are not so cheap and worthless as you think them and fine noble characters do exist who would overcome that "other self" about which you used to talk. As for sucking her blood, I warrant it you wouldn't. She wouldn't let you. She might suck some of yours away and it wouldn't hurt you to lose some of the bitterness in your veins."

So the Paris experiment was ended, and with it another phase of the education of Henry Adams. During his stay in Paris, Adams regained his equilibrium, as was natural for one who was essentially life-affirming and whose ego, like that of most of the Adams family, was basically indestructible. From now on he would behave toward Lizzie with the gallantry of a knight in the age of chivalry about which he would one day write. He would succeed in mastering the elaborate ritual of courtly love—knowing he would never possess his lady, he would devote his energies and gifts to study and writing. Yet never was she absent from his thoughts, and he stood always poised in readiness to do her bidding, wearing her colors beneath the armor of Porcupinus Angelicus, grateful as a schoolboy for her smile.

Meanwhile, he spent Christmas Eve in Paris and wrote to her with a hint of ambiguity, "I have dined at the antique Lion d'Or with only some champagne of 1874 to keep me company and the idea of how pleasant it would be if you were of the party. But it would be hard on you." (Had Adams somehow learned of her earlier rendezvous with Paul Helleu in this exclusive restaurant and of the poem she had written celebrating it?)

On Christmas Day he dined with Gussy Jones, who introduced him to Edith Wharton and her husband Teddy. This was the beginning of a staunch friendship between Adams and the American novelist. "She surprised me," he told Lizzie, "by her knowledge, especially of Paris, on its literary and artistic sides. She is very intelligent and of course looks as fragile as a dandelion in seed, an American product almost as sad to me as Puvis de Chavannes."

10

"The Tame Cat"

By January 1892 Lizzie Cameron had accepted Henry Adams in the role of tame cat, which he had originally proposed. If he complained, she petted him with extravagant praise, "You are so good you almost make me cry. Why did you send all those lovely pictures? You are really too good . . ."

If Adams grumbled to her, "Washington without you is commonplace enough. I think I will go back to the South Seas for I see more of you there than when I am here," La Dona soothed him with morsels of the latest gossip that he loved.

When Lizzie complained that he did not write to her often enough, he retorted, "You scold me for not writing. How should I write? The first law of tame cats: under no circumstances must they run the risk of boring their owners by writing more than once a month or so. You never consider that a tame cat's business is to lie still and purr."

Since both La Dona and her tame cat were equally restless, they were constantly on the prowl—he from Paris to Scotland to Washington that year, she from Washington to Beverly to South Carolina. Sometimes they just missed each other, as when she wrote, "I wanted to come Saturday but Donald decreed otherwise and I arrived to find you gone by two minutes." At this misadventure, Adams growled, "This is getting to be a marked thing and both awkward and public. As you come I go. My train will, I suppose, leave the station precisely as yours draws in. Another fortnight then. How many fortnights in the average calendar?"

Now Lizzie confided to Adams a secret that her husband had hidden from her. "Donald has bought St. Helena Island below Beaufort S.C. and will build a cottage there. He hasn't told me anything, but I always 'drop on him' as the boys say. The cottage will be great, I am sure." Wistfully she added, "I wish he would give Martha a bit of land, we would go there and live." Don's new island contained an ancient cotton plantation and was located at Coffin's Point in St. Helena Bay, halfway between Charleston and Savannah. During the Civil War St. Helena Island had been the dumping ground for the last shipload of African slaves that was headed toward the southern markets, which were by then closed to slave trade. Hence all the "darkies" on the island were descendants of these freed slaves.

"The Tame Cat"

Before building his guest cottage, Don maintained a large houseboat for guests. Manned by a Norwegian crew of seven, the ship had many of the luxuries of an ocean-going liner and would ply the Atlantic as far as Jacksonville, Florida, where it picked up guests, then carried them back to St. Helena, which John Hay described as "a sweet island of soft sunshine and magnolias."

The main house at St. Helena was a white frame mansion, three stories high, encircled by a large veranda. It had a center hall, archways framed with graceful fluted posts and intricate rosettes. The house was surrounded with crape myrtle and magnolia trees. Once he was established in his Southern stronghold, Don would become more sociable. When he planted a grove of pecan trees, they flourished, confirming the legend, "Everything Don touches turns to gold."

One of their first guests at St. Helena was Henry Adams, who came in February and described his visit: "We exercise by lying on the beach, roasting oysters or potatoes in bonfires and crabbing in the creek." The party of eight he described disdainfully as an "idle, useless, wasteful set."

In June, Lizzie agreed to go with Martha to Adams's house in Beverly, which delighted him. "The idea that the house is dark and empty is always a nightmare to me and yet I want no one there who is not somehow a part of my old life. When you are in it, I am contented." Yet he would not join her there when she asked him, maintaining, "I've given up the game and only keep the cards to deal them to my friends. If I were to appear at Beverly, it would only spoil your hand too."

Occasionally her tame cat would arch his back in stubborn resistance, as when Henry Adams that June refused to accept an honorary degree from Harvard. "No work of mine warrants it," he declared. President Charles W. Eliot tried unsuccessfully to make him change his mind, commenting, "You are not conferring this degree on yourself. It is the act of the university." Henry's brothers John Quincy and Charles were irate, and the latter protested that their brother was "showing with almost insulting aggressiveness that he has outgrown his own poor mundane family and that the etherealized intercourse of the Hoopers, La Farge and Mrs. Cameron alone satisfied his lofty soul." Clearly the Adams clan were as resentful as Clarence King of the influence of La Dona over Henry Adams.

In Beverly, Lizzie learned that her tame cat had been hurt in Washington. Adams had badly sprained his ankle "when my horse, walking through a meadow, sat down on me like a cat, catching my ankle under the saddle." Lizzie was all tender solicitude, "You poor dear. How could you go and hurt yourself in my absence and have no one at all to worry you and look after you? Are you making light of it? Are any bones broken? I wish I had you here to take care of—why wouldn't you come? Martha thinks you ought to be moved up here where we can take care of you and be your legs for you. The only drawback to being in your house is that you won't come to it. Wire me if you cannot write. *I must hear.*"

In his reply, the convalescent Adams described his step as "crab-like." Continuing to check on his progress, Lizzie urged Adams to "go about and not play the misanthrope—it is good for you even if it bores you." In contrast, she described her solitary existence at Beverly, in the company of her decidedly misanthropic husband. "I am shut up like a hermit in the ever-narrowing arch of trees on this dear hill and refuse all invitations and return no hospitalities. Still, Washington brings up my average and it doesn't yours."

However, the Camerons did accept one invitation from John and Clara Hay in their summer home at nearby Newburyport. It was on a Sunday, and Senator Cameron was growing bored. As Lizzie explained, "We are going because Don can't play poker on Sundays and I am to see if I like abandoned farms enough to buy one."

John Hay described their visit to Adams. "We have had celestial visitors—the Camerons for two days to our delight and amazement. Don was grumpily good-natured and La Dona radiantly lovely. They pretended to like everything and commissioned me to ask the price of the farm. Their visit put everything up 50%."

By now, although no one mentioned it to Lizzie, Martha was becoming something of a problem. Precocious, overindulged, she demanded her mother's full attention. Even the doting Henry Adams, when she was four, exclaimed in exasperation, "Martha has become a big, obstreperous girl beyond my powers of amusing or being amused. Children are an illusion of the senses. They last in their perfection only a few months and then, like roses, run to shoots and briars." A year later, Hay, sourly eyeing the precocious child, remarked, "Martha seems to me a rather humorous, middle-aged woman who, before speaking, asks herself how she shall best convey the impression that she is a sweet, serious charming child of five." But Lizzie was unaware of this criticism. Determined to have Martha's portrait done, she chose her cousin Rosina Emmet Sherman, a minor artist, to sketch her, then confessed to Adams, "I suppose you will faint with horror. Don't scold me. I must have something of her. I'm hoping for a likeness. . . . I'm so afraid of you that even this sketch will keep me awake nights until you tell me you don't mind." On its completion, she groaned, "it is quite awful. She looks like a paper doll."

Like any careful mistress, Lizzie devised errands for her tame cat, requesting him to pick up a pair of new shoes for her in London. "Ask the girls to bring them in—they are bigger than yours. Then I wish you would go to Paris and get me clothes. Otherwise you will have to look at my old ones all winter. I am too close to pay McKinley prices."

Life at Beverly in the summer of 1892 was surprisingly peaceful. Father and small daughter were becoming great friends just now, Lizzie reported. "He is much flattered by the fuss she makes over him. He drives about the countryside damning the Yankees and even has notes of admiration for their more salient good points. Senator Eustis and one or two choice spirits are at Manchester so he has an occasional poker game. I am so pleased that all goes well."

Knowing Adams's interest in Senator Cameron's political machinations, she told him of "a new man from Pittsburgh" named George Schiras who had been named for appointment to the U.S. Supreme Court. Although Schiras was considered a "very good man," he and his friends had made the mistake of promising $100,000 to Cameron for his next political campaign. With sarcasm, Lizzie noted, "Donald had an access of morality and talked of defeating him. We convinced him it was very bad policy and got him to leave Washington and let it go through. They tell me Schiras is fairly young, has ability and an agreeable family. The latter I will judge for myself. I know my Pittsburgh."

For Adams's eyes she reported the details of the summer wedding of the Cabot Lodges' daughter Constance to Augustus Gardner, of which the family did not approve. "If I live to be 100," she told him, "I shall never forget the look on Nannie Lodge's face. Such a grim determination and suffering. Quite tragic." Then the alert Mrs. Cameron intercepted another look, on the face of Dr. Sturgis Bigelow, a cousin of Clover's who had become a Buddhist monk, as he watched the bride approach. "I will always love Sturgis for the look in his face when he saw her. It was like God's in its infinite tenderness and pity. Why didn't you tell me he loved her? Rev. Phillips Brooks married them. Connie was lovely and Gussie looked about as sodden and dissipated as ever."

The whole eastern seaboard was suffering from a heat wave in July. "People die like sheep," Lizzie reported. "Children have convulsions and men go mad. The Coroner had more work than he could handle." But Mrs. Cameron and Martha were luckier than most. Airily describing herself as one of the "lazy useless drones of life," Lizzie donned her coolest Parisian batiste negligee and "lay in a hammock, reading and fanning and enjoying myself absolutely. I loved it." Beside her played Martha, who was wearing "her latest Samoan costume, growing brown all over—a lovely golden color which would have carried you back to the South Seas."

In the fall, Adams was back from Europe, carrying the shoes Lizzie had ordered. "Shall I send them to you or take them to Washington?" he asked. "I really have nothing to do there but to see you and though the ghosts are dreary enough the so-called living are 10 times worse!"

But before they could meet, he received a message from the Samoan chief Tati Salmon who was arriving from San Francisco, so, setting out to meet him, he found he would miss La Dona. "Forgive me for running away. After all, you know it is my only serious occupation and this time it is not far. If I thought you cared, I should care more."

The tame cat was always grateful for a letter from his mistress. "It arrived with a promptness that always makes me wonder and a kindness that makes me sad. This sadness is an involuntary tribute to you, a kind of hurried recognition of the impossible possibilities of this imposssible world. I shall follow hard on this letter and once more you will see me returning to the old haunt as gay as a magpie and as devoid of any consecutive idea."

But La Dona's pet feline was uncertain of the warmth of his reception. "As before you will not know what to do with me and will be more afraid than glad to see me and will be rather relieved when I vanish again in some new spot. The game is a little monotonous . . ."

Although Lizzie was frequently away from Washington, she remained unfailingly devoted to her widowed mother. She would instruct her coachman to stop every day at her mother's house in order to take her for a drive and frequently left her mother a supply of books which her companion would read to her.

Early in the winter of 1893, the Camerons took their usual winter trip to St. Helena. While she was there, Lizzie received the crushing news that her favorite brother Henry, while on a sea voyage, had died of a heart attack at the age of 49, leaving a wife and young family in Cleveland. She wrote at once to Adams, "I am scarcely steady enough to write. The absolute uselessness and wanton cruelty of such a death! It is so wicked I cannot submit. I cannot accept it. Mother is crushed and ill. His poor wife and children are not even trying to bear it. I am off to Cleveland tomorrow and Mother comes later for the funeral." Yet amid the whole family's prostration, Lizzie remained indomitable. "I alone am on my feet," she told Adams, "and am cheerful and mad."

Of her brother Henry, who had been 13 years her senior, she wrote tenderly, "I've never known anyone who was so much to so many people—a keystone. That we loved each other is my sole comfort. Do you know what I mean? He was father, brother, counselor, protector—I dare not look into the future."

Adams had seen the news of Henry's death and was "distressed that I can neither do nor say anything to help. I don't know where to look for you or where to go to search for you. I want desperately to know whether you will go north or have done, whether you will return to St. Helena, whether you want me there, whether I can be of any use. I say nothing of condolence. Death is not to be consoled. Some people submit or think they do. I have never been able to do even that."

Now La Dona could grant the wish of her tame cat to be of use to her. At her request, he departed at once for St. Helena—to stay with Martha until her mother could send traveling orders from Cleveland, where she was attending Henry Sherman's funeral. Arriving in March at St. Helena during an unusual cold spell, Adams found Martha "wonderfully well. Mr. Cameron seemed recovered from Washington and was cordial and communicative. He says you thought of my bringing Martha on. Everything remains waiting on your wishes. I am ready to start at an hour's notice to you—or to wait a year for you—or to go to China with you. All is one to me."

But a snag developed in the plans. Martha did not want to go, and her father backed her up. Adams stood helplessly by, awaiting orders from Lizzie. The child was allowed to have dinner with the grown-ups and devoured her ice cream. Even the excessively cold weather did not bother her.

A telegram arrived from La Dona ordering Adams to conduct Martha to Cleveland. But Adams faced a dilemma. "I will bring Martha up next Monday if I can. I would promise certainly if it depended on me and would pay no regard to anything else. But the command does not belong to me." Senator Cameron, it seemed, objected to Martha's "being exposed for some hours to a driving north-east storm with the thermometer at 50 degrees and no protection at the end." With unaccustomed optimism, Adams continued, "By tomorrow I hope the weather will clear and his objections be removed. Then I will start without fail." Eventually Martha set out in the custody of Dordy for an uneventful trip to Cleveland, while her father remained behind.

By now, the tame cat was accepted as the possession of the entire Cameron family. In May 1893, Adams was the guest of the Camerons on a trip to Chicago in the senator's private railroad car for the opening of the World's Columbian Exposition celebrating the 400th anniversary of Columbus's discovery of America. Returning after a two-day visit, Lizzie was exhausted, but she and Don and Martha were due to start for Europe in June, and she barely managed to get aboard the liner. Adams watched her departure with anxiety. "She signalized her departure by going completely to pieces. She had to remain shut up in her stateroom complaining of a painful back and an attack of nerves. Don't tell her mother. I was a good deal alarmed," he confessed.

In London she revived, and they went on to Paris, where, she reported, "The apartment was quite stunning and impressed Martha into whispers temporarily." Lizzie found herself, to her disgust, surrounded by "social climbers, especially a Mr. Robinson, who is thicker than honey and more clinging, but I flatter myself it was because we knew three Dukes." Don complained of boredom and took off to meet Henry Adams, with whom he planned to visit Chamonix briefly.

In August a cable from Washington informed Lizzie in Paris that her mother, five months after Henry Sherman's death, had suffered two strokes and was lying near death. Lizzie was frantic to return to Washington. "I am in the utmost suspense," she wrote, "and of course filled with 1,000 different ways of reproaching myself for being here. I am packed and ready for the night train." When she finally arrived, after the sea voyage and a trip by train to Washington, she found her mother fully conscious "but suffering horribly, so I can only pray for a speedy end." Lizzie had her mother moved to Lafayette Square so she could nurse her. Although she wished to die, Mrs. Sherman lingered, feeble and helpless, for several weeks, while Lizzie spoke of bringing her to St. Helena for the winter. But in October 1893, she died.

That year, Adams, whose family had recalled him from Europe to rescue their holdings during the financial panic of 1893, was in his element, forecasting universal doom. "I am in a panic of terror about finance, politics, society and the solar system with ultimate fears for the Milky Way and the nebulae of Orion. The sun spots scare me. Ruin hangs over the Pole Star. Of course this means the approach of old age and senility."

In September, Senator Cameron made one of the few speeches of his career on the floor of the Senate, opposing the repeal of the Sherman Anti-Trust Act, for which Lizzie's Uncle John had been responsible. Cameron's political lieutenant Matthew Quay told him it was a good speech and that his wife must have written it. Actually, Adams had had a hand in it, although he would not admit it. Adams reported gleefully, "All the papers are full of violent diatribes against Don who is as pleased as a hen with one chicken and absolutely chirrups with delight at having laid his egg."

In December, Lizzie again sprained her ankle, but, unwilling to play the role of invalid in a year that had seen the deaths of her brother and her mother, insisted on going to the theater on crutches, escorted by Henry Adams.

Lizzie invited Adams to spend the rest of the winter with them at St. Helena, and in January 1894 he arrived. But Adams and Clarence King had for a long time been indulging in an old dream of taking a trip to Cuba. King was recovering from a nervous breakdown, for which he had recently been hospitalized in Bloomingdale Asylum, and he was eager to be off. Always short of funds and too proud to accept money from Adams, he nevertheless planned to go. (He did not object to borrowing money from the wealthy John Hay.) When he discovered that Adams was visiting at St. Helena, he wrote sarcastically to Hay, "I am waiting for Adams to tear himself away from the arms of—South Carolina, where he is 'doing time' with the Camerons."

Finally, Adams tore himself away and met King in Tampa, whence they set off for Santiago, two middle-aged adventurers whom Adams described as "bald-headed, grey-haired or at least 'sable-silvered,' like Hamlet's father, literary and scientific gentlemen of a respectability that appalled even the Knickerbocker Club and themselves."

The departure of her tame cat saddened Lizzie. "You have deserted me," she wrote to him, "after solemnly promising to spend the winter with me here. If hasty, I'd say that one promise more or less made and broken by one of your sex mattered little." She could not in honesty say this of Adams, for he had never broken a promise to her. "But," she had to admit, "everlasting truth prevails that you are of your sex a specimen apart and that you are as true as the North Star. So it simply means that someone else needs you more than I, a perfectly false assumption."

As always when he was absent, she appreciated his qualities most keenly. "Lately I've been thinking about what you have been to me," she mused. "I was in the darkness of death til you led me with your gentle guidance into broad fields and pastures. Even sorrow and trouble lessen under your light—a light so calm and still I wonder if any man was ever so big as you. I must not flatter you, though, or you won't be as dear as you are."

She discussed with their friend Chandler Hale the possibility of their going together to join Adams in Cuba. But she hesitated. "We feared you might not have room *and* that we might not be quite welcome to Mr. King."

Now that he was gone, she realized how much of a moderating influence her tame cat had been in the warring Cameron household. Both Rachel Cameron, who made no secret of her dislike of Lizzie, and Jim, who was openly hostile, were now at home, and the senator was ailing with one of his unspecified illnesses. With a touch of bitterness, Lizzie noted, "Jim and Rachel never dispute my claims upon their father in illness, whatever they do in health."

She described for Adams an appalling weekend when Rachel and some friends arrived and the island was struck with a howling northeaster that lasted for four days, forcing the entire party to remain inside. Rachel, who was jealous of Lizzie's friends, was especially furious at the presence of the glamorous P. B. Mary Leiter. So she and her friends began uttering a series of rude remarks that called forth rejoinders from Lizzie and her friends. The affair ended with each side adjourning to separate parlors, "like a lot of whipped dogs skulking off in corners together, all of us feeling childish and miserable. I am so ashamed and mortified," Lizzie continued, noting that if only the weather had cleared "we could all have taken to the boats and the beach. It is a history of utter childishness of which I fear you will hear more. I am crazy to join you in Cuba but it's no use now. We miss you awfully."

In the summer, Lizzie and Rachel, in an uneasy truce, traveled together to Europe, with Rachel insisting on going to Scotland, while Lizzie wanted France. Senator Cameron, who always humored his daughters, sided with Rachel and promised to buy her a castle at Inverness in Scotland, where Clan Cameron had originated. "If you knew how I hated that cold and unknown Scotland," Lizzie complained.

Under Adams's guidance, Lizzie had developed a taste for Flaubert, and now she reported, "I'm reading the naughty but spicy letters of your friend Gustave Flaubert. I find in him touches of you minus your sweetness. Did you know that Guy de Maupassant was his son? It appears to be an open secret in Paris among literary men."

Adams and Hay were off vacationing in the wilderness of the Grand Tetons in Wyoming, when Senator Cameron brought Lizzie the word that Adams's brother John Quincy II had died of apoplexy. "My very dear," wrote Lizzie, "my heart goes out to you. I cannot bear to think that you are suffering another shock, another pang. Are you so far that the news will not reach you? I am anticipating a thousand evils for you, including the complication of business troubles. I know he was very dear to you—he was like you and that is enough. It is now that I ought to be with you."

Two days later, she wrote again, "I want to write to you all the time—to say something to console you and I have nothing at all that will reach you ever."

On his return to civilization, Adams learned of his brother's death from Edward Hooper, Clover's brother. He was struck by the irony. "As usual death takes the useful and active ones, while it leaves the useless and lame ones to hobble along behind the procession as long as the band will play. I might have broken my neck a dozen times a day this last week—but death chooses my brother in his bed. He was only 60—I thought him safe for 20 years."

For a while the tame cat wandered about dejectedly alone. "I have succeeded in getting rid of everything but myself," he wrote to Lizzie. "I go to Washington to see if you have written. Possibly someone may want me. This is so extraordinary an idea that I reject it at once. If I find no letter, no wants and no you, I shall start again."

Responsive to his suffering, La Dona wrote, "My dear Dordy: Sometimes I wish you liked your fellow beings just a little better and did not repel all sympathy quite so much. I know the loss of your favorite brother costs much and I'm sure you are paying your debt of sorrow alone. I wish I were with you—not that I could do you any good. It is for my sake that I wish it."

Adams's reply was stoical. "John's collapse has given me what they call on trains 'first call for dinner'. I am not hurried by the notice for I have been all ready these last four years but I want to do some few odd jobs first—one is to travel."

Lizzie told him she was sailing for home in November, so Adams was at the dock to meet her only to find Senator Cameron instead, who informed Adams that she was not on the ship. "I'd rather not repeat that disappointment," Adams told her, "so this time I shall wait for you here [in Washington]. I want to see you and to see Martha. I am tired of you both for not coming here."

During the winter of 1895, Lizzie was "as fresh and young as ever," according to a letter from Hay to Adams. She went often to the opera and described to Adams the voice of Nellie Melba in *Lucia di Lammermoor*. "It is surer, fuller and more true than a flute. The Mad Song makes me quite curl with pleasure." Lizzie noted with her practiced eye that Mrs. Harry White (the former Margaret Rutherford, who was the wife of the American diplomat Henry White) "fit Donald and Cabot both in her pocket and she flatters them both. She is a very intelligent, handsome and appreciative woman." These qualities are apparent in the notable portrait of her by John Singer Sargent.

Adams was vacationing in Mexico that winter and he sent Lizzie a comic word portrait of himself that was as vivid as any likeness by Sargent. He described himself "in a riding-suit of leather with a superb adornment of white leather frogs and buttons all over me; a sugar-loaf Panama hat; heavy steel spurs and a serape wrapped around my shoulders; all on top of a mule which ambles along at just the rate of four miles an hour."

Although Lizzie seldom wrote directly of her husband's irascible disposition, Adams, who knew it well, could understand. As a tame cat of the Cameron household, he had witnessed the constant turmoil that Lizzie endured in her husband's presence. So when Lizzie and Don decided to try a whole summer traveling together throughout Canada, Adams was dubious. Nor was he surprised when she wrote to him in September. "Our summer together has not proved a successful experiment. I would like to remain here [in Canada]. But we leave tomorrow." She remarked that her husband looked bored, while as for herself, "I am *au bout de mes forces*—how much better if I had gone to Europe!"

By now, nine-year-old Martha was becoming aware of the tension between her parents. No longer did she idolize her father, although he spoiled her in every way. Toward her mother the growing girl felt a strong loyalty, and Lizzie noted with dismay that "Martha returns his devotion to her by a treatment which resembles his to me. She may revenge me yet." Martha was showing an open indifference to her father despite all his attempts to win her affection with expensive gifts and treats. She flatly accused him of being unkind to her mother, which, when Lizzie heard, she tried to overcome by talking to Martha about filial love and duty. Martha listened solemnly, nodding agreement, then plaintively asking, "But why does he treat you that way?"

Lizzie felt an even greater regret for her "lost summer" when she received Adams's letter describing his visit to the Benedictine Abbey of Mont-Saint-Michel off the coast of Brittany. "I gnash my teeth when I think I might have been with you and have seen all that with your eyes. Our traveling in Canada is very hard. No sleep or food." In Roberval they saw three black bears that had been taken from the woods. Martha was entranced, and the senator talked of buying one to send home to Dordy. "We all spoke of how you would love them," Lizzie sighed, then added, "I live on your letters so give me life."

News reached Senator Cameron that the Baltimore newspaper, *The Sun,* was predicting the collapse of his political career, so off he sped to Washington, leaving Lizzie and Martha to feel a huge sense of relief. "Already I feel as if the summer was a bad dream," Lizzie wrote to Adams. "But after all, how can I tell that he does not suffer more than I? It is so peaceful and nice now that Don is gone." Smilingly she watched as Martha began to discover the world of books, and remembered her own childhood "when the world seemed so vast and I had such a hunger for those rows of bindings which seemed doors onto a great world."

Hardly had she recovered her equilibrium when she received a peremptory wire from Don to meet him in Washington and go with him to Hot Springs. "So we packed up and here we are." Wistfully, she added, "I'm crazy to be in Washington when you arrive but of course I'm dependent on the matter of my fate, in the little as in the big things of life. With his restlessness he may break up here at any time. How if you came down here? We could go back together."

In April 1896, the Camerons, with Adams as their guest, visited Mexico, and Adams cynically remarked, "Senator Cameron was delighted by the attentions shown him. Politicians, to be successful, must partake of the infantile temperament of extreme babyhood. Under the influence of epaulettes and brass bands we have stayed a week in this sink of Hades."

The following month, Adams planned to go to Europe with John Hay. Lizzie dreaded his departure. "I watched for you with the usual lump in my throat, too chokey to even tell you how lonely I already feel in anticipation. We shall miss you terribly."

She described for him a carriage ride that she took with his eccentric brother Brooks to the Soldier's Home. On the way home they were caught in a torrential rainstorm, and "Brooks valiantly mounted the hood and stood balancing himself like an acrobat on the steps with the horses going full speed and our wetting was very slight."

Her spirits were low as she thought of Adams's ship steaming out of New York harbor toward England. "I think of you every hour of every day, always with longing and gratitude beyond expression. I shall watch and wait for your letter and long for you. If I can come out, so much the better. If not, you will come to me won't you? Martha sends her love and I—and I . . ."

Don Cameron's drinking, which had persisted for years, was getting worse. Lizzie noted, "He seems to me very feeble and unless he is much better I shall not attempt to break away. I am impressed—and oppressed by his condition. This last spree has left him very poorly indeed."

So she decided to forego her European vacation again and tend to her ailing husband. But his strange whims, which her mother had so often deplored, were increasing. First he toyed with the idea of accepting an invitation from General Miles to visit him in Yellowstone, and Lizzie told her tame cat breathlessly, "If he does, I shall come to Paris at once but oh, dear, I have little hope." Then Don changed his mind, decided they should go to Bar Harbor, stopping en route with the Lodges on the North Shore, then go on to Donegal, his farm in Pennsylvania.

During their visit to the Cabot Lodges at Nahant, Lizzie exclaimed, "I wonder how you endured the noise and violence of them all last summer. I never heard such wrangling and Nannie's rather worn face is now explicable." One day Brooks Adams came to visit her. "I was touched and flattered at his coming all the way from Quincy to see me. I can't get over it. Of course I am his slave for life."

Finally, they set out for Donegal, and she wrote resignedly, "A curious whim of Don's—but a situation is never hard when faced and now I have accepted it."

But her sacrifice of her summer was in vain, for she found that her husband was "just as cross as ever and he is also so much better that the suspicion enters my wicked mind that it is a trick. If so, a successful one."

On the train to Donegal, Lizzie, who was sitting alone in the car, was so affronted by the impudence of the conductor that she demanded to know his name in order to report him. When he caught sight of her railroad pass, "the way he crawled was sickening." From her position of privilege, she wondered, "What do you suppose people do who only buy their tickets and haven't a known name? It makes one ill."

When she met Don at the station, she saw that he was in his "now almost normal condition. He looks terrible." But in an attempt to conciliate her, he had improved the farm "for the city dame." She was touched by "the few little puny flowers stuck in the ground, fly screens on the doors and a new carpet on my bedroom floor. Above all he had removed the pig pen from its old spot too close to my aristocratic nose. I almost felt the situation demanded a tear."

The farm woman who did the cooking was so intimidated by all the preparations for Mrs. Cameron's arrival that she threatened to leave. All of Lizzie's diplomacy was called on, for the woman did far more than any city cook, even making butter. "It took me several days to convince her I was not dangerous. Everybody was 'afraid' to wash our clothes, do our rooms—but now everything is adjusted."

With the extravagant gesture of a rich man, Senator Cameron sent to Harrisburg, 30 miles away, for fresh vegetables, fruit, and butter, although, as Lizzie noticed, "We are in the heart of the richest country in the United States."

"The Tame Cat"

When a neighbor woman asked Lizzie if her husband had "run to flesh," Lizzie reported to Adams, "It was my one and only spasm of sanity in Lancaster County."

Mrs. Cameron was puzzled at the lack of family feeling among the senator's family. "Don and his children are within 45 minutes of each other and ignore each other. Rachel and the MacVeaghs in Paris did the same thing. Rachel hasn't written a word since she went to Europe. When she sailed, her father did not so much as see her off. He went to Harrisburg and did not even call Jim. At no time has he ever written me—except incidentally. *They are strange people but are not considered so here."*

The heat in Donegal was overpowering. "Martha is grey white," her mother wrote anxiously. "But Donald, of course, eats, sleeps and is perfectly well and perfectly oblivious of anyone else's discomfort or anger. We spent yesterday with ice bandages on Martha's head."

But Lizzie was not the niece of General Sherman for nothing. She would not stand by and watch her daughter wilting in the oppressive heat. "So I had to take a stand. He is kicking like a mule of course but he must kick. Don't think I'm complaining. I am understating the actual situation." Finally the heat "has broken even Donald's will. He is now anxious to get us off somewhere." She enclosed a clipping from a New York paper which showed that from the 5th to the 12th of August there were 621 deaths and 1,255 prostrations from the heat in greater New York. So the three Camerons departed for St. Helena to recover.

By early spring of 1897 the Cameron marriage was clearly disintegrating. Recognizing the unmistakable signs of impending political defeat, Senator Cameron had decided not to run again, leaving the field to his lieutenant Matthew Quay. The prospect of his retirement was more than Lizzie could bear. Having him constantly underfoot, being dependent on his unreasonable whims, enduring his irascible moods, was proving impossible. Like many a Victorian lady in a similar impasse, she found refuge in a "nervous breakdown." As Adams noted in horror, "her heart went all to pieces." The attending physician spoke of "a valvular weakness and weakness of the muscle itself." She was ordered to remain quiet for at least six months under a doctor's supervision. After being confined to bed for a few weeks, she was allowed to sit up in a chair for 15 minutes only.

Just at this critical moment, Senator Cameron decided to put up the Lafayette Square house for rent. As Adams reported, "When she was at the worst and every worry was a matter of life and death, Mr. Cameron let their house to the new vice president [Garret Hobart] from May 1 for four years. So she had to break up and remove all her things and plan to go away at a time when she could not even sit up. Naturally she had one relapse after another and when I came away on April 12th I did not believe I should ever see her again."

But Lizzie was still indomitable. She did not want to miss her trip to Europe and a reunion with her tame cat. So she persuaded her doctor to allow her to go, "if I take a nurse and stay in bed. He recommends physicians in

Paris and London and advises the Isle of Wight climate for moisture and no tendency to stimulate." She also persuaded Adams to await her arrival in England, since she intended to sail with Martha and Rachel on 5 May 1897.

Adams in London was astonished at the power of women over circumstance. "What can't a woman do if she will? I think it will kill her but I am bound to remain until the matter is settled." While she was on the Atlantic, he wrote to Hay, "She somewhat more than risks dying on shipboard as her brother did," and he considered the possibility that he would have to bring a motherless Martha home—"wherever she can find a home."

His fears were unfounded, however. Aboard ship, Lizzie's spirits lifted and she felt stronger. "We are almost in, Dear Dordy," she wrote to him, "and the sea is tranquil and blue. It has been a wonderful voyage but I have stayed in bed in a craven manner. It is so cold and wet and my large stateroom has an electric lamp. The girls [Martha and Rachel] are blooming."

Resolutely she informed him, "I am determined to make a good try at mending our broken-down machine. If it won't go, I can adjust and begin again. But I *must* try. That is why I came."

While Adams in agitation was awaiting her arrival in England, as always expecting the worst, and while she had, as usual, no word from her husband, Lizzie began to muse on her relationship with Henry Adams. "It is curious," she wrote to him, "how one shuts up like a jackknife when anything becomes real or sensitive. There is a long history of mental weakness and mental struggle. I have often wanted to tell you but couldn't. I cannot talk to you even to yourself. Above all, I cannot say anything of all that I feel to you. But, some day, I shall go down on my knees to you and humbly kiss your hand. Even then, you won't know the smallest portion of it, very dearest."

Adams met her at Southampton, rejoicing that "she was alive." He had ordered "an invalid saloon and bed" for her on the train to London. He settled her in Brown's Hotel, urged her to go at once to bed, then departed for his own hotel nearby. But Lizzie disdained the bed. Instead, she sat down at once at the writing desk to dash off a note to him. "I cannot give you any news for my hat is not even off. But London smells of London and of fog and smoke and there are coal fires in every room. We have very nice rooms with a barrel organ playing under the window. They are forbidden in Paris. The Channel was like glass. No one with any self-respect could even think of sea-sickness." This was a playful jab at Adams's chronic sea-sickness.

During this trial separation from her husband, Lizzie gradually recovered her strength, guarded by her tame cat, who showed her a solicitude never displayed by Don Cameron. Of course, Adams's predictions were gloomy. "Mrs. Cameron revived rapidly after the voyage—and overdid. She is really making no progress I can see. The doctors all say she must rest absolutely for six months. She may need a year of rest, but there is no incurable trouble, only nervous collapse, the slowest of all things to repair."

Since Lizzie yearned to go to France, Adams set about finding a suitable spot in which to install her along with the five Hooper nieces. After a month of house-hunting, he found a "queer old house" in Saint-Germain-en-Laye, a charming town in the Île de France outside Paris, and "Ill as she was she took the only house the girls fancied and did all the work of setting up the establishment." The house was shaded by huge cedars, purple beeches, and ash trees and had a distant view of Marly and the curving Seine. Adams supervised the houseful of women as they studied French conversation and history together. He insisted on feeding them constantly. "I try to fatten them all for they came here as gaunt as so many razor-backed pigs in Carolina."

During a brief stay at the Hôtel de Voltaire in Paris, while Adams was house-hunting for her, Lizzie had befriended a tall, cadaverous young man who turned out to be the artist Aubrey Beardsley. He was at the height of his fame for his fantastic and erotic drawings which were used as illustrations for books and which had caused a *succès de scandale* in the quarterly journal *The Yellow Book*. At the age of 25, the unfortunate genius was suffering from rapidly advancing tuberculosis. On his doctor's orders, he had just left Paris, accompanied by his mother and sister, for the seaside resort of Dieppe. Oscar Wilde, who described Beardsley as having "a face like a silver hatchet with grass-green hair," was staying at the nearby Hôtel de la Plage, having recently been released from Reading Gaol.

From the Hôtel du Casino in Dieppe, Beardsley wrote a note to Lizzie in his tiny, elegant handwriting. "My mother is writing to you and I feel I must also send a little note to thank you for your kindness. I am much better for being in Dieppe and my doctor has given me permission to winter in Paris. I was frightened to undertake a longer journey." The doomed Beardsley would return to Paris for the winter, as he hoped, but he would be dead within a year.

Since her Lafayette Square house was still occupied by vice-presidential tenants, Lizzie headed for New York, where she hoped to regain her health and spirits. Lonely and displaced, she wrote from there to her tame cat, "I wish I were with you. I ought not to have said that. I want you to feel, you know, that I am not unhappy in the least, that I am well and have my time well filled. Will you believe that?" When he replied he was lonely too, she retorted, "You alone in Paris are not really so chill as I am in New York with never a minute to call my own." The pace of the city irritated her. "If you want only a spool of thread, you must stand in line in a crowded shop, pushing and jostling and bruising."

To please Adams and to enjoy herself, she spent a Sunday afternoon with John La Farge in his 10th Street studio and reported, "He is charming and said the cleverest things, yet apologizing for his dullness because his weak health kept his head buzzing. But he looks better than a year ago. He works, in short periods, then lies down in between. He complains of literally collapsing if he works 15 minutes too long."

Christmas in her New York hotel, although "covered with flowers," was difficult for Lizzie and Martha. "We tried to forget that it was a hotel and that the chimney was small. La Farge sent me his book [*Reminiscences of the South Seas*] and Olney sent a box of roses. There were many gifts for Martha, and from Mexico came a chihuahua dog, smaller than this sheet of paper." The lonely child was enchanted with her new pet and carried it around in a basket. "Very Valois," her mother remarked. "Martha is sewing a blanket for it with the utmost gravity and delight. It is better than a doll."

Lizzie told Adams that she dined out alone and spent much of her time with Martha. "I am wonderfully well, so please say to yourself that New York was the best thing to happen after all." But soon the invitations began to pour in as her New York friends, including the Stanford Whites, discovered she was there. "Anything is better than staying in the hotel so I accept them all."

On New Year's Eve she wrote, "The eggs I am walking on have not smashed but the tension keeps me so absorbed I cannot concentrate on anything else. The only other side is society. In that narrow and limited field I hear no topic of interest even mentioned. It is a smiling, easy, non-malicious society so far—véry hospitable, pleasant and with an intense interest in Mrs. Wharton's furniture. All of New York is reading her book. [Edith Wharton's *Decoration of Houses* had appeared on 3 December 1897.] I lunch and dine, go to plays—yet after a night's sleep it is all completely effaced." Ten days later she boasted, "As I am now perfectly well I don't fear anything much, even winter at Donegal."

When Adams wrote to her of his disenchantment with the year 1897 which had just passed, she agreed. "It seemed natural that I should feel it too. You are right. Where *are* we now? I'm sure I don't know."

11

Surrenden Dering

In February 1898 Henry Adams went off to Egypt with John and Clara Hay, and Lizzie wrote to him yearningly from Washington, "Egypt lies in my imagination as dark and remote as the time of Moses. I am homesick for you and Paris and the happy solitude and busy idleness." The pointlessness of her social round struck her most forcibly whenever he was away. She described for him her frequent dining out "with howling swells and crowned heads as thick as blackberries and so many jewels—that to have none gives cachet. Rachel and I fritter away our days exercising and making calls and I see no one to really talk to and *all is vanity.*"

Her husband's disposition had not improved since his retirement from the Senate, and Lizzie reported that "Don looks white and old." As in many a loveless marriage, their precarious relationship was at its worst when they were alone together, and in a curious way Adams served to restore a certain balance. The taciturn senator enjoyed Adams's company and trusted his judgment as he trusted few others'. And Lizzie was always more at ease in the reassuring presence of her tame cat.

The society in which the Camerons moved, noting their frequent separations and their mutual indifference, was rife with rumors of a pending breakup. On a visit to New York that winter, Lizzie had an unpleasant encounter with the press. Although Senator Cameron kept to an iron-clad rule of "no interviews," one Manhattan reporter, because of a servant's error, managed to get upstairs in the hotel where the Camerons were staying. "He was looking for Donald," Lizzie wrote, "and was investigating a telegram from Washington saying that I was seeking a legal separation from 'my owner.'" Seeing the senator's wife instead of Cameron himself, the reporter "was overcome with contrition and bowed himself out. But that is what I can expect, I suppose."

Although she attempted to shrug off these recurring embarrassing incidents, nevertheless the situation was distressing to La Dona. However strongly she may have wished to be free of her husband, she had, according to the laws of that time, no legal grounds for divorce, and a legal separation would have required a consent from Don which he was clearly unwilling to give. Her total dependence on him for support, her reliance on his whims whenever he wished to travel, her ignorance of his movements during his frequent long absences—all of these irritations increased her restlessness, causing her to engage in a frenzy of activity that she alternately despised and enjoyed. "I am sitting here," she wrote to Adams, "dressed in turquoise velvet with all the jewels I possess, waiting to dine with the howling swells and after to a concert with Melba . . ."

She was invited to dine with Edith Wharton, whom she found "the most interesting woman I see. Very intelligent and pretty to look at too." The two women took an immediate fancy to each other which later grew into a lasting friendship. The novelist shared with La Dona an iron will and an aristocratic reverence for breeding. And of course Edith Wharton was pleased with Lizzie's educated interest in her works.

The Italian portrait painter Giovanni Boldini was having a vogue in the United States, and Lizzie attended a showing of his portrait of their friend Stanford White. With mixed feelings, she wrote to Adams, "Sargent never was so cruel! It is a fighting Irishman, brutal but so awfully like . . ." Adams himself referred to the painter as "that skunk Boldini . . ."

Lizzie, whose taste in art had been developed under the influence of Adams and La Farge, was serenely confident in the presence of artists. She remarked to Adams, "It amuses me to see how much more easily I can talk their talk than that of the rich and vulgar. I seem to drop into dialect." The passion of the *nouveaux riches* to have their portraits painted in New York had led some enterprising if mediocre artists, both American and European, to devise a marketing approach to their work. As Lizzie noted, "Four French painters are here painting them as they are. I never saw such pictures—the dealers bring them out under a guarantee. It is too funny." The guarantee offered to the sitters was an agreement that if they did not like their portraits, or felt they were not a good likeness, their money (prepaid) would be returned.

Lizzie's plans, as usual, depended upon Don, and he had not spoken. She wanted to take Martha away, but she did not know where to go, now that their Lafayette Square home was occupied by tenants until 1901. She considered Adams's "friendly house" across the Square. "But what would Mrs. Grundy say?" Then Don indicated that he might accompany her and Martha to Europe in the summer, and she was thoroughly dismayed. "He is growing very deaf," she told Adams, "is fairly amiable, very devoted to Martha and occupies himself with the typewriter all the time." Senator Cameron had a financial investment in a new typewriter, on which he hoped, using his Midas touch, to turn a substantial profit.

"Oh how I want to see you *just now*," she added. "The summer is long in coming and what will it bring?" She soon found the answer. The uneasy truce with her husband could not last. "He has gone off to Donegal for a week with his sulks," she reported. Before his return, Lizzie planned to visit Boston, "so we'll have a fortnight to simmer down. The burden falls on Martha who is terribly distressed. I am more convinced that my return was a mistake—but here I am."

Surrenden Dering

When Adams sent her a copy of *Cyrano de Bergerac*, the new dramatic sensation by Edmond Rostand, she was delighted: "It came this morning. I have read the first act—it reads very well, and must suit Coquelin, down to the ground. A sort of d'Artagnan character, only more so, with the swagger of Baron Munchausen. All my friends were impressed, for I possess the only copy of *Cyrano* in New York. My reputation for intellectuality is well established."

Arriving in Boston, where she liked to recall her days at finishing school, Lizzie told Adams of the Sunday dinner party at Mrs. Jack Gardner's to which she arrived late "because the 'Blue Laws' don't allow traffic during church hours. Mrs. Jack was lightly arrayed in a striped dress of yellow brocade and an ermine cape. One look at her face—heavy-eyed with swollen lids—and I saw the reason for the cape. She was ill with influenza." Afterward, as she was driven to her hotel, Lizzie heard the snow "creaking beneath the carriage wheels," and she shivered. "When I found myself in Louisburg Square," she wrote to Adams, "I felt sixteen but such a worn sixteen. Was it really this cold when I was sixteen?"

Lizzie confided to Adams a new anxiety—it was Martha's size. The 12-year-old girl was tall and big-boned like her father and was, in Lizzie's word, "enormous. Something of the lack of shape Alice Hay used to have. It is very distressing to me." She could not miss, either, the contrast with Alice Roosevelt, a playmate of Martha's who, at 14, was pretty, flirtatious, and slender. "She [Martha] is very sensitive about it and wants me to ask the doctor if there is anything wrong with her that makes her grow so fast. It is a great pity." To prove to Adams that her life was not entirely frivolous, Lizzie added, "You have made me a purist. At a ladies' lecture on architecture, the speaker mentioned the Gothic. I tried to explain that it was not just ornament but fundamental construction. But they refused to listen."

Now recovered from her recent breakdown, Lizzie set off with Martha for Europe. Her passport was signed 22 March 1898 by her Uncle John, the secretary of state, and it read, "Mrs. Cameron, accompanied by minor child, maidservant and governess. Height: five feet eight inches; forehead—high; hair—brown; eyes—blue-grey; nose—straight; chin—round; complexion— light; face—oval."

Gleefully, John Hay announced that she was "off to conquer England." While not aspiring to victory on such a scale, Lizzie was embarking on one of the most strenuous summers of her life. Her husband and Henry Adams had set up "a sort of syndicate" for renting Surrenden Dering, a huge country house in Kent. Here Hay, the U.S. ambassador to Great Britain, would establish his "summer embassy." With Lizzie as hostess, Adams, Cameron, and Hay would entertain "swarms of guests" from America. It was a summer of patriotic fervor among the Americans. The United States had just declared war on Spain on 26 April. Lizzie's brother-in-law General Nelson Miles was commander in chief of the U.S. forces, and Hay was about to be named secretary of state. Secretaries from the U.S. Embassy in London scurried back and forth with the latest dispatches on the Spanish-American conflict, which

Hay would later call "a splendid little war." For Adams, Surrenden Dering offered a box seat at this newest act in the drama of history as the United States grew overnight into a world power.

The name of the house puzzled everyone. "Dering" was the family name, but "Surrenden" was never satisfactorily explained. According to Abigail Adams (later Homans), the teen-age daughter of the late John Quincy Adams II whom Uncle Henry had brought here to spend the summer, "The younger secretaries at the embassies in London used to think it funny at times, as we were still at war with Spain, to forward mail to 'Surrender Daring,' Pluckless, Kent—but it only confused the literal-minded postmistress at Pluckley, so that after she made several complaints, the joke had to be frowned upon."

Two hours' drive from London, Surrenden Dering, which Henry Adams described as "about the size of Versailles," was an Elizabethan manor house that stood foursquare on its grassy terrace overlooking the Weald of Kent. It had numerous large, stately rooms, a courtyard, stables, gardens, and a park filled with deer. Afternoon tea was held every day on one of the lower terraces. The number of bathrooms was not equal to the number of bedrooms, so the guests often had to make do with Sitz baths and large jars of hot water. Over this huge "American summer hotel on the Paris highroad," La Dona presided with grace and efficiency.

Several keen observers were watching her with admiration. First, of course, was Henry Adams, who from his serene eminence as co-host, marveled at her competence. "One's energies are exhausted in housekeeping," he noted. "I have never seen such a steady stream of guests or such constant efforts of entertainment. On Sunday we were twenty at table. Americans take all our time and all our rooms, coming in whole families."

Another observer was the young, sharp-eyed Abigail Adams, who missed no detail of the "complicated caravanserai." In her book *Education by Uncles*, she writes that the house was comparatively empty when she arrived. Besides her uncle there were Don, Lizzie, and Martha Cameron, Lizzie's nieces Rosina and Annie Hoyt, John and Clara Hay, and their sons Del and Clarence. Among the regular visitors were Ralph Palmer, "a queer, charming, cadaverous old fellow, a mine of information," who was a friend of Adams's since Civil War days; Mrs. Oswald Charlton, the former Mary Campbell of Quincy, who had married a British diplomat; James Bryce, the author of *The American Commonwealth*; the beautiful Mary Leiter Curzon, with her little girl; and the two sons of the Michael Herberts. So "there was quite a nursery of children to fill the big house."

Abigail Adams was impressed by the tall, dour Senator Cameron, "that energetic, red-blooded American," who, "scorning tea and perhaps all things English, had managed to produce from somewhere a pair of long-tailed trotting horses and a buggy with which he amused himself by tearing about the staid Kentish countryside and frightening the ponderous native work horses." Noticing Abigail's eagerness, Don often invited her to ride with him at top speed, but since "he often got lost and was impatient of asking questions, these expeditions were frequently quite exciting." The senator, who was an incorrigible chauvinist, especially when a war was going on, insisted on having sent over from America, at enormous expense, his favorite fruits and vegetables, including corn and watermelon, neither of which the cook had ever seen before. "She struggled fairly successfully with the corn, although she deplored the manner in which it was 'gnawed' at the table, but the watermelons defeated her, for she boiled them and served them as a horrible gelatinous pulp. Even the Senator, who was really a good sport at heart, had to laugh, and the disgruntled cook redeemed herself by proving to be quite a competent hand at sugared sweet potatoes."

Abigail Adams perceived that the solitary Cameron was not a conversationalist and buried himself in American newspapers. "He wasn't interested in chitchat and eschewed politics as a conversational gambit. As for Uncle Henry's whimsical philosophical musings, he mistrusted them profoundly. He was not often open or companionable, but sometimes an unexpected cordiality would break down the crust of shyness in which his queer self-distrust wrapped him and he would burst out into real volubility and even affection. He was in many ways a very intriguing character."

She described Martha as "a pretty little girl about eleven years old with a straight nose, blue eyes and the fattest of yellow pigtails." Martha was often seen with Henry Adams, who had hired two chubby brown ponies and, with Martha on a leading rein, rode almost every day. But above all, it was Lizzie who caught Abigail's imagination and instilled in her a lifelong admiration. For, in watching Lizzie Cameron, she sensed that she was observing a thoroughbred in action.

> Mrs. Don Cameron was on the whole the most socially competent woman that I have ever met. With perfect self-confidence she could tackle any situation and appear to enjoy it. She was not perhaps strictly beautiful, but she was such a mass of style and had such complete self-assurance that she always gave the appearance of beauty and she gave everyone a good time when she set out to please. She was not only the hostess for this big and compelling caravanserai, but she ran it as well, and I doubt if many details escaped her eagle eye. . . . She checked on all the expenditures and knew minutely what was going on, for there was a good deal of the Yankee in her.
>
> She never discussed the below-stairs problems except with Mrs. Charlton . . . When those two got together talking over the intricacies of the English domestic system, it was the greatest fun in the world and made the tedious business of running a great establishment seem like some huge joke. Mrs. Cameron, while looking over the bills, would ask Mrs. Charlton, "What percentage of graft is considered legitimate in a house of this size, for I refuse to be bothered with it unless it is all out of scale?"—and then Mrs. Charlton would start in on the ridiculous side of some of the hard and fast unwritten domestic usages which had to be considered, and we would all end up perfectly satisfied that Surrenden was worth the rake-off no matter what the scale. It gave you a pleasant cozy feeling that you were all having a good time together.

There was also a third observer of the Surrenden Dering menage—one of the most acute critics of social manners in the late 19th century—the novelist Henry James. His new home, Lamb House in Rye, was only a few miles distant, and he was warmly welcomed by Adams and Mrs. Cameron on the one or two occasions when he was able to visit the manor house. Henry James wrote to a friend, "I have had Henry Adams spending the summer not very far off—in the wonderful old country house of Surrenden Dering, which he has been occupying in the delightful way made possible by the possession of Shekels, in conjunction with the Don Camerons."

With his novelist's gaze, James studied the complicated interplay among the guests and particularly between Henry Adams, his lifelong friend, and Elizabeth Cameron, whom he had met long ago in Clover Adams's drawing room. It was the kind of relationship that he delighted to write about, and the situation appealed to him enormously. In his notebooks, he declared that he was "somehow haunted with the *American* family as represented to me by Mrs. Cameron." Clearly the idea had captured his imagination, and he might well have written of Henry Adams and Lizzie Cameron as he had once written of the Washington Bonnycastles, whom everyone had recognized as Henry and Clover Adams, in his story "Pandora's Box." But finally he set the idea aside reluctantly, feeling that it demanded "a large comprehensive picture."

However, as a stern social critic, James could not resist passing judgment on Lizzie. Perhaps out of an old loyalty to Clover or out of an antipathy to strong-willed women, he described her as "hard, considering her prettiness, grace and cleverness." Scrutinizing the behavior of Henry Adams in this comedy of manners, he wrote that he "envied him as much as was permitted by my feeling that the affair was only what I should *once* have found maddeningly romantic."

He continued to ruminate on the fascinating duo, and three years later, in a letter to Henrietta Reubell, he gave it as his considered opinion that "Mrs. Cameron sucked the lifeblood of poor Henry Adams and made him more snappish than nature intended." Yet despite this harsh assessment of Mrs. Cameron, Henry James would change his mind a dozen years later and become both her advisor and her admiring host.

Meanwhile, on 13 August 1898, John Hay received from President McKinley the offer of the post of secretary of state, two days before the signing of the armistice between America and a defeated Spain. Hay could not make up his mind at once to accept, so he wrote two contrasting replies, before deciding which to send. He enjoyed too well the comfortable, easy life at Surrenden Dering, and he wrote of his hosts, "Don is the finest type of old Tory baronet you ever saw. His wife makes a lovely chatelaine. Oom Hendrik [Uncle Henry] has assumed the congenial function of cellarer and chaplain."

Finally, Hay reluctantly accepted the cabinet post, and at once Adams's friends began to insist that Adams should step into the vacant post of ambassador to Great Britain which his father had once held (then with the title of U.S. Minister). Although Adams showed a calculated indifference toward such an appointment, he wrote to Milnes Gaskell, "All my life I have lived in the closest possible personal relations with men in high office. Hay is the first one of them who has ever expressed a wish to have me for an associate in his responsibilities. Evidently something is wrong with Hay—or with me." Such deliberate coyness was characteristic of Adams, who, like his grandfather and great grandfather, was too proud to push his own candidacy.

But Elizabeth Cameron suffered from no such inhibitions. She wrote to her former gallant, John Hay, in Washington in October, "Tell me secrets. Tell me if 'Dor' is to be Ambassador." Again in November, she wrote to Hay, "You know that 'Dor' is our candidate."

On 5 November 1898, Adams sailed for home and wrote, "The Camerons will pass the winter in Paris. I left Mrs. Cameron established there at 50 Avenue du Bois. Mr. Cameron starts his tour of Europe for the sale of his typewriter—a rather dull amusement for her but he takes it seriously and expects it to make money." On arriving in Washington, Adams learned that the ambassadorship had gone to a Republican lawyer, Joseph H. Choate. Clearly the appointment had been taken out of the hands of his old friend, for as Adams noted, "Hay's office was pawned in advance, both in patronage and politics. He was not even allowed to appoint an Assistant Secretary nor to name even the instruments he had at hand—meaning Rockhill and me."

To Lizzie Cameron he wrote professing his relief at not receiving the appointment. "You will appreciate how glad I am of it. To refuse him [Hay] my help would be most disagreeable to me but to accept office would be misery. What I like—for I am, as you have often truly said, a mass of affectation and vanity, is to have people make me pretty speeches, which they do, and to grin behind their backs, as they do behind mine."

Henry Adams's chance for political office had now passed. Justice Oliver Wendell Holmes, who would become an intimate friend of Adams's, remarked to the writer Owen Wister, "If the country had put him on a pedestal, I think Henry Adams could have rendered distinguished public service." "What was the matter with Henry Adams?" Wister asked. To which Holmes replied, "He wanted it handed to him on a silver platter."

So the fateful summer was over, the company dispersed. Adams resumed his role of tame cat and wrote, "It has been a God-send for me to creep into other people's kitchens—this summer, the Camerons—and I try to make myself very, very small so as to hide in the corner and not give trouble or have to be sent to bed for bad manners."

12

The Lady And The Poet

In the last year but one of the dying century, Elizabeth Cameron, looking radiantly younger than her 42 years, first met the poet Trumbell Stickney who was 26. It was a fateful encounter for them both, and it would change forever her relationship with Henry Adams.

Paris, during the summer of 1899, was sadly disheveled. While the city was preparing for the forthcoming international exposition that was scheduled to open the following April, it resembled an aging beauty who has put herself in the hands of her masseur, her coiffeur, and her corsetiere in an indomitable attempt to prepare herself for the ball.

Henry Adams, trim in his summer white and his neat Van Dyke beard, was installed in Mrs. Cameron's fifth-floor drawing room at 50 avenue du Bois de Boulogne (now avenue Foch). He had just returned from a tour of Italy with the Henry Cabot Lodges, and he darted a disapproving glance at the city's disarray. "Paris," he wrote, "is as odious as possible. The principal streets are torn up and the river is limed with ruin and the open places are closed and covered with iron skeletons painted red. All is dirt, dust, noise and nudity. A few more weeks or months will see everything cleared away for the Fair. The French have their own feminine way of doing things but sometimes they get it done and I think they mean to sweep everything troublesome out of sight for next year. Out of such a chaos, something worth seeing ought to come."

This chaos Elizabeth Cameron was leaving to Adams. As she entered the gold and white drawing room—exquisitely tailored for travel, with an enormous feathered hat perched on top of her dark hair—she was for him the embodiment of feminine loveliness. He watched her closely, his air of playful gallantry not quite concealing his silent yearning. Even while he was addressing her with elaborate decorum as "my dear *proprietaire*," she remained his constant preoccupation—she was his *petite amie* who was still unattainable. For years, the skeptic Adams, who had only to enter a room to command the conversation, had enjoyed startling his listeners with the assertion that "the woman is superior to the man"—an opinion not widespread at the end of the 19th century. But Adams was serious. He had always idealized women, in his writings and his life, and to him Mrs. Cameron represented the feminine superiority that had intrigued him all his life.

With Lizzie the story was different. Born with an instinctive knowledge of the art of pleasing men, she had no illusions regarding male superiority. But she accepted their adoration and allowed them to play the role of her protectors, although their need of protection may have been greater than hers, for she was a natural survivor. This role of protector Adams had willingly assumed in the beginning. But after the suicide of his wife Clover, his grief and his longing had met her need, and they had been drawn together in a growing intimacy. In Adams she found an unfailing gallant, who worshipped her with words, flattered her with exquisite gifts—a man whose consummate tact made him a perfect intermediary between Lizzie and her difficult husband. With Adams's watchful presence, his readiness to do her bidding, his worldliness which was her shield, and his tenderness which was her warmth, life for La Dona would have been bleak indeed. Henry Adams offered her all that she had never received from her husband. She basked in his adoration, and that should have been enough. But clearly she was seeking something more.

Toward Lizzie's daughter Martha, Adams showed an abject devotion that he dared not display toward her mother. The tall, solemn, wide-eyed girl was 13 now, and she still wore the pigtails of childhood. Her constant traveling about in her mother's wake, in addition to her natural diffidence, allowed her to make few friends of her own age. She was nearly always in the presence of her elders, and it was only in Dordy, who seemed ageless to her, that she could confide. They used to play a game in which Dordy acted the part of Martha's little boy, and the young girl, who was already beginning to overtop Henry Adams, would scold and pet and mother him. But with other grown-ups, including her mother, Martha was taciturn, with a scowling, inscrutable, Cameron air which Adams perceived was really a defensive cover for her adolescent uncertainty. Standing awkwardly at the outer edge of Lizzie's circle of admirers, Martha would always feel overshadowed by her enchanting mother. The girl's quiet intensity and adolescent gawkiness brought a tender smile to the face of Henry Adams as he drew her to him for a farewell embrace. Lizzie was carrying her off to one or two fashionable European resorts in an effort to escape the torpor of Paris in the summer.

Adams would remain here, as usual, for the summer and fall. He was burrowing into the history of the Middle Ages in preparation for writing *Mont-Saint-Michel and Chartres*, then alternately returning to the 20th century to savor the teeming life of Paris in the fashionable restaurants and theaters that were still open during the city's renovation. Upon his hostess's return in November, in time for the "Little Season," Adams would gallantly evict himself to find other accommodations farther along the avenue du Bois or on the Champs-Élysées. He always delayed his return to Washington until January, because he could not face life in Lafayette Square during the month of December, the anniversary of Clover's death.

Each year, Henry Adams and Elizabeth Cameron followed this elaborate minuet of approach and withdrawal. Adams spent the months from

January to May in Washington. On his return to Paris in late spring, Lizzie departed on her travels. When she returned in November, he withdrew to temporary quarters until January. The ritual was designed by Adams to preserve the facade of respectability that had to be maintained in those last years of Victoria's reign, in this land of the Third Republic. What went on behind the facade was known only to the players in these courtly games of love. However impassioned, the players must always be discreet. To emphasize their respectability, Adams, at 62, addressed his hostess in public as Mrs. Cameron or "my dear *proprietaire*." Yet privately he deplored the charade, complaining to her, "I am so damn respectable, the more I struggle for a reputation for vice, the more I am conspicuous as a pattern of sexagenarian respectability. It's disgusting."

But not all of Lizzie's friends were so formal. Clarence King, the irrepressible geologist for whom she felt suspicion and small liking, referred to her as La Dona, using the Italian word for "lady" in a play on her husband's Christian name. The Scottish diplomat Ronald Ferguson called her Mrs. Decameron, in another bit of name-play that titillated her hearers. But most of her circle called her Lizzie—especially Bernhard Berenson, who had his own view of Adams's courtly ritual. (Berenson dropped the "h" from his first name during World War I.) In a society where divorce was still frowned upon, Berenson recognized the variety of discreet arrangements that flourished among the wealthy Americans in Paris. Berenson—or B.B., as his friends called him—was himself an American expatriate who, having begun his career under the patronage of Mrs. Jack Gardner, had become an expert on the art of the Italian Renaissance. A member of Adams's exclusive circle, Berenson shared with him an intellectual as well as an emotional kinship. (His own liaison with Mary Smith Costelloe culminated in marriage at the end of 1900.) Intuitively he sensed the nuances of the Adams-Cameron relationship, recognizing that Lizzie, who dazzled every man she encountered, had hopelessly captivated Adams. Berenson concluded, "Lizzie Cameron was the material, if not the spiritual center of Adams's existence for the last 30 years of his life." Just as clearly, Berenson perceived Adams's constitutional uneasiness about his Jewish origin. This B.B. accepted with a shrug, observing, "We had much in common but he could not forget that he was an Adams and he was always more embarrassed than I was that I happened to be a Jew." Adams's pose as a hater of Jews was part of the prevailing anti-Semitism that had infected to some degree most of the American expatriate society in which he and Lizzie moved. It did not die easily. At first, Lizzie was on her guard with B.B.. But gradually she was won over by the urbanity of this small, keen-eyed genius who would grow, in age, to resemble her Dordy. Soon she had accepted him—indeed, she was turning to him, this most understanding of men, who was eight years younger than herself and who would become her only confidant besides Adams.

Meanwhile, B.B., as a connoisseur of art and of human relationships, watched with amused detachment as the little comedy of manners enfolded before his eyes.

In this summer of 1899, "hot as forty hells," the very air of Paris was sti-

The Lady and the Poet

fling. Oscar Wilde, released from a British prison, was living wretchedly here under the name of Sebastian Melmouth, dining on cheap food and absinthe in the more infamous Left Bank cafés. Defiantly he was forecasting his approaching death with the words, "It would really be more than England could stand if another century began and I were still alive." Wilde, who had blazed across two continents a decade before, was now reduced to accepting $250 for *The Ballad of Reading Gaol,* the despairing poem he had written in prison.

Adams, in his role of professional cynic, could not publicly admit enthusiasm. Yet his friends saw through his pose, as when Cecil Spring-Rice wrote, "I wonder where you are and if you will be unhappy enough to throughly enjoy yourself." But even Adams could not resist the enchantment of Paris. For in this momentous *fin de siècle,* the city glowed with a kind of phosphorescent decadence and burned with a fierce energy that had nurtured the giants in art and letters and science—Cézanne, Monet, Renoir, Rodin, Bernhardt, Coquelin, Rostand, Mallarmé, Zola, Bergson, the Curies. Now a new wave was cresting. Marcel Proust was beginning his study of this complex society which he would delineate in *À la recherche du temps perdu.* The young Pablo Picasso arrived in 1900. Alongside its artists, Paris boasted some of history's most famous courtesans—Liane de Pougy, Cléo de Mérode, and Caroline Otero. The city attracted hordes of Americans—expatriates of genius like Henry James and Edith Wharton, James McNeill Whistler and Mary Cassatt, John La Farge and Augustus Saint-Gaudens. It drew also pursuers of wealth and titles—the wives and daughters of American tycoons who sought the elegant worldliness of the salons where conversation still flourished and where a noble if impoverished husband might be captured for a determined debutante.

Despite the decadence, which Adams eyed with fascinated disapproval, despite the avaricious landlords, the uncivil Parisians, and the lazy servants of whom he complained, Adams wrote, "Paris is still the most ornamental sepulchre for the still living." And Henry Adams was triumphantly "still living." In this fateful summer, after four years of traveling through the French cathedral countryside, and delving into libraries and museums, he was beginning to write *Mont-Saint-Michel and Chartres,* the first of his pair of masterpieces. Playfully he warned Lizzie, "I am a sexagenarian Hamlet with architectural fancies." The previous week he had dragged Henry Cabot Lodge about the countryside for two days. Doggedly the historian and the senator peered into every stone cranny of the 12th-century churches. "Your rooms," he told his absent hostess, "are becoming a school of Romanesque architecture."

As a historian with the eye of an artist, Adams was responding to the cult of the Middle Ages that had already inspired works by French, British, and even American writers—Renan, the apostate who was in love with cathedrals, John Ruskin, Alfred Tennyson, Walter Scott, Dante Gabriel Rossetti— even the irreverent Mark Twain. The sculptor Auguste Rodin was also writing a lyrical study of French cathedrals. But none of these books would equal the book that Adams was beginning.

All during that summer, amid the "heat the dirt, the noise and nudity,"Adams worked on his manuscript. Avoiding company for the most part, he pored over hundreds of photographs of 12th-century churches, which he spread about on the period chairs and Aubusson carpets of Lizzie's apartment. Amid his labors, two American visitors came to sprawl on the floor, studying the clutter of photographs with informed curiosity.

The first was an old friend—Augustus Saint-Gaudens, the gaunt, bearded sculptor who was drudging away in a studio on Montparnasse. In his artist's smock, the silent Gus was surrounded by a noisy group of fellow artists, good-naturedly offering him contradictory suggestions. The work on which Saint-Gaudens was putting his interminable last touches was the equestrian statue of General William Tecumseh Sherman, which was to have the place of honor at the forthcoming World's Fair. Begun in 1892, this heroic sculpture, cast in bronze and gilded with three layers of solid gold leaf, stands today near the 59th Street and Fifth Avenue entrance to Central Park in New York City. Adams undoubtedly knew the identity of the model for the stone Angel of Victory who precedes the mounted general, striding along, her elegant head held high, her arms outstretched, with one hand holding the palm of victory. According to family legend and studio gossip, it was Elizabeth Sherman Cameron, the favorite niece of "Uncle Cump" Sherman. Gossip also related that Gus Saint-Gaudens, a notorious woman chaser, had been in love with his model.

One hot July afternoon, Adams visited Saint-Gaudens in his studio to find him suffering from "just old melancholia—the oppression of life and the fear of death. He also complained of insomnia." Recognizing in the artist his own symptoms, Adams assumed for a time the role of "Porcupinus Angelicus"—the angel with prickly quills which Saint-Gaudens had once playfully designed to show the dual nature of his friend. To dispel the sculptor's "infantile terrors," Adams dragged him down the hill for a stroll in the Bois, then took him to dine on the Champs-Élysées. The irony of the situation appealed to Adams, who later told Lizzie, "That I, of all people, should act as a tonic!"

His second visitor, Adams informed Lizzie, was a new friend, "Joe Stickney who comes down every week from the stars." Twenty-six-year-old Joseph Trumbull Stickney was the son of an expatriate New England family that for years had moved restlessly about Europe like figures in a novel by Henry James. Joe, or Trumbull as his mother called him, was six feet four, handsome, and "with a figure supple and graceful as a Greek runner's." He had deep gray eyes set in a sad, bewildered face. Although women swooned over him, he regarded most of them disdainfully as "stuffed corsets." He was a poet of promise, and he played the violin. Stickney had graduated magna cum laude from Harvard and was studying at the Sorbonne for his *doctorat ès lettres*, the first American student to receive one. Living in an apartment on the rue d'Assas near the Luxembourg Gardens, Stickney was drawn into Adams's orbit by their mutual friend Bay Lodge, the son of Senator Henry Cabot Lodge.

Frequently that summer the three Harvard exiles, Adams, Stickney, and Lodge, strolled the torn-up boulevards. They pondered the ancient questions which the two young men were just discovering and which their mentor had for years delighted to play with. They made an arresting trio — the two tall youths flanking the middle-aged scholar in his silk hat, who affected a slight strut to compensate for his lack of height. Bay Lodge — his nickname derived from the childhood Bay-Bee — was bronzed from the Italian sun and ruggedly built. He affected a large black sombrero and wore his grandfather's gold watch chain hung about his neck. Stickney, who towered almost a foot over Adams, strode along with an athlete's grace, oblivious of the sidelong glances of women.

Gravely, but with a wicked glint in his eye, Adams guided their discussions with the same skill he had used in his classes in medieval history at Harvard. The iconoclast was stimulated by the young men's pessimism which reflected the teachings of the Sorbonne sociologist Emile Durkheim. He listened to their pronouncements, read their verses, and smiled a little at their disillusion. During one session, the three scholars formed their own society — a gossamer invention which Adams called the Conservative Christian Anarchists and which allowed them to range freely across the realms of thought from their strangely triangulated base.

Although both young men were indignant that their times were out of joint, Adams noted that Stickney was more oppressed with melancholy. Years later, his classmate and fellow poet William Vaughn Moody would write of Stickney, "Throughout his life, despite his fortunate circumstances and real happiness, there weighed on Joe a nameless oppression, a sense of the futility of wordly outcome, a shadow of pain and bitterness on all the fair face of things." This enduring melancholy of Stickney's ran much deeper than the fashionable *fin-de-siècle* malaise.

After visiting Stickney's family, Bay Lodge thought he knew the reason. They exuded an atmosphere of "utter gloom and inanition, utter unenthusiasm and lifelessness. The whole family are quite forlorn and I don't see how Joe stands it." Perhaps this gloom originated with Mrs. Stickney, Joe's mother. The dominating, middle-aged widow of Austin Stickney, a classics professor at Trinity College in Hartford, she was conscious of being descended from the colonial governor of Connecticut Jonathan Trumbull. After meeting her, Lizzie Cameron confided to Henry Adams, "Mrs. Stickney is New England transplanted to Europe. She is a generalissimo — totally unlike her children in physique and mind. If it were not for the family she produced, she would be distinctly ordinary." Of Stickney's older sister Lucy, who was stalking a husband, Lizzie reported, "Lucy is her mother's own daughter — selfish, sordid and a snob. She is of that unhappy analytical temperament which drives a man wild."

But despite the revulsion that both Lizzie and Bay Lodge felt for Mrs. Stickney and Lucy, this was the family that had produced Joe and to which he was still bound by filial duty. Although Joe Stickney and Bay Lodge had been friends since Harvard and enjoyed together the life of the Latin Quarter, they differed widely in temperament and gifts. The extroverted Lodge loved to indulge in self-dramatization. His family and friends considered him a prodigy, and when his first book of poems *The Wave* was published (with some influence exerted by Theodore Roosevelt), they seriously compared it with Shakespeare. Rebellious and talented, Lodge was described by a family friend, Mrs. Winthrop Chanler, herself a writer, as "a rather unkempt and uncouth boy" who had suddenly emerged into "an immensely attractive and accomplished youth who loved to growl against the comfortable world of the well-to-do. He ranted that government, religion and family life were all shackles—I found his opinions not very original, merely symptoms of intellectual adolescence. Of course he would soon have to walk the tightrope between youthful rebellion and family responsibility." Lodge, with the backing of his adoring family, could afford to indulge his passion for poetry. Stickney, on the other hand, could not. "He had to earn his bread," as Lodge noted.

Stickney was more self-confident in experience than Lodge. His years of European wandering had induced in him a feeling of rootlessness that vanished when he reached Paris. Here the exile was at home, reveling in the Greek, Latin, and French studies of the university. He soon attracted the notice of the Orientalist scholar Sylvain Lévi, and together they translated the *Bhagavad-Gita* from Sanskrit. Rejecting Christianity, Joe was sharply disapproving when his sister Lucy embraced Catholicism. Shane Leslie later wrote of him, "He was a pure pagan and wished to turn me against the Catholic Church which fascinated my Sundays."

A note of melancholy pervades many of Stickney's lyrics:

> It's growing evening in my soul,
> It darkens in.
> At the gray window now and then
> I hear them toll,
> The hour-and-day-long chimes of St. Etienne.

Lodge was melodramatic even in his ambition. "If I haven't it in me to be a poet, what a tragic farce my life will be!" he exclaimed. Stickney was quieter, with a clearer vision, a stronger lyricism. In his paganism, he was like a Norse faun whose ears had caught the sound of a distant music which his poet's intuition told him would be brief. Sadly he wrote of "a wretched little lad—he has the fright of time."

As the hot summer melted into the haze of autumn, Adams felt the old urge to depart. But he wrote wistfully, "I don't want to go home. Washington is repulsive." He was loath to leave the two young poets, his far-from-finished manuscript—and most of all Lizzie. But with a faint premonition of disaster, he added, "Still I suppose it is best to go."

Yet he lingered, "basking in the warmth of the 12th century." Stickney consulted with him on the verse drama *Prometheus* that he was writing—about the legendary Greek hero who stole fire from heaven and brought down destruction upon himself. Adams privately noted the intellectual refinement of the poem, which would later appear in the *Harvard Monthly*.

Later that month, Lizzie Cameron returned, beguiling Adams from his melancholy. Dordy caught Martha in a hearty welcoming embrace, then gathered up his photographs, his folios, and his unfinished manuscript and withdrew to the nearby Élysée Palace Hotel.

Joe Stickney, gazing down into the Luxembourg Gardens from his rooms, idly noted to his friend Moody, "I've got to go and call on Mrs. Cameron who has been put on my track by Bay."

Lizzie was ripe for this meeting with the young poet. Despite the surface excitement of the past season, she was bored. Neither the court ball in Brussels, where she was presented to King Leopold, nor the dinners with the Jack Astors and the George Vanderbilts, nor a meeting with Edith Wharton, whom she instantly recognized as "the most interesting woman I see," could relieve her of the prevailing ennui. It was a disease she may have caught from Henry Adams, who was always complaining of "this constant weariness of self-self-self" even while he managed to enjoy himself hugely.

The uncertainty of her husband's plans was another irritant. For news of him she had to turn to Adams, who was one of Senator Cameron's few correspondents. This peculiar triangle never ceased to fascinate their friends. Although Lizzie's affection for her husband, if it had ever existed, was dead, her dependence on him for the money to maintain herself and Martha remained. She was a model of a devoted mother — Adams jestingly called her "mama pelican" for the female bird which denudes her own breast to supply feathers to warm her offspring. But this stern maternal devotion sometimes weighed heavily on Lizzie, as when she had to refuse the Lodges' invitation to accompany them to Italy, a trip which Adams had taken with them instead. Plaintively, she had written to him, "How can I go with the Lodges to Italy? What about Martha? It would be sensible to leave her in Paris but that would make her unhappy. She is such a spoiled thing."

Even the literary offerings of her distinguished admirers failed to amuse Lizzie. Their middle-aged outpourings lacked the dewy quality of youth. Adams's closest friend, John Hay, the secretary of state in McKinley's cabinet, who still considered himself a literary man, wrote to her:

> You like novelties. This is novel. Did you ever get a letter written in a Cabinet meeting? I have said all I had to say. Day and Root are good for the next hour and so I will talk with you. Do you remember when you dined with me, talking of Samoa so long ago? Little did either of us dream that I should have to negotiate the partition of Samoa.... There is something unreal, something *tant soi peu divine* about all my knowledge of you. That you should be the most beautiful and fascinating woman of your generation, the most attractive in wit and grace and charm and yet be so good to me is a thing I never realize and find it hard to believe when I am away from you. Are you going to come home and let Dobbitt [Henry Adams] take care of me this winter?

Hay's hyperbole was gratifying to Lizzie, but not to be taken seriously. He was, after all, happily married to the stately Cleveland heiress Clara Stone who for years governed their household, disciplined their children, and protected him from small annoyances. And Hay was the same age as Adams.

It was youth that Lizzie yearned for, in the bloom of her seductive power.

Although she looked a decade younger that her 42 years, the fact that she had a tall young daughter growing into womanhood made it impossible for her to deny for long the passing years. Age swiftly overtook women of that era — even the fortunate ones like Lizzie, who were sheltered from the rigors of poverty and constant childbearing. All the distinguished men who paid court to her with ritual gallantry meant less to her now than did Stickney, this new Prometheus who had not yet succumbed to the "fright of time."

Henry Adams, lingering uneasily in Paris, saw her mood of yearning with dismay. In a melancholy outpouring to his equally gloomy brother Brooks, he wrote, "What one really wants is youth and what one really loses is years. Life becomes at last a mere piece of play-acting."

Although the actual meeting of Lizzie and Stickney was unrecorded, the events that followed it were not.

As the anniversary of Clover's death passed, Adams wrote, "I have lingered here dreading the voyage." Finally, on 5 January 1900, he sailed from Cherbourg after an anguished parting from Lizzie in which he realized anew that every parting is a taste of death.

Lizzie, who could never suppress for long her coquettish instincts, now behaved as if she were pushing him from her with one hand while beckoning him back with the other. After he left, she wrote to him immediately, "I don't want you to leave my Paris. The flavor goes out of the city when you do. Nothing is left but the shell." A few days later, she was lamenting that 10 days must still elapse before Adams's first letter could arrive. Clearly she was acutely bored and lonely. She sighed across the ocean, "You and America seem very far away. After you left I could not face people so I went over and wandered in the Luxembourg Gardens" (onto which, as she knew, Stickney's rooms looked). Seated on an iron bench in the snow, hugging her fur muff close to her face in the January cold, whe peered up the hill to watch the great dome of the Pantheon appear and disappear through the shifting fog. As she wondered where Adams was at this moment, she trembled with an inner chill that matched the weather's bite. Languidly she rose and wandered back along the quai until she reached the Cathedral of Notre Dame. In the vast interior she sat disconsolately, listening to the organ and feeling "very lonely, very miserable, one-sided and lame without the best half of me."

But Lizzie was by nature buoyant. A few days later she was sufficiently restored to dine with "Our Duchess." This was one of the many ambitious American heiresses who had married a European title, to the amused contempt of Adams, who mocked, "What a power is a title! Everyone ends up by flocking around a Duchess and incensing her."

In the flattering candlelight of the Duchess's table, which was massed with flowers and loaded with sterling and crystal, Lizzie was seated next to Stickney. Her dark hair was piled high above her forehead, her rounded shoulders rose from a modest décolletage as she shimmered in her blue satin gown. But whether her stays were too tightly laced about her slender waist or whether the poet's presence was too heady for his dinner partner, Lizzie suddenly succumbed to one of her "attacks" at table. This was one of those imprecisely diagnosed, ephemeral seizures that afflicted ladies during the twilight of Victoria's reign.

Raising one graceful hand to her forehead, Lizzie sagged limply against Stickney's shoulder. With admirable presence of mind, the tall young man sprang up (after all he had a mother and two sisters to whom such seizures were not unknown). Gently he eased Lizzie to her feet and supported her to her carriage, calling out sharply to her footman, *"Au Bois! Tout de suite! Numéro cinquante!"*

As their carriage clattered through the wintry night, Lizzie, nestling against his shoulder, revived a little. When they arrived at 50 avenue du Bois de Boulogne, the concierge informed them implacably that the "occasional" lift was broken.

"So," Lizzie reported later to Henry Adams, "Joe had to drag me up five flights of stairs." Drooping and fluttering, the beautiful wounded bird was half carried, half hauled up the 120 stairs by Stickney's strong arms.

Before Henry Adams, who was back in Lafayette Square, could receive Lizzie's account (however modified) of her new adventure in Paris, the post had brought him a letter from the lady's husband. The gruff senator from Pennsylvania, wintering in St. Helena, wrote to Adams in order to exchange news of his wife and child with their "protector." "Your hostess," he began, "reached home when I was north. I am very much pleased with what you say about Martha. I don't think the accounts I get from her mother are fair. She expects too much from the child and does not do her justice." A solitary man who nevertheless hated solitude, Cameron invited Adams to pay him a visit. A few days later, he wrote cryptically, "I find myself growing selfish with the advancing years." At this news, Adams, who had heard Lizzie wail frequently about her husband's shortcomings, must have smiled wryly.

From his second-floor study that looked across the park to the White House, Adams could revel in his nearness to the "center of the web." Here he watched the intricate weaving of the strands of power as practiced by his friends Secretary of State John Hay, Senator Henry Cabot Lodge, and Vice President Theodore Roosevelt. Yet there was something lacking to his enjoyment. "If you were only here," he wrote to Lizzie, "the machine would be all right." He complained that he was "solitary beyond tears, a hermit in a crowd."

But Lizzie was not really listening. In her Paris drawing room, she was marveling at her new Prometheus, Joe Stickney, who had arrived unannounced, lighting up her world. Ingenuously she wrote to Adams, "I saw Mr. Stickney. He came over and dined with me and it was delightful. He half promised to come and pay me a visit. He interests me very much. I do not know if he would wear but I am willing to try." At this announcement, Adams must have heard a first ominous warning.

Lizzie continued, "We have planned some excursions together . . ." This Adams translated to mean afternoon visits to the Louvre or the Musée de Cluny, with mother and daughter escorted by the poet who was almost halfway in age between them. The excursions to museums were in part intended to edify Martha. But the gangling adolescent quickly complained of boredom as she trailed listlessly along behind the animated couple through the endless marble corridors. Unlike her mother, Martha was not able to lose herself in the contemplation of beauty, in marble or in the flesh. She felt instead the old sensation of exclusion as she watched her mother weaving a spell about Stickney.

Noting Martha's indifference to art and pleading "restlessness" (but perhaps intending to sharpen Stickney's interest by a brief absence from Paris), Lizzie set off with Martha, in mid-March, for a visit to Biarritz. The weather at the resort was wretched, as she declared to Adams. "The Ides of March again! I should think Caesar might have been glad to be stabbed if Rome were as cold and grey as Biarritz!"

Back in Paris when Adams's next letter reached her, Lizzie was startled to learn that he had preserved all her letters. Uneasily she replied, "I had no idea you kept them. Why not destroy them at once? Surely it is better. As for yours, I shall do the same thing. No publisher or compiler will ever get hold of them."

With an innocent air, she suggested that Adams should visit her husband. "Don has written cheerfully from the Island. I am always hoping you can go there. It would help things along a great deal, I think."

That Lizzie, who could not stand for long the company of her husband, should suggest that Adams seek him out in solitary St. Helena in the belief that it "would help things along" must have amused Adams. But he did not go.

A week later, Stickney went off to visit his family, and Lizzie, now without an escort, turned again to Adams, telling him, "Without you I am no good. I have no energy, no force, not even amiability which you used to think my strong point. I lean on you very hard and you supply all my momentum."

All this time, poor adolescent Martha found herself carted about Europe like an unwieldy piece of luggage. She was a quiet, intense girl, lacking her mother's gay poise and regarding strangers with her father's watchful gaze under level brows. Lizzie saw with dismay that Martha had almost no friends, and she lamented to Adams, "Poor Martha—she is so lonely. It is a little pathetic."

Lizzie bought Martha a French poodle, which they named Kiki. The lonely girl was delighted, and a few nights later, Lizzie, putting her head inside the door of Martha's bedroom, saw her asleep, clasping the poodle in her arms, with the black curly head resting on Martha's shoulder, one beady black eye regarding her alertly. "We've certainly got our $50 out of Kiki," Lizzie exclaimed to Adams.

The 14th of April 1900 marked the opening of the Paris Exposition, which Adams had earlier described as "an architectural Inferno of unfinished domes, Greek temples and minarets." To the French citizens this world's fair was a triumphal assertion of their national power. The prevailing friendship between France and Russia had led them to build an ornate new bridge across the Seine which was dedicated to the memory of the Russian Emperor Alexander III. At the same time, a smoldering enmity against the British Empire had caused Queen Victoria virtually to boycott the fair. On opening day, 118,000 visitors poured in through the arches of the Grand Monumental Entrance, which was nicknamed "The Money Box." Viewers swarmed over the 270 acres of the exposition, which was spread across both banks of the Seine. Dozens of gleaming white buildings stretched the length of the Champs de Mars, reaching from the Louvre to the Trocadéro. The crowds admired the marble elegance of two permanent new buildings—the Grand Palais, beneath whose great glass dome stood Saint-Gaudens's statue of General Sherman, and the Petit Palais, which was displaying the art of the past. As one journalist wrote, "Art is the only priesthood in France."

The sculptures of a leading member of this "priesthood" were on view in Le Pavillon Rodin, on the corner of place de l'Alma. Financed by a group of admiring French bankers, the building housed 171 works in marble, bronze, and plaster by Auguste Rodin. Striding about inside the gallery, the short, chunky peasant with close-cropped hair and luxuriant beard fixed his piercing gaze upon the visitors who came to gape, at one franc a head, at his monumental works—*Balzac, Le Baiser* (The Kiss), *Les Bourgeois de Calais* (The Burghers of Calais). For years, Rodin had been slaving in his studio, winning little recognition and much adverse criticism. Now, as a result of this expertly mounted display of his works, he was at last achieving the recognition that would lead him to be ranked as the most original sculptor since Michelangelo.

Eager to attend the exposition, Adams returned to Paris in May and settled into an apartment close enough to the Trocadéro for easy visiting of the fair. Unlike the elegant apartment at 50 avenue du Bois, his temporary headquarters were in a *rez-de-chaussée* that belonged to an English lady, and were furnished coquettishly in soft green and pink. "It suits my complexion," he wrote to John Hay, "and has an extra bedroom for you when you come." Every day he visited the great Electricity Building, which he called "Hall of Dynamos." Here he stared in fascination at the 40-foot dynamos which in 1900 were producing a prodigious 15,000 horsepower. To Adams, they seemed a kind of 20th-century moral force that represented infinity. He compared their enormous energy with the creative force of the Virgin of the 12th century and concluded, "All the steam in the world could not, like the Virgin, build Chartres."

That spring, Stickney was still away, so Adams had his "dear *proprietaire*" to himself. She was at her most alluring, and Adams wrote contentedly, "I see no one but Mrs. Cameron and Martha . . ."

But Lizzie could seldom stay still for long. Gathering up Martha and Mademoiselle and the maid Cooper, she set off to take the waters at Pougne-les-Eaux. In this scenic health spa, tourists revived their flagging energies and reduced their waistlines by drinking endless glasses of warm mineral waters and eating sparsely.

Not by accident, Stickney turned up at the resort, but his bewildered look returned when Lizzie asked him, with pretty helplessness, "Perhaps you could find a suitable house for Martha and me?" When he could not, she was understanding. "I suppose Mr. Stickney knows of one but is frightened to death of the responsibility, which I appreciate. Poor boy . . ." So she decided not to settle down after all but to "float around without plans." Enjoying this nomadic life, she wrote to Adams, "We are off in the morning to Spring Lake at Thun."

Early in August, Lizzie learned that Bay Lodge, the senator's impetuous son, had eloped with Bessie Davis, Joe Stickney's dark-haired cousin and the granddaughter of Senator Frederick T. Frelinghuysen of New Jersey. A large society wedding had been planned for them in Boston. But as the gifts came pouring in, Bessie and Bay eloped and were married in the First Church of the Advent in Boston with only the necessary witnesses present.

Lizzie was all outraged propriety in her letter to Adams. "They are both fools and I have no sympathy for them. I don't like their entrance into life on a lie, nor Bay for persuading her to act on it. I am disappointed. The world is full of fools. I have written to him twice. I should have an answer tomorrow. If not, I will go my way East or South and pay no attention." Lizzie was lingering here, she added, to please Martha, "who has found some outdoor-type English girls with whom she is learning to row." With her new friends, Martha climbed the surrounding mountains, and Lizzie approved. "It will do her good—she is lazy." Lizzie also reported with distaste that she was being pursued by an elderly Frenchman "covered with decorations—who wants to row me in the moonlight and discuss art!" Next, Martha found "an English baby of five who adores her. She needs companions," Lizzie noted regretfully, "she depends on me too much."

After a few days they moved on to Baden-Baden, which Lizzie exclaimed "is so like the Riviera!" She described the sunsets to Adams. "You never saw anything out of a Turner to compare with the colors—violet and gold and through the deepening violet a yellow moon rose." As Martha took up the study of Italian with a tutor, her mother promenaded along the veranda of the hotel, where she picked out a familiar face—the dissipated young marquis de Ruden, whose father she knew. But the young man was traveling with a boisterous party, and Lizzie suspected that the overdressed female member of it was "not a lady—so he fights shy of me."

Lizzie's letters failed to match the regularity of Adams's, and he complained often at receiving no letter from her. Now Adams wrote to her vaguely, which surprised her, for he was always a marvel of the specific, "Stickney has gone off to wherever he is going." His destination, as Lizzie had suspected, was Baden-Baden. The poet greeted Lizzie with a triumphant smile, as he tried to shrug off his ubiquitous mother and two sisters. The Stickney trio seldom gave the couple a moment alone, and finally, in a mood of defeat, Joe announced that he would escort the family party to Milan. But at the last moment, Mrs. Stickney vetoed his plans when she realized that all the shops in Milan would be closed on the feast of All Souls. They must remain in Baden-Baden, she ordered, until the end of the week. Flushed with chagrin, Stickney protested in a low murmur, while the three women grew shrill in disagreement. At length, they departed, Mrs. Stickney with her mouth set in a grim line, Stickney looking more bewildered than ever, the two girls trailing sullenly behind. Lizzie watched these skirmishes with glee, as she reported to Adams, "I see that our family is not alone in its little quarrels and disruptions."

Adams's reply was succinct. "Really I am lost without you." To which Lizzie answered, "It is curious how incomplete everything is without you. You double my eyesight, my understanding and my appreciation."

Her next news was somber—Uncle John Sherman was dying in Washington. "He is at the end now," she wrote. "He is not happy and I'm sure he'd rather have it finished." in her sadness, she grew introspective and deplored her habits of extravagance. "I'm a poor woman now. Even Martha is finding that out. I'm afraid I cannot have a carriage. I wonder how I spend so much money? I always knew I was a poor economizer. I have a sitting room here and I have no business to. That's where I am so extravagant. Space and privacy must be paid for."

Meanwhile, Adams, failing to receive her weekly letter, became agitated. "I was near one of my panics last night, with no news of you." Lizzie, who had in turn received no word from the wandering Stickney, moved on to the Grand Eden Hotel in Pallanza. Next morning, as she strolled along a sun-dappled lane, dressed in frothy layers of white lace and carrying a white parasol like the lady in a painting by Monet, she caught sight of a tall figure approaching her, with a young woman hanging on his arm. Before they could greet each other, Lucy Stickney ran forward and gushed, "Oh my dear Mrs. Cameron! We just now decided to leave Munich. I had a bad throat and Joe said he *should* be in Paris and..." But Lizzie was not listening. Over Lucy's head her eyes met Stickney's in a look of recognition. Later, Lizzie told Adams, "The entire Stickney family blew in. They fill the air with enchantment. We do excursions together."

For ten days Joe lingered, like a victim tied to a chariot that is pulled by two opposing horses. From one side he felt the tug of his studies at the Sorbonne; from the other, the pull of Lizzie's will. But Lizzie was less bemused than he. So she did not miss the poet's struggles with his mother. "He says he will go to Paris on Friday," she noted, "but he will go when his mother tells him. She is a generalissimo—it is admirable."

Four days later, Lizzie noted, "Stickney is gloomy at times. But apparently he has conquered and he goes to Paris on Tuesday." Finally, as originally planned, they all left, heading for Milan, then Paris. Now Lizzie was able to draw a light breath of relief. "Martha and I go back to our old ways of living outdoors all day." Mrs. Stickney, who disapproved of fresh air, had preferred to stay indoors, huddled before the fire in Lizzie's sitting room. Now, in an effort to cheer Adams, Lizzie praised some verses he had translated for her, remarking, "To think of Bay Lodge and Mr. Stickney setting up as poets while you..."

A cable brought the expected news of Uncle John Sherman's death. "It means," she wrote to Adams, "the death of a thousand childish recollections—and it puts one in the front rank. For him I can only be glad. But so ends the family distinction. There is no one in the next generation to revive it. I doubt if the third generation can produce anything better. You Adamses [she added, with a touch of envy] transmit your energy and strength as few do. But I suddenly feel old and gray." (This statement belied the evidence of her mirror, which reflected her bright eyes and fresh features under a crown of soft dark hair.)

Adams, reading between the lines of her recent letters, fell prey to his old demon ennui. "I wish I hadn't lost my taste for tobacco and champagne. That is worse than your going away. Thank God I appreciated my vices while they lasted and never regretted my indulgence in them. What a weird life it is! And to think that your Uncle John was never bored! I wonder if God the creator was bored when he made such a world." Later, in mild reproach, he added, "My 12th century is my single resource and chiefly because it never knew ennui. When it was bored, somebody got killed."

By now, Mrs. Stickney and Lizzie were on visiting terms, so Lizzie decided to follow them to Milan, where they had established themselves. Here, for Henry Adams's sake, she would attend High Mass at the cathedral and visit the Ambrosian Library. "Libraries and churches always mean you," she wrote. "I realize each day I am only half a person without you. When it is 6 o'clock I am as restless as a cat. Why did you go? Nothing goes when you are not here. I don't even read the newspapers without you to translate them for me."

Lizzie made no mention of Stickney. Instead, she reported her decision to return to Paris the following week. With that charming imperiousness that men found irresistible, she issued to Adams (who had returned to Paris) her "final order — to dine with me in Paris next Tuesday — and I will talk you blind at 8 o'clock. Suspecting that the prudent Adams was fretting about her extravagance in all this gadding about, she assured him, "I have paid all my debts so don't be cross." The impracticality of their living arrangements in Paris bothered her, and she protested, "We should at least arrange a boarding system for it is too absurd for me to be eating alone at one end of the Avenue and you at the other."

On her return, they dined at Paillard's, and in the candlelight Adams noted a new abstraction in her manner, a wistfulness in her violet eyes. As always when her behavior upset him, he assumed his pose of cosmic despair. He wrote to Sister Anne (Bay Lodge's mother), "I cannot doubt that God will very soon bust up the whole circus and proceed to judgment and then you know best what will happen to the U.S. Senate. Personally I am not interested, having made my arrangements for Paradise through the Virgin Mary and the 12th century Church." This was an allusion to his "Miracles of the Virgin," which was his tentative title for the book that would eventually become *Mont-Saint-Michel and Chartres*.

In writing to John Hay, Adams was more savage in mood. Inscribing the envelope with the words "Private, most privately private," he wrote, "I am a waif on the waters of eternity and I care not one sour French grape how soon or how late this damned humanity breaks its neck." Later, he exclaimed, "Woman is the Jap of the sexes — shrewd, wily and 9 times out of 10 she gets what she wants."

The reason for his mood of suppressed rage was plain to both Bernhard Berenson and Bay Lodge. The urbane Adams was jealous. Imperturbably looking on, B.B. could foresee the end of the story. But to young Bay, still in his honeymoon euphoria, it was unthinkable that his revered Uncle Henry, whom he had watched for years surrounded by adoring ladies, should now sit, silent and wretched, because of one lady's behavior.

In the gaiety of Mrs. Cameron's dinner parties, the regular guests joined — Berenson, Stickney, Bay and Bessie Lodge, and Henri Hubert, a gossip-loving anthropologist who was a friend of the two poets. Adams alone did not share in the lively laughter. Instead, he watched sardonically as Lizzie focused her charm on Stickney, who was no longer sad but dazzled. When pressed, Stickney declined to play the violin because he was "out of practice." Bay Lodge soon failed to enjoy the game. Instead, he writhed inwardly, reporting to his mother, "Mrs. Cameron takes a huge interest in Joe. She spoils and flatters him absurdly — it is rather unpleasant to watch when one is fond of him — and he takes it all like a lamb."

To all guests, especially to Adams, it was painfully clear that Lizzie, who had previously eluded her pursuers, was now herself discreetly in pursuit — a little breathless in her infatuation for this poet whose youthful beauty she could not resist and which Adams, with all his gifts of mind and heart, could not hope to match.

"Paris is very damp, dark and dusky," Adams complained, as the date of his departure neared. In wintry mood, he held aloof from the dinner conversation. In fact, as Bay Lodge noted with distress, "Uncle Henry was very rude to Joe on several occasions. It was quite pathetic." Everyone was growing faintly embarrassed, perhaps recalling Adams's dictum, "In the grip of sex, no man has ever thought."

Watching Stickney as he basked in his hostess's adulation, Lodge was critical of his friend. "Joseph has changed a great deal," he wrote. "This is also *entirely confidential*. He seems to me like a man who has been spoiled by women and taken it seriously which is unpardonable in a man of his intelligence."

But intelligence played a small role in this drama of the emotions. Lodge scornfully referred to the pair as "The Lady and the Poet" and could not fail to note the developing intimacy which wholly excluded Adams.

"Certainly they are very intimate," Lodge wrote, then added from his own wishful thinking, "I doubt however — and I say this with genuine regret — that there is anything to bring a blush to the cheek of innocence."

This certainty was not shared by the worldly B.B..

The elaborate efforts of Stickney and his hostess to conceal their movements struck Lodge as "rather stupid — for one can suspect things." But in fairness he conceded that the subterfuge was due to a well-founded fear of the displeasure of Mrs. Davis, Bessie's mother, who would certainly be shocked at a romance between an experienced hostess like Lizzie and a young unmarried student who happened to be a relative of Mrs. Davis.

Although Lodge had convinced himself that Lizzie was "the more ardent" of the two, he had to admit, "I haven't an idea how much she cares for Joe or he for her." Then he stubbornly insisted, "But I am sure she cares more."

Berenson was not so certain. With his eye for detail, he had noted that Stickney was spending very little time on his studies and most of his hours either attending on Lizzie or writing verse to her such as:

> Like a pearl dropped in dark red wine
> Your pale face sinks within my heart
> Not to be mine, yet always mine.

"Mrs. Cameron," Lodge complained, "takes small pains to conceal the fact that she likes the attentions of a young man. The whole thing makes Uncle Henry pretty sick."

In this unhappy state of affairs, Adams could only retaliate by vowing that, after he left for home, he would never return to Paris. The hollowness of this threat struck young Lodge, who pointed out, "If Mrs. C. wanted him to come back he would come soon enough. There are fools and knaves everywhere and I don't see why, because his proprietor is both, he should swear never to return to Paris."

No longer able to conceal his indignation at her treatment of Uncle Henry, Bay Lodge confronted Lizzie. "My dear Mrs. Cameron," he began, "it is such a pity that Uncle Henry will not come back to Paris . . ."

To his dismay, Lizzie was "brutally cheerful." Laughing lightly, she spoke of Adams, "but without any kindness." Afterward, Lodge added for his mother's benefit, "She even told me he was losing his mind and gave little instances of his lapses of memory. This struck me as hardly fair play. The whole thing is pretty tragic and I don't think either Mrs. Cameron or Joe have dealt with him fairly."

In nihilistic mood, Adams was writing, "I know nobody and go nowhere and see nothing." On 10 January 1901, he sailed for New York, leaving the field to his rival.

Lizzie's gaiety was undimmed. Perhaps, in her infatuation with Stickney, she failed to see the depth of the wound she had inflicted on her departing Dordy. She continued to write blithely of the winter's social sports. "I went to a concert with Stickney and the Lodges last night. This week Walter Gay is exhibiting his paintings." Then, in a devil-may-care reversal of her earlier self-reproach, she added, "I am *criblée* with debts but what does that matter? If I live I can pay them and if I don't Donald will have to." With a smiling shrug, she added, "I wish he could hear that reasoning."

By now, as she witnessed their happiness, Lizzie had overcome her disapproval of Bay's and Bessie's clandestine wedding. She helped them move into the apartment near the Trocadéro that Adams had offered them, with the services of his manservant, as a wedding gift. The beautiful Bessie, she noted, had no maid but did not seem to mind.

The Lady and the Poet

Lizzie was captivated by them. "The radiance of that pair is something to see. I am tired of all our practical outlook and those two mad people enjoying their youth and their love without a thought for that awful tomorrow is rather splendid to see. He adores her—it shines all through them both. It really made an impression on me."

Indeed, the impression on Lizzie was lasting. The newlyweds' bliss forced her to remember her own honeymoon. Writing to Lucy Frelinghuysen, an old friend who was Bessie's maiden aunt, she declared, with unaccustomed fervor, "Really Lucy, when I see their youth and love and enjoyment I forgive—and envy—their folly. Everyone shakes their head but dear me! I believe it is they who are wise to love and enjoy without thinking of tomorrow." With sudden candor, she revealed the desolation of her own marriage. "Neither you nor I, Lucy, have tasted what they are living on now— don't you regret it?"

It was this thirst for the unknown sweet that was impelling her, half consciously, toward Stickney.

On 21 January 1901, a funeral bell tolled for all that self-contained society. After a reign of 64 years, Queen Victoria was dying. Lizzie noted matter-of-factly, "The Queen is dying. There is astonishingly little excitement. It didn't even affect the stock market much."

In New York, Henry Adams felt the prick of his historian's sense. "Even I, who for some years belonged to Victoria's Court in what was supposed to be its best time and could never see anything but selfishness and bourgeoisie to admire in the old woman and who never received from her or her family so much as a sign of recognition, am a very little touched to see her disappear so tragically, broken hearted at the wretched end of such a self-satisfied reign and nobody care. The stock market itself is hoarse with croaking the entrance of Edward VII."

Briefly installed at the Knickerbocker Club in New York, he took pains to inform Lizzie of the social whirl he was enjoying.

> I found myself in a mad cyclone of people. Miss Marbury and Miss Elsie de Wolfe received me with tender embraces. The latter begs me to repeat to you her earnest desire to meet you in Italy in March or April. Marion Crawford is bringing out a new play. [His *Francesca da Rimini* would be produced by Sarah Bernhardt in the following year.] I dined at Mabel's with John La Farge who is in excellent form, going to die, very talkative and inquisitive and naturally very pleased with his promotion into Officer of the Legion of Honor. Really New York is amusing. I am dying to write another satire.

Lizzie's reply recounted an evening she had spent with the Bay Lodges, who were still installed in Adams's apartment. "After dinner," she wrote, "Bay lashed himself into noisy enthusiasm and was all over the place in his argument—illogical, contradictory and fiery. Stickney grew quieter and quieter as the argument went on, never leaving the main road and keeping the point always in sight." Watching them with a mysterious smile the langorous Bessie "spoke only once or twice, more wisely than fiery Bay whose noise was like Teddy Roosevelt's without his genuineness."

Lizzie's feelings for Lodge were touched with annoyance. "He is writing but God knows what." Then, to reassure her absent Dordy, she added, "All these nights I have dined alone with a book propped up in your fashion. I fell upon Henry James' 'The Marriages' which I read at a sitting."

During the past year, Lizzie had sat for her portrait to the fashionable Swedish painter Anders Zorn. Now she received a photograph of it, and she was dismayed. For the photograph relentlessly recorded what a viewer of the oil painting might miss—a note of inescapable vulgarity. In the sitter's calculated pose there is a suggestion of the predatory which Zorn evidently considered the essence of the *femme fatale*. Despite the romantic details of the background—a flowering branch against the wall, an apricot sofa, the lady's ivory satin gown bedecked with flowers, the lady herself stands out as a kind of female temptress—self-contained and coldly seductive. In fact, Zorn had portrayed Lizzie, in the guise of a lady of fashion, as a sleek, exquisite lion-tamer poised to crack an imaginary whip.

Angrily, she wrote to Adams, "Its defects come out so strong in the photographs that I dare not send one over to you. If you know where Zorn is let me know and I'll send him one and I hope it will shake him. He really must alter it."

Like any artist who painted what he saw, Anders Zorn must have encountered this reaction before. Expecting a flattering likeness that will coincide with the subject's own image of herself, she is abruptly confronted with a wholly different picture. The effect is jarring.

Further contradicting the portrait's realism was the romantic mirror that Stickney's verse now held up to her:

> Love, I marvel what you are!
> Heaven in a pearl of dew,
> Lilies hearted with a star—
> All are you.

These two portraits of Lizzie made a remarkable composite, like one of those period photographs in which a woman, seated with her back to the camera and facing a double mirror, was photographed so that her face was shown from several angles, but never facing directly front.

As Lizzie mused over these contrasting likenesses, Adams wrote to her with typical self-deprecation, "By way of relief from boredom I have returned to verse and have written a long Prayer to the Virgin of Chartres which I will send you presently to put in your fire. It is not poetry and it is not very like verse and it will not amuse you to read but it occupies me to write, which is something—at 62."

This "Prayer," which Adams was sending only to her, was an extraordinary gift. It remains a work of art in miniature and it prefigures the masterpiece on which he was working—*Mont-Saint-Michel and Chartres*. From his long immersion in the spirit of the Middle Ages, Henry Adams had developed his unique interpretation of the Virgin. This Bostonian of Unitarian ancestry saw, in a great sweep of historical imagination, that during the age of faith when France had proudly claimed the title "Eldest Daughter of the Church," Mary the Mother of God had reigned supreme. He recognized that she "even embarrassed the Trinity—it was the reason why men loved and adored her with a passion such as no other deity had ever inspired." Adams contended that the Virgin was the single most powerful force in the world in the 12th century—greater even than the Father or the Son or the Holy Spirit. She had so powerfully dominated the imagination of all her children—artists and sculptors and architects, kings and common people, that, simply and directly, like some great natural force, she had herself inspired the building of the great Gothic cathedrals. All the great churches—Chartres, Amiens, Coutances, Beauvais, Rheims, and Notre Dame—were built to please her. "At Chartres," Adams wrote, "one sees her give orders and architects obey them—but very rarely a hesitation as though the architect were deciding for himself. She was the greatest energy the world has ever known."

Long before he finished the book, Adams wrote "Prayer to the Virgin of Chartres," a poetic summing up of the spirit of the book, composed in a series of quatrains reminiscent of the poetry of François Villon.

The "Prayer" details Adams's long imaginary spiritual pilgrimage as "an English scholar with a Norman name." He sees himself praying before the Virgin in the company of Peter Abelard, chanting the "Ave Maris Stella" along with Saint Bernard, following the penitent King Louis barefoot over the snow. He describes the Pilgrims as "the greedy band crossing the hostile sea" and describes their loss of faith—"I did not find the Father, but I lost, what now I value more, the Mother—you." Within the poem is a second prayer, "Prayer to the Dynamo," in which Adams points to the ascendancy of science and prophesies with astonishing insight, in 1900, the lethal power lurking in the atom. He concludes with the plea:

> Help me to see! not with my mimic sight—
> With yours! which carried radiance, like the sun . . .
>
> Help me to know! not with my mocking art—
> With you, who knew yourself unbound by laws . . .
>
> Help me to bear! not my own baby load,
> But yours; who bore the failure of the light,
> The strength, the knowledge and the thought of God, —
> The futile folly of the Infinite!

This poem was Adams's most passionate outpouring of his longing to believe, of his enslavement to the Virgin, who dominated his imagination as she ruled her 12th-century children and as she informed his book *Mont-Saint-Michel and Chartres*.

Why did Henry Adams send this "Prayer" to Elizabeth Cameron and to no one else for eight years—this prayer which was found in his wallet after his death?

Lizzie was his pupil, without doubt. She owed much of her education to him. He had introduced her to Gothic architecture as he read selections from the first draft of his work to her and to the uncomprehending Martha. But despite Lizzie's starry-eyed pose of listener, Adams surely could not have expected her to act as a serious critic of his work. He knew that her interest in religion was essentially superficial—she delighted in the beauty of Gothic cathedrals but she cared little for their *raison d'être.*

But long ago Lizzie had captured his heart and she had unwittingly set him on the road to *Chartres.* Fifteen years earlier, a childless widower returning from Japan, Adams had come upon La Dona, then a young mother who was holding her infant Martha in her arms. In this radiant pair he had glimpsed, perhaps for the first time, the enduring appeal of the mother and child and he began to sense the enormous power of the Madonna throughout history. For a few years, Lizzie had encouraged, then rebuked his growing passion. For a few months, she had seemed to reciprocate. But she remained always unattainable. And as both mother and child grew away from him, Adams the historian found himself turning back toward the mother of God, to begin his long celebration of the Virgin of Chartres. His yearning and his worship informed his "Prayer" as they later filled his book.

But why, in what mood of desperate hope, did he send it to her at this moment? Now, as he saw her affections straying toward a younger man who cared nothing for the Virgin, did he perhaps nourish the illusion that in reading his poem she would also read his heart?

Certainly he knew she would never consign it to her fire. No woman would—least of all Lizzie, who loved to collect the poetic outpourings of her suitors. He sent it to her with the flattering note, "Here is my Prayer. No one but you has seen it. No one but you would care to see it."

Reading this richly mysterious celebration of the Virgin must have been more than a little overwhelming for Lizzie. For years, she had willingly followed his direction in her reading. Under his guidance, she had deepened and enriched her taste in art and letters. But she was not prepared for this—indeed, she was baffled and uncertain and a little worried.

In her reply, she began by brushing aside his vow never to return to Paris. "Of course you will come back. I have never heard such nonsense. Where else is there to go?" She thanked him warmly for the priceless Chinese vase he had left her. "Your Ming makes the place look like a museum. It is gorgeous. I feel rich and proud."

Subtly flattering, she continued, "You yourself are as mysterious as the Sphinx. You have depths that frighten me when I get a glimpse into them." Finally she reached the subject of the poem. "The Prayer you sent me stirred me profoundly. I know that the trouble it stirs up in me does not settle for hours and that I turn back and read it again and again. *Are* you as weary as that? Can one be? Have you all of the fatigue of the generations that preceded you to bear? But your Virgin is dethroned—they knew what she stood for but it is too pagan for today and no one understands."

"No one understands"—the words must have sounded a knell for Adams. Had she truly missed in this poem his longing for an earlier age of faith? Had she misunderstood his yearning for the lost legacy of Christian affirmation? And had she failed to see his human need, not only for the 12th-century madonna, but for his own "La Dona"?

Lizzie was stirred, but she was also uncomprehending. Perhaps, gripped by her own need, she could not bear to recognize the depths of yearning that the poem revealed. So she turned quickly from the mysterious to the practical. "We are off to Italy," she wrote, "if Don sends the money. I think he will for he must have made a lot this winter." By way of justifying her trip to the South, she added, "I can't seem to stop my cough or get on my feet since the attack of ptomaine. Nothing but change will set things straight."

Alluding to Stickney, she observed, "Bay Lodge finds Mr. Stickney grown 'very reflective.' Of course by that he means 'older' and I have a guilty feeling that I have done it. Dear, dear—think of me aging a man when his great attraction is his youth—to me I mean."

The season of Lent had begun. Lizzie, who was not notably devout, reported, "I used Ash Wednesday and its penance in going to see Mrs. de Wolfe, Elsie's mother, an awful old woman, vulgar and pretentious beyond words."

Her financial dependence on Donald Cameron irked her. "I wish a burst of feeling would strike Donald into a check," she exclaimed. Then she waited, chafing, as the weeks passed and "no word from Don. I don't understand why he did not write to you. It is the first time that has happened." Eventually the check arrived.

In mid-Lent, Lizzie received, by pneumatic post, a light-hearted request from Stickney and Lodge, who addressed her as "Divine Lady": "Tomorrow is Mi-Carême and La Vieille du Départ. Therefore it seems that you and I should foregather in your room, for wheresoever two or three are gathered together—they come to the Boulevard successfully. Lunch at half past 12 at 45 Rue de Bac. We shall gape open-mouthed for you and food."

Mi-Carême, or Mid-Lent, was a one-day pause amid the rigors of Lent, when the young in heart forgot their penances and converged in laughing groups on the boulevard Saint-Michel to toss great handfuls of confetti. In the churches, the priests changed their black vestments for rose-colored ones. Gaily, Joe Stickney, Bay and Bessie Lodge, Lizzie, and Martha joined the merry-makers. It was the eve of their departure for the South, and such a journey demanded a formidable amount of packing. Aided by her maid, Lizzie handled it expertly. "I am in a whirl of preparations," she wrote to Adams. "We go to Sicily, then Rouen—Martha and I—we go alone as Cooper can't leave Kiki."

Lodge duly reported their departure to his mother. "Mrs. Cam and Martha have gone to Sicily with Mr. and Mrs. Caulfield and Frank Griswold. Joe and his sisters go to Florence next week. I get a room for myself and begin a novel."

From Naples, Lizzie expressed her irritation at Don. "I am still in uncertainty about his plans. Does Don mean me to re-let that house, to go home or stay here? I'm tired of Europe but what else is there? Don writes to Martha but he says so little. I'm tired of it all." Then, threateningly, she added, "I could cut a straight swathe if it were not for Martha."

When Lizzie arrived in Palermo, the site of the famous Cathedral of Monreale, she heard from Adams. "I hope you have prayed to the Virgin for me at Monreale. I'm glad you have seen it. Perhaps you will catch the faint phosphorescence of the Virgin's light and will feel why one wants to pray to her rather than the Dynamo." He had written movingly of the mosaics at Monreale in his *Chartres:* "No art—either Greek, Byzantine, Italian or Arab—has ever created two religious types so beautiful, so serious, so impressive yet so different as Mont St. Michel watching over its northern ocean and Monreale, looking down over its forests of orange and lemon on Palermo and the Sicilian seas."

In her reply, Lizzie ignored the beauties of Monreale to protest again his vow never to return to Paris. She reminded him that she had renewed her three-year lease on the apartment at No. 50. "But if you are not there I cannot stay. Where is there to go? You must reconsider. Or find a place I can go to. After all, I am not wedded to Paris. How about Sicily? The whole island is covered with fruit trees in bloom. It looks like Paradise."

But for Lizzie, Paradise beckoned from Florence. Early in April, she wrote to Adams from that city, "Stickney is here." For the next six weeks, she wrote no more. It was the first break in her letters to him since their correspondence had begun fifteen years before. Adams continued to write to her with the old regularity and a growing anxiety. All during April and into May, he fretted. "Still no letter. I am seriously uneasy." He told her that recently, while he had been sitting alone at dinner, he thought he heard Martha's voice calling "Dordy." Although he smiled at his "advanced imbecility," his fears would not subside. "Of course I'm worried," he wrote, "for I imagine you broken down in Italy. I shall expect to hear from you. For the first time I begin to feel poor and peevish like a child left out of a game." When this did not move her, he wrote again. "It flashed on me that you may have stopped writing because you thought I was coming in May. Anything for a peaceful mind."

As always in an illicit romance, there were observers—to watch, to speculate and report. Henri Hubert wrote to Bay Lodge in Paris, "They were very much occupied with inspecting points of interest in this charming resort—together." They must have made a handsome picture in Florence—Stickney, who was the model of an Edwardian poet, stooping protectively over the radiant lady under the white parasol, strolling past the ancient palaces in the spring sunshine.

From Hubert and other gossipers, Bay Lodge pieced together a report for his mother, to whom he wrote with an unbroken frequency that any mother might envy. "It appears," he informed her, "that on the memorial margins of the Arno, Mrs. Cam and Joe flirted together daily for about six weeks—very busy." A few days later he added, "Stickney and Mrs. Cam are still in Italy disporting. The scandal is for you alone."

Trumbull Stickney

Elizabeth Cameron about 1900

Was it indeed a scandal? Lizzie was, as always, surrounded by chaperones—Martha and Henri and the Caulfields, and in the background Bernhard Berenson. But despite their presence, any lady bent on romantic adventure could have eluded them. The question is, Did Lizzie, who had been trained from girlhood in the habit of discretion, overstep the conventions now?

Undoubtedly, she did. She had traveled to Florence in pursuit of a love that she had not experienced either with her husband or with Henry Adams. Her defenses had melted under the spell of Stickney's sad, bewildered beauty. Now she was faced with this ardent young man who, having finally broken away from his family, was hot to assert his manhood. Undoubtedly she yielded to his pleas and her own inclinations. And in her willing surrender to a mutual desire, she completed one more chapter in her education.

Naturally, she never told. Nor did he—directly. His letters to her have been lost, and only a few pages of his sonnets, written in his tiny handwriting, on notepaper marked "J.T.S.," were found among her papers. But his published lyrics sing of the young man's rapture:

> You are to me the full vermilion rose
> That love, with trembling arms uplifted, crowned...

In another verse he muses on:

> That face
> for the mere memory I would die.

And returning to an earlier figure he declares:

> As a pearl in red wine cast
> Grows like a drop of moonlight there
> Your face possesses my despair.

Too soon, their idyll ended. The raptures of the Florentine night faded quickly in the daylight of "that awful tomorrow." To her surprise, Lizzie found that it was less difficult to renounce this fulfillment of passion with Joe Stickney than to renounce her first unconsummated love for Joe Russell. That infatuation had taken place 24 years before, yet it was Russell, not Stickney, of whom she still dreamed.

Practiced in handling difficult situations, Lizzie now took the lead with Stickney. Strolling beside him over the Ponte Vecchio, she gently pointed out to him, with sweet reasonableness, that the affair must end. Neither of their lives could contain the complications of a continuing liaison. They must return to Paris and they must part.

In vain, the poet, who had been so briefly transformed by happiness, pleaded with her. Lizzie was determined, and finally she won his agreement. He resumed his melancholy air, and his expression became more bewildered than ever.

In early May, the lovers traveled part of the way back to Paris together, then took separate trains, for appearance's sake, before they reentered the city. Their entourage had preceded them.

On Lizzie's return, she found a pile of letters from Henry Adams, who had been writing to her with his usual growing alarm. "I've had nothing from you since April 10," he complained. In another letter, he wrote, "So Mr. Cameron has called you home?"

Lizzie, now ensconced in the familiar luxury of the avenue du Bois apartment and gaily unrepentant, wrote to Adams as if nothing had happened. She exulted, "I saw much of Berenson in Florence. Imagine me with Berenson!" She was quick to set Adams straight about her husband. "Don did *not* summon us home. He merely wrote he was not coming over so I decided to go to him." She added, "I'm so glad you saw Don in New York. He seems pleased that we are coming home."

Reverting to Adams's vow to abandon Paris forever, she asked plaintively, "Now what am I to do? I am going to America and perhaps for good. Since you won't return to Paris why should I? And in that case don't you want me to bring a lot of your things home to you?" (Among his "things" were some exquisite porcelain, a painting by Claude, and some priceless furniture.) "Do give instructions. If this partnership is not to continue, you must certainly have your things."

Lizzie was not surprised to learn that Adams would, after all, return. When he wrote that he was sailing for England on 15 May, and would arrive in London on the 22nd, she seized the opportunity. "Please go to Hanford, 24 Sloane Square and buy me a dozen pairs of very fine open-work lisle thread stockings, tan-colored and size nine. I wrote them but had the usual insolent answer. So you must buy them for me and save my self-respect."

Her self-respect was intact, although Bay Lodge thought it should be otherwise. Disapprovingly, he told his mother of her return. "Mrs. Cam is going home to Washington. I imagine, with the glittering realization that she better had and she talks of not coming back. Stickney will be home next winter also. The mask—if one there be—is, I'm sure, principally on her side."

With the stern judgment of outraged youth, Bay Lodge saw only the externals. Berenson knew better, for Lizzie confided in him, tremulously, since she could not confide in Henry Adams. With a touch of the melodramatic, she saw this as the end of her youth, as she declared "that awful tomorrow has arrived." From now on, she lamented, she must resign herself to playing the role of Madame de Maintenon, who as the mistress and secret wife of Louis XIV had witnessed the power but missed the glory. At this unflattering image of her relationship with Henry Adams, Berenson made no comment.

B.B. also watched the chastened Stickney as he returned to his studies at the Sorbonne. Before his excursion to Florence, Joe had been writing an ambitious poetic drama based on the life of the Emperor Julian. As the editors of his posthumous poems would note, "Trumbull Stickney was unable to give this splendid fragment the time and attention required. Though he subsequently returned to it, it was unhappily never finished."

But Stickney's love affair was finished. The bittersweet love he had tasted had deepened his melancholy and furnished him with new poetic insight. Musing on his experience, he wrote, "We learn by suffering and we teach by pity." He also produced a hauntingly lovely poem in the manner of Verlaine, "It's autumn in the country I remember. . . ."

But the richest fruit of this springtime idyll was his sequence of love poems entitled "Eride." The title is his Frenchification of the Greek name for the goddess of discord. According to legend, Eris, who was angry at not being invited to a wedding on Mount Olympus, threw into the happy gathering an apple marked "To the Fairest," thereby setting off a mortal strife that led to the Trojan Wars.

In Section IV of "Eride," Stickney writes with a sense of doom:

> No, no, 'tis very much too late.
> I thought it mockery that you said
> You loved me; but a certain fate
> Lowers your voice and bows your head.
> I tell you, your desire is to wake the dead.

He confronts her with the stark question:

> For what were gained if I were yours?
> Fever and frenzy of the blood,
> The endless pleasure which no surfeit cures,
> Endless desire, hunger, feud—
> And at the end of passion, solitude.

He shows a mournful recognition of the claims of others:

> So are our lives. I love you more.
> But other hearts by destiny
> Must needs possess what they adore
> And have it, to live with and to die,
> To strangle or soothe with kisses. Not so I.

With Byronic despair, he continues:

> If I have wronged you in the days
> Bygone but unforgotten now,
> I make no pleading for your grace.
> My tongue is bitter. Leave me, go. . . .
>
> Like this love of ours, that lying dead
> Clamours for burial. It is time,
> It was time in much earlier days,
> Before we soiled our lips with crime,
> That you and I went our two ways.

The note of doom that sounds throughout much of Stickney's poetry was a grim forecast of his end. Later that year, he finished his studies and, with matchless skill, defended his thesis in two languages before his academic judges at the Sorbonne. Receiving his *doctorat ès lettres,* he returned to teach at Harvard. One year later, at the age of 30, he was stricken with a brain tumor. Blind and in agony, he stumbled toward an untimely death in 1904.

For Lizzie, the affair was indeed finished. She referred to Stickney occasionally in her letters to Adams, and a few years later to Henry Wilkinson. "I sent a Kodak to Lucy Stickney who is delighted to have them. She is living more and more on the memory of Joe—bless him!"

The effect of the affair on Henry Adams was noted sourly by Bay Lodge. After Adams had returned to Paris in late May 1901, he attended a dinner party in Mrs. Cameron's apartment at which the lady was flanked by her two poets. Lodge, who had not forgiven Lizzie for her high-handed treatment of Uncle Henry and his fellow-poet Stickney, described the changed atmosphere in a letter to his mother:

> Uncle Henry is here and we see almost nothing of him, in fact only twice. Once we dined with Mrs. Cameron. Uncle Henry seems to me older—after dinner he enfolds himself in the smoke of his cigar and says nothing. Then Mrs. Cameron seizes the floor and—entre nous—I've been horribly bored both times I've seen them together. It's curious how she produces the same effect when Joe is about— i.e. makes him a bore and silent. Joe is a totally different man when he's alone with us and when she's around. We planned expeditions together—we tried it once and it wasn't funny.

But Adams, at 63, was a philosopher as well as a historian. When Lizzie had wired him birthday congratulations in February 1901, he had replied, "If you knew the fantastic, opera-bouffe, idiotic, grotesquely convulsing, laughable depths of sadness of a 63rd birthday you would forget even to be seriously kind." Watching her now, at 43, still restlessly searching for a love that would always elude her, he reasoned that if she could never fully accept the love that he so freely offered, she could at least be kind and he could share that kindness.

Meanwhile, he had his Virgin of Chartres to whom he turned with all the tenderness of an adoring skeptic.

Adams remained Lizzie's "protector," writing to John Hay, "Mrs. Cameron sails for New York on June 29. Will you get her a house near you at (Lake) Sunapee for she knows not where to go?" Then, with false joviality, he added, "Mrs. Cameron is good-natured enough not to show I am more of a bore though, I think, somewhat less of a jackass than I was when she stood still in her teens and we first met."

Lizzie and Martha sailed for home, and Adams sent her a letter to read on board ship. "Tomorrow you arrive. Of course it will be a fiery furnace."

Adams, during these past three years, had endured much and had understood everything. His devotion to her was still unwavering. But he was not prepared to play the role of martyr. In hardly veiled fashion, he wrote to Lizzie concerning their mutual friends Senator Henry Cabot Lodge and his wife "Sister Anne." The senator had been unwilling for his wife to leave him alone for three days, and she had accepted his wish. "I thought mama was chiefly to blame," Adams wrote, "The voluptuous passion of martyrdom need not end in vice. Some natures cannot exist without the gratification of the perfectly sensual appetite for self-sacrifice, like the early Christian martyrs. But it is more fatal than rum."

On a lighter note, he added, "Stickney also came to dinner. . . ."

13

Lizzie And The Artists

By the turn of the century, Lizzie Cameron was dividing her time between two worlds. As John Hay observed, "Her two poles of motion are Paris where she would be and D[onegal] where she wouldn't." At Donegal she drooped like an exotic cattelya planted in the desert, but in Paris she bloomed like the same orchid transplanted to a greenhouse. *The Washington Post* noted her success:

> Mrs. Donald Cameron and her charming daughter Miss Martha, are spending the winter in their apartment in the Avenue du Bois de Boulogne. Mrs. Cameron is distinguished as being one of the most brilliant and delightful hostesses that America has ever furnished to the French capital. Her personal beauty and charm, combined with her scintillating wit and intellectual qualities, make her peculiarly fitted to cope with the manifold requirements of Continental society. . . . Few of our countrywomen have ever had the same amount of admiration and appreciation from these same people that Mrs. Cameron has deservedly won!

Among the "manifold requirements of Continental society" was the necessity of dealing with the leading portrait painters whose studios and reputations were in Paris. With her sensitivity to beauty, which Adams had taught her to cultivate, and with her skill in the management of men of talent, she found it easy to communicate with such artists as John La Farge, Augustus Saint-Gaudens, Paul Helleu, John Singer Sargent, and Auguste Rodin. The artists were drawn to the scintillating hostess who, while not precisely beautiful, created an air of beauty. But when it came to painting her, they found, as had John La Farge, that she was a difficult subject to capture.

When she was in her thirties, Lizzie had found herself pursued, literally and artistically, by Augustus Saint-Gaudens, who would become the foremost American sculptor of the period. The scowling, red-headed Saint-Gaudens, with his bluff features and earthy humor, had an eye for female beauty. He had been at work on a bust of General Sherman with which he was dissatisfied, so he approached the general's niece to persuade him to pose for an equestrian statue that he intended some day to execute. But Sherman was not easily persuaded. He wrote to Lizzie,

I can't help smile at your picture of my sitting on that hobby horse of Saint-Gaudens' for an indefinite time, which he would build up 50 years hence. He promised to give me two sittings a week for all of January and he would let me off. It is now March and the bust is still unfinished. Today is positively the last time. He is convinced that my bust is the very best work he has done. Let him finish the bust and trim enough for the statue business. I already have a good oil painting of myself, seated on my favorite "Duke" at the house in Atlanta. This, together with the studio Saint-Gaudens, enables him to prepare a plaster cast of "Horse and Man" to be held by him until I am gone—then enlarge to life size. This is well understood by all artists. No general ever did or will sit for an equestrian statue.

The huge bronze statue of General Sherman on horseback, preceded by the Angel of Victory, which stands today at the 59th Street entrance of Central Park in New York City, is one of the sculptor's most notable works. Although Saint-Gaudens did not receive the commission to execute it until 1892, he was planning it long before. With patriotic determination to celebrate Sherman's memory, Saint-Gaudens was constantly dwelling on it in his imagination. He intended it to be his masterpiece—heroic in concept and scale, to immortalize a great victory for the Union. After considering various possibilities for this work, Saint-Gaudens decided that he would create a monument that would be far grander than General Sherman's literal notion of "Horse and Man." Instead, he conceived of three figures, twice the size of life, which would include horse and rider and angel to form an artistic unit. Besides being a bronze portrait of the general, the statue would symbolize peace with victory.

Angels were in fashion in the 19th century—in art and in literature—from the weeping angels adorning mortuary tombs and the graceful winged messengers in religious paintings to the literary "Angel in the House" celebrating the wife of the poet Coventry Patmore or the nickname "Angel of Devastation" given to Edith Wharton by her friend Henry James. So it was artistically inevitable that the contemporary practice of depicting women in the form of angels, complete with upswept wings pinioned to their shoulders, should have influenced Saint-Gaudens in choosing an angel as the symbol of Sherman's victory. And it was psychologically probable that he would have looked to Sherman's niece, whom he had known since girlhood, as an early model for his angel. Sherman family legend relates that Saint-Gaudens studied and sketched Lizzie's tall, lithe form and her clear-cut features many times even as he tried, in his clumsy fashion, to woo her. It was the sculptor's habit to use a number of models for his heroic statues, for he was not seeking an exact likeness, which he rejected as "too personal." Often he blended several models in his mind's eye, and his son Homer Saint-Gaudens declared, "I believe that every woman of beauty who was near him impressed his work."

Since he was a perfectionist, Saint-Gaudens was seldom completely satisfied with his work. He continued to change and rework it, sometimes for years, even while the statue was being moved to the exhibition hall. In his 27th Street studio in New York City, in 1897, Saint-Gaudens was still working on the Sherman. He placed a nude model upon the sitter's stand from whom he fashioned a clay figure for the Angel of Victory, then remorselessly slashed into the clay to give a natural look to the drapery, which he would add later. As he worked, he sang or whistled snatches from Italian opera. Watching him in fascination was the rising young Swedish artist Anders Zorn, who eventually proceeded to make two etchings of the sculptor in his studio, one showing Saint-Gaudens sitting on the edge of a couch, with the rump of the reclining nude model visible behind him. Later, Saint-Gaudens sent this etching to Mrs. Cameron as if to suggest that although he was still working on his Victory, this time using a nude model, he had never forgotten his first, fully clothed model.

In the finished bronze figure of the Angel of Victory, who strides forever just ahead of General Sherman, seated on his horse, there is a clear likeness of the youthful Lizzie Cameron. Crowned with laurel, her left hand holding the palm of victory, her right arm raised like some Angel of the Annunciation, she has the straight nose, firmly rounded chin, and clear-eyed gaze that characterized the general's niece. As the statue was described in *The Nation* in 1903, "The angel seems newly alighted on the ground from above. She half walks, half flies, with a certain fierce wildness of aspect, her rapt gaze and half-open mouth shows her a seer of visions. On her bosom is embroidered the eagle of the United States. She is an American Victory."

The sculptor was very proud of his Angel, calling it "the grandest Victory anybody ever made." Southern viewers, who felt only bitterness for General Sherman, mocked it with the words, "It's just like a Northerner to send a woman ahead of him—so nobody could shoot," or "Who but a Northerner would let a woman walk while a man rides?"

The Sherman statue held the central place at the exhibit of contemporary art in the Grand Palais at the Paris Exposition in 1900. It was awarded the Grand Prix, and Saint-Gaudens was named an officer of the Legion of Honor.

He remained an admirer of the general's niece, and once when he was staying in Gramercy Park in New York, he received a ticket from Lizzie for a performance of his favorite Wagnerian opera at the Metropolitan Opera House. In his reply, he wrote, "I always wanted to hear *Parsifal* but could never gather executive ability enough to buy a ticket. Now like a good angel you send me one."

Long after his death and shortly before her own, Elizabeth Cameron wrote to her niece Cecilia Reber about Saint-Gaudens's famous Adams Memorial at Rock Creek Cemetery. "You speak of St. Gaudens. He never said 'This is my model.' He certainly would never admit that he worked with a model. The heavy folds of the grey blanket were to illustrate the idea of secrecy, of mystery. The heavy-featured boy was an Italian who worked in his studio."

Toward John La Farge, Lizzie felt a special affection mingled with admiration. Under Henry Adams's guidance, she had recognized that this painter, who had a special gift for the creation of stained glass, was a man of immense learn-

The Sherman Monument
sculpted by Augustus
Saint-Gaudens

Saint-Gaudens's study for
the head of the Victory

ing and subtle discrimination. All the members of the Adams-Cameron circle agreed with the astute Margaret Chanler when she wrote, "La Farge was different from others, not only in degree but essentially in kind. His head seemed carved in ivory centuries ago by a Chinese artist. He wore very thick glasses but he saw everything. He had read everything. After listening to him, one was forever wiser."

La Farge was also something of a hypochondriac, but his ailments and his helplessness in the face of practical problems roused the protective instinct in La Dona. She, who habitually made errand boys out of her distinguished courtiers, gladly ran errands for him. Occasionally, when she was in Paris and the hard-working La Farge was slaving in his 10th Street studio in Manhattan to support his large family, he would write and ask her to carry out some commission for him. His gratitude was touching, as when he wrote,

> Like a squirrel in a cage I look out on another sort of life in pleasant places of air and light and space. The squirrel is fed (or his little ones are) if he is willing to stand in a little circular cage and he sometimes thinks he is running up trees but really he is only scrambling in a pit to earn nuts for that day. This is the story of my last months of illnesses. But during those grey months I had a vision of a graceful and gracious person doing "chores" and "commissions" for me in freedom and far away in Paris. And I was tempted to invent things to have you get for me that I might think, shut up in my prison, that I have the most elegant free service and help outside. It is still a temptation to invent something. I expect to hear soon about you from Mr. Adams.

When La Farge invited Lizzie to attend an exhibition of paintings with him, she found herself watching his reactions to them. Later she recalled, "I can almost see the tender sardonic smile of La Farge as he looks at the productions of his artistic descendants. He had a kind word for each one, though some were quite awful. He seemed to see what they *wanted* to do—the idea in their minds, more than the achievement."

In his courtly manner, La Farge gravely invited La Dona to his studio to inspect a large painting that he was executing for the courthouse in St. Paul, Minnesota. "If you like it," he wrote, "tell Adams about it and if you don't—and it is not much of a thing except in size, you won't tell him." Although Lizzie learned that La Farge had turned down Adams's request in 1887 to do a portrait of her, she readily accepted the explanation he had offered to Adams. "A face like Mrs. Cameron's has all sorts of difficulties—there is a distinct interior which contradicts the exterior at moments—or rather, there are changes which make one wonder whether they are not really most important." Lizzie sensed that his hesitation to undertake the portrait was due to a reason which would have flattered any woman—that he was unable to probe the mystery of her personality.

In his turn, La Farge recognized the influence that La Dona exerted over Henry Adams. One time he wrote to her with a note of urgency, "As to Adams, did you ever persuade him that his work and play on the Middle Ages ought to be kept and published?" Certainly the artist who had been the sole companion of Henry Adams during two long South Pacific voyages must have realized that it would take a unique person indeed to "persuade" Adams to do anything unless it was his own firm intention. So La Farge was especially delighted when Adams's book *Mont-Saint-Michel and Chartres* was issued in 1904.

Lizzie Cameron, who spent much of her time with the Beautiful People of La Belle Époque, many of whom she judged as "rich and vulgar," was quick to appreciate the genuine quality of this man. She agreed with Adams when he summed up his friend. "La Farge was a great man. This is rarely true of artists—or of publishers, bankers or business men. Take away the brush from Sargent or Whistler or the pen from Balzac—what have you? But La Farge, like Saint Francis of Assisi, *needed nothing but his own soul to make him great.* Both were deeply religious, both were noble and gentle men."

La Farge spent many summers at Sunnyside Place in Newport. Lizzie frequently visited the fashionable Rhode Island resort, which she described as "the most complete City of Pleasure in the world," and, in a spirit of playful protectiveness, she would invite the artist to dine with her. She described one of these luncheons to Adams. "Mr. La Farge lunched with me all alone yesterday and was delighted, though he elaborately explained to me that he was very ill, no good to anyone, never ate lunch, but would call while I ate mine. He ate everything I gave him and was talkative and cheery. He brought his book *An Artist's Letters from Japan* to Newport and expects to stay here. I can't see that he looks worse than usual." Lizzie noticed that for the first time he spoke with affection and tenderness of his large family, especially of his youngest son, John, who was that day being ordained a Jesuit priest. "He became quite affectionate over him . . ." The artist lived frequently apart from his family, in New York City, while his wife, Margaret Perry La Farge, and her numerous, talented children were often in Newport, Rhode Island, or Glen Cove, Long Island. As the Jesuit son, John La Farge, wrote of his father in his autobiography *The Manner Is Ordinary,* "Father found himself increasingly absorbed in his work. It took him from home and with his absence from home came a rift in the web of domesticity . . . It finally dawned on Mother that she no longer completely possessed her John." It was during these frequent absences from his home and family that La Farge traveled with Adams.

By the summer of 1905, the artist's eyesight was failing, and Lizzie watched in pity as he groped when he came to steps or even a doorsill—a sure symptom of near-blindness. Lizzie reported, "In that way he seems old and uncertain. He came here to dine last night, talking of his health and his egg diet—he ate everything and second helpings. He has brought his work here to Newport—the stained glass for Columbia College Chapel. Whether he really works or not I do not know but he *thinks* he does." Noticing that the artist seemed suddenly very weary, she ordered her carriage and drove him to his home at Sunnyside Cottage, where she ordered his Japanese servant to put him to bed.

Adams, too, was aware of La Farge's physical decline and wrote sadly, "La Farge is shrunken, the stoop is becoming a hunch, he looks wrinkled and white. But he is still ten years younger than me and in mind is as young as he ever was!"

With John Singer Sargent, the American portrait painter living in London who "expressed too perfectly the taste of his own day," La Dona's relations were less cordial but admiring. Sargent, who had been born in Florence of American parents, settled in his Tite Street studio in London in the late 1880s. At first he was regarded with suspicion and his work was called "eccentric, bizarre, avant-garde and influenced by Impressionism." Soon, however, the tide changed, and he became a huge success. Consequently, he was lionized whenever he returned to America. Everyone who was anyone had to be painted by Sargent—it became a seal of success. The duchesses and countesses who had sat for him abroad were followed by a scramble of American ladies—and their husbands—who sought immortality.

Of course, Adams could not agree with the crowd. He was both fascinated and repulsed by Sargent's work, which often seemed to lay bare the soul of his sitter, although the artist maintained, "I chronicle—I do not judge." For the temperamentally secretive Adams, the portraits were too revealing, even though they generally caught an undeniable likeness. When Adams caught sight of Sargent's portrait of Asher Wertheimer, a London art dealer, he exclaimed, "Sargent has just completed another Jew. A worse crucifixion than history tells of." And Lizzie's reaction, when she attended the Buffalo Exhibit of Contemporary Painting, was similarly unflattering. "Whistler was immense and Sargent at his screaming worst. That Stokes picture [the dual portait of Mrs. Isaac Newton Phelps Stokes and her husband] should condemn him forever."

But La Dona had been quick to admire Sargent's impressive frieze of Old Testament prophets that adorned the new Boston Public Library. For this, the artist had used as his model for the prophet Malachi their mutual friend the emaciated French artist Paul Helleu. And when, in 1901, Lizzie was invited by U.S. Ambassador to Belgium Bellamy Storer and his wife, Maria Longworth Storer, to be presented at a court ball in Brussels, she wrote excitedly to Adams, "Quite an excitement! I am flying around trying to jew John Worth into a really pretty dress just as I jewed Sargent into a good academic portrait." Presumably she had succeeded in purchasing one of Sargent's academic works for a reasonable price.

Adams's ambivalence toward Sargent's work remained unchanged. Sargent had recently painted President Theodore Roosevelt, an experience of which the painter later wrote, "I felt like a rabbit in the presence of a boa constrictor." The presidential portrait was being held at the framer's, and no one was allowed to see it until the day of the public unveiling. But Adams managed to get permission to go to the framer's shop and to enjoy his own private showing. His reaction was grudgingly favorable. "The portrait is good Sargent and not very bad Roosevelt. It is not Theodore but a young intelligent idealist

John La Farge

Auguste Rodin

John Singer Sargent self-portrait

Augustus Saint-Gaudens

with a taste for athletics which I take to be Theodore Roosevelt's idea of himself. It is for once less brutal than its subject and will only murder everything in the White House. Indeed, it offers nothing to criticize except Sargent." Adams's friends John Hay and Henry Cabot Lodge sat for Sargent, and of their portraits Adams declared, "These two works put Sargent quite by himself. I am really pleased for once to admire without qualification."

It would have been fitting for Adams himself to pose for his portrait by the leading artist of the time, just as he had called on Richardson, the leading architect, to design his home. As the Sage of Lafayette Square and one of the nation's most distinguished historians, he certainly qualified as a subject. But Adams had a queer inverted ego, an ingrained secretiveness that made him unwilling to stand before the public view in a full-face portrait by Sargent or any other painter. What likenesses of him have survived—the black and white photographs, the sketch by John Potter, the watercolor by Mabel Hooper La Farge—are nearly always in profile, as if he could not directly face the public gaze. Similarly, it was his dread of biographers, whom he called "murderers," that led him to write *The Education of Henry Adams,* which is not a self-portrait at all.

Although La Dona usually followed Adams's lead in matters of art, nevertheless in this instance she recognized the importance of a portrait by Sargent. With a breezy willingness to overlook personal prejudice in the interest of history, she tried to cajole Adams into changing his mind. For a moment he hesitated when he wrote to her, "You have a sort of feminine faculty for making things seem worthwhile." Then he mused on the matter, "Sargent himself best knows his own merits and defects. Everyone parades his taste at Sargent's expense. Sargent gibbets us all with his everlasting condescension and patronage. We bore him. He paints it."

The truth was that Sargent had small use for Henry Adams, and he certainly had no need of further commissions as he was winding up his busy 1903 visit to the capital, after painting a number of Americans of varying distinction. But the burly artist was a patriot and a gentleman—he once refused a knighthood from King Edward VII, which would have required him to become a British subject, stating simply, "I am an American citizen." He decided to pay a customary call on Adams, "but without enthusiasm." The artist was received in the upstairs library, and what followed, as reported by Charles Merrill Mount, was a "scene of pure comedy": "The two men sitting in the quiet of Adams' library, inwardly glaring. Adams never penetrated to the contempt for him that Sargent concealed, the complete boredom in his company. Adams didn't realize that the purpose of the call was to give him a chance to speak up if he wanted to be painted like Theodore and John Hay." But Adams did not speak up. Later he wrote of their meeting, "At last the man I sought, the coruscating limelight of enthusiasm. Holy Virgin, how useless civility is when you have an artist to handle! Still I did my little phrase book and he looked as irresponsive as ever and so he soared to heaven—Sargent is stodgy."

Clearly the visit was not a success. Adams was confirmed in his refusal to sit for Sargent; the artist was confirmed in his dislike. Later Adams wrote with simple candor, "I never would let Sargent paint my portrait. I knew too well what he would do to me. I am too much of a coward." Lizzie Cameron was not so intransigent. Although she never sat for Sargent—she had already sat for Anders Zorn—she would turn, years later, to Sargent for his professional advice and receive a gracious reply.

But none of her previous encounters could have prepared La Dona for the experience of dealing with Auguste Rodin. This "immortal peasant," as his biographer Anita Leslie calls him, required all Lizzie's persistence, her imperiousness with men, and her ability to "drop into dialect," especially French dialect.

In the summer of 1895, Henry Adams had met Rodin. The French sculptor had the build of a peasant—"broad, stocky, strong as a bull with large hands and thick sensitive fingers." He wore his grizzled hair close-cropped, and above a bushy red beard his eyes were piercing. "Despite his heavy appearance," writes Anita Leslie, "he was sensitive and alert like a forest animal. No one ever domesticated Rodin. Claudel said he had the sincerity of a big dog, as happy and unselfconscious but with no affection in his nature. He cared for no one and nothing except the cruel taskmistress Art."

In the mid-nineties, Rodin's work was still the subject of controversy—he had not yet arrived at public acceptance. Only his fellow artists and a few discerning critics such as Henry Adams recognized the primeval force and artistic originality of the sculptor. But Adams, as a New Englander, was still a little defensive about Rodin's work when he wrote to Lizzie, "I do know that the shops offer no good pictures and that I am going, as a last resort, to call on Rodin and try to buy one of his small bronze figures. They are mostly so sensually suggestive that I shall have to lock them up when any girls are about, which is awkward. But Rodin is the only degenerated artist I know of whose work is original." A week later, Adams made his way to Rodin's studio at 182 rue de l'Université, which was made out of two converted sheds turned over to him by the French government. Among the jumble of marble figures, plaster and clay models, Adams stood, ambivalent as always, admiring and rejecting at the same time. He examined the works in marble, especially "a Venus and dead Adonis which he is sending to some exhibition in Philadelphia and which is too, too utter and decadent, but like all his things, hardly made for *jeunes personnes* like me and my breakfast table company." Yet he could not resist their power despite their "decadence." "Surely the meanest life on earth," he wrote, "is that of an age that has not a standard left or any form of morality or art except the British sovereign. I prefer Rodin's decadent sensualities. But I must not have them and though rotten with decadence I have not enough vitality left to be sensual. Victoria and our age are about equally genuine. We are beyond even vice."

Earlier, Adams had attended the annual opening of the Salon and reported that he found "little or nothing except Rodin's *Eve* and Saint Gaudens's *Sherman*." That Adams should pick out only these two highly dissimilar pieces for praise shows the breadth of his artistic perception. Saint-Gaudens's *Sherman* is excellent of its kind — 19th-century heroic statuary, surrounded by all the conventional symbolism of the period. But Rodin's *Eve* is an example of the new spirit that transcends period and speaks without artifice to the deepest human emotions. The bronze *Eve* is, according to the art critic Richard Ormond, "one of the most beautiful incarnations of the female form since the Greeks, full of robust life and in a natural attitude, suggesting her presentiment of coming motherhood as well as her natural anguish at thinking of the sorrow to which the coming generation is destined. The face is beautiful and tense with thought, the arms are folded over the breasts, one hand being raised as if to shield her face; the other grasping her left breast as if in pain or anxiety."

Studying the small bronze replica of *Eve*, Adams conceived the notion of buying it. Of course, he wanted Lizzie to meet Rodin and view his selection, partly out of his natural wish for her to share his experience of genius and partly out of a canny suspicion that La Dona would be more effective in business dealings with this unpredictable Frenchman. Adams realized that "Rodin is not in the least dishonest, only a peasant of genius, grasping, distrustful of himself socially, susceptible to the flattery of beautiful or fashionable women. He is buzzy about his contracts, keeps no books or memos, forgets all he says, hasn't the least idea of doing what he promised. If there were not a marble block in his way I doubt if he would remember to get it out of his way by executing the order."

So Adams turned to Saint-Gaudens to introduce La Dona to his French colleague. Obligingly, the American sculptor arranged to take her to Rodin's studio at 10 o'clock on a July morning. But finding himself unwell, he sent Lizzie his card, noting, "If you will present yourself with my card, you will be well received. *Cela va sans dire.*" Lizzie's reception at Rodin's was all that Saint-Gaudens had anticipated. The "immortal peasant" was delighted with La Dona. As Anita Leslie has observed,

> Rodin's morals would make an interesting study for Freudians who believe that all artistic energy is the result of sublimated or repressed sex. Like many artists he loved woman in the abstract but in practice made quite a different matter of it. To Rodin all the women he met were merely objects of delight, to be enjoyed, modeled and then forgotten. In his youth he adored Venus. Now he adored the reality—little gazelle-eyed creatures, easily obtained, easily forgotten. They came to pose and stayed to love—attracted by his fame.

But Mrs. Cameron was no little gazelle-eyed creature, as Rodin quickly learned. This elegant wife of a Pennsylvania senator was a lady and an American, and Rodin had had experience with *them*. When the young American dancer Isadora Duncan, who was impressed by his fame, came to his studio and danced barefoot for him, he tried to seduce her. Flatly she refused, leaving the Frenchman to exclaim with a shrug, "*Ah, ces Americaines . . .*"

As Lizzie tried to conduct some form of orderly negotiations for her friend M. Adams, the French sculptor began his siege. He sent her dozens of messages—hastily scrawled *cartes bleus,* anguished notes, written in his almost illegible handwriting and his unpolished French, delivered by messenger or by *carte pneumatique.* His object, hardly concealed, was to achieve a rendezvous with her, in his studio or in her apartment. Occasionally he would revert to Adams's order for the bronze Eve. "I ask your indulgence," he wrote in one note. "The bronze Eve will be ready—perhaps next week or perhaps this week. I want to bring it to you in person. Friday I will also be at my exhibit on the place de l'Alma for it is not closed until 3 P.M. On the 27th November there will be a lecture by M. Edmond Sicard—I will be indeed flattered if you wish to go there with me."

A fortnight later Lizzie expressed a wish to come to his studio, and Rodin was ecstatic. "I am overcome at the visit which you wish to pay me with one of your friends," he wrote. "Since the morning is convenient for you, do you wish to decide on Thursday morning or tomorrow [Wednesday] around 11? Can you come alone? I am your most expectant slave." Lizzie came, but accompanied by Martha. A few days later Rodin wrote to her, "Do you wish me to come on Friday or Saturday to pass the evening with you as you have suggested? I was very flattered by your visit and still more to be able to please you. The bronze is at the patina and I hope, as soon as possible, I can show it to you and bring it myself before your departure."

Rodin's visit to Lizzie's salon is described in witty detail by Henry Adams in a letter to Mrs. Cabot Lodge. "Martha is gaudy with a Parisian accent to scorn the Comédie Française. Her mother sits on the Louisquintsiest chairs with Anders Zorn's portrait behind her and talks wicked flattery to Rodin and Helleu and Edmund Saglio and any old *arrivés* that are handy while Martha reads Racine to me in the schoolroom and teaches me to *vibrer.*" Meanwhile, Adams noted, Joe Stickney was left with Henri Hubert to "study in a corner," and later Edith Wharton made an appearance and Brooks Adams arrived, uttering mournful predictions.

Although he was the center of attention, Rodin must have seen that here he was one among many and that his only chance of seeing Lizzie alone would be in his studio. So he continued to try, informing her that the bronze *Eve* now "has a new patina which seems superior to me. Your taste guides me well." Rodin could on occasion resort to the flowery compliment, as when he added, "I am always under the influence of your charming benevolence toward the artist who sends you this expression of his soul."

Two days later he wrote, "Tomorrow—Friday—toward five o'clock I wish to come to see you. I remember that Friday is your 'day.' I have worked on the marble which will soon be finished. I will need the address of M. Adams."

By now, Adams had expanded his order from the single bronze *Eve* to a half-dozen small figures, some of which were on commission from his Boston banker friend Henry Higginson, the founder in 1881 of the Boston Symphony Orchestra. Adams was particularly taken with the figure *Déséspoir,* a seated female figure, showing a woman whose head is hanging between her outstretched arms, which are clasping one raised foot, with every lineament expressing the anguish of despair. The sculptor had originally included *Déséspoir* among the throng of human figures making up his monumental door *La Porte de l'Enfer* (The Gate of Hell), which also included the famous *Le Penseur* (The Thinker). But he had detached it from the group to make a powerful freestanding figure. Adams had also chosen a bust of Alcestis and a rendering of *Les Bourgeois de Calais,* the heroic monument that depicts six hostages roped together as they walk toward their death. On this work the sculptor had been working for a decade, and today it is ranked as one of his greatest.

Adams realized that to place an order with Rodin was one thing, but to obtain its delivery or even its price was another. So he entrusted this task to Lizzie. After undergoing persistent prodding, the sculptor wrote to her triumphantly, "I found the price list. It is as follows:

Déséspoir (pour vous)	1900 francs
Alceste	2000 francs.

He added, "I think perhaps we spoke to you of the bronze Déséspoir and the Burghers of Calais. But they are not marked. Instead I have proposed for you one like the great bronze of Madame Johnson, I believe (the great lady who resembles you)." The price list continued:

Fugit Amore	4000 francs
La Terre et L'Illusion	2000 francs.

Then Rodin added, "Forgive this list which is so dry and accept my ardent and affectionate sentiments." Because Adams had suggested some changes in the statue of the goddess *Ceres* which he had ordered, the artist added a postscript: "The marble Ceres is perhaps a little modern in expression, but I think the sculpture has value. In modeling, if we make all the changes, something would be lost I think. I will do it and be happy—some of the changes but I cannot guarantee it." At the top of the price list he had scrawled, "Twenty-five hundred francs for the bronze Eve." The following day Rodin received his money from Mrs. Cameron. But a month later, Adams was writing Lizzie plaintively from Washington, "My Rodin does not arrive." Then he continued in a minor key, "My lease in Paris is for a year but I have nothing to do there. I am not sorry for an excuse to leave it. If you are not there, there is no reason for staying. Life is an intolerable bore except when one is in love." Adams's habitual melancholy was undoubtedly exacerbated by Lizzie's involvement in the Stickney affair, which he could only deplore but not prevent.

A week later, due to a misunderstanding with his landlord in Paris, Adams in Washington was horrified to find that the apartment on the avenue du Bois was closed to him, Lizzie was locked out, and all of his possessions in Paris were now the responsibility of Mrs. Cameron. To Lizzie he wrote on 18 February 1901: "You poor martyred angel. I am white with wrath. By abandoning my furniture, my manuscript [*Chartres*], Rodin and you to those monkey-children of apes, I can escape with life. Kelley must pay off Mrs. Markwald, rescue my traps from the apartment, have them stored, shut it up, pay Jean, recover the cast of the Rodin which is lost and make my printer surrender my manuscript. Now what next? With Paris closed, where am I to go?"

Lizzie was less disturbed. She found other quarters in a delightful little three-story duplex apartment at 6 square du Bois de Boulogne and set up her salon again. Soon Rodin was writing to her, "With great joy I accept for luncheon next Sunday noon at your house. This will be a delicious moment among my bad ones. I have thought of you often. But amid the turbulence of my thoughts your face has brought a happy moment." The luncheon was a great success. Lizzie had invited a group of French artists, for whom the presence of the great Rodin was a drawing card. Delightedly Lizzie described the occasion for Adams, "How the lions roared! They sat here til after four, talking amazingly of each other and their brother artists. I had Rodin, Menard, the Paul Helleus and André Saglio to lunch. William Gay came without Walter who was ill. How brilliant my lunch—I felt I had a salon. Rodin came out very well, much better than I expected."

The loudest lion of the group was now the captive of La Dona. Soon Rodin was writing to her again, begging to see her, now that he was over his recent illness. "To my great joy I am a little less martyrized now and so I will come to see you. Permit me to come to your house on Monday next at five o'clock which is your hour. I will tell you how I have treasured in my memory the souvenir of your bounty and that every time I think of it, it is with the terror of appearing indifferent. My profoundest respect and the eagerness with which I am your slave . . . " A few weeks later, he again tried to entice her. "The bronze is here at the studio. Do you want to come here to see it? Do you want me to carry it to you at your home or to its destination? Your friend M. Adams came and wants several more works."

Adams had visited the Rodin studio in the company of Bessie Lodge, the bride of the poet Bay Lodge, and he wrote to Lizzie, "Michelangelo has a pronounced feebleness for handsome women. He was very gracious to her and she to him." A week later, Adams told Lizzie, "Henry Higginson credits me 1000 francs to buy some Rodin bronzes. You've got to select four or five bronzes for I won't and I can't bargain."

Despite Rodin's extravagant assurances of devotion to Mrs. Cameron, the sculptor still had not produced the bronze *Eve* that Adams had ordered months before. Now Adams wanted several more works, and it was Lizzie's task to pursue him. Fortunately, she was willing to put up with his endless delays. On 23 November 1901, ten months after he had been paid for the statue of Eve, the sculptor wrote to La Dona: "I am very happy to know you are in Paris and yesterday I thought about going to present my compliments to you at 5 o'clock. But I could not. I had too many people at my place—is it possible to go to see you on Tuesday at 5 P.M. or on any other day at any hour you suggest? I am also happy that you want some more bronzes from me, on the part of your friends. I am installed—almost—at Meudon and I will hope for a visit from you one fine day there or at my studio in the rue de l'Université any day except Tuesday or Thursday. This week I will be there all afternoon."

Three days later, Adams, as he was preparing to depart for Washington, was making another try. In exasperation, he explained to Clover's niece Louisa Hooper, "I've fixed Rodin for tomorrow. I will worry him out of all the bronzes I can squeeze." Needless to say, he did not succeed, and he had to leave for Washington empty-handed. The game of hide-and-seek went on, with Rodin continuing his unsuccessful pursuit of Lizzie while Lizzie attempted to secure the bronzes. In January 1902, she descended on him in his studio in order to find the *Déséspoir* for Adams, who wanted it as a gift for Helen Hay. Anxiously, she queried Adams, "Will that do for Helen? If not, a monster and a girl which seem to me sufficiently indecent."

In May, Adams was back in Paris seeking the elusive Rodin, but, as Adams complained, "He is still cavorting about Europe flattered as never before, oblivious to work." Next, Adams ordered Lizzie to draw from his account 5,000 francs for Rodin and "use what you want of it until he wants it or pay for my bronze and take it away." Lizzie finally succeeded in wresting the *Déséspoir* and another bronze from Rodin, and the sculptor wrote to her, "I am happy to have been able to please you with the bronze Déséspoir. My thanks for the sum of 1500 francs. . ." Hardly believing his good fortune, Adams wrote, "Mrs. Cameron has carried off two Rodin bronzes. They are safe. Rodin promises two more this week." Finally, in June, Adams caught up with Rodin and demanded a price list.

> When he sent a memo of his prices, [Adams reported to Henry Higginson] I was startled to find that he had doubled his prices and said nothing of the objects ordered a year ago. Then, Mrs. Cameron sailed in and asked him flatly what it meant. He sent the following:
>
> | Frère et Soeur | 2200 francs |
> |---|---|
> | Vulcain | 1500 francs |
> | Poète | 1500 francs |
> | Burghers de Calais | 2200 francs |
> | Alceste | 2600 francs |
> | | 10000 francs |
>
> Je perd 5000—
> [I am losing 5000 francs]
>
> Who was furious on receipt of this rustic epistle was Milady Cameron [chuckled Adams]. But as she had planned to go the next day to England to meet her husband and pass the summer there, she had only time to write him a pretty sharp note.

Lizzie left the note with Adams, who called in Joe Stickney to translate it into impeccable French. This was a gesture undoubtedly wasted on Rodin, for the peasant genius's handwritten notes suffered from weak grammar and uncertain spelling. However, the note from Lizzie and a covering letter from Adams were despatched to the rue de l'Université. In his stiff note, Adams declared: "With regret I leave the question of loss of commission for which I feel responsible, owing to my desire that Higginson send me 5,000 francs for bronzes to be shown in Boston to a person who loved your work. Of course I can't allow a loss either to you or Mrs. Cameron or Higginson. If there is any loss it belongs wholly to me. So you must send here to Mrs. Cameron whatever work has already been ordered and done and I will send you a check for whatever amount you name. Two bronzes as delivered will be paid at your price. I will write Higginson I can't carry out his wishes for the rest."

The Frenchman showed himself puzzled at the double-barreled attack from Madame Cameron and her friend Monsieur Adams. He held the notes a few days, then wrote to Adams ingratiatingly, "I am touched at the courtesy of your letter and Mme. Cameron's. The marble bust [of *Ceres*] a little modern, with hair and drapery is 8000 francs. I find it a complete work of art. There are two bronzes at Mme. Cameron's. Three will cost 3000 francs [that included 1000 for the *Alcestis*]—for I am doing my best that your generosity will not go to your disadvantage."

"I am not responsible," Adams noted, "for the great master's grammar. But he has conceded more than we asked."

On a sweltering day in mid-July, the burly sculptor, dressed in his work clothes covered with marble dust, arrived at Henry Adams's door, accompanied by his studio assistant. Together they were struggling under the weight of the massive statue of *Alcestis*, which they delivered to the astonished Adams. "I can't understand," Adams later told Higginson, "why Rodin didn't write since I promised to take whatever he gave and pay what he liked. Evidently he mistrusted me or he wanted to show what a gentleman he is, for he wasted a couple of hours on a stupid errand an American sculptor would have sent an Irishman on. In he came like a country peasant" into Adams's well-appointed drawing room, and here the French sculptor and the American historian confronted each other.

The interview began awkwardly. Adams expressed his admiration of the bronze *Alcestis*. Rodin professed to admire only the patina, the "bronze dress" of the lady, since "he did not wish to seem to admire his own work."

Then the master sculptor made his grand gesture. He pulled out of his pocket "a little bronze seven inches high—just the distance between his huge thumb and forefinger." It was a work which Adams described as "An excessively Rodinesque bronze gem, unpolished, but about the most frankly undressed pair he had ever made. This, he said, was a substitute for the Burghers of Calais."

With Gallic enthusiasm, Rodin exclaimed, *"Que c'est beau—le patine, je veux dire"* (How beautiful it is, the patina, I mean). Apparently he was trying to show how fine it was, lest Adams should think it was insufficient. In an effort to equal Rodin's noble gesture, Adams declared, "I exhausted my vocabulary of superlatives in echoing his. We each acted our part a little clumsily but we didn't break down. He was glad to be let escape so easily. I was glad to be off so cheaply—instead of 5 bronzes at 5000 francs I have four at 4000. Instead of buying for you [Higginson] I am buying for myself. According to his present scale, those four pieces cost 7000 francs. When one deals with an artist, $200 or $300 takes on the proportions of a hippodrome. I will keep the bronzes, marble and all, with pleasure or send them all to you.

"I've had a good $500 amusement out of it . . ."

Both Adams and Rodin were reasonably satisfied. Adams had acquired several priceless works of art, and Rodin had acquired an important American patron. And Adams had been shaken out of his chronic ennui.

But what they both missed, during the long chase and in the final *opera buffa* encounter, was the recognition that, despite language and cultural differences, each of these two artists, outstanding in their respective fields, possessed the same love and veneration of the art of the French Gothic that would lead each of them to produce a literary masterpiece. Since Rodin knew almost no English, it is unlikely that he ever read Adams's *Mont-Saint-Michel and Chartres*. And Adams, although competent in reading French, because of the general dislocation caused by the Great War, probably never saw Rodin's book *Cathedrals of France,* which was published in Paris in 1914. It was Rodin's only book, and the French text, with its accompanying sketches taken from his notebooks, record his impressions, both artistic and spiritual, of the Gothic cathedrals, both the famous and the less known at Rheims, Chartres, Laon, Amiens, Le Mans, Etampes, Nantes, Nevers, and Soissons. The book, which was published in France three years before Rodin's death and issued in an English translation in 1965, is a series of lyrical meditations on French Gothic architecture and sculpture, which the author sees as synonymous. As Herbert Read states, "The writing again and again rises to heights of eloquence that are essentially poetic but it is always a poetry inspired by a sensuous contact with the living stones."

Both Adams and Rodin, whose lives were almost the same in length—Adams, 1838-1918; Rodin, 1840-1917—were enraptured by the same magic. Where Adams wrote, "Whatever Chartres may be now, when young it was a smile," Rodin wrote, "Chartres has become a hymn of praise for eternity. Chartres is wise with an intense passion. Before this Cathedral my first impression is total astonishment." And Adams countered with, "To us it is a child's fancy, a toyhouse to please the Queen of Heaven, to please her so much that she would be happy in it—to charm her til she smiled."

Just as Adams had worshipped the Virgin as "the greatest artist, as she was the greatest philosopher and musician and theologist that ever lived," so Rodin responded to the divine mother: "The Virgin triumphs in the high pediment; the coronation of Woman, divine gesture to which, with all the angels, all men concur as enraptured servants. The triumph of gentleness, apotheosis of obedience, masterpiece of advice to women. This radiant one holds her child, the Son of God. And is not the child of every woman always the son of God?"

As for Lizzie Cameron, who had briefly touched the life of Rodin as she had permanently influenced that of Adams, she had played her role superbly. She had dazzled this artist who was one of the greatest creators of female beauty since Michelangelo—Rodin of whom it was said, "he was not afraid of the impossible problem of showing emotion by motion in static marble."

Like any great artist, Rodin had the last word. As an old man he observed, "I have loved women so much it is pleasant to discover that I regard them only from the viewpoint of sculpture."

14

"A 12th-Century Monk"

Henry Adams spent the last years of the 19th century and the first years of the 20th in completing *Mont-Saint-Michel and Chartres,* a soaring celebration of the spirit of the Middle Ages and the creative energy of the Virgin.

By a delicate irony, which Adams perhaps recognized, the original inspiration for this book was his worldly madonna—La Dona, who herself had no understanding of the Mother of God who dominated Adams's imagination. In his *Education* he would write, "Adams owed more to the American woman than to all the American men he ever heard of." If, as is probable, the "American woman" meant Elizabeth Cameron to him, then surely it was inevitable that Adams, in his pursuit of her, having been demoted to the role of "tame cat," should turn for emotional sustenance to the original madonna of whom Lizzie was a fallible descendant.

While he was working on *Chartres,* Adams described himself as "a 12th-century monk in a 19th-century attic." Although his Paris "attic" on the avenue du Bois seemed a rather elaborate setting for a medieval monk, his labors on this history of the art and architecture, history, and philosophy of the Middle Ages showed all the dedication of the humblest scribe in a monastic order. Since 1895, when Adams had begun his ten-day tour of the French cathedral country in the company of the Lodges, his imagination had been captivated by the images of the Virgin's power that he glimpsed in all the Gothic churches—at Rheims, Amiens, Rouen, Le Mans, Chartres, and Paris. As he would write in *The Education of Henry Adams,*

> For Adams the virgin was an adorable mistress who led the automobile and its owner where she would to her wonderful palaces and chateaux, kindly receiving, amusing, charming and dazzling her lover as though she were Aphrodite herself . . . . He was only too glad to yield himself entirely, not to her charm or to a sentimentality of religion, but to her mental and physical energy of creation which had built up these World's Fairs of 13th-century force that turned Chicago and St. Louis pale . . . . So he went on wooing, happy in the thought that at last he had found a mistress who could see no difference in the age of her lovers.

Adams explored the Norman Cathedral of Coutances and the Benedictine Abbey of Mont-Saint-Michel, which he called "my dear Coutances and my divine Mont-Saint-Michel." The abbey was built in 1066 on a rock rising 250 feet above the sea off the coast of Normandy. He reported that the two sons of Senator Lodge dragged him up and down walks, moats, cliffs, and beaches. The trio investigated every niche of the granite abbey of St. Michael of the Sea-in-Peril, so called because the treacherous 50-foot tides that swirl twice daily against the giant rocks have claimed unnumbered lives. The Romanesque church is perched on the craggy top of the island whose sloping sides contain a huddle of ancient stone buildings that once housed an order of Benedictine monks. Their motto *"Laborare est orare"* (To work is to pray) is a fitting one for an order that performed the monumental work of erecting an abbey in such a seemingly impossible site. The monks had fostered the legend, in the age of faith, that the abbey had been built at the order of the Archangel Michael himself.

"The Archangel loved heights," Adams would write in the opening page of his book, as he described the statue of the militant defender of the faith. "Standing on the summit of the tower that crowned his church, wings upspread, sword uplifted, the devil crawling beneath, and the cock, symbol of eternal vigilance, perched on his mailed foot, Saint Michael held a place of his own in heaven and on earth which seems, in the 11th century, to leave hardly room for the Virgin of the Crypt at Chartres, still less for the Beau Christ of the 13th century at Amiens. The Archangel stands for Church and State, and both militant. He is the conqueror of Satan, the mightiest of all created spirits, the nearest to God."

Within the shadow of the archangel's wings, pilgrims and tourists for more than nine hundred years have journeyed across the dangerous waters to view the great Romanesque abbey and sometimes to join the Benedictines in their observance of the monastic hours.

Adams felt a special affinity for the Archangel Michael. Had not John Hay dubbed Adams "Porcupinus Angelicus" and commissioned Saint-Gaudens to design a medal depicting his dual nature? And did not Adams, the small but imposing figure with the soaring imagination, also love heights, both actual and figurative? He was, after all, an Adams and so destined to loom above the crowd.

Guardedly, Adams had approached the work, which would cost him years of unremitting labor, although in 1899 he estimated to Lizzie Cameron that "it would cost a year's work and about $1000." He immersed himself in a study of the Romanesque style of architecture with its heavy masses and rounded arches and contrasted it with the pointed arches, soaring lines, and flying buttresses of the Gothic style. He made these two widely different architectural styles the dominating spirits of his book just as they dominated the Middle Ages: the masculine spirit as epitomized in the militant Archangel Michael, defending the faith against all foes, and the feminine spirit of loving mercy as found in the Virgin presiding over Chartres Cathedral, whom

Adams recognized as "the greatest energy the world has ever known, the generative power of sex." From its inception as an appreciation of medieval churches, the book grew into a celebration of the philosophy, history, and art of the Middle Ages and the unique role that the Virgin Mother of God played in the history of mankind.

Concentrating his prodigious energy on his research, Adams visited cathedrals and museums, accumulated hundreds of photographs, swallowed whole libraries of learned books. He steeped himself in the history of the Crusades, the legends of Charlemagne, the chansons of Roland, the architecture of Amiens and Coutances and Chartres, the theology of Thomas Aquinas and Bernard of Clairvaux. On sunny days he toured the French countryside in his chauffeur-driven, 18-horsepower Mercedes Benz in search of stained glass, declaring, "My idea of Paradise is a perfect automobile going 30 miles an hour on a smooth road to a 12th-century cathedral." Day after day he sat for hours in the Cathedral of Chartres, raptly regarding the incomparable windows and the exquisite carvings in stone and in wood. "I am somewhat like a monkey looking through a telescope at the stars. At least I can see that it must have been great." Studying the Cathedral of Coutances, he remarked, "The squirming devils under the feet of the apostles looked uncannily like me and my generation."

To La Dona he explained, "My 12th century is my single resource chiefly because it never knew ennui. When it was bored somebody got killed." Lizzie retorted, "For my part I am very glad the 12th century is so far away and that things move on. I like a bathroom and I'm glad I can have strawberries and can reach Rome in 30 hours in a heated car. See how unsympathetic I am!"

Yet, lest he think she did not really care about his new enthusiasm, she added, "Of course I want to be with you. I want to see medieval France and Germany and stained glass with you and have you tell me all the things I ought to admire."

Still too engrossed in his research to begin writing, Adams told her that he was contemplating "a drama of the Second Crusade with Queen Eleanor of Guienne as heroine and myself to act as St. Bernard and reprove her morals." He did not begin the first draft of his book until the fall of 1899, then shelved it during his annual winter visit to Washington. It was at this time that Adams noticed that "Martha is beginning to be dangerously handsome."

By mid-May of 1900, Adams was back in Paris, devoting himself to studying the legendary miracles of the Virgin, "using Thomas Aquinas like liquid air for cooling the hot blood of my youth." The international exposition had just opened, and Adams noted, "Paris is full of Americans, from Pierpont Morgan downwards, Paris is really an American city and perhaps that is its future. I am a colonist battling with the savage natives." The "colony" of which he spoke was the large American enclave whose members devoted their considerable wealth and leisure to the pursuit of endless pleasure.

Meanwhile, Lizzie was prodding her reluctant daughter to leave the safety of her adolescent cocoon and emerge as a social butterfly. But Lizzie wrote to Adams despondently, "I always said that though infinitely old I am younger than Martha."

This youthful spirit of Lizzie's and her habit, whenever she traveled, of attracting a variety of European titles amused Adams. "What a gift you have," he wrote to her. "If you could only give it to your poor little girl Martha and her little boy Dordy! You pick up nobility wherever you go. What title do you intend to take? Countess? Princess? Duchess?" Slyly he was poking fun at her discreetly veiled ambition for a titled husband for Martha, during a period when many American mothers, with substantial money and social aspirations, were openly seeking European counts and princes and dukes for their daughters, sometimes with disastrous results, as in the case of Consuelo Vanderbilt.

During the summer of 1900, Adams labored on his first draft of *Mont-Saint-Michel and Chartres*. In one of his daily letters to Lizzie, he wrote, "Tell Martha that my metaphysical chapter is nearly done and I want to send it for her to read and tell me what she doesn't understand so I can correct it." This exaggerated flattery could not fail to please both Martha and her mother. By October, he was appealing to their joint facility in the French language to read his free rendering into English of the Old French ballades "to see if it hitches anywhere." Responding to this request, Lizzie replied with enthusiasm, "Your verses are exquisite. It gives one quite a feeling to realize that Thibaut was writing with such delicacy of sentiment over 600 years ago. In what have we progressed? Your rendering is beautiful. You have the poetic quality strong—I wonder why you didn't do more."

As a confirmed skeptic, Henry Adams was approaching his study of the Catholic Church during the time of its greatest influence on civilization with the mind of an admiring unbeliever who could never accept the dogma of the Church but who nevertheless could not resist the attraction of the Virgin. He defined his attitude to the medieval scholar Henry Osborn Taylor. "Dear brother in the 13th century: I think you even believe a little, or sometimes, in human reason or intelligence which I try to do in vain. You respect the Church, I adore the Virgin."

Meanwhile, the mother and child, Lizzie and Martha, were vacationing in the Swiss Alps near Vallorbe, in the shadow of the Jungfrau. La Dona decided that Martha, despite her distaste for it, needed exercise, so she planned a mountain-climbing expedition on one of the more manageable hills near Lauterbrunnen. The two ladies, with Martha carrying Kiki, set out unaccompanied, each wearing a long skirt, a snug jacket, and a warm cape covering the whole outfit. Lizzie carried a white parasol to avoid sunstroke, a Baedeker to point out the sights of interest, and a leash to restrain Kiki. Martha carried a Kodak, a picnic basket, and a package of knitting wool. It was a warm day, and as they began their climb, the sun grew hot. Soon their capes came off, their jackets went into the basket, and the poodle's tongue hung out. Lizzie took off her cape, rolled it into a cushion to which she attached the picnic basket, and placed the unwieldy burden on her shoulders in a kind of backpack. They struggled up 3,000 feet, but by then Martha was recalcitrant and refused to climb further. So, red-faced and clutching her camera, Martha, followed by Lizzie still valiantly gripping her parasol, began the descent, which Lizzie described as "a hard run, with knees bent and all brakes on."

Lizzie was unsympathetic to Martha's anguish. "You know her courage," she told Adams with sarcasm. "Her fears emerged as we got into the valley. Her howls grew louder and she finally dropped flat in the middle of the path. She refused to go on—it was only the first of her collapses. How I laughed! It was so characteristic. But of course she had to come on, there was no alternative. Finally we reached Lauterbrunnen—we had walked only five miles but the descent of 3,000 feet on a path of loose rocks gave us blisters and stiffness. The whole expedition makes us feel as old as you talk."

While Adams was continuing his visits to 12th-century cathedrals, Lizzie took Martha on a pilgrimage to Lourdes, the grotto where the French peasant girl Bernadette Soubirous had seen a vision of the Virgin and which had now become a tourist attraction. Lizzie described it for Adams. "The grotto is a wide shallow cave which holds 30 people and votive candles. Overhead are canes and crutches, with none of the tinsel of the modern church. All is bareness and simplicity. All these poor crutches—the whole thing is very touching indeed. But the squalor and filth of the town is like Cripple Creek after gold was discovered."

In April 1901, before starting out for Florence to meet Stickney, Lizzie complained to Adams that, as usual, she had heard nothing from Don. "I am still in uncertainty. Does Don mean me to re-let that house [in Paris], to go home or to stay here? I'm tired of Europe but what else is there? Don writes to Martha but he says so little. I could cut a straight swathe if it were not for her. . ."

Adams in his reply was able to tell her he had recently seen Senator Cameron but had no idea of his plans. Just before leaving New York to sail for London, "the last person I saw and breakfasted with on my way to the dock was your husband. He seemed in a very good humor—he was not caught in the squeeze. He insisted on introducing me to Henry Clay Frick. . ."

Before they parted, Don asked Adams numerous questions about his daughter. In his reply, Adams spoke so warmly of "her perfections" that he found "it choked my voice with tears." Cameron told Adams that he feared his daughter was suffering from "precocious development," to which news Lizzie made no reply.

For a time during the year 1901, Adams set aside the writing of *Mont-Saint-Michel and Chartres* partly because he was unsettled by Lizzie's behavior with Trumbull Stickney and partly because he wanted to await La Farge's opinion of his manuscript, which he sent to him, asking for "further guidance and suggestion before burning the stuff." On reading it, La Farge was quite overcome by the work, which Adams still called his "Miracles of the Virgin." In discussing it with Adams, the artist's voice became "quite husky with admiration."

When, in late summer of 1901, Adams resumed his work on the manuscript, ensconced in Lizzie's Paris apartment, he managed to find time each day to write to her and Martha. Sitting at Martha's desk, he could not resist teasing Lizzie obliquely about her aspirations for her daughter. He pictured himself in Martha's chair, reading the correspondence between Empress Maria Theresa and Ambassador Marcy concerning Marie Antoinette and the diamond necklace. (This priceless jewelry which Cardinal de Rohan had purchased for the French queen—although she later denied it—became a *cause célèbre* which resulted in a famous trial and was regarded as one of the proximate causes of the French Revolution.) "It leaves the Queen without a tolerable quality or excuse and proves that she intrigued with Cardinal Rohan for the necklace. And all the time I was thinking that you were Maria Therese and Martha at 15 was sent off to be Queen and what would have become of her? Really I hope she would not have been so weak or vicious or false. Perhaps if Marie had not turned out so badly as Queen her mother would not have been so imperial an Empress. I wonder! Some day when you are fifty and Martha is married and I am in a bath chair, read the book and consider the problem."

During the following year, while Adams was continuing his labor on *Chartres,* and after the Cameron-Stickney romance was over, Joe Stickney brought to visit Adams his gifted friend Shane Leslie, a cousin of Winston Churchill's who was studying at the Sorbonne. The young Irishman was entranced with the historian. "He was the wisest and most cynical of Americans, the great Henry Adams," wrote Leslie. "I had the sense to listen to him with delight, which touched the wise and weird old man. He was at his zenith, talking exquisitely about blue china, the modern dynamo, Chartres Cathedral and Mrs. Cameron. It was sheer luck lunching with him and hearing his fine talk on Mont-Saint-Michel and Chartres with Paris gossip thrown in like garlic into a salad."

Leslie and Stickney continued to visit "Uncle Henry" whenever their university studies would allow, and Leslie recalled that one day Adams pronounced to him in awe-inspiring tones, "You must come to a conclusion sooner or later whether the center of the universe is masculine or feminine."

Clearly Adams himself had no doubts that it was feminine. His conversation and his book were informed with this conviction. "Nature regards the female as the essential, the male as the superfluity of her world." Once he remarked, "American history is so dull, there is not a woman in it." But in his private history, he was ruled by a woman, and all the pages of his book - *Chartres* reflect this.

By 1902, Adams had nearly finished the first draft of his manuscript, and he longed to read it aloud to his most attentive audience—Lizzie and Martha. Now that she was back in Paris, Lizzie was established at her new address at 6 square du Bois de Boulogne—a small duplex apartment that had its own front door and a kitchen that was below street level and opened into a little courtyard in the rear. The front entrance opened into a square hall, with a door on one side leading to her salon and on the other to a small dining room and a library. A little winding stairway led to the wide, sunny bedrooms on the top floor. Surrounded by tall ancient trees, the elegant little house and its quiet mews might have been set in the French countryside instead of in the heart of Paris.

Visiting Martha that summer were her cousin Elizabeth Hoyt and her friend Gladys Rice of New York, both of whom were studying landscape gardening. The two girls were enormously impressed with Martha's mother. Years later, when she was Mrs. Van Wyck Brooks, Gladys, in her memoirs *Boston and Return,* recalled Lizzie vividly. "We were both in dread of Mrs. Cameron's disapproval, which was rarely stated halfway. For she was a person of unlimited experience in every imaginable situation of a lofty and glamorous sort." The wide-eyed teenagers had heard stories of Lizzie's salon on Lafayette Square, her visits to the great houses in England, Austria, and Hungary, and her attendance at shooting weekends at the country places of the nobility. To their delight, she described for them a ball that she had attended in an ancestral castle. The guests, she explained, entered a ballroom lighted by flaming torches, which were held aloft in the hands of uniformed flunkeys, who stood motionless against the walls, wearing powdered peruques and gold-braided scarlet liveries.

"But Mrs. Cameron," interrupted Gladys, "didn't the flunkeys get dreadfully tired, standing there hour after hour without moving?"

"It was part of their duty not to betray their feelings," La Dona replied crisply. "Those were, of course, well-trained servants."

The girl was stunned. Such a matter-of-fact viewpoint seemed merciless to her and made it difficult to resolve the balance of right and wrong, because "Mrs. Cameron was used to deference in the matter of her opinions. It seemed not possible to believe her mistaken. Her pronouncements were final."

Lizzie reminded Gladys of the goddess Pallas Athena, "with her steady forward gaze and unsmiling mouth and the habit she had of command." She seemed a "goddess imbued with wisdom. Had Pallas Athena been imbued also with warmth of heart. . .?"

During the third week of the girls' stay, Henry Adams arrived in Paris and came at once to call. Before his arrival, Gladys had noticed that almost every morning's mail had brought a letter addressed to Mrs. Cameron in his "round hand of carefully constructed script. She herself spent several hours at her desk during the week, writing to 'Uncle Henry,' the nickname [which had] become almost universal . . ."

Gladys confessed that she fell at once under his spell—

> his curiously short stature, his darting forward motion like that of a small boy intent on finding what lay ahead, the rapidity combined with the inconsequence of his gesture. When he chose to rest, deep in a chair, slumped, one leg crossed above the other, he seemed momentarily to retire, to shrink as does a hibernating animal, to become almost anonymous. . . . His abstract utterances as well as his queries appeared only indirectly to issue from the man himself, small as he was, unimpressive as a physical being, the sharply pointed beard that he wore concealing much of his facial expression.

This was a memorable summer for the two girls. Martha was away for a visit, but Mrs. Cameron kept "an authoritative eye" on them. She set them to work at embroidery, a genteel occupation that she considered "quieting to the spirit of a young woman in the making." Over her embroidery, Gladys watched Adams surreptitiously,

> fascinated but fearful of being singled out as an inept target for the swift thrusts of his interrogating mind, I saw that he was not unkind or caustic. Rather, he was a seeker, passionate, eager, trusting, longing to believe in the treasure he now and then found. And the smile that at moments enlivened his eyes seemed to moderate the oracle's rights to stern order.... [Gladys was invited to become a niece, joining the sisterhood of aspirants for his favor.] I learned, however, when Uncle Henry turned to the manuscript for the book later given the title of *Mont-Saint-Michel and Chartres*, he favored nieces as an institution.... I was entirely willing to be a niece in wish, to play, 'for the time,' the enviable role that Alice in Wonderland played for Lewis Carroll.

The select little audience listened raptly as Adams read from his manuscript. Dressed in a sapphire velvet tea gown, Mrs. Cameron sat in her favorite brocaded armchair, while the two girls sat erect, on either side of a tall reading lamp, toying with their needlework, while Adams, leaning forward in his zeal, read the story of religious architecture and its influence on the 12th and 13th centuries in France.

Gladys Rice showed a remarkable understanding of Adams's intentions as she heard his slightly husky voice, with its clipped British pronunciation, read from his Chapter Six, "The Virgin of Chartres." "I came closer," she remarked, "to the mysteries that veil the Virgin and her child and, little by little, to the man who wrote of them, the man who, wrapping his arms close about them, sought to solve the enigma of life itself."

Dropping her embroidery in her lap, Gladys peered at the face of Henry Adams, looking "for a sign of the suffering that must, I know, lie in his heart. But I could not find a trace in the tidy, aloof aspect of the little man beneath the reading lamp." He came presently to the Virgin of Chartres, his Lady of Love. On and on he continued, "as though to pronounce aloud the words written with his pen brought verification of his thought." All three of the women felt, hearing the timbre of his voice in the hushed room, that he enjoyed dwelling especially upon the Virgin, upon our Lady of Chartres whose essence he perennially strove to touch.

Adams paused to turn the pages until he came upon the sentence in Chapter Seven, "The Church at Chartres belonged not to the people, not to the priesthood, and not to Rome; it belonged to the Virgin." Quietly he laid aside the sheets of the manuscript. The reading was over for the evening.

In April 1902, Adams wrote to Lizzie triumphantly, "I am perfectly square with the Virgin Mary, having finished and wholly rewritten the whole volume!"

During this time in Paris, Lizzie was entertaining Adams's friend Margaret Ward Chanler, who had, among her ten children, a daughter Laura who was Martha's age. An unspoken rivalry existed between Margaret Chanler and Lizzie Cameron. "I feel great sympathy for Mrs. Chanler," Lizzie confided to Adams, "she is a beauty, yet I don't like her." And Laura Chanler would later report, "My mother did not like her either. They were too different." An author and a literary critic, Mrs. Chanler was happy to be numbered among Uncle Henry's "nieces." A devout Catholic, Margaret Chanler may have resented the fact that it was La Dona to whom Adams chose to read his manuscript of *Chartres*. And when in 1908 she learned of the existence of his "Prayer," she begged him for a copy—probably suspecting that Lizzie Cameron had seen it earlier but not realizing that he had sent it to La Dona as soon as he had finished it.

Whatever the reasons, the two women disliked each other. And Laura Chanler, who became a lifelong friend of Martha Cameron's, was instinctively hostile to Martha's mother. "I didn't like Mrs. Cameron," she says.

> There was about her a smell of artificiality which even as a small child I could detect in those friends of my mother who were trying to impress *her* by exclaiming over *me*. Mrs. Cameron was too worldly—she was very different from my mother. I cannot understand her so-called charm. Of course I never saw her with Henry Adams. Yet she was generous. She gave me a Cartier watch which I lost and expensive jewelry. She was different from Martha who was tall and straight and typically Scotch. Martha didn't like jewelry, she hated exercise and preferred to bury herself in books. She was straightforward and direct but of course she was dominated by her mother. She was not outgoing—yet I liked her. We were good friends. . . .

Now that Adams's work on his manuscript was completed, he resumed his old pose of anonymity—omitting his name from the title page and referring to his book as "my declaration of principles as head of the Conservative Christian Anarchists, a party numbering one member." Still rankling at the disappointing reception accorded to his *History*, he decided to order a private edition of 100 copies. But the volume must be worthy of its subject, for, as he wrote to Lizzie, "My only hope of heaven is the Virgin. If I tried to vulgarize her and made her as cheap as cowboy literature I should ask for eternal punishment as a favor." Adams turned the manuscript over to the printing firm of J. H. Furst and Company in Baltimore and ordered 100 copies at a cost of $1,000. But on 7 February 1904, a great fire swept the city and destroyed the business district at a loss of $150,000,000. Adams learned that a portion of the printer's copy had disappeared. This "snarl" caused additional work for the author and a delay in the printing so that the book was not finished until December 1904.

From the selected readers who had received their copies of *Chartres* came immediate approval. Henry James praised "its easy lucidity, its saturation with its subject, its charmingly taken and kept tone. Even more than I congratulate you on the book, I envy you your relation to the subject." His brother William James rhapsodized, "From beginning to end it reads as from a man in the fresh morning of life with a frolic power unusual to historic literature. . . . Where you stole all that St. Thomas, I should like to know!"

Saint-Gaudens wrote, "You dear old Porcupinus Poeticus. . .You know (damn you), I never read, but last night I got as far in your work as the Virgin, Eve and the Bees, and I cannot wait to acknowledge it until I am through." Charles Warren Stoddard wrote, "You are a brilliant ornament of the Church and ought to be canonized."

Adams had sent copies of the book to his close friends, his family, and his nieces, as well as to leading libraries. A few went to outstanding women's colleges "to unsettle young Protestant women" and a handful to Catholic churches "to irritate a priest or two by teaching his parishioners some dogma." Concern for the theological accuracy of his book led him to send a copy to Bishop Thomas Shahan, rector of Catholic University, who received it, Adams reported, "like a red-hot poker. The poor man squirms for fear of getting into a scrape and I expect to get into the Index." But, as he well knew, Adams was in no danger of ecclesiastical reprisals. On the contrary, the book was recognized as one of the most authentic studies of the Middle Ages by the Thomist authority Étienne Gilson. Later, Adams wrote, "I care far more for my theology than for my architecture and should be much mortified if detected in an error about Thomas Aquinas. . . ."

Later still, Shane Leslie would observe, "With *Chartres,* Henry Adams introduced medieval religion to Boston which had previously adjudged it part of Irish ward politics."

Of course, La Dona was delighted to receive her copy of *Chartres.* Excitedly, she wrote to Adams, "I told you so about your book! It is the best thing done in modern times and it will creep into the ken of literateurs and you will find yourself 'boomed' in a new line. Don't you like it? Isn't it fun?"

In reading her copy of *Chartres,* Lizzie, whose intuition was keen, may have caught in certain passages a reflection of herself. For Henry Adams, the skeptical historian, was writing about the Virgin of Chartres in the language of a man in love. Four years earlier, he had sent La Dona his "Prayer," the poem that suggests that his worship of the madonna and child had developed from his earlier enchantment at the sight of Lizzie holding the infant Martha. Just as an author's first and sometimes later novels are regarded as partly autobiographical (Adams's novel *Esther* had described Catherine, the character based on Lizzie, as "the Madonna of the prairie," so *Chartres,* his unique evocation of the Mother of God, had its roots in Adams's experience of women. His portrait of the Jewish maiden who lived in the 1st century owed something to the American matron of the 20th century. Just as Lizzie's form and features had influenced Saint-Gaudens in creating his Angel of Victory, so her mind and spirit influenced Adams in writing *Chartres.*

Adams described the Virgin as "intensely human but always Queen." He declared that she was "above criticism. She made manners. Her acts were laws." As if he had known her well, he wrote, "She was by essence illogical, unreasonable and feminine. She was not in the least a prude. To her sin was simply humanity."

For an acknowledged skeptic who professed no religious affiliation,

"A 12th-Century Monk"

Adams sounds in his passages on the Virgin like a devotee of the cult of Mariolatry:

> The Queen Mother was as majestic as you like; she was absolute; she could be stern; she was not above being angry; but she was still a woman, who loved grace, beauty, ornament....She was the greatest artist, as she was the greatest philosopher and musician and theologist, that ever lived on earth, except her Son who, at Chartres, is still an infant under her guardianship. Her taste was infallible; her sentence eternally final....She was the mother of pity and the only hope of despair....The Virgin will wait; she will not be angry; she knows her power; we all come back to her in the end.
>
> She remains the most intensely and the most widely and the most personally felt of all characters, divine or human or imaginary, that ever existed among men . . . not to dwell too long upon it, one admits that hers is the only Church. One would admit anything that she would require. If you had only the soul of a shrimp, you would crawl, like the Abbé Suger, to kiss her feet.

It is the language of a man in love.

15

Lizzie And Martha And Don

*W*hile Lizzie had been absorbed in her affair with Trumbull Stickney and later in her serio-comic encounters with Rodin, her daughter Martha had been growing up. By the age of 14 she already overtopped Henry Adams, who found himself looking up to her as he did to her mother. With her Cameron height and her adolescent gawkiness, the young girl was more reserved than ever and found consolation chiefly in Adams, since she had no close friends of her own age.

Although Martha resembled her father in build and disposition, Senator Cameron took little responsibility for her upbringing but left all decisions to Lizzie. On the few occasions when he was present in their Lafayette Square household, he refused to be drawn into a discussion of her future. Some evenings while Lizzie was upstairs in the drawing room entertaining Henry Adams, Don could be found downstairs sprawled before the fireplace, sulkily throwing rolled-up newspapers into the grate.

During Lizzie's springtime stop in Palermo in 1901, on her way to meet Stickney in Florence, she had not been too preoccupied to notice that Martha had attracted the attention of young Lionel Rothschild. A student at Cambridge University, the 19-year-old scion of the wealthy banking family was vacationing in Europe, accompanied by his father's secretary. La Dona was impressed with him yet at the same time taken aback for she still held to her anti-Semitism, a prejudice that she had acquired in part from Adams, who was always vocal in his anti-Jewish utterances, even though he counted several Jews among his acquaintances. But the virus of anti-Semitism had been especially prevalent in France since 1894, when Alfred Dreyfus, a Jewish officer in the French Army, was convicted of treason and exiled to Devil's Island. Five years later, the verdict was annulled, the prisoner was brought back for retrial, again condemned, then later pardoned. French society was split into two camps by the Dreyfus affair, which heightened the bitterness against the Jews. Hence Lizzie, while hardly aware of it, shared this prejudice and was consequently horrified at the thought of a possible Jewish suitor for Martha. She told Adams, "Our funniest pick-up is one of the London Rothschilds, the veriest little sheeny you ever saw but bright as can be and strangely enough, very sympathetic and simple. He talks to Martha—heaven save the mark! But would you believe it? I like the boy. A Jew too." Nevertheless, Lizzie lost no time in snatching Martha away. Back in Paris, she noted another sign of Martha's growing up. "Martha is being put into my last year's clothes, to her pride and delight," she wrote.

When Lizzie's wanderings brought her to New York, she was surprised to find Don waiting for them at the dock. "He grows stouter around the waist. But I never saw him look so young and well. He seems full of money but he says he is just getting out even. Don is so amiable I think he is glad we are here. Nothing is too much for him to do." Cameron's mood fluctuated with the state of his finances—when "full in pocket," he was agreeable, but when the market dropped, he resorted to alcohol and sulks.

Arriving at Donegal, Senator Cameron, holding Martha by the hand, dragged her and Lizzie "through four miles of thick, deep clay mud" to show them his latest surprise—he had renovated and enlarged the farmhouse. Don was indeed glad to have them back. But Lizzie dreaded his return to his usual ill temper, spurred on by his older children. A few years before, she had complained to Adams, "When Don writes, it is always from the Island although he has been in New York twice that I know. But I do not think he ever wishes us to return."

But for the moment, Cameron was the model of a devoted husband. "He is more lamb-like than I've ever seen and clings to us so and is such a chatterbox that he must have been very lonely without us." Lizzie noticed that her husband was showing a new devotion and admiration toward his teen-age daughter that seemed to her "pathetic. If Martha is not my revenge she is at least my justification. Her relations with her father are very pretty. She knows just how to handle him and at the same time is both respectful and very affectionate. His admiration of her is even exaggerated it seems to me."

The weather at Donegal was so hot and humid that Don decided to move them to Beverly—not to Adams's house but to a cottage on Pride's Hill. Lizzie went on ahead and set up house and hydrangeas on the piazza. She found "a dear old darky" to provide meals to suit her husband's demanding taste. This was important, for "if the cook suits Don, that is the main thing. He has an appetite always, so he growls less at his food." Martha's ponies, her dog Kiki, and the carriages arrived, followed by Senator Cameron. For a time all was idyllic. Lizzie reported to Adams, "This place is one of the good things of the world. Don is in a wonderful temper. I'm afraid he cannot keep it up. It is unnatural..."

Four days later, the domestic climate returned to normal. Lizzie complained, "Whenever Don is with us, it ends in our living as secluded a life as your friends the Cistercians. I go nowhere, see no one and am not 'at home' in the afternoon."

Although several of Don's business associates were vacationing nearby, he refused to see them. Having retired from politics, which was his first love, he was content to remain inert for days at a time. The ebullient Lizzie was appalled. "What an extraordinary person he is" she wrote to Adams. "He sits in his smoking room about six hours a day and on the piazza the rest of the time, doing absolutely nothing after the papers are read. It is no worse —it is not so bad as his life at Donegal or the Island —for at least here he has us to speak to and without undue vanity I think we are more companionable than Uncle Simon [Don's retarded brother] or Tom Lee [the handyman]."

La Dona admitted that she was baffled by her husband's temperament. "I have never seen a person so pitifully bored as he is and yet so life-loving. Without apparently one interest in life the thought of death would be horrible to him. He is the primitive instinct and nothing more. I could not exist that way. Fortunately he is amiable and Martha can always stir him a little." Don's strong attachment to his daughter sometimes made Lizzie resort to using the child as a go-between, for he would respond to Martha even when he ignored his wife. After his retirement from the Senate, he had been for a time "reduced to submission and contentment with home." During a brief visit with them in Paris, where Lizzie had placed Martha in a convent school, Senator Cameron one day had agreed to take the carriage to fetch the child and returned home looking sheepish as he led her, dressed in white and wearing a white veil, into their apartment. Lizzie had watched them ruefully. "To what base uses he is reduced."

But established in Beverly for the summer, the retired senator, who had never been considerate of others, was not prepared, at the age of 68, to accommodate his wife. Although the Camerons received many invitations to dine with their North Shore neighbors, he refused to eat out. It meant nothing to Don Cameron that Beverly Farms, with its surrounding area, was one of the most exclusive resorts in the country, where "rich people are like huckleberries on the shore, with their coaches, their victorias and 35 horses in one stable —beef-packers, promoters —they are all here." As far as Don was concerned, he would have been happier eating alone at Donegal or St. Helena. The ennui of their self-enclosed existence was broken on 14 September 1901 by a visit from Henry Adams's brother Brooks and his wife Daisy who drove over from Quincy. Since there was no daily delivery of papers at Beverly, the Camerons' news of world affairs depended on the occasional visitor. The ordinarily crusty Brooks Adams, who had few friends, burst into the Pride's Hill cottage, voluble with excitement. "Teddy Roosevelt is President of the United States!" he shouted. He told his startled hearers that President McKinley, who had been wounded a week before in Buffalo by an assassin's bullet, had died in the night.

The news, he declared excitedly, had great implications for Don Cameron and for himself. An enthusiastic supporter of Roosevelt for many years, Brooks Adams now pictured himself in the role of *éminence grise* for the new chief executive. As later described by Arthur Beringause, "The volatile, exuberant, sentimental Brooks displayed all the happy reactions of a gambler whose horse has just led the pack at great odds. Popping up and down in his seat, talking all the while, finally he insisted on sentimentalizing the occasion by going off to look at the cottage where he had spent part of his honeymoon. The wonderful day was also the anniversary of his marriage.

Lizzie and Martha and Don

Mrs. Cameron was amazed. Never had she seen Brooks Adams so humane, so nice, certainly never so animated and so absorbed as he was in the great topic of McKinley's assassination."

Theodore Roosevelt himself had been stunned by the realization of his sudden elevation, and his political enemies reacted in horror at the prospect of "that damned cowboy" in the White House. Henry Adams, visiting in Stockholm, wrote to John Hay, "Behind all, in my mind, in all our minds, silent and awful like the Chicago Express, flies the thought of Teddy's luck." But for Brooks Adams the prospect was most pleasing. Constantly harboring political ambitions, he conspicuously lacked the political knack of winning votes. Now, unexpectedly, he saw himself with the levers of power almost within his grasp. Intoxicated with dreams of political appointment, he wired his congratulations to Roosevelt in a paraphrase of Macbeth: "Thou hast it all now: King, Cawdor, Glamis, the world can give no more..."

Their mutual enthusiasm for Roosevelt had created a bond between eccentric Brooks Adams and dour Don Cameron. Lizzie wrote with amusement to Adams, "Don and Brooks are that chummy. They now write each other to tell what a delightful day they spent together. Brooks and Donald agree so thoroughly that the latter has invited Mr. and Mrs. Brooks to spend the winter with him on the Island!"

Unhappily for Brooks Adams, his dream of political office never materialized. Despite his undeniable intelligence and loyalty, his queer eccentric manner and his invariable bluntness (unlike his brother Henry's more polished thrusts) may have seemed too much of a political liability to the Rough Rider president. Nor did Don Cameron fare better. Although Roosevelt invited Don to visit him in Washington, an invitation at which Don was "greatly pleased," no appointment was offered. And now that old Simon was dead, Don was no longer involved in Pennsylvania state politics. Urged by his political cronies to run for governor, he refused, at which La Dona was delighted.

"I am thankful," she wrote. "*Think* of spending four years in Harrisburg."

The question of Martha's future was weighing on Lizzie. For a long time she had been carrying most of the responsibility for her, but without any financial authority. Their rootless wandering about Europe, trailing a succession of governesses for Martha's instruction, was proving unsatisfactory. Without any permanent home, and lacking the educational and social discipline of a regular school, Martha was becoming headstrong, vain, and unhappy. "Martha feels desperately let down in this quiet spot," Lizzie reported from Beverly. "But it won't hurt her — it's time she got back to work as soon as possible. She has been admired and she knows it and is a little too cocky and vain now." Yet she was rather frightened of the attention that Martha attracted. "Boys flock to her and she carries herself as proudly as Rachel did. I actually feel dismayed. Martha has made some English friends — nice healthy girls who tramp up mountains and like it. It will do her good. She is lazy."

Now that she finally had her husband on the premises, La Dona was determined to settle the matter of Martha's future with him. Tentatively she suggested that they should settle in Beverly and find a private school in Boston. Senator Cameron's reply was noncommittal, "Time enough for that when her education is finished." Adams, whose own education was never finished, may have smiled at this.

Lizzie could only interpret her husband's remark as meaning more of the same wandering about Europe for them. She told her tame cat that "Don's own future, as far as I can make out, is definitely planned — it is Donegal and St. Helena. But he simply turns Martha and her future over to me and will let me do for her what I wish within certain limits. Washington is never mentioned except for Martha who always assumes we are to go there and meets no contradiction." La Dona was increasingly vexed with her husband's avoidance of parental responsibility and puzzled over the limits of her own responsibility to him. "Dear me," she wrote, "how complicated life is. There are two rights, two duties — one to him and one to Martha and they lie in opposite directions. I cannot make them meet. I don't seem to know what to do next either." She noted that Martha was done with Paris, "as far as French is concerned." The young girl's facility in French was the envy of her American peers. But this left Lizzie with a new destination to choose. "Shall I go to Berlin? Or Munich? Or Rome? Or Paris once more? You and I," she wrote to Adams wistfully, "must have a long talk this autumn. I sometimes think of taking her home to Boston and putting her in a regular day school where she could make friends. How would that do?"

As always, Senator Cameron refused to inform Lizzie about his financial status, although, from her financially straightened youth, she had learned how to manage money. But since he would never discuss money with her, she decided to spend it as freely as possible. She knew that he was a very wealthy man, with a diversity of business interests, but she never knew his exact income. When in August 1901, the stock market had plunged, she told Adams, "The steel strike knocked prices down. Don had to put up more margin all around. He has made a great deal of money as far as I can make out. He seems easy in pocket." Out of his ample fortune he paid all the household bills and allotted his wife and daughter the sum of $800 a month on which they were to live. But given the luxurious style of living to which Lizzie and Martha were accustomed and the increasing material needs of this growing daughter, Lizzie felt that she needed more — at least $1,000 a month. "I think I manage very well on what he gives but no one could convince Don of it."

Senator Cameron departed for St. Helena with the question of Martha's future still unresolved. Lizzie took her back to Paris for the winter, and here the girl's French poodle Kiki became ill. "Martha is facing her first grief," her mother wrote. "Kiki is slowly dying, wasting away, so weak he cannot stand. He collapsed and Martha cried herself sick. We both had a rocky night. Poor Kiki cannot recover. He is French to the end — kind, courteous, affectionate — poor little doggie." A few days later the dog was near death, and Lizzie observed bitterly, "But Martha really won't care. Only Cooper the maid and I will miss him. I don't think Martha cares for anything in the world beyond the surface. She is very happy this winter — so lovely in her white crepe you would be proud of her."

The little dog had to be chloroformed, and Lizzie reported "Martha cried a little — then had her dancing class. But I miss him — I feel so lost." But Lizzie was mistaken, for her daughter, despite her reserved manner, was equally shaken by the death and began to look "pulled down." So Lizzie took her to Biarritz to take the waters. While they were both drinking and bathing in the salubrious waters, they heard from Don only once, "and that scrap of a note was cross." Although both Lizzie and Martha wrote regularly to him, they received no answer. "I hope," Lizzie remarked spitefully, "that he is freezing on the Island."

The pointlessness of her nomadic life struck Lizzie with renewed force. "Me and my wreck of an existence," she wrote to Adams "What a smash-up it was! I wonder how it will turn out for Martha. Certainly Don is not an element to be counted on, so we must leave it to kind chance and go on in the same old way in Paris. I wish [she told Adams hopefully] that you could see him and find out if he intends coming here this summer — or if we are to go back there and do everything all over again? I wonder where he is now. It all depends on Don. Martha had a cable to meet her here to approve of our trip. We still know nothing of his plans and our plans necessarily depend upon him."

This constant uncertainty about her future because of her husband's lack of communication was noted with sympathy by Henry Adams, who blamed it in part on Cameron's financial activities. "Mr. Cameron is so greatly interested in his many speculations that he cares for little else and finds America much pleasanter in flush times than Europe."

As soon as Lizzie and Martha received the senator's financial blessing for their trip, they joined a party of friends for a yachting tour of the Mediterranean, sailing to Venice, Constantinople, and the Greek islands. Lizzie, who was always susceptible to beauty, described for Adams "the lovely shadows as violet as Monet himself could paint. When you and I make our fortune and take that yacht we will spend three months there."

Suddenly Senator Cameron ordered Lizzie to meet him in London, for he was planning a trip to Russia, the country to which President Lincoln had once sent his father Simon in diplomatic exile. But once they had arrived in London, he changed his mind. Instead, he decided they would go to Scotland, and he dispatched Lizzie on a house-hunting tour. In July, she wrote to Adams mournfully from Edinburgh, "It is as cold as winter and pours in sweeps and gusts of east wind. A cheerful spot at best — in this weather it is as enticing as a penitentiary." Adams was amused at the grandiose ideas of Don Cameron and advised Lizzie, "Why not take Balmoral? It is hideous but Mr. Cameron seems to want a royal residence."

Finally, Don decided to rent Castle Interlochy at Fort William in the Highlands, where Clan Cameron had originated. He summoned Adams to join them, and Adams described the scene to Mabel Hooper La Farge. "The moors and mountains are Scotchier than ever. It was all Mr. Cameron's doing, who suddenly came over, bent on having a castle. Of castles the land is full but he chooses to come to Cameron country and no sooner were they established than I was bidden to help fill the towers. So I came," he added with sly humor, "and brought all my Church philosophy with me to study in the air of Calvinism." Adams was at this time finishing his manuscript of *Mont-Saint-Michel and Chartres*.

He described the countryside: "My window looks across the valley up among the mountains along Loch Eil and in intervals of Thomas Aquinas and the mountains of Grace, I can enjoy an occasional ray of sunshine on the moors.... No one is here except Mr. and Mrs. Cameron, Martha and her cousin Edith Hoyt and their French music mistress, but we make a fairly complete family. The castle is big enough for a regiment but as yet no guest has appeared. It is six weeks since I came here and I have seen some six hundred varieties of storm and rain."

Their visit was plagued with accidents. Adams sprained his ankle, and before he could recover, Senator and Mrs. Cameron, while riding along a country road in their carriage, with Don holding the reins, were thrown out of the carriage into a ditch. Bruised and battered, they were both confined to bed, and the house was filled with the bustle of nurses and the arrivals and departures of the local doctor. Sixteen-year-old Martha took over the management of the household, and Adams observed with pride, "She keeps house and bosses us all very much, including her father who has been quite angelic and pleased as a lord to be in his own heather on which he never sets foot. It is as good an amusement as another to play laird when one has none of the bother and all of the fun. So all the Camerons come to call and Mrs. Cameron officiates in all public capacities for the clan and Martha thinks it immense fun. All the neighbors take Martha quite seriously as cousin of the first big chief Cameron." But Adams found the jest not so amusing, "not being a Cameron." As the invalids improved, Martha and her friend Nancy began rehearsals for a one-act play to amuse the castle's invalids. The two girls dressed in coats and trousers belonging to the senator and shirts, shoes, and stockings belonging to Adams. A few days later, the invalids were out of bed and the restless Don headed for London, "perfectly well and hugging his crutches."

When September came, the little party broke up, "Mr. Cameron is on the ocean hurrying westward. Mrs. Cameron and Martha are in London, hurrying southward. I have run northward here to Tillypronie [Scotland]."

Lizzie decided to take Martha, accompanied by her new governess Miss Worthington, to Germany, where she would establish them in a private home in Carlsruhe for two months so that Martha could learn the language. While there, Lizzie took Martha to the opera house to hear a performance of *Don Giovanni*. Lizzie found the orchestra "fine, but the singing was execrable." Her daughter was entranced when the statue of the Commendatore came to life and invited the Don to dinner. Lizzie announced to Henry Adams, "I got much amusement from listening to Mozart and his naive methods after hearing Wagner and our friend Charpentier." A few nights later, Martha decided to play hostess for her mother, so she took her to a concert, but the two ladies

Martha and Elizabeth Cameron

Surrenden Dering, summer of 1898
Left to right, standing: J. Donald Cameron, Henry Adams, Spencer Eddy (a secretary at the U.S. Legation in London), Adelbert S. Hay; seated in rear row: John Hay, Clarence Hay, Edith Hoyt, Helen Hay; seated in front: Martha Cameron, Alice Hay. John Hay's four children were part of the "complicated caravanserai" at Surrenden Dering.

were more absorbed in the audience than in the music. Excitedly, Lizzie looked out from their box seats and spotted royalty. "We saw Prince Max and his wife — thrills of excitement in democratic Mrs. Cameron!" With disdain she described the audience, "who looked like their under-housemaids." Then she added gloomily, "Martha has grown and quite overtops me. She is larger, too, alas, and her complexion has gone to the bow-wows."

At Christmas, Martha rejoined her mother in Paris but, Lizzie complained, "all her girl friends are gone except Gladys Vanderbilt." At her mother's urging, Martha sat for her portrait to Lizzie's friend Paul Helleu. The finished three-quarter-length portrait in pastel shows a wide-eyed young girl wearing a pinafore and resembling Alice in Wonderland. As a Christmas gift, Lizzie presented Martha with "two whacking big pearls." She confided to Adams that she wanted four more, "but they are getting very costly — $300 each. At that rate Donald must buy them hereafter."

When the holidays were over, Martha was reluctant to return to Germany but, accompanied by Miss Worthington, she went. Hardly had they left when Lizzie received a wire from the governess marked "Urgent — Martha desperately homesick." So Lizzie hastily packed her trunk and caught the Orient Express, leaving Paris at midnight and arriving in Germany exhausted. Here she found her unhappy daughter, who was ill from the German food. But as Lizzie surveyed the situation in the German *pension,* she grew exasperated. The big, reserved, determined girl had become a silent adversary. Martha was taciturn like her father, and like him she made small effort to please. She loved to read, hated exercise in any form, and despised coquetry. Her lack of friends of her own age made her chronically dissatisfied, and it irritated her mother, who exclaimed, "You can lead a horse to water but you cannot make a Cameron horse be friendly." She recalled that during the four years that Martha had been at the convent school in Paris she had snubbed every French girl who tried to be friendly—"all the children felt that she wanted to keep aloof. Why, I have made more friends here in five days than Martha will make in five months. I try to accept that lack of social faculty... ."

Despairing of continuing Martha's German education, Lizzie decided to take her on holiday to the German resort of Bad Nauheim, which was a favorite spot of hers. Without warning, on the second day, they encountered Trumbull Stickney, whom she had not seen since Paris. The poet-scholar had received his degree with distinction from the Sorbonne, and she was delighted to see him looking "bronze-colored and more cheerful and gay than I've seen him in years." Martha, who had never responded to Stickney's charms, grumbled, "This place isn't all it's cracked up to be."

During this German visit they met a talented young architect from New York, Henry W. Wilkinson, who was halfway in age between mother and daughter. His health was poor, and he was visiting the spa in the hope of regaining it. Martha was drawn to "dear old Wilks," and Lizzie admired and befriended him. Soon the young man was half in love with both of them.

When they moved on to St. Moritz, Martha sent him a postcard showing their hotel and remarked, "This place is a hole. I miss Nauheim." They had arrived at their luxurious hotel at the Swiss resort only to find that the rooms that Lizzie had engaged were occupied by the Vienna Rothschilds. This situation she found intolerable, so she sat down firmly on her luggage and refused to budge. "If it had not been a Rothschild I might have conceded," she wrote to Adams. "But I held my own. I felt like a sponge grown soggy when I left." But she obtained their rooms.

At 17, Martha was proving almost as difficult to manage as her father. The lonely adolescent was frequently bored and gloomy, and Lizzie fretted at her fits of profound depression in which she begged to leave. Lizzie blamed Martha's disenchantment with Switzerland on the fact that "here a young girl is of very little account and is relegated to the background. American children are used to being the pivot of all interest and movement but I don't know that we can alter civilization on their account. I am willing to leave but she must decide where she wants to go. She doesn't want to go *anywhere*." Adding to Lizzie's woes was the governess, whose "lack of tact amounts to genius and her unselfishness takes the fussy, buzzy form. There is no fault to find with her except *trop de zèle*. She is a benevolent mosquito!" Then plaintively she asked Adams, "Do you think you could invent an excuse for getting rid of her?"

In November 1903, Lizzie was called home to Cleveland by the news that her sister-in-law Hatty Sherman had just learned that her son Henry, a student at Yale, had fallen 40 feet to his death. Lizzie exclaimed, "Some fate strikes down every man in this family and leaves the women alive and healthy!" She rushed off to Cleveland to stay with the bereaved mother, then invited her for a stay in Harrisburg. Here she looked on in silent sympathy while the grief-stricken Hatty Sherman paced the floor for hours until she was exhausted. Wistfully Lizzie wrote to Adams, "For once I have been of use and it is gratifying to feel I could do something."

Lizzie told Adams that she had finally received a letter from Don acknowledging a miniature of Martha that she had sent him, "although he says he hasn't seen her in so long he doesn't know if it's a good likeness or not."

16

A Husband For Martha

While Henry Adams had been engrossed in writing *Mont-Saint-Michel and Chartres*, Lizzie Cameron was absorbed in the most serious work of her life—finding a suitable husband for Martha. Expecting and receiving no help from her husband in this critical pursuit, she turned naturally to Adams. But Adams understood that his role would be merely to support whatever choice Lizzie made, for he already knew her ambitions. When the girl was only 15, Lizzie had asked his advice about Martha's future, and Adams had replied with his usual perception, "I hope you may gratify your worst and lowest instinct and see Martha rich and marry her, if you like, to your own dear Englishman." Adams had caught the unspoken message underlying many of Lizzie's social maneuvers.

Although in the early 1900s a titled Englishman represented the peak of many an American mother's social aspirations, Lizzie was too realistic to seek merely a title—which could mean an idle young aristocrat with no career and no intellectual pretensions. During the days when she presided over her salon in Lafayette Square, she had met many titles that were also allied to brains among the young diplomats on Embassy Row. She remembered them well. And they remembered her, too.

For the capture of a suitable mate, Lizzie had groomed her daughter well. She had given her lessons in dancing, in deportment and etiquette, in French and German. She had stressed the importance of appearance to Martha, who as her father's daughter had small interest in clothes. Now the young girl was tall and handsome and carried herself with grace. Over the years, Lizzie had established connections in international society—whether in Washington or London, Paris or Rome, the social circle was well defined. Now, under her mother's expert direction, Martha would be properly launched, even though the young girl herself would have preferred the pleasures of the library to the unknown dangers of the ballroom.

When Martha was invited to the Lochaven Ball, a major social event in Scotland, at the home of a Cameron connection, Lizzie watched her daughter narrowly. She noticed that the girl was becoming infatuated with her youthful escort. After one quick evaluation, Lizzie decided that he was unsuitable, so she skillfully disengaged the pair, remarking to Adams, "It is just a question of distraction."

Rome in the winter months was a popular destination for well-to-do Americans, for it offered a busy social season. So Lizzie engaged a villa for the winter of 1903-4. As usual, she had heard no word from her husband, but Adams informed her that Senator Cameron, wintering on St. Helena Island, had written to invite him down for a month, so at least she could keep track of her "owner" through her "protector." Surveying the social scene in Rome, La Dona noticed with a mixture of amusement and anxiety that her daughter was beginning to attract masculine notice. "She is tasting the dangerous pleasures of being admired. She has rows of little men around her and, curiously enough, one mature one who seems quite infatuated." This was a young Englishman, and Lizzie was reassured. "Fortunately he is of a race which produces gentlemen and our own ideas of what is decent."

From Martha's infancy, she had been guarded by an overprotective mother whose domination had caused the girl to grow up both timid and indecisive. But since she was also a Cameron, Martha had inherited a certain stubbornness that Lizzie dreaded. For there was no telling what unsuitable choice Martha might make if left to herself. So Lizzie saw to it that this did not happen. "I cannot leave Martha alone for an hour," she complained to Adams, "so I am very cross." Lizzie managed to hold at a distance each successive admirer, "and I think she does not even suspect. But one never knows with a young girl." Lizzie was instantly on the alert whenever a young man appeared. "I keep my eyes wide open on both of them until I think the danger is past. But there are moments of great uneasiness," she confessed to Adams. "Dear me—when I *think* what is ahead of me! I realize that my little girl is now a big one and I feel quite wobbly." She admitted to suffering sleepless nights over Martha, and she told Adams, "Putting this all on paper makes shadow into substance. It is only my nerves and the dreadful anticipation which makes it fairly visible. *You* understand, don't you?" Certainly the childless Henry Adams could understand La Dona's apprehension about the future of the girl he cherished as if she were his own. But he also realized that there was very little he could do but listen, and he told Lizzie, "Martha never will grow up. She is no older now than in 1886. You are the one who pays the bill in nervous wear and tear." With an air of foreboding, Lizzie exclaimed on Leap Year Day in 1904, "Calamity can only strike through a husband for Martha!"

Lizzie also sought reassurance from Henry Wilkinson, who had won Martha's admiration as well as her own. In her relations with the architect, who was talented but impecunious at the start of his career, Lizzie was alternately the bountiful patron and the perennial coquette. She confided in him, commissioned his services, and enthralled him.

While their days in the Roman villa passed quietly and no eligible suitors appeared, Lizzie wondered, "Perhaps Rome is a mistake. But Martha doesn't think so—she doesn't want to go back to America! It will seem 'provincial' she says." As Lent approached, the social pace quickened—the two ladies were invited to the elaborate court ball that would honor King Victor Emmanuel and his queen. Lizzie regarded the royal palace as "one step more elegant than the White House," and even the reserved Martha seemed delighted to be there. The king was so tiny that he looked, Lizzie observed, "like Hop-o-my Thumb beside that splendid Montagnard piece of flesh and blood. She is magnificent, not as Queen, but as woman and *très femme* in manner and speech. I don't believe that he is as tall as Queen Victoria. He has no legs. . . ." When Lizzie was presented to the monarch, he asked her to dance, and off they set across the ballroom floor, the tall, regal Lizzie and the tiny king.

American visitors to Rome, whatever their church affiliations, considered an audience with the pope a social necessity. One day at noon, Prince Alliere, one of Martha's young men, rushed into their villa, proudly waving tickets for a general audience with Pope Pius X, who had been seated on the papal throne for less than a year. The papal audience was set for 3 P.M. within the walls of the Vatican, and papal etiquette required that all the ladies who were to be received must be garbed in black, with neck, arms, and head demurely covered. "So we flew around," Lizzie reported, "to find black clothes and lace for our heads." Lizzie found a black dress of her own for Martha and was horrified at the results. The poor girl looked awkward and miserable—"like a cook *en dimanche*," Lizzie groaned to Adams. "I've never seen anything so funny and hideous. But we found everyone else in the same senseless dress and we got through it."

Amid the ritual pomp that surrounded the simple, sad-faced man in the white cassock, the visitors were presented to him, and some knelt to kiss the fisherman's ring. At her first encounter with a Roman pontiff, Lizzie was not impressed. "The Pope is sweet and benevolent, but not an intellectual and certainly not a high-bred one. He is a peasant and knows it. But he doesn't look corrupt and loathsome like so many priests." (Within fifty years the peasant pope would be canonized Saint Pius X by the Catholic Church.)

As Lizzie scrutinized Martha's social behavior, she was disappointed to find that there was far more Cameron than Sherman in her manner. "Martha isn't a whole success," she confessed to Adams. "She is a partial one like Rachel." (Martha's half-sister Rachel Cameron had always been difficult to manage, but she was finally married off to Senator Eugene Hale's son Chandler.) "Martha," Lizzie decided, "is both less simple and less polished than I expected her to be. Nature, not nurture, you'll say."

During the Roman spring, Martha suffered a bout of measles, during which she ran a fever of 104 degrees. Lizzie was upset and called in doctors and nurses. But a fortnight later the girl was "quite rosy again and showing great interest in another of her little men. But oh dear—she was playing with dolls so short a time ago."

Young Lionel Rothschild turned up in his new touring car, and Lizzie agreed to chaperone the pair on a motor trip. When another young admirer named Moltke appeared, Martha shyly asked her mother, "I wonder if Dordy will despise him because he isn't clever?" Lizzie admitted that the young man behaved perfectly—"he almost asks my permission to look at her." "But he has gone," she reported with relief, "to Denmark so she is safe for two or three months. The weak part is he shows taste and discrimination."

Clearly Lizzie was torn by conflicting emotions in her role as the mother of a marriageable daughter. Naturally she wanted Martha to marry well—someone who could provide for her and enhance her social position; but her own arranged marriage was a constant reminder that such an alliance could bring about the calamity she feared. She also recognized that this project would be costly. As she explained to Adams, "Martha is very expensive, so whether we can go on living on $12,000 a year or not I do not know. At first, you remember, I had $800 a month, then $1000 but now . . ." Donald, she pointed out, had recently suffered a big loss in the stock market and was experiencing what she called "a rich man's panic." But for this misfortune she felt small sympathy. Instead, she gladly accepted Adams's offer of his Mercedes, with which she planned to make a motor tour through Italy, and wrote, "What an angel you are to let me have it!"

Sadly watching her as she wandered restlessly about without any fixed center, Adams showed his sympathy for her in a letter to Mrs. Lodge, who was in Washington. "If you care to get Mrs. Cameron back you can probably do it by finding her a house. If you know of any let me know. She can have my house if she likes but that would oblige me to stay here." But Lizzie did not require this sacrifice of him. In the fall of 1904, she and Martha went to New York, where she took an apartment at The Lorraine on 45th Street, "for some fabulous price."

Although La Dona complained of being a "pauper," she managed to buy an electric car for Martha in the conviction that if the girl had a car of her own "she could run about more freely—and I may sell it when the season ends." Of course Lizzie, as well as Martha, took lessons in driving it.

Lizzie had always been an art lover, and now that she was in New York she could attend numerous exhibits. At an opening in a gallery on 57th Street, she came upon Adams's brother Charles Francis, who did not recognize her. "But I insisted on being known," she told Henry, "and we spent an hour together. He goes to Egypt next month. I found him delightful as a companion but looking a great deal older than you and I. What a keen, intelligent face he has!"

By December 1904, Martha, who had passed her 18th birthday in June, was ready to be introduced to Washington society. From New York, Lizzie wrote to Adams in Lafayette Square, "Will you tell Edith Roosevelt that I want to go to the Diplomatic Reception on the 12th of January?" A White House reception, with all the royal trappings that Theodore Roosevelt insisted on, would make a suitable debut for Martha. Adams obeyed, and on her return to Washington Lizzie supervised all the practical details. But after the affair, she was disappointed in Martha—as she told Adams, "It is curious to see how little social instinct she has. I have to push her into everything."

For the summer, they went to Newport, which Cecil Spring-Rice called "the refinement of vulgarity." While they were there, Lizzie learned of the death of John Hay, and she wrote at once to Adams, "I cannot bear to think what a difference it will make in your life." With rare self-criticism, she continued, "I will try not to be cross and disagreeable. I cannot be what he was to you but I can be less cranky than I often am. I will go to the funeral if it is a private one." She recalled for him the old Huron idea of immortality, "where the shadows of warriors, with shades of bows and arrows, chased the shades of game through the shades of the forest. This," she added, looking disapprovingly around her at Newport society, "is a picture of American social intercourse. Instead of spirits, it is only the shades projected by their imaginations. The men are horrors and the women are 'animated' and the mingling of the two is a ghost's dance and a shadow of pleasure."

A week later, still trying to console Adams for the death of his closest friend, she wrote, "Long ago we talked of the complete isolation of sorrow. No one can penetrate it, no one can help. The chamber room has remained closed. But you come out ennobled and I—impotent, worn, defiant and challenging. What a rich nature you have . . ." "But oh," she pleaded, "don't give up. You and Martha are my universe and I dread blows from one or the other. No one else has the power to hurt me now. And you know that my nerve has gone. Don't hurt me by giving up."

Lingering in Newport, she awaited some word from her husband, although she did not really expect it. "Donald is sulking again with one of his unexpected turns. He wrote a very disagreeable letter to Martha on her birthday and to me he doesn't vouchsafe a word. I fancy his children have been at him and so I let it pass ignored." But by now she was thoroughly weary of her nomad existence. Back in Paris, she decided that she and Martha needed a home—she intended to have one. With a combination of cajolery and threats, she finally persuaded Don to let her reopen their house at 21 Lafayette Square. Soon she was writing to Henry Wilkinson to send her drawings and cost estimates for renovating it. She described to the architect how she wished to redecorate Martha's bedroom, in a manner of royal elegance, "with a Louis XVI bed with crown and curtains, a console with marble top for a nightstand; Louis XVI chairs covered with the material of Louis XVI curtains. If you are an angel, you will have some patterns of green wallpaper for the sitting room ready for me to see."

Wilkinson answered that he had ordered new brackets for the dining room and salon, some side lights, and the green wallpaper. "But don't become too wedded to Paris," he cautioned, "just as you are leaving, I beg of you." To which Lizzie replied, "Let the side lights go. I am very short of money. I have bought a lot here. Will arrive the 25th November." On her return, she expressed her approval of Wilkinson's efforts, and, throwing prudence to the winds in the matter of decorating, asked Adams in Paris to buy some pictures that she coveted and to get some samples of 15th-century cretonne at Le Bon Marché. "But don't unless you *want* to do errands to fill your time."

Adams was aghast at the nature of her request. "I won't," he wrote. "You can't afford it. You are ruinously extravagant—you with an empty apartment to pay for. I'm ashamed of you. No, you must not buy pictures but you may have any of mine you like. I owe you one already—do you want my Madame Louise?" (This was the portrait of his grandmother, Louisa Catherine, wife of John Quincy Adams.)

By December 1905, Lizzie was back in Washington and delighted with the redecorating Wilkinson had done. She wrote to him, "The dining room is lovely. And the bay window is a triumph and does you credit—and oh, Wilks, I am so proud! I am now crazy to have you see it. Martha's room is equally successful. The green papers are all too strong but *faute de mieux* we can use them. Perhaps you can find some grey-green somewhere."

Don arrived for the Christmas holidays, professed his admiration for the refurbished rooms, and admired everything equally. "It did not keep him here though," Lizzie added, "he went back to the South the day after Christmas." Martha added her own reactions to "Dear old Wilks" and thanked him for the collection of green pottery he had given her. "The scarab looks quite lovely in my celebrated green room and gives it a very chic note of antiquity and Eastern-ness. Thank you a thousand times. Daddy came up from the South for three days and was in a generally beatific mood. Christmas Day was the most beautiful ever seen and matters in general were very pleasant. We long to see you . . ."

In the spring of 1906, Lizzie received a long-awaited wire from Whitelaw Reid, the American ambassador in London, stating that he planned to sponsor Martha's presentation at the Court of St. James's. This was the signal for a flurry of excited buying by La Dona, and on 1 June 1906, Martha Cameron, now almost 20, was formally presented, among a group of eager debutantes, to His Majesty Edward VII.

At the presentation Lizzie was in her element—more regal in her bearing than much of royalty itself. She described the affair to Wilkinson. "I know you like the glories of this world and Martha and I have been in them. Of course I had to go too—that is etiquette. Martha for once was beautiful. The richness of her dress, the length of her train and the white plumes made her look regal. When she came in, the King leaned forward and whispered to the Queen to attract her attention." (Whether Queen Alexandra heard him is not known, for she suffered from deafness.) "Martha's dress was of white gauze, heavily embroidered in silver, made with a high belt, Empire style, which gave her length of limb. Her court train was of cloth of silver, covered with tulle embroidered in Empire wreaths of silver. It was lovely."

Their old friend Whitelaw Reid treated the Camerons "like nobles," Lizzie reported with satisfaction. "We were third to pass in and had seats on the Ambassadresses' benches close to the Queen. We saw the whole procession." The presentation was followed by invitations "everywhere. I have so many old friends in England and they never forget one. On Whitsuntide we went to Rufford Abbey, a party of eighteen, principally M.P.'s." Their schedule included dinners, balls, and luncheons, including a formal dinner with King Edward VII. "And we visited Montague House, filled with art treasures and souvenirs of Monmouth their ancestor—Chamberlains, Curzons, Balfour,

James Bryce were all there. Now our glory is over. Going to Nauheim will seem a dreary end for Martha after the glories of London."

As Lizzie had foreseen, when they reached the peaceful resort of Bad Nauheim, Martha collapsed, worn out from the festivities. Her mother was worried: "She is very weak and her spirits are low. I hardly know how to cheer her." Gradually she recovered, and soon Lizzie was writing Wilkinson asking him for a couple of prints of Martha standing amid the roses. "They are always taken from me by her admirers."

Now Lizzie received a check for $300 for money that she had loaned to Wilkinson when he was temporarily low in funds. She begged him to take back the money, "which I do not need from you who do, just to gratify your stupid pride. Hang it all! Let me send it back. I would do so in this letter if I were not afraid of hurting your old Yankee feelings."

Suddenly Martha had a new admirer whom she had met in London, and Lizzie knew at once that he was serious. He was the 29-year-old Scottish diplomat Ronald Charles Lindsay, the fifth of six sons of James Ludovic Lindsay, the 26th earl of Crawford and Balcarres. Six feet four, brilliant and handsome, he was also penniless. With four older brothers, he had small chance of inheriting either the 14th-century title or the family estate. In view of this, he had entered the British diplomatic service after passing a competitive examination and was at the moment stationed in the British Embassy in Washington.

Clearly this alliance would represent a Pyrrhic victory for Lizzie. Ronald Lindsay had many of the attributes she sought in a husband for Martha—except the title and the income. Observing how strongly attracted he was to her daughter, Lizzie insisted on a temporary separation, with the stipulation that his letters to Martha must pass through her. As she confided to Wilkinson two months after the court presentation, "Lindsay is languishing in Lenox [Massachusetts]. I think Martha has made up her mind he won't do. I hope so. We are going to Denmark to visit some friends. Lindsay writes me charming and well-written letters. But I said from the first they could not correspond so it all comes through me. I wonder who the next will be?"

Naturally Adams in Washington was invited to meet Lindsay, and he liked him at once. But Lizzie was concerned with basics. With maternal realism she pointed out to Martha that on the income of a "penniless" young diplomat she would have to revise her standard of living radically. "By dint of helping her pare down her needs to her income I think she will find her young man less bewitching," she told Adams.

Martha, who all her life had been pampered and protected and who had never made a major decision by herself, was acting bewildered now as she was confronted by this importunate suitor who would not accept a refusal. In the wings, her managing mother hovered, and soon the girl was assailed by nameless fears that attacked her whenever she had to make up her mind. Growing up overdependent on her mother, she dared not travel anywhere alone, was shy with strangers, and frequently lapsed into undiagnosed ailments.

A Husband for Martha

In the hope of dissuading her from choosing Lindsay, Lizzie relentlessly pursued the theme of poverty in her talks with her daughter. Pretending to believe that the match was already settled, Lizzie reminded Martha that, after she was married, she would have to live on Jefferson Place, an unfashionable address worlds removed from Lafayette Square. And she would have to discharge her maid and make do with her mother's cast-off clothes. "If it is a real case," Lizzie observed grimly, "it will stand. If it isn't she had better be frightened off. I fear he is weak. . . ." But Lindsay turned out to be strong and decisive, and he was as persistent in his courtship as Martha was vacillating. First she would decide that "he won't do" and Lizzie would rejoice. Then Lindsay would appear and cause Martha to change her mind. This would be followed by Martha's developing a new ailment. In June 1907, Lizzie wearily capitulated, writing to Adams, "perhaps Martha had better marry Lindsay after all. He hopes to leave America on June 20 and be in Paris in early July. So you will see him before we do. The change in Martha is quite wonderful. She has gained weight, her color is back. But any exertion brings on backaches. . . ."

Lizzie and Martha were invited again to visit Rufford Abbey, where Lizzie mentioned "odds and ends of people who seem extremely dull except for the mother and a lovely girl who is a Lindsay." The ancient abbey had a ruined chapel and a crypt dating from the 12th century. To Martha's horror, the Cameron ladies were assigned to the "ghost room," which legend claimed was visited by the skeleton of a monk. The terrified girl hardly slept at all, although her mother kept a light burning through the night. "But she was in a panic," Lizzie noted.

Although Lizzie confessed that the visit bored her, she was pleased that Martha seemed happy. Ronald Lindsay arrived and with his boundless energy insisted on driving them through the Scottish hills in an open car. It was pouring, and the ladies were soaked, which did not improve Martha's mood. "We have never been so wet," groaned Lizzie. "How long Martha will be able to stand this I don't know." Next the girl announced that she and Lindsay would attend the Highland Ball, with Lizzie enlisted as chaperone. La Dona complained. "Dear, dear, for what am I being punished? For marrying a Scot. . . ."

In March 1908, Lizzie took Martha back to St. Helena, where Don was entrenched. Soon they had a visitor, the young diplomat Larz Anderson, whose father General Nicholas Anderson had been their neighbor on Lafayette Square. Sailing his houseboat along the South Carolina coast, Anderson entered Pirate's Creek and proceeded through the marshes that surrounded St. Helena Island. He recognized Senator Cameron's boat at the dock and further inland saw the "white road stretching back to higher ground and the plantation house."

> As we neared, I caught sight of Mrs. Cameron coming down the walk. A strange boat in this out-of-the-way place was exciting. Then the Senator appeared. We went up with them to their house and sat in the shade of Cherokee roses. Mrs. Cameron was as nice as could be and did all to make us welcome. It seemed strange to

see her in this remote spot where there were nothing but darkies. One thousand of them had been killed in the great tidal wave of 1893 and voodoo is their religion. Yet she seemed as much at home as when I last saw her in her charming apartment in the Avenue du Bois de Boulogne.

Donald Cameron, now 74, spent much of his time brooding about his finances, although he admitted he was in better financial shape than when he had left the Senate. As Lizzie told Adams, "He was carrying $400,000 and his securities dropped by 50% so he is dead bent on selling the St. Helena house if he can." Since the house still carried a $70,000 mortgage, it would not be easy. "How I wish he would sell it," Lizzie mused, "but no one is so maniac as to want it. He is very busy writing descriptions of its manifold beauties. The future looks very dark [to him] but we've lived through other things and can weather this, even if it means a summer at Donegal." Lizzie was eager to placate her husband, since so much was at stake for Martha. But when she learned that Don had departed for Washington without telling her, she was furious. She wrote to Adams, "If I had known, of course I should have gone there and had another glimpse of you. But I am trying so hard to please now that I dared not ask—or thought it unwise."

She stayed on in South Carolina, and her husband returned in a more cheerful mood because he had heard rumors that oil and gas had been discovered on his property in West Virginia. "When he hears these rumors he grows as inflated as if the gas were in him," Lizzie commented. Meanwhile, Martha was still dangling her suitor, and Lindsay's letters were mournful. Lizzie was irritated with her daughter. "She is certainly not going to marry him now and to let him hang on is so completely unfair. He had better give up all idea of it."

Apparently Don had communicated his "rich man's panic" to Martha, who was resisting her suitor on the grounds of money. Lizzie declared, "If her affection for him cannot stand that she had better give him up altogether." In fairness, Lizzie admitted, "Our shortages are only comparative. We really have all we want. But her nerves make the worst of everything." Suddenly she appealed to Adams, "Why don't *you* talk to Lindsay?"

Adams was wholly sympathetic to Lindsay, and he was growing impatient with Martha's vacillation. "Lindsay is the only satisfactory and sympathetic young man I know and I only wish I were a girl and would marry him myself." To rouse Martha's competitiveness, he wrote, "I will try to marry him to Laura Chanler if you go back on him. He is pathetic too and pretty solitary. Poor Lindsay." The young man, after receiving a discouraging letter from Mrs. Cameron, had sighed, "Very well . . ." and Adams had wondered where to send him. "When one is beaten one goes somewhere else, but I hardly recommend Paris. It is exasperatingly gay and horrid."

In her turn, Lizzie was exasperated with them all—Martha and Lindsay and Adams. "Good heavens, man," she wrote to Adams, "you do not suppose I am opposing Lindsay? On the contrary, I wish Martha would marry him. So does she. But Cameron-like she is resisting to the end of her strength.

Edith Wharton

Martha Cameron

Above: Martha Cameron as presented
at the Court of St. James's

Left: Ronald Lindsay
portrait by John Singer Sargent

I can see her mind working. She is determined she *won't* and for the present she certainly won't. But if she sees him again she *will*. There it all is in a nutshell. He is the only man she likes—but she is afraid—of the unknown, of England, of a boring life, of leaving me, of everything. You can say all that to Lindsay if you like."

A week later, Martha was "very nervous. She seems to have dismissed Lindsay and is sorry that she did. What a pity," Lizzie mused, "that either he or she can't have a fortune left to them." Since La Dona was mortally afraid of poverty for her daughter, this increased Martha's anxiety. She tried to explain to Adams: "I cannot urge her to go into a life of deprivation and when I see what money can do in an illness, how imperative it is—I am too frightened of poverty to admit she could face it. But of course," she added self-righteously, "I am not lifting a finger pro or con. They must settle their own affairs. Only it frightens me silly for her."

So the romance dragged on all summer, with Martha hesitating, Lindsay persisting, Lizzie lamenting, and Adams listening. Then Lizzie asked Adams, "If I can go to Europe in the fall, am I justified in taking Martha?" Somehow, she felt this departure might end the affair. She insisted that she "liked Lindsay and realized that a girl could drift into marriage with a man she sincerely likes and respects and be very happy. But to face poverty, strangers, a nomad life! I think she needs more enthusiasm. They would be awfully poor and moving poverty is worse than stay-at-home poverty."

Suddenly it occurred to La Dona how tiresome all this must sound to Adams. "Dear me, how tired you must be of all this. I have gone on so many times. My letters are one long wail. I should think you would hate to receive them."

As he regarded the little comedy from a safe distance, Adams could be more objective than Lizzie. He told her that before leaving Paris he had written to Martha "as much as a crabby old man ought to say," namely that Martha, who was now 22, should not marry until she was 25—"or 27 was even better. A woman does not get her courage til then or her head. But whether Lindsay will wait so long I do not know." Although he recognized Lizzie's anxiety, Adams could only recommend patience. He had not yet talked with Lindsay on the matter, but he did agree reluctantly that if Ronald were in Paris on his return he would talk with him—"but it is not in my line and I fear doing harm."

From Donegal, Lizzie reported that Donald was not well and had suffered another attack of dizziness. When she tried to make him go on a diet, it made no impression. "He has had an iron digestion all his life so he can't understand the need of prudence now." Martha was still pining for Lindsay "or his equivalent. She's in no condition to marry now. Her nerves are wretched. She sleeps and eats badly and has troubled dreams!"

On returning to Paris in 1908, Adams received a visit from Lindsay. Shyly the young man forced himself to ask Adams the great question, "Do you think there is any chance that Martha will marry me?" Adams smiled. "In my experience," he said slowly, "any man can marry any woman if he has tact and patience, for the woman in most cases cannot help herself." Then the two men discussed the situation "all around and at length," and Lindsay went off professing to feel better. "Naturally," Adams wrote, "I had no greater wish than to avoid speaking with authority or giving advice or appearing to represent Martha or you. My question was whether he cared enough to wait and work. I spoke of two years as reasonable. He spoke of getting transferred to London and taking a career in the Foreign Office. As they knew, the British diplomatic service frowned on marriage for junior officers who might be stationed in remote outposts.

Although he offered no advice, Adams did hint that everyone was favorably disposed to Lindsay. "I insisted on the uncertainty, the impossibility of forcing the situation and the value of patience, good temper and steadiness and I even suggested that by the chance of fate he might turn out as the single staff of us all. The effect of the talk was meant to be encouraging. I have no right or authority to discourage him. Lindsay is so pathetic, patient and sympathetic that I cannot endure to give him pain." Then he mentioned pointedly that Clover's niece, Ellen Hooper, was engaged to John Potter and "he has nothing to live on any more than Bancel La Farge [the artist's son] or Lindsay."

Lizzie and Martha were summering in 1908 at a house in Beverly near Adams's. "This place I like best in America," she wrote. "It is a taste I owe to you, dear man, as I owe everything which makes life tolerable."

Soon afterward, Lindsay rushed in to Lafayette Square to see Adams. He was disturbed about a letter he had received from Mrs. Cameron. Patiently Adams explained to him, "Mrs. Cameron is *au bout de ses forces.* She must come over here with Martha and the situation will settle itself."

Amid all this turmoil, Adams's chief concern was for La Dona. As he told her, "My anxiety has always been about you not Martha. As long as she can depend on you, she will get on somehow. Lindsay can do nothing unless he resigns and becomes an American son-in-law. [Embassy rules prohibited staff members from having a "foreign" wife.] Lindsay has been chargé d'affaires in the Paris Embassy and he is the only man who does anything."

Life with both Don and Martha was wearing on Lizzie. Martha was fine when all went well, but under any stress "she goes to pieces, is morbid, introspective, and studies everyone's motives. I felt sure," Lizzie wrote, "that she was fretting for Lindsay. Now I'm not so sure." On the other hand, Don at 75 was growing less vigorous and consequently even more difficult. "I'm not sure he can be left alone," Lizzie fretted. "But where can I take him? We cannot go into dreary exile and if a place is civilized Donald avoids it. If there is life, he won't go. If it were only Martha, I could manage it but Donald will complicate it fearfully. His attitude on finances shows how broken and changed he is." With a touch of her old imperiousness, she added, "Ronald must not come over until I send for him." Regaining her self-control, she added, "I am all right and finally realize the worst is still to come. I must keep well."

In August 1908, Lindsay's chief insisted on retaining him in the diplomatic service, from which he had asked to be transferred, although the chief, Lizzie pointed out, "doesn't like married men."

During that summer, Martha had visited a young couple in the Beverly neighborhood and had seen enough to lose any illusions about marriage. "The childbearing horrified her and the immutability of the bond terrifies her. She is afraid of England, particularly the women . . ."

In the fall, Lizzie was called to Southampton, Long Island, to nurse her sister Lida Hoyt, who was dying. Martha was sent to visit relatives in order "to spare her." Lindsay was fretting in London, and Don Cameron was at Donegal nursing his finances.

After Lida's death, Lizzie took Martha with her to Paris, where they settled into an apartment at 53 avenue Montague. Lindsay was invited to visit them. Martha suddenly decided that she didn't want to see him, so she wired him not to come. But the young man had already started, and in the morning Martha received a *carte pneumatique* announcing that he was arriving that evening.

But Lizzie was wearily certain that Martha would balk. "Before spring she will chuck the whole thing and make us infinite trouble. His people are too charming—it is impossible for them to be more cordial. If she behaves badly I will be mortified. She is nervous, white and drawn and has lost her purse—this brings bad luck."

Every night for a week, Lindsay came to the Paris apartment to dine. Every night, Lizzie was gracious and Martha hardly spoke to him. Finally, on Friday evening, Martha rose abruptly from the table and started to leave the room. This was too much for Lizzie and Ronald. "The two worms turned," she wrote to Adams. "We told her plainly what we thought of her. You know Martha. Suddenly she turned around and told him she would marry him." So it was settled, and all was for the moment blissful. "You have never seen two happier young people. It made even me sentimental to see them."

Both Martha and Lindsay wanted to cable Dordy the news at once, but Lizzie vetoed it, instructing Martha to write to Adams—but to him alone, "for she wants no one else to know it." After his long siege, Lindsay was transformed. "You never saw a more beaming image of happiness. He goes to London today but will return and we will go back with him. He wants to show Martha to his mother."

"Then," Lizzie added ominously, "we must face Donald when we return." Of course, both Lizzie and Adams knew that Martha would change her mind. Within a week, "she had one of her violent reactions today at having accepted Lindsay and fretted herself ill. In the meantime we had received a letter and a wire from his family. So she felt caught in a trap. But Lindsay's arrival cleared the air—he sobered her."

Prodded by her mother, Martha wrote the news to her father at Donegal, but Lizzie was nervous about his reaction, so she asked Adams, "if you would write to Don at Donegal recommending the young man?"

Adams greeted the news of the engagement with a knowing smile. "Your letter," he told Lizzie, "surprised me by telling me what I already knew, for the engagement was as certain as though I had witnessed it. Martha is entirely absorbed in it and in him. She had long ago made up her mind and only found a sort of pleasure in holding off the idea and looking at it and hemming it and embroidering it as women—and men—like to do. Meanwhile I am not thinking so much of them as of you. But if I know Martha she will keep you sufficiently occupied. I am immensely relieved. He is a man you have confidence in. If we are mistaken about it we are mistaken about the whole world."

Adams then wrote to Martha, to whom he had sent hundreds of letters since she was an infant. "Although I have no voice in the matter he was your own unaided choice. If I were you, I would not exchange him for any of the young men now marrying my young women. You have a very nice lover indeed and I wish I too were young. You've got all that is worth having in life and all that I should care to live it over for. Do not shirk at enjoying it."

Adams informed Lizzie that he had carried out her request of writing to Senator Cameron, who was "junketing in his boat in South Carolina. To my great relief he did not reply. If so, I would probably be told to mind my own business."

Meanwhile, Lindsay told Adams that the Camerons had invited him to visit them in Washington during his holiday in the last three weeks of December 1908. "Martha will carry me around Washington tied to the wheels of her chariot which is a 1909 model Columbia electric car." Then he added, "Dear Mr. Adams, will you put me up? I have proposed myself to you so often and found so kind a welcome as a result. We sail the 6th December—it will be the greatest fun. My entire family have fallen in love with Martha and she likes them so much." The Lindsay visit passed without incident, and Adams observed that "Martha seems more placid and happy than I ever knew her. It is her mother who suffers, worries and is broken up."

To Mabel La Farge, Adams wrote, "Martha is to be married in April, I gather, and go to London. Quentin Durward [a young Scottish guardsman who was the hero of Walter Scott's novel of that name] and she seem very happy and peaceful."

In his thank-you note to Adams, Lindsay wrote, "The days I spent in your home were the happiest of my life—yet. I am so pleased at all the letters of congratulation—it is impossible to express my thanks and pleasure briefly."

Of course, some of Lizzie's friends were not so sanguine. Cecil Spring-Rice wrote to her, "It must be a terrible blow to you but he is as good a robber as could be found." Then, referring to a health problem his daughter had, he added, "I wonder if it is better not to have children. You have Martha taken from you. I can sympathize."

Few of her friends except Adams understood Lizzie's ambivalence. Certainly she had made every effort to have Martha "taken from her." She was delighted at Martha's choice. But without her daughter on whom to focus all her emotional energies, her life would seem strangely empty.

There was also the worrying question of Martha's mood swings—from extreme happiness at being engaged to dark depression with a half-hearted intention of sending Lindsay away. Perhaps the young woman could dimly perceive that even her fiancé was subject to her mother's fascination.

Although Lindsay was twenty years younger than Lizzie, and was always proper in his behavior toward her, Martha could not fail to see how his face lit up when her mother entered the room and how easily they fell into conversation about the world of diplomacy in which she felt too uninformed to participate.

After Lindsay left for London, Martha became ill. A doctor was called in who pronounced, "It is the suspense which is making her ill." Then Lindsay received three letters from Lizzie reporting how unmanageable Martha had become. "It is a pity," she wrote, "you didn't get married at Christmas. If you were here, all would be right. I think long engagements are a mistake." Lindsay was astonished at this declaration and wrote immediately to Adams, "I must hurry over double quick to America and assume charge of Martha as soon as possible." He mentioned that Mrs. Cameron wanted the three of them to spend the summer in Switzerland, but he was perplexed. "If I don't work in the summer I shall have to stay in London in the fall. Martha should spend a very quiet summer in London. Can you put us up? Write and say if I'm doing the best thing."

Arriving soon thereafter in Washington, Lindsay took command, and he and Lizzie decided the wedding would take place within a month—on 18 March. Adams wrote to Mabel La Farge, "Martha says she is to be married in 10 days and as she has no outfit her mother must go over to London to fit her out. Mrs. Cameron has been shaken by the strain of the last few years and she is as little fit to go about alone as I am."

After her hurried trip to London for Martha's trousseau, Lizzie made plans for a very quiet home wedding. She commandeered Adams's house to accommodate the Lindsay and Sherman relatives. Adams complained half humorously to Mrs. Jack Gardner, "I am turned out of my house but only for tonight. Can you make me an hour for breakfast or dinner tomorrow? You shall have all that is left from weddings . . ."

The hostility of the Cameron family remained implacable. Although Lizzie had insisted that Martha invite her half-brother Jim Cameron, his answer in so many words was that "he would not speak to Mrs. Cameron or set foot in any house where she was."

The wedding took place on Thursday, 18 March 1909, at half past noon, in what *The Washington Post* called "the prettiest home wedding of the year." The ceremony was performed by the Reverend Mr. Roland Cotton Smith, pastor of nearby St. John's Episcopal Church, sometimes called the Church of Presidents. The best man was Martha's cousin Lieutenant Sherman Miles of the U.S. Army. The bride was unattended. She was dressed very simply in a severe suit of gray cheviot, with a short skirt, a close-fitting half-length coat, worn open and showing a white lingerie blouse. *The Washington Post* described her hat as "trimmed in rough straw, a mushroom sailor in Chinese blue, an ensemble of great simplicity, comfort and common sense. It shows the splendid type of girl the Earl of Crawford will have for a daughter-in-law and the Hon. Ronald Lindsay, former secretary of the British Embassy, is as winning as his bride."

A Husband for Martha

The couple departed on their honeymoon, and three days later Ronald Lindsay was writing to Henry Adams from Oatlands, Virginia.

> Of course I've never been on a honeymoon before so I don't know how to compare it with others. But I should say, on the whole, favorably. Martha has assured me many times that she is perfectly happy. Then, after mature consideration, she has definitely settled that marriage is a failure and she has done wrong in ever marrying me at all. Still the weather is fine and that is the point most in doubt. Our house is pretty and comfortable. I think even Martha will strike a balance sheet with the surplus appearing on the right side.

Lizzie was prostrated from the excitement but sailed at once for France. Adams noted that her first reaction was "to hide herself in her apartment in Paris, then slowly to emerge from her Niobe state."

17

"The Roman Matron Business"

After Martha Cameron's wedding, her mother gave up the house in Lafayette Square forever. Both Henry Adams and Lizzie Cameron knew that they were witnessing the end of an era. The closing of her salon caused Adams to indulge in a mood of nostalgia tinged with gloom. He wrote, "This town has been much upset socially by farewells and tearing of ties. Life is absurdly dear at the price one pays for it . . ." To Lizzie the move brought an even more poignant sense of loss, for her home on Lafayette Square had been the scene of her happiest days as a young mother, a reigning hostess, and the center of a romantic court.

Now she fled to Paris and took luxurious refuge in a large apartment on the top floor of the Hotel Crillon, high above the place de la Concorde, which commanded a sweeping view of the city. Adams, in his mildly satirical tone, described La Dona's behavior. "She has picked herself up and does the Roman matron business now with fine effect." In fact, he was concerned about her, for he saw that Lizzie, who was now 52 years old, was completely adrift. Although the timorous Martha would still try to cling to her mother, as she had for all of her 23 years, nevertheless, the young woman was now the responsibility of her husband, who was showing a strength and patience that were clearly required. But Lizzie was without any anchor—her home was gone, her daughter was married, her husband at 76 was as indifferent as ever. Only Henry Adams remained. If Lizzie had seemed a wanderer before, her travels, however erratic, had nevertheless had a purpose—the launching of Martha. That purpose was fulfilled. Now her search must be to find herself, a more difficult task in a pleasure-loving Edwardian age.

"I think," prophesied Adams, "she will get natural again in a few months but where or how she is to live the Lord may know." For the moment, she was languidly joining in the social activities of their brilliant little expatriate American society, which included Adams, Henry James, Edith Wharton, Ambassador and Mrs. Henry White, watercolorist Walter Gay, and Bernhard Berenson.

Suddenly Martha arrived, supposedly in search of Parisian clothes. "And diamond tiaras," observed Adams. "Her father gave her one and her pelican-mother another." But the bride of two months, complaining of exhaustion, was planning to stay with her mother until her husband succeeded in finding her a suitable home in London. Martha, who had achieved, with small effort on her part, what her contemporaries considered a "brilliant" marriage, was now confronted by the reality of married life. And she could respond only by crumpling into chronic invalidism. Ever since infancy, she had been emotionally dependent upon her mother and, having reached a supposed maturity at 23, she was still unable to break away. Dutifully, Lizzie tried to insist on the necessary separation from her by supporting Lindsay's efforts to make Martha into a self-reliant wife. But Lizzie had never admitted to herself that she was emotionally entangled with her daughter. In dismay, Ronald Lindsay watched as the imperious LIzzie, who could command an army of gallants, clung to her daughter even as she tried to send her away.

Henry Adams, of course, had been observing their mutual dependency for years, and Martha's impending collapse did not surprise him. He tried to encourage them both, writing to Lizzie, "Martha is suffering from nerves. Of course she can, like so many others of our friends, shut out all contact with the world. But the whole of her life depends on her nervous strength." Six weeks later, Lizzie was still complaining of sleeplessness, and he wrote to her, "I am sorry you can't make a successful effort to conquer your insomnia. I am callous to all but *foudreyeux* [struck by lightening] catastrophes. If you last five years you will outlast me and I ask no more of the universe."

The next day, he wrote sternly to Martha,

> Until you yourself are well and strong I don't see how you can deal with your mother. Things must begin with you. If you be vigorous-minded like a true Scotchwoman, you and your mother will not just go on dragging each other down. I don't know what is the matter with you but it is the same thing as with me. The same complaint affects us all sooner or later. Some of us sink sooner than others under the shock of getting old. In me it is a foolish irritability. In her you see what form it takes. Soon you are going to lose Ronald [to a new assignment]. But if you can only get courage and health enough to run him and yourself, then you can run us all.

But Martha did not heed his words. When Lindsay came over to Paris to bring her back to London, "looking as charming as ever and putting all other bridegrooms to shame," Martha insisted that she was unable to accompany him. "She is anything but stalwart," Adams remarked, "and she must go very soon and try to get some strength somewhere. I don't know where but it will have to be a mountain I suppose."

It was to the Bohemian resort of Marienbad that Lizzie took her daughter. Soon Adams visited them there, "running from invalid to invalid." But La Dona was not really an invalid. She had come in a state of emotional exhaustion to this quiet retreat, and in semi-isolation she was forcing herself to examine her situation. After a period of self-scrutiny, she turned to her own family in Cleveland. She poured out her feelings to her nephew Hal, who was a lawyer.

Your letter makes me feel that I am complaining which indeed I did not intend to do. I suppose the truth is that not only my nerves, but my *nerve* has a little given out. I cannot settle down anywhere and I have nothing to do—which is the worst of all. We all need some sort of occupation. My sleeplessness gives me nights of worry, for those are the black hours. Altogether I just sat down one day and wailed. It seems to me that nothing had better be done until I come back and try to tackle it myself first. Then if I fail, I will appeal to you for help.

During all the years of their loveless marriage, Senator Cameron and his wife had never had a formal separation. Now La Dona was ready for one, but on her own terms. To help her in dealing with her husband, she judged that her brothers-in-law Colgate Hoyt and General Nelson Miles were "worse than useless." So she was turning to Hal Sherman for help because "Donald likes you and if it comes to that, he would listen to you."

She referred bitterly to Jim Cameron, the senator's son, "whose hatred, fanned by his sisters, is now vindictive. He is absolutely controlled by his sisters and they have or think they have some cause of complaint of which I know nothing."

Lizzie spoke of her husband with an attempt at understanding. "I honestly think that Donald *means* to do well. But his one passion in life is now accumulation. For that he has given up home, comforts, even the decencies of life and he thinks I can do the same. And I am not to benefit by the accumulations—he has told me that. It is all for his children who are already rich."

Showing the vein of iron that characterized her during a crisis, Lizzie continued:

> I am trying my best to get well and steady in nerves, then I shall join him and try to arrange matters. If I cannot, then I must appeal for help. It isn't that I am afraid of poverty. It is the outside effect of being put in such a situation by a very rich man. His children stop at *nothing* in their abuse of me. It cannot really hurt me as long as he does not give it color. But the moment he does it becomes serious. That part of it I will not for a moment accept. If I can only make him see that, then I think that he will do the square thing—I *think* he will.
>
> But this mania of old age to have a large fortune is a passion —and it may dominate him.
>
> Donald is very cunning and I think he can outwit us all. But I do not think he wants a public separation any more than I do. I may handle him that way.

So Lizzie outlined her problems to her sympathetic nephew Hal. What followed, according to Cameron family legend, was a mutual agreement between Lizzie and her husband to maintain separate lives, with Lizzie making her permanent home in Europe, thus relieving the Cameron family of a hated embarrassment. For this concession, Senator Cameron would settle a sizable sum on her for life, through the establishment, in 1914, of a Cameron Trust. Martha was also a beneficiary in this trust, sharing with her half-brother James and her five half-sisters. The trust was administered by Don Cameron's son, James McCormick Cameron, and his grandnephew, J. Gardner Bradley, Sr.

"The Roman Matron Business"

The amount was not disclosed, since no written records of the agreement were kept. This was not unusual practice for Bradley, since, as one Cameron family descendent recalls, "He never kept any details on this in writing, any more than he wrote down anything on his coal mine operations in West Virginia. Uncle James was also secretive, yet he gave Simon's papers to the Library of Congress." In the absence of any documentation, both Senator Cameron and Lizzie apparently relied on the strength of each other's word to maintain the bargain.

By the last week of September 1909, Lizzie was tired of Marienbad, so she took her daughter back to Paris, where they were met by a beaming Ronald Lindsay, who had finally found a house for Martha in London's fashionable Cadogan Square. Adams looked on wistfully as both mother and daughter set about furnishing it, "plunging into it with an interest and happiness that made me feel almost myself again and back in 1870." On reflection, he added, "Of course it does not make me young again and still less does it rejuvenate Mrs. Cameron. She does get your usual bitter mama's pleasure out of playing the pelican and denudes herself of one feather after another until she must inevitably freeze to death on the nest. I see no pleasure in it for the uncle Pelican. When Mons. le Pelican comes home from his afternoon stroll, he finds tea a little weak."

When it was time for Lindsay to return to his work at the Foreign Office in London, he went alone, since Martha insisted that she was still not strong enough to travel. Because she was never able to travel alone, this meant that she would stay with her mother in Paris indefinitely.

In August 1909, tragedy had struck the little group of expatriates, with news of the death of the poet Bay Lodge, the father of three small children and the husband of dark-eyed Bessie. At 36 he had been stricken with a heart attack and had died in the arms of his father, Senator Henry Cabot Lodge, on Nantucket Island. Lizzie heard the news from the Lodges and sent the grim message to Adams, who was vacationing briefly in Switzerland.

Adams, who had known and loved George Cabot Lodge from infancy and had encouraged him in his writing, now wrote his condolences to Bay's widow and recalled his own tragedy

> How hard I found it to feel I was not alone. Even in the worst depths of solitude I was surprised to find that everyone, beyond childhood, was nursing or hiding some wound that was never spoken of but made the deepest feeling in life. What we really mourn is our own youth and the love it brought. Sooner or later it passes for us all but memory lives on it and nothing else...Nothing helps except to think of the happiness we have had and even that is a kind of self-torture. I am old enough not to try to make the suffering less. The woman and the child are the wonder of my old age. You are the true poems, the best he ever did.

Still mourning Bay's loss, Adams wrote to Lizzie, "I have gone through every possible loss and can lose nothing more except my life which all these amputations have reduced in value to a very small interest."

November came and Martha had not rejoined her husband. Adams noted, "Here is Martha who threatens some day to get well and here is her mother who is going home and looking for a steamer to take me with her." In December La Dona brought her daughter to London to rejoin Ronald Lindsay, and Adams agreed to follow for the holidays. Staying at a hotel in Belgravia, Adams visited the young couple in Cadogan Square and observed, "Martha's house is very pretty and furnished only with her mother's spoils from Washington." Martha had apparently recovered her health, and Adams noted before sailing for home, "Martha is much better and she seems to have become altogether absorbed in her Ronald and her house and her housekeeping and the English." Martha's recurring health crises whenever she was faced with responsibility and her resiliency when she had someone to lean on were familiar to Lizzie, who remarked, "Martha and Ronnie have gone off to a Court Ball, Martha crowned with a huge tiara. Give me one delicate woman to outwear two strong ones!"

By 1910, Adams had become a member of Edith Wharton's inner circle. According to Kenneth Clark, Mrs. Wharton, who was now an international figure, "had a dislike of disorder, was formidable, intelligent, well-disciplined, well-read in four languages. When bored she would listen with icy contempt, her mouth shut like a trap." Her home in Paris, which Adams called her "saloon," was a large, richly furnished apartment in an old mansion at 58 rue de Varenne, which she had rented from the George Vanderbilts. In her book *The Decoration of Houses,* which was published in 1897, she had stressed the virtues of simplicity. Yet here she was living amid Vanderbilt opulence—crimson Aubusson carpets, rare antiques, Chinese porcelains and bronzes. "It is decorated much as yours was," wrote Adams scornfully to Lizzie, "in the worst style of the Second Empire with a sort of German atmosphere, like stale tobacco, pervading it. Such an apartment as women seem to like. You would adore it."

For some time the members of the Adams-Cameron circle had been intent on bringing together Mrs. Wharton and Bernhard Berenson. An adviser to the international art dealer Joseph Duveen, B.B. was the acknowledged "authenticator" of Renaissance paintings. Berenson was "perched on the pinnacle of a mountain of corruption," wrote Kenneth Clark. "The air was thinner up there—but he could not get down." B.B. had once been introduced to Mrs. Wharton, but finding her disagreeable (he later learned this was due to shyness), he had resisted another meeting. But one day, as B.B. was leaving Adams's apartment at 50 avenue du Bois, Mrs. Cameron arrived by prearrangement, bringing along Edith Wharton. Introductions were gracefully acknowledged. A few nights later, Adams asked B.B. to dine with him at Voisin's, the fashionable restaurant. On his arrival B.B. was shown, not to Adams's usual table on the ground floor but to a room upstairs, where Adams greeted him and took him to a table by the window where they found Mrs. Wharton, her lover Morton Fullerton, Mrs. Cameron, and Martha Lindsay. This was the beginning of a staunch friendship between Berenson and Edith Wharton.

Lizzie was by now intimate with Mrs. Wharton, who called her "Dearest

Lizzie" and confided the emotional and financial problems that her husband was causing her. Teddy Wharton was showing signs of emotional instability and had been caught mishandling her funds. Undoubtedly the quick sympathy that sprang up between the two aristocratic ladies who became fast friends but never rivals was based in part on their mutual understanding of the misfortunes of love. Edith Wharton's marriage, which had never been happy, was nearing its end. She had recently become involved in a passionate but discreet affair with Morton Fullerton, an American journalist of charm and amatory experience. With her novelist's eye, she could discern the ambiguity of Lizzie's relations with Henry Adams. From her own endurance of an unhappy marriage, Lizzie was sympathetic to Mrs. Wharton's plight. So the two ladies reached a quick accord.

It was a brilliant society they moved in—including Henry James, who acted as Edith Wharton's literary mentor and teasingly referred to her as "The Firebird" or "The Angel of Devastation" while he enjoyed her "succulent and corrupting meals"; Bernhard Berenson and his talented wife Mary, who was likened to a figure by Giotto; U.S. Ambassador Henry White and his beautiful wife Margaret Rutherford White; French novelist Paul Bourget; the fashionable portrait painter Jacques-Émile Blanche; watercolorist Walter Gay and his wife Matilda. "Our little American group here is more closely intimate and agreeable than any now left me in America," Adams sighed contentedly, and after a memorable visit to the rue de Varenne, he exclaimed, "I dined at the Whartons yesterday with Matilda Gay and Mrs. Cameron. We were Paris!"

In February 1910, Edith Wharton decided to move from 58 to 53 rue de Varenne to a larger, unfurnished apartment. To smooth for her the arduous process of moving, Lizzie dispatched her footman to the new apartment, carrying a silver service for twelve, with four dozen dinner knives, blue glass salt cellars and pepper pots. In appreciation, Mrs. Wharton wrote, "I bless you whenever I look at my beautiful couverts."

Lizzie wrote to Adams in Washington that she had recently lunched with Mrs. Wharton, "who is translating her *Ethan Frome* into French. Teddy cabled that he intended to go to Bermuda. I hope he *will* go." The two ladies continued to exchange confidences, news, and gifts.

Toward the end of 1910, Mrs. Wharton wrote to Lizzie, "My news is mainly negative and consists in that absence of positive discomfort which is supposed by the experienced to constitute happiness." She thanked Lizzie for a package of tea she had ordered from Washington. "What a friend you are to send that precious package . . ." She sent Lizzie a gift "which brings you my love and I hope it will blend with the pale green of the loveliest of drawing rooms."

Even as Edith Wharton was contemplating divorce, Lizzie's own marriage was a source of dismay to her. Despite the agreed-on separation, when Lizzie was staying briefly at Sloane Square in London she suddenly encountered her husband. In annoyance, she wrote to Adams, "Don came in this morning as beaming and pleasant as if he had not let nine months go by without a sign of life."

After a reign of only nine years, Edward VII had just died. Together,

Lizzie, Martha, and the visiting Elizabeth Hoyt listened to the church bells of London tolling the death of the king, and together watched the magnificent funeral procession. On receiving an account of the funeral, Henry Adams declared, "It takes away what little breath is left to a simple modest Parisian."

By December 1910, Henry Adams's lease in Paris was not renewed, so he decided to move from 23 to 80 avenue du Bois de Boulogne, a few doors from Lizzie Cameron's apartment. He called on Lizzie's managerial abilities, and within a few days he was writing, "My new apartment fits me like a bear-skin fits a monkey. Still the jump is made and I am enormously astonished at my own energy. I hadn't supposed I could do it. In fact I didn't. Mrs. Cameron did nine tenths of it but I showed quite startling and youthful vigor in letting her."

Elizabeth Hoyt was a frequent visitor at Lizzie's Paris apartment, trying to fill the place in her aunt's affection left by the absent Martha. Elizabeth, who called her aunt by the family nickname Dilly, was an energetic young woman who was very different from her languid cousin Martha. She had been the first woman in New York State to acquire a driver's license, and she and her aunt loved to dash around Paris in Lizzie's open-top Peugeot. La Dona, who still felt responsible for her niece's social formation, took her to numerous social affairs, and Elizabeth complained of "one stupefying dinner with a mob of people with incomprehensible foreign names, hurried greetings and vaguely familiar faces whose names I lost forever. There was a long table covered with horrible roses and abortive fruit."

The two ladies planned a motor trip to Ajaccio, Corsica, and the only thing that marred their happiness was "the lack of a male escort." Lizzie's niece lamented "the wonderful rides up mountan gorges and through forests which of course we cannot take and parts of the country we cannot go without that hitherto useless creature." The fact that their driving would be done by a male chauffeur in livery did not apparently compensate for their manless state.

In Lizzie's Peugeot they climbed the Sicilian hills through a dense pine forest. When they reached a clearing, they encountered a torrential rain and a driving wind. Since the driver could not manage to put up the car's open top, his passengers were soaked by the freezing rain. "Our furs and tweeds leaked furiously," Elizabeth Hoyt recalled. Finally, they drew up before a small inn, where they were greeted by two friendly women proprietors who "undressed us like children and wrapped us in blankets and dressing gowns." Lizzie and her niece hung their wet undergarments on a line before the open fire—a row of steaming corsets, combinations, and drawers, and sat there sipping their tea. To their consternation, the chauffeur, still in his soaking uniform, entered the room. Impassively, without uttering a word, he carefully turned each one of the ladies' garments hanging on the line, then left the room.

Meanwhile, Martha wrote to Adams from the British Embassy at The Hague to which Lindsay had been transferred, and for once she sounded cheerful. "We are getting on so comfily and happily. Mother is South. We've had a terrible domestic row with the French chef whom we finally fired. Ronnie has his nose to the grindstone. Dear little Dordy, do write me soon."

"The Roman Matron Business"

Still on their motor tour, Lizzie and her niece drove up from Italy to the South of France, where they met Edith Wharton at Cannes. Lizzie described the scene for Adams. "The Americans here are impoverished like us or they are the riff-raff whom one does not know. And Teddy Wharton is on the ocean. Poor Edith — I wonder what she will do with him . . ."

One day while the two ladies were sitting, fully dressed, beneath a huge umbrella on the beach at Cannes, Gladys Rice heard Mrs. Cameron describing her recent stay at Bailey's Beach in Newport. "Why, my dear," Lizzie addressed Edith Wharton, "the young people actually lie — not sit, *lie* — beside each other on the sand. It curdles the blood to watch this sort of abandon." Gladys noticed that Mrs. Wharton said little — probably, she thought, because she was too busy taking notes for her next book. Lizzie continued

> with that strained and sharp quality in the timbre of her voice as though from too long and too severe a denial of the softer pleasures, "Now and then you see a girl who has removed her stockings entirely. Such an action began, I dare say, with an attempt to get the sand out, rolling them down for this purpose. Well, they've stayed down and doubtless will for good and all. The world, our world at home, is becoming a decidedly slipshod place. Manners everywhere appear to be disintegrating.

From The Hague, Lizzie received a cablegram from Ronald Lindsay that Martha had suffered a second miscarriage. She told Adams, "Martha had another mishap and is flat on her back. I think this time it is a disappointment. Nettie hovers over her like an angel so I am easy in mind." A week later, she wrote, "Martha has given me an anxious week. I am in readiness to go to The Hague if Ronnie telephones. It sounds like her breakdown of last year without colitis — pure nerves and inability to digest. And spells of fainting when she gets up — she is very panicky."

By March 1911, Martha was taking her first automobile ride since her "mishap," and Lizzie noted that "she bore it well. She wants to go to England for Easter. I may join her there. Ronnie is looking very badly. I fear the climate may not suit him." When Lizzie returned to her pied-à-terre at the Crillon in Paris, she found a letter from Martha's friend Gladys Vanderbilt offering her an apartment. "I call that luck," Lizzie wrote, "Here I am a whole month earlier than I expected with my house paid for a whole year and even the servants paid up to April 15. There is nothing like capturing a Vanderbilt."

Having sprained her ankle again, Lizzie hired a carriage for 600 francs an hour. "At least I can get around." She told Adams that Edith Wharton had just returned to Paris with her ailing husband, "looking fagged and worn. Teddy is on her hands. They all tell her he is physically well but I find him looking the reverse."

Meanwhile, Martha and Ronald Lindsay had rented a vacation home in Dorset to which they could return when he was on leave from The Hague. It was an 18th-century manor house called Stepleton set in a valley surrounded by small rolling hills in the countryside made famous by Thomas Hardy. All three of them fell in love with Stepleton, with its square solid lines, its eastern and western wings, and its eight bedrooms, which gave it a hospitable spaciousness. Wistfully, Lindsay wrote, "Stepleton is a priceless possession but formidable to maintain. I am glad at least one thing gives Martha unmixed happiness."

Elizabeth Hoyt recalled Stepleton as "a delicious place—great stretches of green meadows broken by clumps of trees such as one sees only in England, a garden moldy with age and neglect, winding lanes with high hedgerows of wild rose, clematis and hawthorn. Once Tudor in style, it was rebuilt and added on to in Georgian days."

Joining the Lindsays at Stepleton, Lizzie noted that "Martha looks pale and wan but she is in better shape than this time last year." "The woods are filled with primroses and violets," exclaimed Lizzie, "& there are buttercups along the lake." (This picturesque small lake was filmed for a scene in the British movie *Tom Jones*.)

Now that they had found Stepleton, Lizzie's "two poles of motion" became Paris and the English countryside. In the summer of 1911, from Lamb House, his home in Rye, Henry James invited her to come and bring their mutual friend Henry Adams for a visit. "The honor of receiving you will be one of the proudest in my life and any day whatever now will absolutely suit me." Lizzie invited him to Stepleton for a return visit, and in his reply James stated, "This place has been much more interesting since you were here and I shall arrive with the glamour of your visit still all hanging about us to mingle with the glamour (I don't mean for *you*) of mine."

In April 1912, Adams, who was now 74, was back in Washington planning his annual visit to Europe. He booked passage on the return voyage to Europe of the White Star liner *Titanic*, which was making its maiden voyage from Liverpool to New York through the North Atlantic. But on 15 April, the "unsinkable lifeboat" struck an iceberg off the Banks of Newfoundland and sank, with the loss of more than 1,500 lives. "In half an hour," wrote Adams, "just in a summer sea, were wrecked the Titanic, Pres. Taft, the Republican Party and I. We all foundered and disappeared." Adams was greatly disturbed by the catastrophe, writing to Lizzie, "By my blessed Virgin, it is awful. This Titanic blow shatters one's nerves. We can't grapple it."

A week later, while dining alone at home, Adams suffered a stroke, which at first seemed slight. He spoke clearly a request that Mrs. Cameron should close up his Paris apartment, then suffered a relapse into a state of disorientation, coma, and helplessness. Once during his delirium he tried to throw himself from a window. Doctors and nurses arrived, and his brother Charles took command. Adams alternated between periods of rationality and delirium and for a while the senility that he so dreaded seemed inevitable.

In Paris, Lizzie was anxious. She set about fulfilling his request and closed the apartment. She superintended the packing of his furniture and the collecting of all his books and papers but found "very few papers and no manuscripts." She sent off a barrage of cables to Adams's physician, Dr. Yarrow, and to his brother Charles, asking when she might come and if she might write. But the Adams family had closed ranks around the invalid. They had no wish for the arrival of Mrs. Cameron.

On 17 May, Charles Francis Adams wrote to her gloomily, "As far as the knowable forecast of the future goes, he will probably for the remainder of his life be in charge of physicians and trained nurses. You ask whether you can write him. Of course there is no objection but your letter will have to pass through the hands of those in attendance. If a letter were read to him I doubt if he would take in its significance. The great thing now is to help him be quiet and comfortable."

By mid-June, Adams was strong enough to be moved by private railroad car to a cottage on Charles's estate, Birnam Wood in South Lincoln, Massachusetts, where doctors, nurses, family members, and nieces all competed in taking care of him. Meanwhile, Lizzie was pleading from Paris for permission to come. But the Adams family were uniformly opposed. Henry Adams's sister Mary Adams Quincy, in Dedham, wrote angrily to her brother Charles,

> Above all things we [his own family] must have the control of everything around him. I object extremely to have *any* woman round him outside his family. I am told Mrs. Cameron is telegraphing to ask if she can come and I have sent her a cable to tell her not to think of it as she could do nothing for him and he would not recognize her.
>
> I tell you fairly [she continued, in growing fury] I won't have her; rather than that I would go there myself and keep her out. There has been disagreeable scandal enough about that affair and we certainly cannot permit people to say that in his last illness she came from Europe to look after him! I oppose absolutely allowing any women with him who do not belong to his family.

Fortified by this uncompromising statement, Charles Francis Adams wrote Lizzie, "Were you here you would be simply another supernumerary in and about the house. Of course there are already sufficient—Loolie [Hooper], Mrs. Charles Francis, my daughter and Mrs. Lodge." He prophesied, with characteristic Adams gloom, "He will be simply a helpless invalid. We have excellent sanitariums here."

Lizzie had cabled Dr. Yarrow for information about Adams's condition. The physician was equally pessimistic.

> He had the seizure some weeks hence, which was either a cerebral hemorrhage or a clot in one of the arteries of the brain. At times he is slightly rational, at other times he recognizes no one. We have to watch him most carefully. He sees the family at all times but interviews are unsatisfactory. I have very little hope for the future. You will see, my dear lady, that if I were to ask him about yourself his mind is as yet in no condition to appreciate any action on your part. One day he might say "Come" and in a few hours he might not be able to see or recognize you.

Even Henry James, who always managed to keep informed on news of their far-flung circle of friends, caught the feeling of opposition of the Adams family, and writing to Lizzie from the Reform Club in Pall Mall, expressed himself with uncharacteristic directness. "I can't help feeling with a pang or at least a groan that your going over to the dire American midsummer may be involved. To speak crudely and familiarly they clearly—by all their gestures—'don't want you' (and by they I mean simply They). So that if your dear Henry should have difficulties of communication, expression or even perception, they will overflow with superiority."

While Lizzie continued to wait for someone in South Lincoln to bid her to come, she was the headquarters in Paris for news concerning Adams's condition. Berenson wrote to her from I Tatti, "Your news fills me with hope and rejoicing. If only he could recover and gladden us again with something like the gloom we love so much, what a difference it would make. In my heart of hearts I cannot help praying for what I want so much." (This from Berenson, who had been successively a Jew, a Catholic, an Episcopalian, and finally, as he called himself, "A Christianity graduate.") Edith Wharton reported that every day the little group conferred anxiously with Lizzie, demanding to know "What is the latest news of Uncle Henry?"

Almost miraculously, Adams began to improve. His speech was restored. His thinking was as clear and penetrating as ever, and there was little sign of paralysis. As his patient progressed, his doctor could hardly tear himself from his bedside, so fascinating did he find his conversation.

La Dona made up her mind to go to her tame cat. Henry James wrote to her admiringly, "I want to thank you for your kind news and to bless your magnificent journey. It is magnificent—but of course *you* are magnificent. If you do see Henry Adams but once, you will be glad to the last intensity that you have done so and you carry with you the fondest participation and admiration always of yours all faithfully..."

As Henry Adams's condition progressed, Mrs. Lodge wanted to carry him off to her more luxurious summer home at Nahant, a prospect that dismayed Charles Francis Adams, who was convinced that his Spartan regime was responsible for Henry's improvement. When Charles learned that, despite the combined and forceful opposition of the entire Adams family, Mrs. Cameron was coming anyway, his sarcasm was unbounded. "Perhaps," he wrote to Anna Cabot Lodge, "it would fill the bill to overflowing if Mrs. Cameron took advantage of your kind invitation and carried Henry off in triumph and our motor to your castle by the far-sounding sea, there to enjoy a somewhat superannuated honeymoon!"

As if he were unaware of the Camerons' separation, he added, "But all the time where is Don? Where—oh where?" With another angry slash, he exploded, "Henry Adams of Washington D.C. as 'co-respondent' and your house as 'locum in quo' will sound good!"

By the middle of July, Henry Adams was able to write to Mrs. Lodge, "I expect Mrs. Cameron here next week or this week perhaps. I do not know how long she will stay or whether she will have to go back to Martha."

On 26 July, La Dona, "all sweet compliance," arrived in South Lincoln, prepared to "devote her life" to her beloved invalid. Adams was as delighted to see her as she was surprised to see that he was almost well. Several times she drove from Boston to Birnam Wood to be at his side, airily disregarding the chill stares of his relatives. But it was clear to Lizzie Cameron that they all— Charles and Minnie Adams, Brooks and Daisy, Mary Adams Quincy, even her devoted friend Nannie Lodge, regarded her presence as an embarrassment. Instead of a ministering angel, she was considered by them, beneath their rigid politeness, as little more than an attractive nuisance. Even Adams, who had so often complained of his relatives while he skillfully evaded them, seemed contented, settled among them and accepting their ministrations. Most critical of her was the perennially scathing Charles. "The Cameron-Adams arrangement is flagrant!" he later exclaimed. "As the expression goes, 'it smells to Heaven' under my very nose."

After a few visits, Lizzie gracefully withdrew, departing for Bar Harbor's livelier social milieu. "Of course I am sorry to have you go," wrote Adams after she had left. But like any recovering invalid, he was now very much concerned with his immediate future. "I can get on well here so long as I am a summer invalid, but if I am sent off to Europe on the idea that I am well the deuce knows how I am to work it. I must have relays of support everywhere." Clearly he was looking to her for support as she had for years turned to him. Learning that she would be in Italy for the winter, he added, "My main hope is that you should be in Rome and I shall want constant news about your movements."

He was more cheerful in October, writing to her, now back in London, "Do I get well or not? I don't know. There is some aphasia but the paralysis retreats." Then he told her of his recent meeting with Isabella Stewart Gardner, who was the same age as he. "She is wonderfully old and wrinkled, far beyond me, but in movement and energy she knocked me silly. She is far the youngest and spryest but"—here he may have chuckled—"a wrinkled old fairy just the same."

Dolefully he reported the death of their old friend the sprightly Emily Beale, reminiscing, "Those years from 1880 to 1885 when you and she were so much and so young and so bright, were the last years of life, when I loved and hated and the world was real."

18

"Death Knocks At Every Door But Mine"

By the winter of 1913, Adams, restored to health, was finding himself increasingly absorbed in the study of French medieval chansons. He had acquired a young secretary-companion, Aileen Tone, who was a capable musician, and for her use Adams had installed a Steinway piano. Once again his home became a center for distinguished visitors. One day there was a new arrival—Father John La Farge S.J., the youngest son and namesake of his old friend, who had died in 1910. In his autobiography *The Manner Is Ordinary,* Father La Farge recalls that a large consignment of medieval liturgical volumes from France had just arrived at Lafayette Square and that Aileen Tone asked him to help her in working out the musical notation. He spent an hour at the piano, explaining to her the basic ideas of plainchant and its notation— enough to enable Miss Tone to sing some of the melodies in turn to Adams. For Miss Tone, it was the introduction to a subject of lifelong interest.

Adams welcomed Father La Farge warmly and, as Aileen Tone observed later in retrospect, with a notable sense of liberation. They sat by the open fire in the big living room while Adams talked long and affectionately about his old friend, the elder La Farge, whose presence he greatly missed. Shortly after the young La Farge's ordination in 1905, Adams had written from Paris to Mabel Hooper La Farge, the young priest's sister-in-law, "Perhaps John will kindly stick me into his Mass. I need it more than you. I've not the least objection to being prayed for. . . . I'm afraid the objection would come from the Church. In all my life I've never met a Church willing to touch me."

As Adams (who was sometimes nicknamed "The Old Cardinal") sat in his low chair and talked earnestly in the firelight, Father La Farge recalls, he indicated that he was inwardly troubled and was searching for a religious faith, yet it was not easy to press the matter further. "One thing none could venture with Henry Adams, not even his nearest and dearest: that was to put to him any questions." But it seemed evident to Father La Farge that Adams's "religious convictions were more definite than his somewhat elusive exterior gave the world to believe. If there is doubt on the matter—and someone can always make a case for skepticism—certainly the benefit of the doubt would seem to rest with one who could write the passionate 'Prayer to the Virgin of Chartres,' which was found after his death in a little wallet of special papers."

Here Father La Farge mentions that Mabel La Farge told him that these verses were shown by Adams to only one friend, "a sister in the 12th century," (This was Adams's name for Margaret Chanler, who was a lover of plainchant.) Aileen Tone, however, had learned of the verses, as did Mrs. Ward Thoron, Mabel's sister, "to whom he sent the only other copy." Presumably none of these women knew that the first fair copy of the "Prayer" had gone to Lizzie Cameron immediately after Adams wrote it.

Just as Adams had buried himself in the Middle Ages when he was writing his *Chartres*, now, in his seventies and with failing vision, he pored over the music of the 12th and 13th centuries with a magnifying glass. These songs of the troubadours and trouvères were written by some of the best poets of their time. As Aileen Tone sang them to him, he quickly recognized the very poems to which he had devoted a chapter in *Chartres*. During his last trip to Paris he had hired the musicologists Henri Expert and Amédée Gastoué to search for these chansons in the Bibliothèque Nationale and the Arsenal, and when they uncovered manuscripts that had lain undisturbed by scholars for more than six hundred years, Adams was overjoyed. "I wish Walter Scott were alive to share them with me!" he exclaimed. "He would have enjoyed the fun of Coeur de Lion and Blondel quite fresh from the Crusades, as good as the west front of Chartres."

In the beginning, of course, no one knew how these songs should be sung. But Adams and Miss Tone accepted the conclusion that they were best expressed in the Gregorian manner, and he encouraged her to sing with greater freedom of rhythm, guided by the literary meter of the poems. "We know too little about the rhythmic notation," the shocked Gastoué said, "and there are too many conflicting theories. Perhaps in 30 years scholars may approach this subject." "But we're singing for pleasure," replied Adams, "and we're singing as artists. Besides, I can't wait 30 years!"

Now that it was decided that Adams was strong enough to return to Paris in April 1913, he looked forward to being with La Dona again. But Lizzie saw less of him than formerly because of her increasing preoccupation with Martha. The young woman was still turning to her mother whenever a crisis arose, and crises were frequent. No place on earth suited her fluctuating spirits for long—certainly not Cairo, where Ronald Lindsay was attached to the British Ministry of Finance. Here she was wilting under the extreme heat, which sometimes reached 110 degrees, until Lizzie decided to carry her off to the Villa Concordia at St. Moritz. Into this Swiss chalet with elaborately carved wooden balconies, which was set on a hilltop with a breathtaking view, Lizzie settled, with Martha and Elizabeth Hoyt, attended by the butler and cook whom she had brought from Paris. To her old friend Ralph Curtis, another American expatriate in Paris, she explained, "The journey was trying but here we are perched on the mountainside and from the first day Martha began to thrive. The usual people are here—fewer Italians who now go up to the Lido—but Bertha and Belmonte and the Countess Piccolomini." The colorful

Italian countess had the villa opposite Lizzie's, and Lizzie watched in amusement as "she enacts the last scene of Camille on a bed with rose colored curtains, lace bedcover, negligee and an audience."

While Martha reclined languidly reading on the balcony, Lizzie and her niece scrambled about the surrounding hills in search of wild flowers. In the evening, thinking that the young women needed diversion, she took them to the ballroom of the Palace Hotel, where they were confronted with the spectacle of the younger generation at play. Lizzie, who was now 56 and had developed the air of a *grande dame*, had begun to realize that the days of Edwardian formality and elegance were over. But this sudden view of the casual manners, scanty attire, and frenzied pace of a society poised on the brink of a war appalled her. She described for Curtis "the slim young girls without an ounce of flesh on their bones, dancing in shocking costumes, shocking dances with shocking looking men. There is a dance which is called The Fishwalk which is so indecent. The worst part of it is that the girls are so pretty—their little feet in perfect shoes twinkle as they fly around. What is the matter with this age of ours? Am I early Victorian that I feel so shocked?" Among the rapidly gyrating dancers she spotted a young German soldier invalided out of service with a bullet still in his body. "They say he has only one lung but he dances as if he had six. On the whole I don't believe it is a gay season."

Amid the mindless gaiety of those "fluffy, fuzzy people" who frequented the fashionable resorts of Europe, Lizzie was among the few who caught the rumble of impending disaster. "These people dance and dine, while close by Bulgaria and Serbia and Montenegro suffer and die. It is like 1789."

Returning to London to help her reluctant daughter prepare for her return to Cairo, Lizzie looked about for a traveling companion for Martha. Her choice fell on Laura Chanler (who would later marry the son of Stanford White). The young woman had just arrived in England, proudly carrying her new nurse's cap from Columbia Presbyterian Hospital in New York. She was eager to begin her nursing career in a country that might soon be at war. She saw that Martha "was still very timid. She would not travel alone and later became queer. At first I agreed to go to Egypt with her but then I changed my mind. When I told them my decision, Mrs. Cameron was wild. We had a serious falling out although there was no confrontation. I never saw Martha again." So Lizzie, although she grumbled, "I am the wrong person for her—I am too interested," had to accompany Martha back to Cairo.

In November 1913, Adams saw the published edition of *Mont-Saint-Michel and Chartres,* which he had had privately printed in 1904. Now it appeared under the sponsorship of the American Institute of Architects and with a "flaming preface" by Ralph Adams Cram. The advance sales broke all the publisher's previous records. "Here I am telling everybody I am quite dotty and bedridden," Adams noted with amusement, "and the papers are reviewing me as a youthful beginner." Later he wrote to Lizzie, "People send me press notices of Chartres...not one has yet been aware that I ever wrote anything else."

Henry Adams
drawing by John Briggs Potter

By the year 1914, international tensions were mounting, as social and political convulsions occurred all over Europe. In June, Adams realized with gleeful horror that many of his doom-filled prophecies were likely to be proved accurate. From his apartment on the avenue du Trocadéro, he wrote to his friend Gaskell, "I've said so long that the world has gone to the devil that I now enjoy seeing the process. He pictured the prevailing sense of hopelessness: "The life is that of the fourth century without Saint Augustine. In those days people—some people—thought they could escape into the next world, but now they know they are going to be drowned, so they dance and play ball. No one cares. I do not exaggerate. No one anywhere, socialist, capitalist or religionist takes it seriously or expects a future. We each hope for ourselves to escape in time but no one looks for more than one generation."

To those who were historically minded like Adams, it was evident that the great age of Western civilization was crumbling, an epoch the likes of which would not be seen again. The assassination of Archduke Francis Ferdinand, heir to the thrones of Austria and Hungary, in the Bosnian town of Sarajevo was the match that ignited the conflagration. Austria-Hungary declared war on Serbia. Germany declared war on Russia and on France, and the German army invaded Belgium. By 4 August, when Great Britain declared war on Germany, most of Europe was officially and actually at war.

Later that month, Lizzie and Martha were vacationing in Venice at the Grand Hotel. To Lizzie's chagrin, "a panicky consul" insisted that they leave the lovely city, which was by now almost deserted. Then Martha became more panicky than the consul and insisted that Lizzie return with her to Cairo. From Venice they hired a carriage to Milan, having heard of a ship about to sail from Genoa. But they found Milan in disorder, "so crowded and noisy, with hundreds of stranded Russians struggling to get home via Constantinople. "The war news is terrible," Lizzie wrote. "Poor France and brave little Belgium. Farms and homesteads devastated and blood flowing in the rivers. But my faith is pinned on that great slow-moving Russian bear which may crush Prussia under its paws." At Genoa they found all the ships so crowded that people were forced to sleep on deck, while in many cases five passengers were squeezed into staterooms built for two. Using her influence, Lizzie obtained "an inside room with four shelves" on the steamship *Nile*, and "we are waiting to see if by bribery and influence we can get a fifth shelf somewhere. The passengers are apes, with apes' habits. I shall dream nights of the plumbing. One bath was used as a receptacle for dirty linen. Other arrangements were unspeakable." After eight days, they reached Cairo, and Lizzie sighed. "I have no plans and no money. I shall simply mark time, living on Ronnie in the meantime."

Meanwhile, 50 miles from Paris at the Château de Coubertin, which Adams had rented for the summer, he and his little dovecote of nieces heard all the church bells tolling. As the tocsin began clanging from every steeple across the countryside, every able-bodied Frenchman reached in his pocket for his mobilization number and reported to the nearest recruiting station. In the face of a German invasion, Adams and his party were now regarded as foreigners. They had to register in the village and obtain their *permits de séjour* allowing them to remain until they could be evacuated to Paris on the first train for foreign residents. At the registry Adams gave his name but was so nervous when asked his mother's name he could not remember it. "What the devil was my mother's name?" he asked a niece. Yet when they reached Paris, he regained his composure—here he was at the heart of things. Although there were no newspapers, he was kept informed through his friends Robert and Mildred Bliss at the U.S. Embassy. The frail but indomitable 76-year-old uncle comforted his young nieces, and for a time they considered staying in Paris. But soon he found that all automobiles were being requisitioned by the government, servants were becoming unobtainable, food was growing scarce. Squads of conscripts marched through the streets hour after hour. The war bulletins became more alarming, and in the absence of newspapers, rumors proliferated. For the safety of his young women, Adams decided to leave Paris. At Dieppe they boarded the last boat carrying passengers across the English Channel and arrived in London en route to Stepleton. Here they found refuge in the Lindsays' home, still staffed with servants, although Lizzie and the Lindsays were still in Cairo.

"We got out of Paris just in time and Stepleton was Paradise," wrote Adams gratefully to Ronald Lindsay, "It was an escape from what verged on Hell." Adams, who had endured many ordeals in his life, was now visibly shaken. "I own that the war has been rather too much for me . . . When one's universe goes to pieces just on one's head, one has to scramble. I see no way out of it. For the first time in my life, I am quite staggered. I have stiffly held my tongue and listened while everyone chatters, but as yet I see no light. I see none in the triumph of either party. If we wipe Germany off the map it is no better."

Meanwhile, from Cairo, Mrs. Cameron was offering her Paris apartment as a temporary refuge for former Ambassador and Mrs. Henry White. To her niece Cecilia Reber she expressed the prevailing hatred of the enemy. "I hope that peace will not be inaugurated until German power is crushed for generations to come . . . Let them be crushed until the militarism of Prussia is downed and a constitutional government established. Then the best side of the Germans will have a chance of development. The average German is a good enough creature—it is the arrogant 'junker' with his gospel of 'might is right' who must be destroyed."

Now safely established in Stepleton with his nieces, while his dear *proprietaire* was in Cairo and his friend Cecil Spring-Rice was in Washington as the British ambassador, Adams received a visit from Berenson. The art historian, who was distraught about the war, motored down from London. "Ever since August first I am unable to think or write—except war," he declared. "I get more excited daily, my nerves are as bad as 15 years ago." Mr. Adams and Mr. Berenson—as they continued to address each other—found comfort in each other's presence as they contemplated civilization—the civilization they had both enjoyed—crashing in ruins around them.

B.B., who only a few years earlier had listened sympathetically to

Lizzie's confidences about her affair with Trumbull Stickney, now wrote to her from Stepleton:

> Dear Elizabeth: I am writing at your desk and in your room. What delightful Tudor-like paneling and what is it doing in this house of such perfect Anglo-Venetian architecture? What a heavenly place it is altogether. I only wish you were here too. We wrote to you repeatedly this summer, but nothing reached you. Mr. Adams had a letter from you this morning and read out a good deal. I find Mr. Adams looking extraordinarily well, he seems thoroughly enjoying this fair haven and regrets leaving. He is in very good form and happily quite as anti-Prussian as myself. He is not so eager and excited as the rest of us and I envy him for I am a wreck over it.

As always, Adams's essential steadiness in the presence of turmoil prevailed and allowed him to comfort the fearful and the agitated who sought his strength.

At Lamb House in Rye, Henry James was in even greater distress than Berenson, horrified at the Great War, which he called "the funeral speech of our murdered civilization." Learning that Adams was in residence at Stepleton, he motored over to visit his old friend. Aileen Tone later remembered "the encounter of the two Henrys, how they threw their arms around each other as if bridging a great chasm." This was their last meeting. It was indeed a bridging of two opposites. As R. P. Blackmur writes in *A Primer of Ignorance,*

> Both men were obstinately artists at bottom. Their relationship was largely personal for neither had read the bulk of the other's work. Their knowledge of each other was on a social not an imaginative plane. But they had enough in common to be complementary. Both were members of a vanishing society and each had kept an astigmatic, selective but sharp eye on what was vanishing, including each other. At the moment their world was blowing up, these two bald men in their 70's found a common ground, each strengthening the other in a common vision of all that had happened, all that they had, by the power of imagination, actually survived. Both felt the stress and horror of war. Under it Henry James broke down. Adams did not. Henry James had only his sensibility and it sucked up horror like a vacuum . . . but Adams had a formed, provisional intellect which guided his sensibility without excess. He was partisan but he kept his head. He knew what was coming—the outward toppling of a collapse which had already occurred. Another world was coming in which he would take no part. He was the morning star fading unnoticed in the thunderstorm at dawn.

In October 1914, Adams left Stepleton and, despite the hazards of wartime voyaging, reached America safely. Back in Lafayette Square, he resumed his letters to Lizzie Cameron, writing with his usual black humor. "Thank God I never was cheerful. I come from the happy stock of the Mathers who, as you remember, passed sweet mornings reflecting on the goodness of God and the damnation of infants."

Lizzie was still in Cairo in January 1915, and she described the city as "a vast camp and khaki clothes the street in brown." She had attended the recent ceremony at which the British government had celebrated the establishment of its protectorate over Egypt. "But the average Egyptian," Lizzie remarked, "is too ignorant to know under whose rule he is and the crowds on the street only showed apathy. They didn't in the least understand what it was all about." Among the British, Australian, and New Zealand troops, the Egyptian effendi "went in mortal terror of the English. They dare not murmur. One night when 'God Save the King' was played in the cafe, they did not rise so the Ceylonese troops threw them into the street. Now they are so afraid of another mistake—they cannot recognize any European tune—that they spring to their feet every time a band plays anything." Lizzie described the warships that she had seen standing by in the Suez Canal and the Red Sea, and suddenly she burst out, "I am so heartily sick of this war and it will last so long. Remember that not a foot of German soil has been touched. All the fighting and devastation has been on Allied territory. The Germans still have the offensive."

Adams, as mentally vigorous as ever, was enjoying his old seat "at the center of the web." He told Lizzie in January 1915, "This morning Cabot Lodge dropped in and fulminated against Woodrow Wilson, as usual, for Cabot raves against that great man who seems, in truth, to be much of the Maryland schoolmaster type." Senator Lodge's furious denunciations of the president one day caused Adams, in the presence of Ambassador Spring-Rice and his wife, to strike the dining table with his trembling fist and icily declare, "Cabot! I've never allowed treasonable conversation at this table and I don't propose to allow it now."

Among the visitors to the Lafayette Square noonday breakfasts was Monsignor Sigourney Fay, a professor at Catholic University and the secretary to Cardinal Gibbons of Baltimore. To Lizzie, Adams wrote with amusement, "Father Fay is no bore—far from it, but I think he has an idea I want conversion, for he directs his talk much to me and instructs me. Bless the genial sinner! He had better look out that I don't convert him, for his old church is really too childish for a hell like this year of grace."

In this same semi-cheerful mood he wrote to her on his birthday, 16 February, "You have laughed at me for 35 years for gloom but now you must laugh at someone else. I am the only gay reprobate now extant."

As spring arrived, Lizzie was still a "prisoner" in Cairo, unable to obtain a cabin on any ship headed for Marseilles, whence she hoped to find a train for Paris. Under wartime censorship she was cut off from news of Europe or America—it took two weeks for the London *Times* to reach Cairo. So the Americans and the British in Egypt listened to a variety of atrocity stories, such as the tale about German soldiers taking over a French convent and holding prisoner 70 French nuns, all of whom they violated and some of whom they murdered.

At last, in August, Lizzie and Martha obtained passage for France and left the intense heat of an Egyptian summer. "The voyage was delicious and once on board we forgot submarines and enjoyed perfect weather." They stopped at Malta, where, in the hospital, they found among the *grands blessés* several young men they had known in Cairo. "One boy who haunted our house all winter had a brain wound and one eye blown out. He was so pitifully ill and clung to us so." They watched the bustle of Marseilles, with German prisoners performing the dockwork and old men acting as porters. Their train for Paris arrived on time, and as they sped through the French countryside, they saw women and children performing the harvesting, assisted by squads of soldiers who had been released for this duty and sent to aid the villagers. Finally they reached Paris. "Paris seems fairly normal," Lizzie wrote, "about as empty and calm as it is every August. Only the one-legged men hobbling about and the incessant buzz and whirr of watching aeroplanes reminded us we were near the seat of war."

But as they headed north, the difficulties of travel were just beginning for Lizzie. Martha, who carried a British passport, had no trouble; "in twenty minutes the British flag got her through." But Lizzie was an American and a citizen of a neutral country. For the first time in her life she found it "humiliating to be an American just now. It took me three days of innumerable trips to consulates and prefectures to get my papers in order. The Germans have forged our passports to such an extent and hyphenated Americans have behaved so badly that we are all suspect. Also we know that our flag won't protect us." The train from Amiens moved very slowly on account of the troop trains and the convoys carrying provisions. At Boulogne and at Folkestone, the two ladies stood in line for more than an hour, holding their luggage and waiting to have their passports stamped. When they boarded the train, they found that all the shades were pulled down because of the danger of air raids. Finally, at 11 o'clock at night, the two travelers reached Stepleton, as grateful for its quiet serenity as Henry Adams had been a year earlier. "The very echoes die away before they reach us," Lizzie noted.

But Lizzie soon tired of her remoteness from the scene of action and returned to wartime Paris, where, in October, Edith Wharton invited her to join in the work at Le Foyer aux Réfugiés, "if you still want a dull job." To this never dull but constantly challenging work Lizzie gave herself with a dedication that surprised even herself. Not only did she handle the everday details of running the Grocery Depôt, she spent countless hours finding clothing and housing for the refugees. She proved to be a highly successful fund raiser, conspiring with Adams and Wilkinson and her many well-to-do friends in America to acquire money and clothes for "my poor." "If you want to help," she wrote to Adams, "send me $50—a cheque on America that I may benefit by the exchange—to buy coal. The problem of buying shoes for 650 children in our rescue homes keeps me awake nights." To Henry Wilkinson she wrote of such horror tales. "A soldier's wife gets 25 cents a day but if her husband is a German hostage she gets no money at all. Last week I ran all over Paris begging for a pair of trousers—the men leave the hospitals with no clothes. The little children are merry and well-mannered but when they are a little older they are so prematurely aged and sober." Thanking Wilkinson for a huge box of children's clothes that he and his wife had sent, she added, "I am so old-fashioned I believe a blessing will fall on your two little boys."

Between 1915 and 1917, Lizzie, working with Edith Wharton and Elisina Tyler, managed to raise more than $100,000 to help the refugees in France. At Lizzie's suggestion, Mrs. Wharton wrote letters to the New York *Herald* and to *The New York Times*, describing their work and begging for money to aid it. "My tongue is so much glibber than my pen," Lizzie explained.

She described for Adams the new friends she had met through Edith Wharton—the Royall Tylers. "He is just the kind you would dote upon. I believe his metier is deciphering manuscripts in the British Museum—15th and 16th century. Personally he is not only intelligent and learned but he has something of the exuberant, joyous quality of Bay Lodge, with a tremendous sense of humor and an infectious laugh." Tyler's wife was the beautiful Italian countess Elisina Palamadessi di Castelvecchio Tyler, who soon became Edith's right arm in the refugee work. "She is Italian, a direct contradiction to all of one's traditional ideas of an Italian woman. A steam-roller is easy compared to her. Clear-headed, executive, practical, she drives us all before her. You can imagine what a team she makes with Edith when they are together."

Early in December 1915, both Adams and Lizzie Cameron learned that Henry James had suffered a stroke in his London residence. "It is slight so far and it affects only his left side," Lizzie wrote to Adams. "If Edith is allowed by the doctors she will go to England but I am sure it will be forbidden as I was when you were ill." Although there was no family opposition to a visit by the "Firebird," Edith Wharton remained in Paris. James lingered for three months and died on 28 February 1916. Adams was stricken at the news. "Harry's death hits me harder than any stroke since my brother Charles' death a year ago. Not only was he a friend of mine for more than 40 years, but he also belonged to the circle of my wife's set long before I knew him or her and you know how I have clung to all that belonged to my wife." James's friends were convinced that his end had been hastened by the war, which he had called "a nightmare from which there is no waking save by sleep."

Throughout the dark winter of 1916, while the Germans blockaded the British Isles and the news from the front was bleak, Lizzie received the new victims of war. "The refugees from Rheims are very superior—patient and cheerful but with an intense longing to go home. They have lost their homes, savings, everything and live in miserable lodgings, some huddled seven to a room. It seems wicked to let them depend just upon that stipend which is given rigorously because the money won't hold out if the war lasts too long. The poor are suffering horribly. I am using every penny I own to clothe and shoe them." One day, as she battled her way through a huge snowstorm, she came upon a pair of men's shoes. "A tiara would not have pleased me so much." Only once did she complain, and that was about the details of running a house which she had always left to her housekeeper. "I can take a house," she declared, "wrestle with the landlord, assemble my women and children and assign rooms, but calculating how many brooms and washcloths per floor is more mental strain than a geometry problem."

Edith Wharton, having heard a false rumor that Lizzie was engaged, wrote to her from Hyères, "Even if you're not engaged to be married, isn't it time you took a holiday too? The Bernard Berensons have written imploring me to come to I Tatti and to 'bring a friend.' I choose you. You looked very tired when I left." Lizzie hesitated, and again Mrs. Wharton wrote, "Dearest Lizzie: Don't think me a bore with my many invitations. I should like to have a little of my idleness with you. You know even Elisina took three weeks in February."

Lizzie's next message from Mrs. Wharton was an excited phone call announcing, "Martha and Ronnie are in Marseilles!" Lizzie was astonished. She knew that Martha had been afraid to leave Cairo because of the submarines, but when Lindsay was able to obtain a leave and they learned they could get passage on a troopship carrying Annamite soldiers and conveyed by a destroyer, "they packed in two days" and set off, having told Mrs. Wharton of their plans in order to save Lizzie days and nights of anxious waiting. When Lizzie saw the two travelers, she exclaimed, "They both looked like the end of a misspent life. Their ship had rescued two boatloads of torpedoed people and zigzagged through the Greek isles. But they are here—and safe." The Lindsays departed for Chamonix for a rest, and before Ronnie returned to Egypt, Lizzie, admitting, "I am getting very tired," joined them in the mountain resort. Soon Edith Wharton, too, arrived, suffering from anemia and an irregular heartbeat. "The doctor says my heart is off the track and packed me off to the mountains so I come to join you. I hope Chamonix is not too high for me."

After her holiday, Lizzie returned with Martha to Paris, where the young woman began work as a nurse's aide in a hospital caring for the severely wounded. "Martha is up at six in the morning and returns at eight at night," her mother wrote proudly, "yet she thrives. She is better than she's been in years—she hasn't time to think of her *petite santé*. She looks very pretty in her nurse's uniform and the men adore her." Her work so pleased the hospital matron that she gave Martha the rank of registered nurse. "The work is not easy," Lizzie reported, "No light cases—only the *grands blessés*—poor shattered and maimed remnants of humanity."

Amid her wartime responsibilities, Lizzie did not forget her relatives in America, especially her favorite niece, Cecilia Reber, who had two bright young sons, Miles and Samuel. As concerned about their proper education as she had once been about Cecilia's, Lizzie wrote to Adams to get information about the Choate School in Wallingford, Connecticut, and sent her niece a check for $500 for their schooling—"in case of my death—we are not a long-lived family." Urging Mrs. Reber to send each of the boys to an established private school, she declared, "Home education leaves out something intangible. Perhaps it is an awakening to self and to personal reliance and responsibility."

As the Great War continued and her native land remained neutral, Lizzie wrote with growing anger to her nephew Sherman Miles, a West Point graduate, "America is rotten with Peace at any Price—and an incurable frivolity and lack of comprehension of serious questions. Woodrow Wilson has succeeded in making us the most despised and best hated nation in the world. Even Greece is not more despised though she is too feeble to hate." Reflecting on the current bloody battles in which the Allied armies were suffering great casualties, she continued, "It seems to me that Verdun and the Somme correspond to our Vicksburg and Gettysburg which marked the turn of the tide. But it took us two years after that to exhaust and conquer the enemy." Prophetically, her letter was written two years and two weeks before the Armistice that ended World War I.

When, on 6 April 1917, the U.S. Congress, responding to President Wilson's demand, declared war on Germany, there was general rejoicing and new hope. From Cairo, where she was again working in a hospital, Martha wrote to her cousin Sherman Miles, "Thank God America is in the war at last. It has been a real grief to every English person to feel that the nation nearest to them was not in the struggle. I think every brave man would want to be fighting alongside those splendid fellows." She told him of her nursing. "I work all day long in the hospital. I am jolly glad for it's enabled me to be quite useful. And the joy of working for British Tommies after those screaming, yellng, querulous, hysterical Frenchmen! However great the pain they never cry out." She mentioned that Ronald was now acting head of his ministry, since his chief was away on indefinite leave. But both she and Lindsay were disappointed that he could not be among the fighting men. "I wish he could have gone off to war—he would have been the happier and better for it all his life."

In a letter to his friend Gaskell, Adams reacted to the news of America's entrance into the war with characteristic ambivalence.

> For once in my life I have found myself wondering how on earth it happened that I was with the majority and had better not criticize or find fault...Meanwhile, here we are, for the first time in our lives, fighting side by side and to my bewilderment I find the great object of my life thus accomplished in the building up of a great community of Atlantic Powers which I hope will at least make a precedent that can never be forgotten...I think that I can now contemplate the total ruin of our old world with more philosophy than I ever thought possible.

In the spring of 1917, Lizzie told her nephew that Martha was again dreading the Egyptian heat. "Martha," her mother noted, "isn't a philosopher so she will probably fret herself to death and increase her temperature to boiling point." But this time Lizzie could not rescue her daughter because of the restrictions of wartime. "I am very cut off from her and we could not reach each other even if one of us were ill."

Now that so many Allied soldiers were in Paris on leave, Lizzie's labors were increased. "From 10 to five I am a businessman and only to be found at my office, then to the YMCA to serve our soldiers tea and talk to them. Our great object is to keep them off the streets and out of the saloons." Scornfully, she described the aviators and ambulance drivers "whose only idea while on leave is to get to Paris and get roaring drunk. And of course," she warned, "they are the prey of young women of bad life and there is much mortification and shame."

When General John J. Pershing, the supreme commander of the Allied

Expeditionary Forces, arrived in Paris, he and his entourage were pelted with roses by cheering crowds of French, English, and American bystanders as he was driven along the massed boulevards to the Hotel Crillon, then on to the home of Ogden Mills on the rue de Varenne. At a formal dinner there, Lizzie was seated next to General Pershing and found him "simple, unpretentious, unpompous and a gentleman." The latter was the highest praise in Lizzie's vocabulary.

After two years of refugee work, Lizzie admitted that she was ready for a respite at Stepleton, although the voyage would be hazardous. Her ship left Le Havre preceded by a protective hydroplane "skimming over the mole and sailing out to sea to clear the way for us." They sailed with no lights and were preceded by a troop transport, with a destroyer alongside. "We did not undress at night but lay down with our life preservers at hand." She was glad of the break but insisted, "I must be back in Paris by September."

At Stepleton, Lizzie reveled in "the peace of it here. Down in this green valley the war is a legend. All the big houses are closed for lack of servants, horses and gasoline. I am quite alone and I like it. I have a dear dog, I weed the garden and knit." While she was in England, she visited one of the great houses, which had once had a butler, a groom, five footmen, and 20 gardeners. "Now two parlormaids do the work. Five old men are left in the gardens. The owner and his two daughters mow, dig, weed, and prune and use wheelbarrows. We all dug potatoes and stored them. In no house is there bread for luncheon or dinner, with only oatcake and biscuits for tea. These are the houses of the rich!"

During this wartime summer, when so many lives were drawing to a close, Henry Adams decided to return to his summer home at Beverly Farms, which he had not visited since Clover's death 32 years before. The large comfortable house, with its many dormers and its fireplace in every room, was set in a forest of oak, pine, and hemlock trees not far from the ocean. Adams wrote to Gaskell, "And now I have returned to the house which I built in 1876 and left in 1885, thinking that nothing on earth would ever bring me back. I live here with my niece as you might live at Wenlock with your daughter, and my only effort is to smile, to look benevolent and to hold my tongue."

In August, Lizzie, acknowledging that "my holiday is almost over," planned to return "across that perilous channel" to her work in Paris. But then she learned that Martha had been stricken with paratyphoid and was in a Cairo hospital in a ward for sick sisters. She was suffering from fever and dysentery, and only her diplomatic connections saved her from going to a civilian hospital "with Greeks and Syrians. How is that for my much coddled child?"

Martha's convalescence was slow, and Lindsay offered his resignation from the Foreign Service in order to care for her. His resignation, after eighteen years of diplomatic service, was not accepted, so he applied for a leave.

Meanwhile, Lizzie was in London while the city was under German air attack. For ten days the people of the city endured a series of air raids. "It was horribly noisy," Lizzie told Wilkinson, with some annoyance. "Shrapnel fragments fell all around us. I think our guns do more damage than Boche bombs. What goes up must come down. In my hotel at the first alarm, we were all made to go down to an inside passage on the lower floor where we huddled—bishops and laymen, ladies and housemaids, till it was over. I felt no alarm, only irritability at the awful noise. The populace is visibly nervous and the 'tubes' were a seething mass of the lower class of people."

Regarding the experience less as a terror than as an inconvenience, she tried to decide her next move. Should she return to Stepleton to await the indeterminate arrival of the Lindsays? "I ought to be in Paris, yet I want to see them both and Martha seems very unwell. I am torn two ways. I long to get back to my work in France but it seems further away."

She decided to wait at Stepleton, and during that fall she was reading a historical study by Charles Francis Adams. To Henry she wrote, "It is curious the faculty you Adamses have of inspiring terror. It must be because you are frightened yourselves and communicate it."

On a clear day in mid-December 1917, with snow on the ground, Lizzie received a telegram from Southampton that the Lindsays had landed after 23 days at sea and were on their way to Stepleton. The little household in the great house was ready for a gala celebration. Lizzie described it to Cecilia Reber. "The fires were lighted, the luncheon prepared. There were flags at every vantage point, flanked by two Union Jacks over the gate where the servants had made an arch of greens with the words 'Welcome Home.' " The 77-year-old housekeeper had laboriously made two flags out of a bedspread and a table cover on which the Union Jack was surrounded by "drunken stripes and crooked stars cut out of calico and basted on in a manner she thought the American flag out to be. Mounted on a broomstick, it made a great effect." Suddenly the Lindsays' car drove around the corner by the garden, while all the villagers and children lined up, cheering and waving flags.

Lizzie was shocked at her daughter's appearance. "Martha is a sad wreck. She looks ghastly. And she has attacks of pain which quite break me up to watch. It is like the tortures of the Inquisition." The doctors in Cairo had speculated vaguely that the pain was due to "adhesions." But the British country practitioner whom they called in diagnosed her condition as inflammation of the entire intestinal tract due to some kind of virulent poison that she had picked up in Egypt. He suggested moving her to a London hospital, where she might require emergency surgery, but this so terrified her and her mother that the patient was allowed to remain in Stepleton.

The winter was bitterly cold and without central heating; "bed is the only warm place." The temperature in the sickroom never went above 50 degrees, but Lizzie managed to cope with this hardship somewhat cheerfully. "We have abandoned the north side of the house and I don't feel the cold too much. I dress as if I were going tobogganing. I am the night and day nurse—we are short handed." Then, half apologetically to Adams, she added, "Ronnie and I don't dress for dinner. How can we? Letters from America tell of 'shortages'—I am malicious enough to feel amused."

In a sudden burst of candor, she confided to Adams, "It is my confounded luck that at the end of life I find for the first time some work I can do and fairly well and I am obliged to give it up for other work for which I have no aptitude. I am held here, with no immediate prospect of getting away. Ronnie has to return to Egypt and I shall probably be kept here indefinitely. This is grumble and I am a little ashamed."

A fortnight later, with Martha showing no improvement, Lindsay went to London to secure a specialist. Despite the shortage of physicians, he found one in uniform whom "he collared by his khaki collar" and brought back to Stepleton for four days of examinations, blood tests, and consultations with the local doctor. Their diagnosis was acute colitis and chronic paratyphoid, with the pain caused by intestinal inflammation. "The doctor thinks her very ill," Lizzie reported. "He skillfully fenced my questions about danger but he told Ronnie he must not think of going to Egypt immediately nor I to Paris and Martha must never return to Egypt. He provided one nurse and another is coming." At this Lizzie sighed with relief, "for I did not see my bed for 15 nights. I was at the end of my strength."

With Lindsay unable to return to his post in Egypt, Lizzie worried about his diplomatic career. "Martha will always be a stumbling block. She will never be quite strong." Learning that a new assignment for Lindsay in South America was being contemplated, Lizzie appealed to British Foreign Secretary Lord Curzon (the husband of her old friend Mary Leiter). From Carlton House Terrace in London, Curzon wrote, "I hear of your acute distress and will gladly do anything in my power to help you so that he [Lindsay] may be kept here until your poor daughter's life is assured."

From London the results of the blood tests revealed that Martha was suffering from tropical dysentery and a probable internal abscess which was in danger of perforation. "Martha is desperately ill. The pain attacks like waves. As one subsides we pour in the vaccine [an injection containing morphine or opium] before the next attack. The house is full of nurses, with consulting doctors flying down from London. We shall be bankrupt!" As the nurses and doctors conferred in the sickroom, "Ronnie and I hang around outside the door like dejected little dogs." Because Martha could not eat the coarse "war bread," the doctor gave them a certificate allowing her two loaves of white bread a week. They bought a cow to provide fresh milk, and the London nurse referred to it as "he."

One sleepless night, as she was going through her desk, Lizzie found a packet of the sonnets that Cecil Spring-Rice had sent her before Martha was born. "I wish I could see him," she wrote to Adams. Shortly afterward she learned that Spring-Rice had been recalled to London "with brutal brusqueness. Springy did not always practice patience in Washington . . . He felt the war intensely, saw it as a struggle in which neutrality was immoral. His nerves on edge, he sometimes spoke too freely." While the United States remained neutral, the British ambassador's outspoken sentiments had proved unpopular in Washington. A few weeks after his recall, he was dead at 59— "of a broken heart," his friends believed. Adams wrote mournfully, "Springy is socially the greatest loss I could suffer, for he had become very much at home and indeed almost dependent on this house for refuge. . . . His doctor has just sat half an hour with me quite enraged because he could find no reason whatever for his sudden death."

Amid the anguish and isolation of her months-long vigil at Martha's bedside, Lizzie yearned for her nephew Hal and her friends in Paris. "I have a longing for my own people." Martha's agony continued relentlessly as it became apparent that the internal abscess was growing. "By God's mercy," Lizzie wrote to Adams, "it broke through the intestinal wall instead of the peritoneum which would have been fatal. But there is a danger of hemorrhage. She is conscious and made fairly comfortable with morphine."

As the wartime food shortages increased, Lizzie recalled the days when she and Lindsay, dining at the Ritz in London, had complained about the preparation of some gourmet dish. "Now Ronnie and I are quite happy with a humble dish of leeks and carrots. I haven't yet been driven to cabbage. (Lizzie detested the odor of cooking cabbage, which she thought "smelled like a sewer.")

By mid-February 1918, Martha seemed a little better. But soon the fever and nausea returned, and she was racked with pain. "We are simply fighting for her life day by day. She knows all and the shadow of a possible operation hangs over her and clouds every bit of hope. Her terror is almost morbid—so is mine—she is not a good subject for a knife. But the local doctor thinks what he tactfully calls 'surgical interference' lies ahead." Finally, an exploratory operation was performed, and the surgeon told Lizzie and Ronald that "the first four days would be critical. After that, if she lived, it would be a series of improvements and setbacks until death released her. He gave us no hope." Against this grim verdict Lizzie opposed the local doctor's opinion. "He thinks she has a fighting chance if we can keep up her strength—and the strength is kept up...Her strength and tenacity of life remind me of her grandfather and her father." Simon Cameron had lived until 90 and Donald Cameron was now 85.

Celebrating his 80th birthday in Washington on 16 February 1918, Henry Adams wagered his doctors that "they can't keep me running for three months." Less than two weeks later, on 1 March, he dictated to Aileen Tone what would be his last letter to Lizzie.

> We shall telegraph today for news of Martha through Elizabeth Hoyt who is still with us and who takes charge of the telegraph. As we have heard nothing for the three weeks since you wrote, it is better for me to say nothing just now and wait with patience for all the news that these days bring, having the enlivening sense that whatever comes is always bad and we are no better for hastening it. You can imagine how my ancient pessimism rebels at the sight of a world infinitely more pessimistic than I ever was and seeming on the whole rather to enjoy it....My quiet house is actually invaded by people who wear all sorts of uniforms and are here on all sorts of errands...but who pretend to regard me with a feigned deference which reduces *me* to dust!...We are waiting with extreme anxiety for your next news, and all this letter is mere chatter to fill up the time....Meanwhile we try to be cheerful and whistle our 12th-century melodies.

But the cheerfulness was hard to maintain as he thought of Martha's suffering and heard the worsening bulletins from the war front. On 21 March, the Germans began their great offensive, using 62 divisions extending along a 42-mile front, to attack the British Fifth Army. Within a week, the British had been pushed back 25 miles, with a total of 90,000 prisoners taken. Then the Germans introduced their long-range cannon, nicknamed "Big Bertha" after the wife of its inventor, to shell Paris 76 miles away. In horror, Adams told Aileen, "Life has become intolerable ... this is no world for an old man to live in when the Germans can shoot to the moon!"

In mid-March, Aileen Tone, worn out from trying to keep his spirits up, reluctantly took a weekend vacation, but "I worried about Uncle Henry every minute." So she returned home, hurrying upstairs to find him sitting with Elizabeth Hoyt, who was reading aloud to him. "I went straight over to his side and knelt down by the low chair and put my arms around him. He was a little man, you know, and I could feel his whole body trembling. 'Never leave me, never leave me,' he murmured and I replied 'I never will.' "

On 27 March, from Stepleton, Lizzie Cameron wrote to Adams a despairing letter that he would never read.

> Martha's life is hanging on a thread. Two days ago we had the fourth consultation and the verdict was the same. Her one chance for life is her youth and vitality. Everything else is against us. She is spared no pain or misery, she is wasted to a skeleton. She has no blood, yet her mind and spirit are bright and grow under extraordinary suffering.... [During the early morning hours] from two until six when "the horrors" come over her ... I have to lean across the bed and comfort her like a frightened child and soothe the pain by sustaining the spirit. It is a grim battle. But nothing matters but that thread of life upstairs. If I can save that, nothing matters.

But Adams, a month past his 80th birthday and trying to carry on as usual, was spared this latest bleak report. On Tuesday evening, 26 March, the night before Lizzie wrote her letter, Aileen Tone went up to Adams's room with him as usual and wound his clock and saw that everything was right. His "Good night, my dear" was as serene and charming as ever. The next morning, she went downstairs at eight and waited almost fifteen minutes for him to come and take his early morning walk before breakfast; then she got anxious, ran up to his room, knocked and called, and there was no answer. She went in and found him "lying as if asleep in a perfectly easy position, eyes closed, perfectly unconscious." When the doctor arrived shortly, he said that Adams had been dead at least an hour. His death was due to a sudden and violent stroke as he was lying in bed. "It was as sharp as lightning and as merciful. There was no look of pain on his face, only the strangest expression of consciousness and will and intellect."

A private service of liturgical simplicity was held in the library of Adams's home on the afternoon of Holy Thursday. Only his family, his nieces, and a few remaining friends of his generation were present. Before his casket, on which rested a spray of lilacs, the service was read by the Reverend Mr.

"Death Knocks at Every Door But Mine"

Roland Cotton Smith, the rector of St. John's Episcopal Church, who had performed the wedding service for Martha and Ronald Lindsay at 21 Lafayette Square nine years earlier. Shortly before his death, Adams had admonished Aileen Tone, "Remember, I am not to be carried into St. John's Church when I never walked into it."

Shane Leslie, Trumbull Stickney's friend, described the scene. "He lay in the midst of all the books, pictures and *objects d'art* you remember, and in the room where Hay, Roosevelt, Cabot Lodge, John La Farge, Clarence King and Saint-Gaudens had so often met." Most of them were gone now, and Leslie noticed "only Harry White, Alice Roosevelt and Jusserand [the French ambassador]."

The following day was Good Friday, and some of Adams's family were still en route to Washington, so the committal service was not held until the morning of Easter Sunday. Perhaps Adams the skeptic would have relished the irony of his being buried on the day of Christ's Resurrection.

Adams was buried beside Clover in Rock Creek Cemetery in the grave that was unmarked except for the bronze figure that he had called "The Peace of God."

After his death, there was found in his wallet the "Prayer to the Virgin of Chartres" that he had sent to Lizzie Cameron:

Gracious Lady:—
Simple as when I asked your aid before;
   Humble as when I prayed for grace in vain
Seven hundred years ago; weak, weary, sore
   In heart and hope, I ask your help again....

But, when we must, we pray as in the past
   Before the Cross whereon your Son was nailed.
Listen, dear lady! You shall hear the last
   Of the strange prayers Humanity has wailed....

But years, or ages, or eternity,
   Will find me still in thought before your throne,
Pondering the mystery of Maternity,
   Soul within Soul,—Mother and Child in One!

19

"*A Great Lady*"

*B*y early April of 1918, Elizabeth Cameron and her son-in-law were guardedly optimistic about Martha's condition. "Things are a little more cheerful," Lizzie wrote. "She is not past the danger point, not by a long distance, but the septic poisoning is diminishing and we think her strength is increasing. She still suffers horribly except when under morphia and the inflammation and ulceration are unabated." A specialist called down from London, who had not seen the patient in three weeks, "pretends that he saw an improvement. In other words, instead of 'one chance in ten' she may now have 'two or three.' I myself who have been so despairing, now begin to believe that youth and strength may pull her through. But I scarcely dare say so." She described their isolation in the Dorset countryside and "the long nights spent in the drawing room waiting to be summoned to see her die." The doctors had warned her that at best Martha would not be out of danger for two months and "would have to be on a couch or in a wheeled chair all summer. But if she lives, nothing matters!" Lizzie exclaimed.

But Lizzie's forlorn hope was not realized. On 28 April, Martha died, one month and a day after Henry Adams's death. Martha was buried on the grounds of Stepleton, and often at night, like a pale wraith, her mother slipped out of the house to prostrate herself on the newly dug grave. Although Martha's death was hardly unexpected, Lizzie's grief was like a sudden torrent, sweeping away all reason. Ronald Lindsay, who had shared the long vigil, found he could not console her. From the neighboring village of Blandford he sent off an urgent cable to her niece Elizabeth Hoyt, who was in Washington working for the Red Cross, which read "Mrs. Cameron nearly out of her mind with grief, sees no one, mourning Martha."

Elizabeth Hoyt, who was staying at the home of Henry Adams, received the cable. A month earlier she had looked down at the still face of Dordy (Martha's pet name for him) and had joined the little group of mourners who followed his body to Rock Creek Cemetery. Someone had shown her the words that Adams had written a month after Clover's death, "No power on earth can annihilate the happiness that is past." Now she must try to persuade Lizzie of this. She applied for a passport that would allow her to visit Aunt Dilly in England, but this was denied because of wartime restrictions on travel. But her superior at the Red Cross arranged for her reassignment to Paris, with permission to visit her aunt at Stepleton for a limited time en route to France.

She reached Stepleton on 7 June. "Here at last I found Dilly waiting for me on the doorstep and piteously glad to see me." Lizzie, dressed in deep mourning, looked suddenly old and vulnerable at age 61. As she clung trembling to her niece, while Ronald Lindsay towered anxiously above them, it was clear to them both that Mrs. Cameron was suffering an emotional crisis bordering on derangement. Storms of sobbing were followed by denunciations of all of Martha's doctors, whom she described as murderers. These in turn were followed by periods of blank despair.

For the first time in her life, Lizzie Cameron showed no trace of buoyancy, no vestige of self-control. Now that Henry Adams, her "dear and best friend," was gone, she was left without any emotional mooring. She found herself shipwrecked before the inexorable fact that Martha, the one being in life whom she loved without measure or restraint, was gone. The life-enhancing unity of mother and child that Adams had celebrated in *Chartres* was broken. Lizzie was now the mother bereft of her child, and she could not accept the loss. To her niece Cecilia Reber, she dictated a note. "I cannot write . . . I am beyond that now except to thank you for your loving sympathy, dear. The world is very dark and my heart is broken."

In the days before Elizabeth Hoyt's arrival, Ronald Lindsay was so concerned by Lizzie's condition that he had stopped off in Paris in an attempt to persuade Edith Wharton to come. Failing to see the novelist, he confided his fears to her friend Walter Gay. On 15 June, Mrs. Wharton wrote to Lizzie, "Walter was so distressed by Ronald's distress at your being alone at Stepleton for a fortnight or more that he came at once to tell me about it and we decided that I must try to get over at once to see you and be with you in the interval." But the matter was not so easily resolved. Although Mrs. Wharton intended to leave at once, she found that her recent six weeks' bout with anemia and a heart irregularity had left her quite unequal to a journey that included the likelihood of a delay at Le Havre or Southampton. Since she was still in charge of refugee work in Paris, she had to be certain that she could return immediately if she were needed. This, Royall Tyler told her, was impossible, and he advised her not to go.

"My first duty, of course, is here at present," Mrs. Wharton reminded Lizzie. "In fact, life is simplified for all of us by the fact that each has an unavoidable duty somewhere and must be there, whatever it costs." She told Lizzie that, in her anxiety for her, the little group of expatriate friends in Paris had debated who should go to her. "Mrs. Mead [a friend of Edith Wharton's whom Lizzie had met] most kindly and gallantly offered to replace me," wrote Mrs. Wharton, and managed to accomplish "the almost impossible feat of getting off to England in three days. I know you liked her and was sure you would be touched by her offer to replace me."

But Lizzie, who was disoriented with grief, sent word that she would not receive Mrs. Mead at Stepleton, even for a day or two. This unexpected reaction, Mrs. Wharton wrote, "quite frankly has distressed and hurt me more than anything that has happened to me in a good many years." She regarded it as shutting in her face "the door that you and Martha always held so wide open for me." She argued that "a delicate woman" risking a wartime journey from Paris to England out of perfectly disinterested friendliness, deserved a rather more kindly welcome. In her own lifetime, she continued, she had endured "a good deal of pretty bitter sorrow" and she had found that "the only out was to do the next thing that came to hand, though so often it comes in the form of seeing someone one may not care to see or writing a letter when one wanted to hold one's peace!"

Then the novelist confessed that "It is hard to express what I mean." Reminding Lizzie of the "horribly painful position" in which she was putting her, she declared, since Elizabeth Hoyt was due to return to Paris on 24 July, "You must come with her, you *will*...There is plenty of work for you too here...*Martha would have wanted that, wanted it above all things*. I don't think I have *ever* written so outspokenly to anyone—but you will understand my doing so, I know."

Despite Edith Wharton's unsparing candor in these two letters, the friendship between these two strong-willed women survived. But Lizzie did not even consider accompanying her niece to Paris. As the days went on, Mrs. Wharton showed her growing impatience with what she called "Lizzie's evil lethargy" and wondered, in a letter to Mary Berenson, "when our sex is coming out of the kindergarten."

All during June, Elizabeth Hoyt watched over her grieving Aunt Dilly and reported, "She is of course utterly broken and despairing...But one thing that matters is that she is *trying*. And that she wants me with her. I do not leave her for a moment all day and we have connecting rooms with the door open all night." As the deadline for her return to Paris neared, Elizabeth Hoyt was urged to take a stand by Edith Wharton, "who writes me constantly, such long letters full of helpful advice and good cheer—and news for Dilly. I feel guilty about my feelings for Mrs. Wharton. I have always thought her hard and she has been *too* nice." Elizabeth summoned her cousin Hal Sherman, the son of Lizzie's late brother Henry, who was also a witness to his aunt's near-suicidal despair. Together they made the necessary plans, and on 4 July she reported, "Hal and I have done the done the deed together....I am going to Paris next week and I am filled with black dread. I am leaving Dilly here alone!" After their departure, Lizzie, attended by her faithful staff, continued to nurse her grief, alternating between restlessness and apathy. She still slept from time to time on Martha's grave, and she became consumed with the idea that, just as Henry Adams had memorialized Clover, she must erect a monument to Martha.

She wrote for advice to her friend John Singer Sargent, who had done a portrait of Ronald Lindsay in 1911. "Alas, there is no other St. Gaudens," the artist replied. "I cannot think of a sculptor who would be sure to portray your high and sad story and I know the standards you have." Lizzie also wrote to the earl of Crawford, Ronald Lindsay's oldest brother, who reminded her of the church-imposed rule that no monuments could be erected inside churches during the war. The decision had to be put off for the duration.

During the last summer of the war, while Lizzie was preoccupied in England with planning a monument for her daughter, in Pennsylvania her husband J. Donald Cameron was incapacitated by a stroke at his country home in Donegal Springs. For three weeks, he lay paralyzed and unconscious, and on 30 August 1918 he died at the age of 85. After the funeral, his daughters ordered that the contents of his extensive wine cellar be emptied into the sewers of Harrisburg.

In an obituary, *The New York Times* mentioned that "Senator Cameron retired seven years ago, placing his property in a trust valued at $4,000,000." The Philadelphia *Public Ledger* called him "a practical politician—pure and simple—who lacked sentiment and never courted popularity. Politics to him was a business like banking. He had no time for anyone who can't deliver the political goods. His assistants were pawns who moved at his bidding. When he was finished, he swept them off the board. . . . His enemies called him a failure as a senator because he spent all his energies to get reelected. In 20 years he introduced eight minor bills none of which became law." In an attempt to show a more attractive side, however, the paper noted that "Don Cameron had multitudes of friends and acquaintances in Philadelphia. Three or four times a year he would go to the old Bellevue Hotel [later the Bellevue-Stratford] where he took an apartment and entertained his friends." The *Public Ledger* concluded "Although the acts of this dynasty were not always creditable and it is doubtful if the Camerons and their tactics would be tolerated today, it is recognized that they played the game according to the rules of their time."

In Stepleton, Senator Cameron's widow made no mention of his passing. Forty years before, on the eve of their wedding, Don Cameron had made a financial settlement "for the care and comfort of my wife Elizabeth S. Cameron." His last will and testament, dated 1914, declared, "I deem it unnecessary in this my will to make further provision for my wife Elizabeth S. Cameron."

From Washington came news that could not fail to please Lizzie. John Hay's biographer, William R. Thayer, wrote: "Henry Adams' *Education* will be published next week. I regard him as the chief figure in American literature from 1880 on. I suspect that you, like other intimate friends of his, attributed *Democracy* to him and Miss Tone tells me she saw *Esther* in your library so you were probably in on that secret too."

The Education of Henry Adams was published in September 1918, six months after the author's death. It contained an editor's preface that Adams himself had written but which at his request was initialed H.C.L. (for Henry Cabot Lodge, to whom in 1915 he had entrusted the book's posthumous publication). The book had no illustrations, for Adams had warned Lodge, "You know that I do not consider illustrations as my work, or having part in any correct rendering of my ideas. Least of all do I wish portraits. I have always followed the rule of making the reader think only of the text, and I do not want to abandon it here." Within three months, 12,000 copies of *The Education* had been sold, more than had been sold of *Chartres*. In 1919, Adams was posthumously awarded the Pulitzer Prize for *The Education of Henry Adams*, a book that the British historian Denis W. Brogan later called

> the most famous of American autobiographies. It is a great work of art and in its first half, at any rate, a nearly perfect work of art.... Adams did not live to see the sudden flowering of his literary fame, a flowering so brilliant that it is a natural temptation to regard the whole history of the great family as culminating in the author of *Chartres* and *The Education*.... He speaks to us as mere Presidents and mere millionaires cannot and he speaks for an American attitude that we tend to ignore, for that critical side of American life that knows how much more the human heart needs than mere material goods and the vulgar success that Henry Adams, to our profit, escaped.

Lizzie Cameron had been familiar with *The Education* from the days in Paris when Adams had read to her from the original manuscript. She knew better than anyone else what the silences in this quasi-autobiography meant, and she understood "that peculiar form of mentality which delights in expressing itself in symbols and paradoxes which may be exactly the opposite from what he means."

From her bridesmaid Julia Parsons, who had witnessed her courtship in Washington, Lizzie received a long letter disapproving of Adams's work, complaining that "he is so cynical, though I think much of it is a pose." Her unfavorable reaction roused Lizzie to a spontaneous tribute. "I am astonished at what you tell me the idea of Henry Adams' book gave you. He was the biggest man, both in heart and mind, that I have ever known. None came near to touching him, none were on his plane. Both mind and heart were as wide as the universe."

During the first year of her mourning and for the rest of her life, Lizzie dressed in black and wrote all her correspondence on black-bordered stationery. She was still receiving tributes to Martha, such as one from Thayer: "She died for France as men and women of France have been dying for all the world. Those who have greatly loved can greatly bear. Take comfort in knowing how much you were to your dear ones." But the one tribute that might have comforted Lizzie because it grew out of Adams's equal love for Martha was denied her. Struggling under the double loss of Martha and Henry Adams, she endured the long days and nights, rallying a little only at the visits of her nephews Hal Sherman and Sherman Miles and her niece Elizabeth Hoyt, as well as of Mary Berenson and Elisina Tyler. Trying to cheer her, Edith Wharton wrote and thanked her for the gift of a hospital bed in Martha's name. When Lizzie sent Mrs. Wharton a fan for Christmas, Edith wrote back, "I am delighted you noticed my fanlessness, you wonderful woman. 'I miss you every hour' as the hymn says."

After four agonizing years, the war ended on 11 November 1918. From Paris, Elizabeth Hoyt wrote to Lizzie jubilantly, "The new world has come."

But Lizzie still clung to her old world. "I am all alone and the days are very long," she wrote to Cecilia Reber. "I need not say how sad I am. I am afraid that I shall live for several years yet. Thank God we are not a long-lived family, but I might easily have five or six years yet and the thought makes me crumble." Her grief was aggravated by the bitterness she felt toward those she accused of murdering Martha. To her brother-in-law Nelson Miles, she wrote,

> You say I have much to live for—can you tell me what? I have no home, no sisters, brothers or children. My friends and relations are sorry for my grief and have shown it faithfully. *But no one grieves for Martha*—even those whom she loved so dearly have not mourned. What is most bitter of all, no one has resented her murder — nor taken any steps to avenge it. No one *cares....*You urge me to come back to America. Why? For what? Where would I go? Do you think I would be better off in a hotel room in New York or Washington than here by Martha?...I pray fervently for death and sit and wait.

Given the depth of her desolation, and in the absence of any sustaining religious faith, it is not surprising that Lizzie resorted to the supernatural to summon up the spirits of Martha and Henry Adams. Various spiritualists came to Stepleton from London, and Lizzie reported to Cecilia, "Strange things have happened. The messages to Sherman were almost agonizing in their intensity and I could scarcely keep from breaking down under their pathos." To the uneasiness of her friends and family, the seances continued. Lizzie, who had shared Henry Adams's skepticism about the world of the supernatural, found herself dabbling in the occult. "It was a curious experience," she wrote to Sherman Miles. "I was very much moved and felt, like Festus, 'almost persuaded.' Death is such a tremendous experience...it cannot fail to make some sort of impression." She ordered a planchette and a ouija board, calling on another niece, Edith Hoyt, to help her operate it and reporting "lucid continued messages from totally unknown people. When the messages come from our own...I have broken down and cried sometimes, so real it seems. But now Edith is gone—she is the 'sensitive.' Well, it's all a question of waiting, isn't it?"

Bitterly she discussed her "dread of surgeons and operations and of falling into such hands as poor little Martha did and of being ruthlessly murdered. ...If such a thing should happen, no one will give a damn. One's life is only valuable to oneself and to no one else....[and] peace is all I can ask for. Certainly it is all I pray for Martha. Peace and oblivion that she may never know how little she meant to those to whom she had devoted her life and had given so much real affection."

Lizzie's air of frozen grief and outrage was disturbing to her friends. Mary Berenson visited her in January 1919, in an effort to console her. But the visit was not a success. The sharp-tongued Mary wrote to her husband B.B. in exasperation, "Dear Mrs. Cameron is as stupid as an owl, that is her greatest drawback," and she noted that Lizzie was full of "formulae of bitterness and despair." Although she sympathized with "the dreadful turn life has played on her," Mary Berenson insisted that "the root of all her trouble is her bitterness. She hates England because she thinks the English doctors murdered her daughter. Poor, dear, unhappy Mrs. Cameron inspired me with such disgust for human intercourse." As Mrs. Berenson was departing, Lizzie begged her to stay. "She says my visit has been the first thing to lighten her woe. But I think I've done all I can, and in spite of the lovely country, it is frightfully depressing here."

Convinced at 63 that she had only a few years to live, Lizzie told her nephew Sherman Miles, "I don't want to leave papers which may be a bother to Ronnie when he clears up my traces. I have all Martha's letters and photographs in a drawer and have pledged Butler [the maid] to burn them as soon as I'm not here so I think we will be pretty effectively wiped out."

After Lizzie made a brief trip to a "cure" in Savoy, Mary Berenson wrote to B.B. from the Hotel des Thermes, Bride-les-Bains, "Mrs. Cameron has gone home. She says people were as kind to her as if there were no broad band of shame across her face." Visitors to Stepleton were frequently startled to hear Lizzie refer to Martha as "here" and assert "I cannot desert her."

Lizzie still heard regularly from Henry Wilkinson, who was now a rising New York architect and the father of a young family. She wrote candidly about age and death to "Wilks," who was 12 years her junior.

> One of the minor consolations is that we all grow old together [she wrote]. If you are an old man, I am an old woman. It doesn't improve me. My temples are white, the back hair is the ugly iron-gray which we all hate and the front locks are a faded yellow brown. I am just like a pie-bald pony. Dost thou like the picture? [Echoing Adams's old motto *"Rien ne vaut beaucoup,* she added,] It is all part of 'nothing matters' and I really mean it. We all know there is nothing but death ahead and what is death to fear? Either we sleep — and we know how blissful is the deep unconsciousness of sleep — or we live on to meet those who are dear to us. Why dread or fear either state?...But if I knew I could die tomorrow, there would be no shrinking. Only joy that it is all over.

By early 1921, the monument to Martha was completed — a marble tablet that "is in very low relief and the hands and face and drapery are delicate." The marble plaque that is set in the wall of the chapel at Stepleton was the work of the French artist François Léon Sicart, one of those whom Sargent had recommended.

Now that the Foreign Office had assigned Lindsay to London, where he was to serve as assistant undersecretary of state in charge of Near Eastern affairs, he spent much of his time at Stepleton. His presence was comforting to Lizzie, since, from the days of his courtship of Martha, Lizzie and he had been staunch friends. Sometimes they had been forced to become allies in dealing with Martha. Through the long ordeal of Martha's dying, they had stood together. Now they resumed their old camaraderie, engaging in spirited discussions about international politics and the recurring Near Eastern crises that within a year would culminate in the lifting of the British protectorate over

Egypt. For his expert handling of these crises, Lindsay won official recognition with the award of a C.B.E. in 1922.

"Moose tall" and imposing in bearing, Lindsay was polite but reserved with strangers. As Henry Adams's grandnephew Dr. John Adams Abbott recalls from a visit during his youth, "Sir Ronald was not a talker, but his silences were amiable. Breakfasting with him alone each morning (Mrs. Cameron did not come down till noon), I tried all sorts of conversational gambits and met only genial monosyllables. One morning he looked up from his kippered herrings and smilingly observed, 'We *do* have such jolly breakfasts, don't we?'"

Early in September 1922, Lizzie received a letter "quite out of the blue" from Brooks Adams, Henry's youngest brother, "a very gifted and uncomfortably clever fellow." She was amazed at its tone, "for I had an idea he did not really like me." The cantankerous Brooks, whom most people shunned because of his irascible, tactless, and dogmatic manner, wrote from The Old House in Quincy. "Life has of late years been very sad for you. . . . I have grown very fond of you as I have learned to know you better. I never did you justice, I fear, during my brother Henry's life." He mentioned the "terrible losses" she had suffered and noted

> how closely you were linked with my brother, There is no one like Henry. . . . I told Aileen Tone (who loved him very dearly, even like you) that the misfortune to a woman of having once cared for a man like him was that, once lost, she would never know another like him. . . . So it was with you.
>
> Why do you live abroad? And how long do you propose to stay? You, toward the end of Henry's life, as I understand from your note to me, looked after his establishment in Washington. Could you or would you be willing to try something of the same sort for me? I am very much alone and am growing very old, quite as old as Henry when he put his affairs in trust.

But Brooks Adams was not entirely alone, as Lizzie knew. For the past three years, while his wife Daisy (née Evelyn Davis) was suffering from mental derangement, in care of doctors and nurses in their Boston home, Brooks in Quincy had been attended by a young secretary-companion Wilhelmina Sellers. "Like Henry," wrote Lizzie, "Brooks has picked a woman to take care of him. His secretary is a nice young woman from Alabama—quite nice and pleasant and intelligent and he dotes upon her. She has a great responsibility on her hands." At age 75, Brooks was the last Adams of his generation, and he still mourned the death of his favorite, Henry, whom he called "the best of us four brothers."

Three weeks later, Lizzie was further astonished at a new proposition from Brooks: "Do you feel like going with me to Porto Rico or the West Indies or some such place? Europe is too cold, besides, I'm sick of it. The same vortex of despair yawns before all of us old men. . . . Have you the slightest impulse to tempt fortune with me? What could you suggest, supposing you were dealing with a sane man like Henry?"

Lizzie was touched by the plight of "dear old Brooks" and a trifle flattered by his invitation. "But," as she told Wilkinson, "of course I did not go." Instead she wrote a letter that consoled him and to which he replied sadly, "I shall never get over my loss any more than you can yours. . . . At all events do your best to live with your son-in-law who, we all know, is devoted to you. Maybe some day we shall meet. . . . I only wish I had you to go with me to the ends of the earth."

Brooks Adams departed to winter in Panama and the West Indies, without Lizzie. By springtime, she learned he was dreading a return to Boston, where his wife was becoming "more insane" each day. "She tried and almost succeeded in setting the house afire. She even manages to escape and run away." Although Brooks had accepted the idea of putting Daisy in an asylum, her family, headed by Cabot Lodge, were opposed. Lizzie pitied Brooks— "he wants to do the right thing but everybody pulls him in a different direction. He can't cope—and if it weren't for that Southern girl . . ."

"Old and weary," Brooks Adams decided to sail for England, where he would take the thermal cure at Bath. In May 1923, he sent Lizzie a desperate note from the Grand Pump Room in Bath. "I do want to see you more than I can say or you will believe. My wife is failing very fast. She probably will not know me. I can't bear to think of it, much less talk of it but I must go to make arrangements for her in some asylum. It has come to that. There are so few people to whom I can speak. So come to see me! You have known deep affliction but you have never known this. This is the worst thing that can fall to the lot of man. Henry lost his wife but that is nothing to this."

He wrote of Miss Sellers. "God knows what I should do without her— for fear some man will take her from me—as indeed human beasts have tried and almost succeeded in doing (she was once engaged but broke it off). My nerves have not yet recovered. Come to us next Wednesday. I am a wreck."

Lizzie could not refuse this pathetic plea from Bath. She found him fairly well, but feeble, and his mind not as clear and vigorous as it used to be. "We talked it all over and I heard all his confidences, then I came home again in a state of pulp. I seldom remember being so exhausted."

During Brooks Adams's stay at Bath, with Miss Sellers waiting on his every whim, Lizzie invited them to lunch with her at Stepleton. Miss Sellers, who is now Mrs. Harris, recalls the meeting, "Mrs. Cameron was quite an actress in her charm. When she was with Brooks she made him feel there was no one in the world but him. Of course Brooks loved this attention. He was walking on air." Although she was now 66 and in mourning,

> Mrs. Cameron possessed every charm of her youth. Every movement, whether studied or not, was graceful. The black she wore was very becoming. She wore her hair straight back, puffed high and with a velvet bow at the back of her neck. She was very handsome, with a slender figure, fair skin and blue eyes. She was taller than Brooks or Henry and she had a splendid carriage. Walking briskly with her head held high, she looked to me like the Queen of Stepleton. I could understand why Henry Adams fell in love with her. You see, she had such enormous charm. She made you feel you were the most important person in the world.

"A Great Lady"

As she had done so often in Washington and in Paris, Lizzie played the role of hostess at her dining table at Stepleton, discreetly served by butler, maid, and cook. She directed an occasional question to Miss Sellers, "But I was too young and Brooks was the one she really talked to. She said what he wanted and needed to hear. 'You were so wonderful to Henry,' she told him."

But the emotional climate cooled abruptly when Lizzie spoke of her contact with the spirit world through a medium whom she had invited to Stepleton. The medium, she told Brooks, had been in touch with his brother Henry and he had spoken about his grave beneath the Saint-Gaudens monument in Rock Creek Cemetery. The incorporal Henry, she insisted, had conveyed his regret that the monument to himself and Clover bore no name, declaring, "This is a mistake. The name should be added." This was too much for Brooks Adams, who knew that the omission of any name from the monument had been Henry's expressed wish. Rising from his chair, he replied gruffly, "Henry should have thought of that before."

Brooks and Miss Sellers were startled when their hostess, rising from the table, stretched out both hands to them in invitation, saying, "Let us go out to see Martha." They hardly knew what to expect as she led them through the chapel, with its marble portrait of Martha on the wall, and out to the grave set among the gently rolling hills.

As they noticed, and as a later visitor William Royall Tyler observed, "Other people died and disappeared and that was an end to it. But Martha died—and died—and continued to die. It was a cult of death."

Like Henry Adams, Lizzie had always doted on babies and young children, and her friends hoped that their presence might distract her from her melancholy. When Elisina Tyler brought her little son for a visit, the occasion was a great success. As the grown-up William Royall Tyler, director emeritus of Dumbarton Oaks in Washington, D.C., recalls, "She spoiled me. As a small boy she seemed to me next to God. I liked her even better than my mother. She took me seriously . . . She gave me a mechanical tiger which growled and a model plane, probably from le Nain Bleu in Paris, which was so special that I was not allowed to use it." The marvelous toy was attached to a screw in the ceiling of the child's nursery, but the resourceful young Tyler managed to bring it down by throwing marbles at it.

Barbara Schiefflin was a young American friend whose husband Charles Bosanquet had proposed to her in Lizzie's rose garden at Stepleton. On a later visit, they brought their ten-month-old daughter, and the baby made a puddle on Lizzie's gorgeous blue rug. The parents were frozen with embarrassment, but Lizzie quickly hugged the infant and cried out to her mother, "Comfort her!" She made no mention of the rug.

Her grandnephews, nieces, and cousins were all equally indulged. "Cousin Lizzie was my god-mother and she gave me a black pony named Allie," recalls Alfred O. Hoyt. "She was a most delightful and talented woman and there was never any question of difference of age as she just took over and time was forgotten." "We used to call her Aunt Lizzie or Auntie Cam and spend the summer at Stepleton or visit her in Paris. My feelings toward her were a combination of terror and adoration," wrote Harriet Sherman Barnes. She was very strict with us as regards deportment (which was terrible). She deplored our American ways and qualities."

Helena Lodge, Bay Lodge's daughter, who became the Baroness de Streel, recalls meeting Lizzie after the war at Edith Wharton's home at Sainte-Brice and coming back to Paris on the local train—Lizzie, Mrs. Wharton, Helena, her mother, and her brother John Lodge. "Mrs. Cameron was wearing a smart new hat and chatted away with us as if she liked us." This impressed Helena, for, as she recalls, "When I was a child, people didn't talk *to* me. They talked *in front of* me." Seated in Lizzie's luxurious Paris apartment, their hostess suddenly exclaimed to the young girl, "I often think your father Bay Lodge was the most attractive man I've ever known." Since Bay had died when Helena was very young, she was thrilled. "This warmed my heart because I scarcely remembered him." When Helena Lodge was to be married, Lizzie gave her a rare Ming celadon bowl which had been given to her by Henry Adams. "I didn't realize then what a lovely gesture it was."

Gradually, Lizzie's animation returned. Even though she wore only black, it was, as Wilhelmina Sellers had noted, "very becoming." As her old urge to travel returned, she wrote to Sam Reber at Harvard that she was considering a trip to Ceylon and suggested, "Think what a storm it would raise if I took you out of college to escort me in my excursion? Would your mother ever speak to me again? I can see the disapproving faces all around." She decided against uprooting Sam and planned instead on a four-month visit to Italy and Sicily, ending in Rome.

In the fall of 1922, Italy was in a state of postwar ferment—widespread labor strikes, social unrest, and a parliamentary breakdown under the well-meaning but ineffectual King Victor Emmanuel III. Benito Mussolini, a former newspaper editor and army corporal, had been organizing his followers, who were mostly veterans of the Great War, into an aggressively nationalistic group called *Fasci di combattimento*. For uniforms they wore the black shirts adopted by the followers of the poet-playwright Gabriele d'Annunzio. The previous year, Mussolini had been elected to the Italian parliament, marking the beginning of the National Fascist Party, Seizing his opportunity in October 1922, he ordered his Fascist troops to march on Rome.

When the takeover occurred, Lizzie was en route by train from Naples to Rome. Excitedly she wrote to Sam Reber, "The train was full of fascisti in black shirts. At every station they got in and were cheered by the crowds." On alighting at the Rome station, Lizzie found a noisy, milling throng but no porters. At 65, she was still resourceful. She seized a handcart and loaded her luggage on it under the admiring gaze of a dapper Italian *signore*. With a deep bow, he asked permission to share her truck, and together "we hauled the truck out to the square." No buses or hotel limousines appeared, but she managed to flag down a stray taxi to get to her hotel.

> Next morning Mussolini marched in with his 100,000 men, all young and strong and disciplined. It was really quite impressive because they used the old Roman salute of uplifted right arm all in

unison and with a rhythmic movement which was really beautiful. It was a revolution—nothing else and but for the wise king it would have been civil war. The Cabinet wanted to resist but Victor Emmanuel refused. He felt that the army could not be relied upon. He knew the feeling that existed against the weak government better than they did.

Called on to form a new cabinet, the triumphant Mussolini gradually transformed the government into a fascist dictatorship.

Before the coup, Lizzie noted that the Italians had been uneasy under the spreading Russian influence. Because of Communist propaganda, she wrote "A war hero dared not wear his medals on the street—troops were hissed, flags were torn down. In twenty-four hours Mussolini has changed that and restored order. Now everyone is delighted. The Italians think this is the most important thing since Garibaldi. The streets today are full of marching bands and it is a national fête. Every man in Italy is now a Fascist. I like Italians but they *are* monkeys.

Seated in her hotel in Rome, Lizzie was suddenly overcome with the memory of "that winter so long ago when you [Wilkinson] were with me here....I broke down entirely, Rome is so full of memories." She recalled their visit to the Spanish Steps, looking into the little walled garden and the little house where Wilkinson had stayed. "I drove up the Janiculum and remembered, in the face of that marvelous view, that you preferred Forty-Second Street. Do you remember that homesick wail?" As she left Rome, she told him, "I hate to leave it now or *ever*."

By June 1923, Martha Cameron had been dead for five years. Her husband Ronald Lindsay was about to be named His Majesty's representative to Constantinople, which would lead to his appointment as British ambassador to Turkey. In this post he needed a hostess, and Lizzie, with her usual adroitness, arranged a match between him and her niece Elizabeth Hoyt. Of this marriage between the 38-year-old Elizabeth and the 46-year-old Ronnie there was no talk of romance, only convenience, as Lizzie announced to Wilkinson on 23 June, "Elizabeth Hoyt and my son-in-law are to be married very shortly here at Stepleton in the chapel." The bridegroom would leave for his new post after the ceremony, and his bride would not join him until fall, meanwhile buying new clothes "for her grand new position which she must learn to live up to." But Lizzie had her doubts about this, for Elizabeth, "who has always been as free as a lance, will feel the restriction of conventions." So it would prove, for the lively spinster, who had developed a career as a landscape gardener, would find it impossible to adjust to the conditions of a marriage of convenience.

Despite her own bitter experience of an arranged marriage, Lizzie had undertaken to arrange this one. Her feelings were ambivalent. She was very fond of this niece, and she could not contemplate the loss of Lindsay. Yet she recognized that this marriage might suggest a betrayal of Martha's memory. To Wilkinson she described the wedding in July 1923. "It was simple to a degree. The two, in country clothes, walked down the garden path to the chapel and came out united. . . . Only the necessary witnesses [Lizzie and the gardener] were there. Martha's marble eyes looked down upon them as they stood at the altar. Then they jumped into Elizabeth's car and went on a picnic! I borrowed a country house for them to honeymoon, and now they are home again. That's all."

But then she revealed her true feelings to Wilkinson.

> Ronnie was the best of husbands to a living wife but like many of his sex he has no use for a dead one. I got Martha's tombstone up just in time! I am going to Kodak it and send it to you. I think you will approve. It is low and like a shrine under a thick clump of yew trees. It is done by a very good architect and is *almost successful.* . . . I ought to be writing of the living and not of the dead. There isn't much to say except to beg you to believe that Martha's mother cannot harbor a mean or petty thought. Martha loved Elizabeth and she gave her everything she could. Now she has given her house, her husband and her name. There is nothing more. I shall have two children to love—we three were the points of a triangle. Now we are a circle. There is nothing I can do beyond keeping a home for them.

From Edith Wharton came a letter offering "all my understanding, sympathy, yes, and congratulations." Mary Berenson, learning of the nuptials, wrote to B.B., "I wonder how Lizzie Cameron feels about that marriage. As wrongheadedly as possible, I daresay, but she seems to be trying to behave decently."

To her nephew Sherman, Lizzie announced triumphantly, "I have bought Stepleton!" She explained that she had given the house to Lindsay with a life tenancy for herself so that he might avoid death duties. After long negotiations, "it is finally done and Martha is safe for our two lifetimes which is all that I can do. But we are paupers for life—there is everything on earth to do to it in the way of structural repairs. We are ruined."

The structural repairs were considerable. The 18th-century Georgian mansion had to be wired for electricity, and as Lizzie observed ruefully, "the dark corners and stairs are no more. But the picturesqueness of the bedtime procession with candles is gone." The heavy stone roof had to be redone after bricks fell from the chimney through the skylight. "Ronnie and I move from one room to another pursued by masons." New bathrooms had to be installed, but the water supply had long been inadequate. Lizzie found that her son-in-law did not share her ideas of modernizing the property. "Ronnie is having great fun," she told Wilks, "but I am in consternation. The truth is that England is static. She is like a clock that has been stopped—at about 1830. Everything he is doing or wants to do is of that period. I murmured something about an artesian well but was snubbed. Julius Caesar never had an artesian well, so why should we?" So, over her objections, a new well was dug, "at great expense, within 10 feet of the old one which gives out every dry summer!" Most urgent, Lizzie felt, was the installation of central heating to replace the great wood- and coal-burning fireplaces which did not protect against the cold of centuries. "This is the only modern idea Ronnie has been willing to adopt."

"A Great Lady"

Amid the domestic chaos, "with the roof off in sections, the floors up in open chasms for water pipes and electric wires, the carpets rolled up in great sausages," the gardener and his little boy caught pneumonia. "They are very near my heart," Lizzie told Wilks, "for they belonged to Martha and the boy was born here." Although they lived in a tiny cottage half a mile away, Lizzie arranged for round-the-clock nursing, as well as for hot meals to be carried from the big house. "The little boy was very ill, having developed pericarditis. His heart was kept beating artificially for 48 hours. It was a very anxious time, for they have become a part of my family." Eventually, the crisis passed, and the boy and his father recovered.

Springtime at Stepleton found Lizzie strolling through the woods, delightedly noting, "The woods are fairly paved with primroses and sweet-scented violets and now the bluebells are making their deep blue lakes all over the woods. They grow in immense patches so at a distance they really look like water."

Lindsay was named ambassador to Turkey in February 1924, and in the absence of his wife Lizzie took on the task of assembling the enormous amount of household equipment for his official residence, "which ranged from high class servants to saucepans and dishcloths, with all the intermediates of china, glass, blankets, linens and liveries." When she finally reached Constantinople, Elizabeth Lindsay described their residence as "about the size of the Cleveland Museum of Art." Before going to Turkey, the Lindsays had been briefed in a cardinal rule of diplomatic behavior, "Be polite to everyone but friendly with no one."

On 1 January 1925, Lindsay was knighted for his services to the Crown. "It takes effect tonight at midnight," Elizabeth Lindsay wrote. "From then on we become the Honorable Sir Ronald Lindsay K.C.M.G. and the Honorable Lady Lindsay. There aren't many women who change their names twice in six months." When Lindsay in full regalia presented his credentials at the diplomatic ceremony, his irreverent wife described him as "looking like a cross between a Christmas tree and a provincial mayor of London."

Although Lizzie and Wilkinson corresponded regularly they had not seen each other in some time. When Wilkinson at 54 expressed his concern at the physical changes that Lizzie might find in him, she retorted "Do you think, by any chance, that the years which have passed over you have left me untouched? I am an old woman, grey haired and worn. My only consolation is that you and I did not love each other for our personal beauty. I prefer to think our souls are still young and unchanged."

In the summer of 1924 Lizzie had fallen ill at Stepleton. "The summer or lack of it broke me. It was like living in an aquarium. I collapsed with my old heart trouble and went to pieces. I thought force of will would get me through the emotional strain but it didn't." Since Lindsay and his wife were due to return to Constantinople, they had to leave Lizzie in bed. "Eventually," she wrote, "I crawled as far as Paris where I spent more days in bed getting enough strength to crawl further on in search of one day of sun." Her search led her to

I Tatti, where the Berensons had offered her their villa at Settignano in which to convalesce. "It is a treasure house of beauty and books," she wrote to Wilks. "I am quite alone. I lie on a sunny terrace all day grilling in real sun—not a pale watery gleam—with a little green lizard for companion and peace sits with me." In her next letter to Wilkinson, she wrote, "You say you cannot understand the *meaning* of pain. Is there one? I don't think so. Something goes wrong with our machinery and we try to remedy it, but there is no *meaning* in the sense of *intention*. How can a good God inflict pain with intention? When Martha suffered so horribly I went over and over it. But I could not find a meaning."

Returning to Stepleton from I Tatti, Lizzie was touched to see that Lindsay, knowing how desolate she would be without a pet since her dog Peter had died, had found for her a little Cairn terrier with which she fell in love. "He is a darling little thing with a wise, anxious little hairy face like Thomas Carlyle."

Now that she was coming to terms with her own loss, Lizzie sent some hard-won advice to Cecilia Reber: "The trouble is that the boys have gone into manhood and you miss them. You miss being needed and wanted. Well, my dear, the play goes on but your role is finished. Your stay in the flies or better perhaps, a seat in the orchestra, where you can applaud when they play their parts well. I don't say it is cheerful but it is inevitable. . . . We all long for our children until it hurts. *But yours are still living*."

In the absence of Adams, she turned often to Wilks, with whom she could be both serious and bantering. Learning that he had the flu, she wrote, "It is like those little medieval devils imaginative people believed in, who sprang out in unexpected places and seized you. It is a form of the powers of Evil. I think, *au fond*, I am a Manichean in spite of theology and Saint Augustine." When he sent her some books by Willa Cather, she wrote, "I enjoyed them thoroughly. I do wonder who she is—what nationality? The name is not American but writers' names never count. They just take any one they happen to like."

Proud of her Sherman heritage, and never relinquishing her American citizenship, she told Wilks, "When I am contemplative, I see the long line of ancestors in bleak New England and wonder how it happens I am back in the old land in a green moist valley where no granite rocks harden my character and resistance."

After two years in Constantinople, Ronald Lindsay was named British ambassador to Germany. With his wife, he reported to Berlin, where "they were not enchanted with the ugliness and vulgarity of the embassy." Already, like Martha, Elizabeth Lindsay was complaining of chronic ill health, and Lizzie exclaimed, "I am sorry for Ronnie—two delicate wives are more than he is entitled to!"

Within two years, Lindsay had a new assignment more to his liking: undersecretary of state and chief of the Foreign Office in London, a prestigious post that would make good use of his diplomatic talents and experience. On his return to Stepleton, Lizzie reported, "Ronnie is as happy as a boy to be home again. He is a delightful companion and we talk politics as hard as I used to 40 years ago. We have been about together a great deal and are very gay. People include me in the invitations which pour in and I accept them."

In October 1930, perhaps with a premonition of misfortune, Lizzie wrote to Wilks: "Those whom the Gods love die young. Are only the mentally deficient and the unfit to carry on the race? Every village has its idiot—it is traditional. But Joe [Stickney] and Martha and Patsy are swept away as if to give place to more morons or idiots." A year later Henry Wilkinson was dead.

Always a voracious reader, Lizzie had been delighted to receive the first of two volumes of *The Letters of Henry Adams* from the editor Worthington C. Ford. "The volume has just come," she wrote to him. "It was unannounced and unexpected. You can imagine how I feel about it. I see by the dates 1858-1891 that I am about to have the joy of reading much of those early years about which I know so little." With a historical perceptiveness that she had developed during her years with Adams, she declared, "For all his self-effacement and modesty, Henry Adams now stands out as one of the great men of his age. Perhaps the greatest of a very remarkable family. His posthumous reputation is largely due to you who have given the world *The Education* and now these letters."

Lizzie, who had once held court over her middle-aged gallants in Lafayette Square, now captivated a new generation of young men who felt no sense of their difference in age from "Lady Cameron." Although she was in her seventies, she displayed the physical and intellectual vigor of a woman in her fifties. When Sam Reber brought down three young men from London, she reported happily, "So now I am enthroned with four men all to myself." And when a contingent of five boys from Groton came to visit, she exclaimed, "They were no trouble at all, only a pleasure. I suppose it is a sign of age that I like youth so much." For their entertainment she hired a "tin Lizzie" so they could visit Oxford and Cambridge.

Among those who still remember her vividly is John Adams Abbott, a Boston psychiatrist who is very much an Adams in appearance. He recalls hearing his Aunt Elsie Adams tell him that Uncle Henry once rebuked Lizzie Cameron for her flirtations "but she only laughed." During a visit to Stepleton, Abbott encountered Lady Lindsay whose wit he found too caustic and for whom he developed an instant dislike, which he quickly realized was mutual. But he responded at once to Lizzie's charm, and as he watched the warmth and ease which the otherwise undemonstrative Ronald Lindsay displayed toward her, he speculated that, as in a novel of Henry James, Lindsay may have been more than a little in love with his mother-in-law.

One of Lizzie's conquests was the writer J. Burke Wilkinson, the son of her dear Wilks. In 1935, young Wilkinson, who was just out of Harvard, came to England on a graduate fellowship at Cambridge. His father, who died in 1931, had told him about Lizzie Cameron, whom he affectionately called "Lady Cameron." But he did not know what to expect. As he drove up the road to her Georgian mansion, he suddenly caught sight of her standing on the steps, her head thrown back, her arms outstretched and held slightly backward, looking for all the world like the Angel of Victory by Saint-Gaudens. She called out to him, "Burke, welcome to your English home." He visited her often after that on weekends, and sometimes they bicycled around the lanes of Dorset. "She had so much charm — you could drown in it."

George C. Homans, Abigail Adams Homans's son, who is a professor of sociology at Harvard, was spending a summer in research at the British Museum in London. At Lizzie's invitation, he spent nearly every weekend at Stepleton. After breakfasting in bed, his hostess spent from 9:30 to 11:30 A.M. in writing letters on her portable writing table. After luncheon, she would summon Bee, the chauffeur, to drive them about the Dorset countryside, where they stopped for tea at various country homes "where she was warmly received." Homans, a lover of the novels of Anthony Trollope, found one occasion to be "just like the Ullathornes' party." When the young man, with American brashness asked a proper old lady who happened to be a countess, "What do you do?" he noticed a stunned silence. But Lizzie quickly covered his gaffe and made no later rebuke. Since she and her guests always dressed for dinner, she sent the butler (the same Bee who acted as chauffeur) to Homans's room to take away his trousers for pressing. "Since it was my only pair of pants I could not go out." After dinner, Mrs. Cameron would talk animatedly of politics and literature while Lindsay said nothing. "She advised me to read the poems of Bay Lodge but she never spoke of Uncle Henry." Homans found her gracious in manner, but with "a vein of iron beneath the surface."

After two years in London, Lindsay was appointed ambassador to Washington, a coveted diplomatic post but one that required consummate tact, patience, and a capacity for interpreting conflicting opinions to two kindred but often dissimilar nations.

Before the Lindsays' departure for Washington, Lizzie had planned a hunters' meet at Stepleton, which Lizzie considered "a historical event" for there had been none since Peter Beckford's day and he died in 1810. Beckford, an early squire of Stepleton, was a country gentleman who was a dilettante before he was a hunting man. As the editor of *Thoughts on Hunting* observed, "He would bag a fox in Greek, find a hare in Latin and direct the economy of his stables in exquisite French.... Never had fox or hare the honour of being chased to death by so accomplished a huntsman." The 18th-century squire of Stepleton is buried, like Martha, in the garden adjoining the chapel. A large crowd of spectators from the country homes of Dorset, as well as a collection of horsemen, attended, and Lizzie described the scene: "The hounds and the pink coats were so pretty on the green turf. I had stirrup cups for them and a table with supplies set against the front of the house. Bee and two little maids passed trays among the horsemen and the crowd of spectators with sandwiches, glasses of port, sherry and brandy." For the grooms and chauffeurs there was bread, cheese, and beer.

By the early 1930s, Lizzie was again visiting France. "Paris—Paradis!" she used to call it. At the age of 74, she resumed her study of French, saying, "It is ridiculous at my time of life but I am so ashamed of the patois I speak."

Stepleton

Elizabeth Cameron and Ronald Lindsay at Stepleton

The French war hero Marshal Joseph Jacques Joffre, whom she remembered as the commander at the decisive Battle of the Marne in World War I, had just died, and Lizzie, seated on a balcony at the Hotel Crillon, "like a box at the opera," watched the funeral. "The French do these things well," she wrote. They demolished the lampposts all the way from the Arc de Triomphe to Notre Dame to create a clear wide space for the parade. "It was cold and misty and the horizon-blue of the uniforms melted into the mist just as the inventor of that particular tone intended. I could see how invisible the troops must be in the countryside." As the procession advanced, she watched the English guards "in scarlet with black tall busbees, the Lord Mayor of London with the mace of office and the escort of Beefeaters and two cardinal archbishops in violet with their long trains carried by attendants. All their priests were in full canonicals of color. The lead horse and the caisson covered with the French flag were moving. Muffled drums and an occasional clarion strain were all the music I heard—then at the door of Notre Dame, Chopin's Funeral March."

In 1932, the Lindsays had a six-weeks' leave with Lizzie at Stepleton. "Ronnie was delighted," and Lizzie observed with satisfaction that "he and Elizabeth are on cordial even affectionate terms. She is happy in this quiet spot and you know how he loves it. She is interested in questions which absorb him and her ability and robust common sense are of real help to him." But under the seeming harmony of the pair lurked Elizabeth's chronic discontent, which she expressed later in a privately published book, complaining, "In this remote and quiet spot the news comes through in the worst and most round-about driblets, especially on week-ends. There are no papers, no post and no telegrams from Saturday mid-day through Monday morning. In the servants' hall last night we heard the radio announcement of the nomination of Franklin D. Roosevelt."

In April 1932, Lizzie had paid an overnight visit to Edith Wharton in her vacation home, Château Sainte-Claire, at Hyères. Once a convent for nuns of the Order of St. Claire, it looked down over the rooftops to the blue waters of the Mediterranean. The two septuagenarians greeted each other warmly— Lizzie was now 75 and Mrs. Wharton, at work on her autobiography, was 70. Both women expressed horror at the kidnapping in March of the baby son of Charles and Anne Morrow Lindbergh. "The arm of the law is paralyzed," wrote Lizzie. "A veritable army of police detectives and municipal authorities haven't found the criminals.... Those poor parents. It is better to be poor and keep one's babes than to be a national hero whom the nation itself cannot protect."

As rumblings of widespread discontent grew louder in Europe and America, she remarked, "The United States, Italy and Germany reiterate the same old inchoate aspirations and no one gets anywhere. As Dordy used to say, 'It is impossible to underestimate human intelligence.' The talk goes on while the world crumbles and we shall all go down in ruins."

Yet at 77 she still responded to beauty, still looked forward to tomorrow. One evening as she wandered in the garden, examining each shoot and tendril, "suddenly I saw the yellow rose of my childhood. I fell on my knees to put my nose into its fragrance."

As she grew older, Lizzie achieved a greater serenity. Although she never "got over" Martha's death, she had fewer outbursts of bitterness, and when her niece Cecilia continued to lament the departure of her grown sons, she wrote to her sternly, "To everyone on earth there comes a psychological moment when the process of readjustment must be made. It is often bitterly hard and nature is apt to bring the crisis at an age when we are less flexible. . . . But one must accept loneliness and even learn, in one sense, to like it. One must *make* a life if one is to keep one's self-respect."

In August 1937, she received word that Edith Wharton had died. "I am shattered by her death," wrote Lizzie. "I am more and more like Holmes's *Last Leaf*" (a popular poem by the poet Oliver Wendell Holmes).

From her familiarity with Henry Adams's ideas on the subject of women, Lizzie was alert to the changing role of women in the period between the two World Wars. To Charles Bosanquet in Northumberland, she wrote, "Whether or not we like it, the situation of the sexes is changing. In America the dominant sex is female. In France it always was. In England women are becoming increasingly vocal. By the time your three little maidens are grown, the government and ministers may be feminine and may be protected by law — or chivalry — from the tyranny of power. Tell Barbara to educate one to be the Chancellor of the Exchequer. We shall never see national economy until women exercise it." Yet she deplored the loss of femininity in the young women she met in London. "Modern life and competition are making women as hard as crabs. In the hotel here [the Berkeley] and in the streets I see my female compatriots with square jaws and hard eyes — and uncommonly vulgar they are too." She believed that "men are more selfish than women partly from the attitude of being lords of creation from infancy and partly from a lack of imagination or more properly speaking a lack of sensitiveness? or of antennae?" With her stern New England outlook on sexual mores, she was quick to condemn a new novel, *The Proposal*, by Gioia Grant Richards, the daughter of Elisina Tyler and her first husband. "You are kind in calling it mediocre," she wrote to Bosanquet. "It may be her commentary on life but how can she—delicate, dainty, and clever, know anything about such filth and moral squalor? It makes me sick when people tell us that, in writing, the author's unconscious is uncovered. Anyway, I have not allowed it on a downstairs table." When she heard that some young American girls were allowed by their parents to "bat about alone" in London, she said, in exasperation, "They have taken a flat in a short street inhabited by another class of ladies—professionals. It is a bad address to have and to give. But how could they know?"

Although Lindsay's term in Washington was nearly up, the Foreign Office asked him to remain until December 1938. Lizzie wrote, "If war doesn't break out, Ronnie is due to retire. He wants to come to England to visit, then back to the U.S. to pack. It seems silly, but it is his idea." But as war tensions mounted on both sides of the Atlantic, diplomats had to remain at their posts.

"Poor Ronnie," she sighed. "There is small chance of his coming home now. His nerves are frayed too."

As Hitler's drive for conquest and his persecution of the Jews intensified, Lizzie observed, "The machine has killed its inventor just as Mr. Adams said it would. Hitler has banned the Old Testament because it is Jewish. Some moderates contend that Jesus Christ was born in Austria so he need not be banished. Unbelievable." Caught up in the general desolation, she wrote, "It is the darkness in November and December which reduces me to despair."

Ronald Lindsay finally retired from his Washington post. "I will be glad to get back to Stepleton and to Dilly," he wrote before his departure, "and I hope to be in time to see her through." He sailed for England on 30 August 1939 and arrived in England just as his country was declaring war on Germany.

At Stepleton, Lizzie at 82 was readying her household to meet a war emergency. Seven American friends were stranded in England without shelter or food, and a contingent of British army officers and 70 enlisted men needed temporary billeting. Graciously, she agreed and, summoning her old powers of organization, she ordered bedrooms prepared in the empty wings, sofas pulled out, mattresses laid on floors. She shut herself up in the panelled drawing room with the officers to map out plans—the men would sleep in any unused bedrooms, the stable, and the attics. She would provide water and sanitary arrangements, as well as a place for the military lorries and bomb shelters and sandbags in the cellar. Above all, she would provide a complete blackout of the 64 windows of the great house. To feed the seven Americans, she resorted to dairy products, "Eggs were plentiful as 11 mouths yawned." The military provided their own rations and soon the Americans departed.

On his arrival, Lindsay was astonished to see what Dilly and the servants had accomplished. "It was a hectic week," she admitted, "for we had to cover the 64 windows with scraps of chintz, chair covers, 'old anything' all lined and interlined with black. We worked day and night cleaning rooms, glueing paper on shutters and doors. But I couldn't manage the skylight," she confessed. "We moved furniture until our backs were broken." Proudly she wrote, "I pat myself on the back and say, 'We Shermans give orders'." The next morning, 3 September, the day on which war was officially declared, was a "lovely sunny morning in which war seemed inconceivable."

As the war continued, she treasured the visits of Sam Reber, who was stationed in Geneva. When he had to leave Stepleton, she clung to him as if she would never let him go. To his mother, she wrote, "I am sad, sad. Simmy sailed last night and I feel bereft. I don't know when I shall ever see him again. I have reached the age when all goodbyes may be eternal ones." But she remained undaunted by the assaults of age or the perils of war. In the spring of 1940, she went up to the Berkeley Hotel in London for a few days "because the chimney sweep has swept me out with the soot. After a severe winter, seven chimneys need to be swept and seven rooms to be 'spring cleaned' after his work is done. Spring cleaning in England is a serious and solemn ritual and I suspect I am looked upon as a heathen because I shorten it."

"A Great Lady"

Lizzie was still remembered in America. In January 1941, Mabel Hooper La Farge, Clover's niece, wrote to Wilbur L. Cross, editor of the *Yale Review* and former Democratic governor of Connecticut,

> My dear old friend Aileen Tone comes for the Washington birthday weekend. I want you to come out for lunch on that Sunday. Aileen is and was beautiful and Uncle Henry loved beautiful ladies, I grant you, but she *sang* him into heaven so there is a double loveliness there. You think we nieces were hood-winked? He was a childless man with a passion for children and my sisters and I had lost our mother very young and our trinity of fathers — Henry Adams, our own father and cousin Sturgis Bigelow brought us up and educated us and we adored him and confided in him from the earliest days. But, I grant you, I was nervous about his ladies of the world, "bloodsucker" as Henry James called one of them.

For Lizzie's 84th birthday in 1941, a family party was arranged, and she was "touched" by the remembrance. "There is a long interim when one prefers to ignore birthdays," she wrote, "then when you successfully round the corner of fourscore, you begin to be proud of each milestone on the road which you can manage to pass valiantly with a straight back and and a clear eye."

Although the war meant the virtual disappearance of servants from the great country houses, Lizzie managed to hold her staff, who remained loyal to their mistress. Since she insisted on maintaining the tea-time ritual, it fell to Lindsay to arrange it. She watched with amusement as her tall, imposing son-in-law, who was used to staffs of servants in his diplomatic posts, "with perfect method carries in the tea table, spreads the cloth, fetches the kettle and food, then takes it out again to the pantry, straightens the chairs, draws the curtains and does the whole blackout. He is housebroken in this servantless land."

Lizzie chortled with approval when she read that Londoners, who had stoically endured fuel shortages, cuts in electricity and gas, bus and cab service and shortages of food, rebelled at the government ban on trains carrying flowers from Cornwall to the capital. "Such an outcry followed that they had to lift the ban. They *must have flowers.*"

In January 1942, Ronald Lindsay was writing to Sherman Miles, "Your aunt's main grievance is boredom. We see few people and are out of the swim. But her spirit is as ardent as 60 years ago." Lizzie was always eager for news of the world, and when the German army invaded Italy she wrote, "The Huns will once again sack Rome. It is Attila in a tank—not on horseback." Recalling the words of her Uncle Cump, she added, "'War is hell' in more ways than one."

When an epidemic of flu broke out in the village, she wrote anxiously, "May this house be spared! How could we carry on?" But she did contract the illness, and Lindsay took over her letter writing until she was better. To Sam Reber she explained, "I indulged in the orgy of the flu. The orgy? The frenzy."

Charles and Barbara Bosanquet drove down from Northumberland to visit her. After a long, intimate chat, they rose to go. She turned to them, Mrs. Bosanquet recalls, with her face transfigured, and speaking with a kind of exaltation, said, "Always remember, God is love!"; then putting an arm about each of them, she whispered, "Cherish one another."

German bombers were ravaging London in June 1943, but the Dorset countryside was, Lindsay wrote, "fairly safe."

> Last week the Germans dropped four "bad shots" on a train pulling out of the railroad station at Somerset and Dorset, enough to make the whole country laugh. It gives me and Dilly a fairly philosophical outlook on the present. Half the house is solid masonry a yard thick and the other half is lathe and plaster that will burn like tinder. Your aunt is very well but I fear the winter. We have all the supplies of fuel we can hope for. But our heating apparatus has gone wrong and it is mighty difficult to fix.

As Thanksgiving neared, Lindsay wrote to Sherman Miles, "Dilly is astonishingly well and vigorous, never smokes now. So long as we all keep well, but old age is our enemy for the average age is 60 and if one of us collapses the Lord knows how we shall carry on. The maids are heroic and hold out but sometimes I wish Mrs. Cameron would allow for more simplifications of life."

On a dark November day in 1943, Lizzie and Lindsay attended the funeral of a neighbor. They were appalled at the sight of "all the men of the district stalking around in black coats and top hats like so many ridiculous crows." Lizzie seized the moment to extract a promise from her son-in-law that when she died she would be cremated and that no one should be at the funeral.

In January 1944, while most of Europe continued to suffer the agony of the war, Lizzie Cameron was stricken with an attack of gastroenteritis, which she thought was another bout of influenza. But three doctors from London conferred at her bedside, and to Lindsay they diagnosed an intestinal obstruction, a cancer that was inoperable in a woman of 86. Lizzie, however, continued to believe she was suffering from the flu and was an obedient patient even when ordered to stay in bed and live on "a diet of slops."

After spending a month in bed, surrounded by every attention, she seemed a little stronger. When her grandnephew Lieutenant Sherman Hoyt, whose unit was stationed nearby, paid her a visit, she rallied and rejoiced in his pleasure, "for he remembers his visit here at the age of seven," she wrote; "he recalls every room, every bowl of lavender. He is tall and dark and slight and the servants are dizzy-wizzy about him.

"Ronnie went around whistling like a boy and rubbing his hands, trying to plan things for the boys whom he almost walked off their legs. He believes in entertaining any guest by making him climb the Hod or Hambledon [two neighboring hills]. Ronnie," she added, "is so fussy about me since the flu that I am scarcely allowed to see Sherman."

Meanwhile, Lindsay was reporting on her condition to her nephew Sherman Miles. "All the time her courage is high, her wits acute, her interests unfailing. If these things could pull the body through, she would live forever. I don't think she is really out of the woods as the pain might come along again but for the moment I am without anxiety. You should hear her whoops of joy when there was good news on the war."

In June, Lizzie was seized "with an access of energy" and, half carried by the faithful Emily Butler, "proceeded to tramp all over the house. But that is over now," Lindsay wrote, "for the doctor never sanctioned any sanguine hopes. Any complication is serious and there are several. She is almost always cheerful but often at the price of exertion. She does not want to go on living as she is—she has always most dreaded this. Old people like us have the right to go on living as long as nature will allow but I don't see why we should be denied the right to die when we wish it."

Lindsay took up the task of writing her letters when she was no longer able to. "With a heavy heart," he wrote to Sherman's wife Julie, "for the first time in all the months of failing strength she cannot write. She was weaker a fortnight ago but now she is peaceful and quiet, fairly comfortable and well looked after. She is now free of pain and always surrounded by masses of flowers." Lindsay explained that, from the beginning, the doctors freely prescribed narcotics by either pill or hypodermic. "She took them extremely well and indeed they often seemed to act like a tonic. She would have her narcotic when necessary and wake up the next morning as bright as a new penny." Complications developed — a mild stroke — and she was unable to move out of her bed unaided. Then her heart began to accelerate — "but it behaved very well," wrote Lindsay, "considering that 30 years ago we always considered her threatened with early death from a weak heart. Dropsy came along too and she hated that. She wouldn't let even a dear old friend come to see her because of her hands. She was very patient always, clear-headed except occasionally as a result of the drugs, always interested but undeniably bored." Once or twice, Lindsay tried to get a nurse but could not because of the war. But, as he knew, "Emily Butler would never have allowed her to do anything if we had got one." Lindsay went to bed one night, worried whether Lizzie would be alive in the morning. "And in the daytime there she was crowing with delight because the American Army had begun a great sweep still in its final progress."

But the disease continued its inexorable course, until in mid-August she sank into a coma. She died on 17 August 1944, still surrounded by masses of flowers. Faithful to his promise, Lindsay took her body to Bournemouth, 20 miles away, for cremation. "I must say it was all done with more decency and taste than I expected." Only Lindsay, the three maids, and Coombs the gardener were present for the simple last service and committal. "And we opened Martha's grave to a foot or two and put there all that remained of her mother."

At her death, *The New York Times* noted, "Mrs. Donald Cameron, famous Washington hostess of the Hay-Adams era, has died at her house Stepleton, near Blandford, Dorset, England. By birth she was a member of one of the great political and military families of the North in the generation that followed the Civil War and by marriage became a member of another."

The words that her son-in-law had written to Sherman Miles were a warmer tribute.

> It was 26 years ago that I promised Marthy always to look after her mother. It would never have occurred to her or to me that it could possibly go on for so long, for hers was a very precarious life; and 26 years later she puts up a struggle—not entirely wishing to—that

has left all the doctors in amaze. The interval has been a quiet life full of kindnesses and generosity and exciting the affectionate admiration of the remoter parts of this remote countryside. It comforts me that, by good luck, she was able to the very end, to live in a manner not unbecoming a great lady.

A year before the war was over, Lizzie's life ended—the life that she had called "reckless" and "wasted," and the mementos of which she had pledged Emily Butler to burn "so that we will be pretty effectively wiped out." But Henry Adams, some of whose writings owed much to her, knew better, when he had written to her in an outpouring of unrequited love, "As I grow older, I see that all the human interest and power that religion ever had was in the mother and child and I would have nothing to do with a church that did not offer them both. There you are again. You see how the thought always turns back to you."

Notes and Sources

All the quotations in this book are documented through letters, books, magazine articles, newspapers, and interviews, as well as through letters to the author.

Abbreviations: EC—Elizabeth Cameron; ES—Elizabeth Sherman; HA—Henry Adams

Locations of letters: Letters quoted in this book are reproduced by kind permission of the owners. All the correspondence between EC and HA is in the Massachusetts Historical Society, Boston. Letters from EC to Eliza Williams Sherman, Nelson Miles, Cecilia Reber, Samuel Reber, and Miles Sherman are in the possession of Julia Reber, Tyringham, Mass. Other Sherman family letters belong to Elizabeth Sherman Hughes, Cleveland, Ohio, and John Sherman, McLean,Va. Correspondence between EC and Henry W. Wilkinson belongs to J. Burke Wilkinson, Washington, D.C. Elisina Tyler's letter about the Orloff affair belongs to William Royall Tyler, director emeritus, Dumbarton Oaks, Washington, D.C. Letters to EC from 19th-century notables are in the Miles-Cameron Papers in the Manuscript Division, The Library of Congress, and in the Library of the National Gallery of Art, Washington, D.C.

Letters cited in the source notes for each chapter date from the chronological period covered by that chapter. Letters to the author, interviews, books, and magazine articles are arranged alphabetically by author; magazines and newspapers, alphabetically by title.

CHAPTER 1, "MY RECKLESS WASTED LIFE" (1915)
    Letters: EC to HA, December 1915, 1905; HA to EC, November and December 1915; EC to Cecilia Reber, January 1915, January 1916; EC to Henry W. Wilkinson, December 1915; Edith Wharton to EC, November 1915, December 1913; Henry James to Henrietta Reubell, 1901; Worthington C. Ford to EC, 1919; Elisina Tyler to Mrs. Pierce, 1929.
    Books: Henry Adams, *The Education of Henry Adams* (Boston: Houghton Mifflin, 1918); Gladys Rice Brooks, *Boston and Return* (New York: Atheneum, 1962); Kenneth Clark, *Another Part of the Wood* (New York: Harper & Row, 1974).
    Magazine: Margaret L. Woods, "An American War Charity in Paris," *Nineteenth Century,* August 1918.

CHAPTER 2, THE ARRANGED MARRIAGE (1877-78)

Letters: HA to Charles Milnes Gaskell; HA to Henry Cabot Lodge; HA to Charles Francis Adams; Marian Adams to Dr. Robert W. Hooper; Eliza Sherman to Mary Miles; Eliza Williams Sherman to ES; Mrs. William T. Sherman to Eliza Sherman; Cecilia Sherman to Eliza Williams Sherman; General William T. Sherman to ES; ES to Eliza Williams Sherman; ES to Mary Miles; ES to Colonel Nelson Miles; Simon Cameron; Henry James.

Letters to author: J. Gardner Bradley, Jr.; Mrs. J. Gardner Bradley, Sr.; Baroness Helena Lodge de Streel; Madame Paulette Howard-Johnston; Hon. Patrick Lindsay.

Interviews: Montgomery Sears Bradley; Cecilia McCallum Parker Bolin; Charles and Barbara Bosanquet; Edward Chalfant; Julia Reber; Samuel Reber; Alice Roosevelt Longworth; John Sherman; J. Burke Wilkinson; Elizabeth Sherman Hughes.

Books: Charles Francis Adams, 1835-1915, an Autobiography (Boston: Houghton Mifflin, 1916); Henry Adams, *Democracy* (New York: Holt, 1880); Erwin S. Bradley, *Simon Cameron: Lincoln's Secretary of War* (Philadelphia; University of Pennsylvania Press, 1966); Emily Edson Briggs, *The Olivia Letters* (Washington, D.C.: Neale, 1906); Frank G. Carpenter, *Carp's Washington* (New York: McGraw-Hill, 1960); Tyler Dennett, *John Hay* (New York: Dodd Mead, 1933); Constance M. Green, *Washington, Capital City* (Princeton, N.J.: Princeton University Press, 1963); Constance M. Green, *Washington Cavalcade* (New York: Dutton, 1948); Ona G. Jeffries, *In and Out of the White House* (New York: Funk, 1960); Virginia W. Johnson, *Unregimented General: A Life of Gen. Nelson Miles* (Boston: Houghton Mifflin, 1962); De B. Randolph Keim, *Handbook of Official and Social Etiquette* (Washington, D.C.: De B. Randolph Keim, 1884); James Laver, *Manners and Morals in an Age of Optimism* (New York: Harper and Row, 1966); Helen Nicolay, *Our Capital on the Potomac* (New York: Century, 1924); Julia Parsons, *Scattered Memories* (Boston: Humphries, 1938); Marianna G. Van Rensselaer, *The Social Ladder* (New York: Holt, 1924); Sherman Genealogy; Emile Zola, *Nana* (Paris, 1880).

CHAPTER 3, THE MEETING (1878-81)

Letters: EC to HA; HA to Marian Adams; HA to Charles Milnes Gaskell; Henry James to Grace Norton; William Walter Phelps; General William T. Sherman to EC; General William T. Sherman to Colonel Nelson Miles; Marian Adams to Dr. Robert W. Hooper; General William T. Sherman to George F. A. Healy; Simon Cameron to EC; Benjamin Brewster to Simon Cameron; General Nicholas Anderson to Larz Anderson.

Letter to author: J. Gardner Bradley, Jr.

Interview: Blair Clark.

Books: Charles Francis Adams, 1835-1915, an Autobiography (Boston: Houghton Mifflin, 1916); Marian Adams, *Letters of Mrs. Henry Adams, 1865-1883,* edited by Ward Thoron (Boston: Little Brown, 1936); Cecelia Beaux, *Background with Figures* (Boston: Houghton Mifflin, 1930); Frank G. Carpenter, *Carp's Washington* (New York: McGraw-Hill, 1960); Anna Farwell de Koven, *A Musician and His Wife* (New York: Harper, 1926); Joseph Durkin S.J., *General Sherman's Son* (New York: Farrar, Straus & Cudahy, 1959); Leon Edel, *Henry James: The Conquest of London, 1870-81* (Philadelphia: Lippincott, 1962); Maud Howe Elliott, *Three Generations* (Boston: Little Brown, 1923); Louise Hall Tharp, *Mrs. Jack* (Boston: Little Brown, 1965).

Newspapers: Cleveland *Leader*; New York *Tribune*; Philadelphia *Times.*

Notes

CHAPTER 4, THE EDUCATION OF ELIZABETH CAMERON (1881-84)

Letters: Marian Adams to Dr. Robert W. Hooper; Marian Adams to EC; Marian Adams to Henry James; HA to EC; HA to Charles Milnes Gaskell; HA to John Hay; HA to James Russell Lowell; EC to HA; EC to Eliza Williams Sherman; John Hay to HA; John La Farge to HA; Benjamin Brewster to Simon Cameron; Simon Cameron to Benjamin Brewster; Simon Cameron to J. Donald Cameron; Simon Cameron to EC; Mary Miles to EC. Henry James; Oliver Wendell Holmes; Henry Holt; Oscar Wilde; James McNeill Whistler.

Books: Henry Adams, *Democracy* (New York: Holt, 1880); Henry Adams, *Esther,* by Frances Snow Compton (New York: Holt, 1884); Henry Adams, *The Education of Henry Adams* (Boston: Houghton Mifflin, 1918); Susan Mary Alsop, *Lady Sackville: A Biography* (New York: Doubleday, 1978); Leon Edel, *Henry James: The Conquest of London, 1870-81* (Philadelphia: Lippincott, 1962); Abigail Adams Homans, *Education by Uncles* (Boston: Houghton Mifflin, 1966); H. Montgomery Hyde, *Oscar Wilde* (New York: Farrar, Straus & Giroux, 1975); L. B. Richardson, *William E. Chandler* (New York: Dodd, Mead, 1940).

Newspaper: Washington *Star.*

CHAPTER 5, PRINCE ORLOFF (1883-84)

Letters: James Russell Lowell to EC; Matthew Arnold to HA; HA to EC; Marian Adams to EC; Senator J. Donald Cameron to Simon Cameron; HA to John Hay; Marian Adams to Dr. Robert W. Hooper; Eliza Williams Sherman to Mary Miles; EC to Mary Miles; Elisina Tyler to Mrs. Hayforth Pierce, 1929.

Book: Cornelia Otis Skinner, *Elegant Wits and Grand Horizontals* (Boston: Houghton Mifflin, 1962).

Newspaper: Philadelphia *Press.*

CHAPTER 6, "POOR CLOVER'S SELF DESTRUCTION" (1884-85)

Letters: Marian Adams to Dr. Robert W. Hooper; Marian Adams to John and Clara Hay; Marian Adams to EC; Marian Adams to Ellen Gurney, 1884, 1885; HA to John Hay; HA to EC; Eliza Williams Sherman to Mary Miles; H. H. Richardson to HA; Ellen Gurney; Mrs. James Eliot Cabot.

Interview: Louis Auchincloss, 1979.

Books: Charles Francis Adams, 1835-1915, an Autobiography (Boston: Houghton Mifflin, 1916); James M. Goode, *Capital Losses* (Washington, D.C.: Smithsonian Institution Press, 1979); *Sixteenth Street Architecture,* Vol. 1 (Washington, D.C.: Commission of Fine Arts, 1978).

Magazines: Marc Friedlaender, "Henry Hobson Richardson, Henry Adams and John Hay," *Journal of the Society of Architectural Historians,* October 1970; Katherine Simonds, "The Tragedy of Mrs. Henry Adams," *New England Quarterly,* December 1936.

Newspapers: Boston *Evening Transcript;* New York *Sun;* New York *World;* Washington *Critic; The Washington Post.*

CHAPTER 7, MADONNA—LA DONA (1886-87)

Letters: HA to EC; HA to John Hay; John Hay to HA; Cecil Spring-Rice to John Hay; Cecil Spring-Rice to EC; Simon Cameron to EC; General William T. Sherman to EC; EC to Mary Sherman Miles; William Whitney to EC; Eliza Williams Sherman to Mary Miles; HA to Theodore Dwight; Abigail Adams Homans to Harold D. Cater, 1922.

Books: Tyler Dennett, *John Hay: From Poetry to Politics* (New York: Dodd Mead, 1933); Sylvia J. Morris, *Edith Kermit Roosevelt* (New York: Coward McCann Geoghegan, 1980).

For a description of Cameron house on Lafayette Square, now owned by the U.S. Judiciary, a personal tour by tour guides; also many individual visits; also an account in *The Washington Post* (undated).

CHAPTER 8, "LIKE A SAD SLAVE" (1887-89)

Letters: HA to EC; EC to HA; HA to John Hay; HA Diary, 6 May 1888; HA to Charles Milnes Gaskell; John La Farge to HA; HA to Martha Cameron; HA to Theodore Dwight; Theodore Dwight to HA; Frances Cleveland to EC; Eliza Williams Sherman to Mary Miles.

Book: Thurman Wilkins, *Clarence King* (New York: Macmillan, 1958).

CHAPTER 9, "IT ISN'T LIFE WITHOUT YOU" (1890-91)

Letters: HA to EC; EC to HA; HA to John Hay; HA to Charles Milnes Gaskell; HA to Rebecca Rae; HA to Anna Cabot Lodge; Theodore Roosevelt to EC; Eliza Williams Sherman to Mary Miles.

Books: *Charles Francis Adams, 1835-1915, Autobiography* (Boston: Houghton Mifflin, 1916); Consuelo Vanderbilt Balsan, *The Glitter and the Gold* (New York: Harper, 1952); Arthur Beringause, *Brooks Adams* (New York: Knopf, 1955); Thurman Wilkins, *Clarence King* (New York: Macmillan, 1958); W. E. Woodward, *Meet General Grant* (New York: Liveright, 1928), chapter on William T. Sherman.

CHAPTER 10, THE TAME CAT (1892-97)

Letters: HA to EC; HA to Charles Milnes Gaskell; HA to John Hay; EC to HA; John Hay to HA; Charles W. Eliot to HA; Clarence King to John Hay; EC to Mary Miles; HA to Charles W. Eliot; Aubrey Beardsley to EC; Charles Francis Adams.

Books: Lloyd Griscom, *Diplomatically Speaking* (Boston: Little Brown, 1940); H. Montgomery Hyde, *Oscar Wilde* (New York: Farrar, Straus & Giroux, 1975); Stanley Weintraub, *Aubrey Beardsley* (New York: Braziller, 1967).

CHAPTER 11, SURRENDEN DERING (1898)

Letters: EC to HA; HA to EC; HA to John Hay; EC to John Hay; HA to Charles Milnes Gaskell; Henry James to William Dean Howells; Oliver Wendell Holmes to Owen Wister; Henry James to Henrietta Reubell; John Hay.

Interview: Blair Clark.

Books: Abigail Adams Homans, *Education by Uncles* (Boston: Houghton Mifflin, 1966); Louise Hall Tharp, *Mrs. Jack* (Boston: Little Brown, 1965).

CHAPTER 12, "THE LADY AND THE POET" (1899-1901)

Letters: HA to John Hay; HA to EC; EC to HA; to Anna Cabot Lodge; HA to Brooks Adams; J. Donald Cameron to Henry Adams; Marian Adams to Robert W., Hooper; EC to Lucy Frelinghuysen; George Cabot Lodge to Anna Cabot Lodge; Trumbull Stickney to William Vaughn Moody; John Hay to EC; Trumbull Stickney and George Cabot Lodge to EC; Henri Hubert to George Cabot Lodge; Bernhard Berenson; Oscar Wilde; William Vaughn Moody; Margaret Chanler; Ronald Ferguson; HA to Mabel La Farge; HA to Louisa Hooper Thoron; Bernard Berenson to Ernest Samuels, 1957.

Books: Henry Adams, *Letters to a Niece and Prayer to the Virgin of Chartres,*

Notes

ed. by Mabel La Farge (Boston: Houghton Mifflin, 1920); Henry Adams, *Mont-Saint-Michel and Chartres* (Boston: Houghton Mifflin, 1913); Margaret Chanler, *Roman Spring* (Boston: Little Brown, 1934); Nigel Gosling, *The Adventurous World of Paris, 1900-1914* (New York: Morrow, 1978); Sean Haldane, *The Fright of Time: Joseph Trumbull Stickney, 1874-1904* (Quebec: Ladysmith, 1970); H. Montgomery Hyde, *Oscar Wilde* (New York: Farrar, Straus & Giroux, 1975); Philippe Jullian, *The Triumph of Art Nouveau: Paris Exposition, 1900* (London: Phaidon, 1974); Anita Leslie, *Rodin, Immortal Peasant* (New York: Prentice-Hall, 1937); Auguste Rodin, *Cathedrals of France* (Boston: Beacon, 1965); Raymond Rudorff, *The Belle Epoque: Paris in the Nineties* (New York: Saturday Review Press, 1972); Ernest Samuels, *Bernard Berenson: The Making of a Connoisseur* (Cambridge, Mass.: Harvard University Press, 1979); *The Poems of Trumbull Stickney*, ed. by George Cabot Lodge and William Vaughn Moody and J. E. Lodge (Boston: Houghton Mifflin, 1905); *The Poems of Trumbull Stickney*, selected and ed. by Amberys R. Whittle, foreword by Edmund Wilson (New York: Farrar, Straus & Giroux, 1966); *Homage to Trumbull Stickney*, ed. by James Reeves and Sean Haldane (London: Heinemann, 1968).

Magazines: Articles in *Harper's Bazaar, Harper's Magazine, Critic, Scientific American, Scribner's*, 1900.

CHAPTER 13, LIZZIE AND THE ARTISTS (1899-1902)

Letters: HA to EC; EC to HA; to Henry Higginson; HA to Louisa Hooper Thoron; John Hay to HA; John La Farge to EC; John Singer Sargent to EC; General William T.Sherman to EC, 1888; August Rodin to EC; EC to Cecilia Reber, 1944.

Interviews: John Sherman, Elizabeth Sherman Hughes, Julia Reber.

Books: Henry Adams, *Mont-Saint-Michel and Chartres* (Boston: Houghton Mifflin, 1913); Margaret Chanler, *Roman Spring* (Boston: Little Brown, 1934); Royal Cortissoz, *John La Farge: A Memoir and a Study* (Boston: Houghton Mifflin, 1911); Abigail Adams Homans, *Education by Uncles* (Boston: Houghton Mifflin, 1966); John La Farge, *One Hundred Masterpieces of Painting* (London: Hodder & Stoughton, 1912); John La Farge, *Reminiscences of the South Seas* (New York: Doubleday, 1912); John La Farge S.J., *The Manner Is Ordinary* (New York: Harcourt Brace, 1954); Anita Leslie, *Rodin, Immortal Peasant* (New York: Prentice-Hall, 1937); Charles Merrill Mount, *John Singer Sargent* (New York: Norton, 1955); Richard Ormond, *John Singer Sargent* (New York: Harper and Row, 1970); Auguste Rodin, *Cathedrals of France* (Boston: Beacon, 1965); *Reminiscences of Augustus Saint-Gaudens,* ed. by Homer Saint-Gaudens (New York: Century, 1913).

CHAPTER 14, "A 12TH-CENTURY MONK" (1899-1904)

Letters: HA to EC; HA to Martha Cameron; HA to John Hay; HA to Brooks Adams; HA to Henry Osborn Taylor; HA to Margaret Chanler; Margaret Chanler to HA; EC to HA; Henry James to HA; William James to HA; Augustus Saint-Gaudens to HA; John La Farge.

Interview: Laura Chanler White, 1976.

Books: Henry Adams, *Mont-Saint-Michel and Chartres* (Boston: Houghton Mifflin, 1913); Henry Adams, *The Education of Henry Adams* (Boston: Houghton Mifflin, 1918); Henry Adams, *Letters to a Niece and Prayer to the Virgin of Chartres,* ed. by Mabel La Farge (Boston: Houghton Mifflin, 1920); Gladys Rice Brooks, *Boston and Return* (New York: Atheneum, 1962); Shane Leslie, *American Wonderland* (London: Michael Joseph, 1938); Auguste Rodin, *Cathedrals of France* (Beacon, 1965); Eugene Emmanuel Viollet-le-Duc, *Discourses on Architecture (Boston: Osgood, 1875).*

CHAPTER 15, *LIZZIE AND MARTHA AND DON (1901-3)*
  Letters: EC to HA; HA to EC; Martha Cameron to Henry W. Wilkinson; HA to
John Hay; HA to Mabel La Farge.
  Letters to author: Blair Clark; J. Burke Wilkinson.
  Interviews: Blair Clark; members of the Sherman family; J. Burke Wilkinson.
  Book: Arthur Beringause, *Brooks Adams* (New York: Knopf, 1955).

CHAPTER 16, A HUSBAND FOR MARTHA (1904-9)
  Letters: HA to EC; EC to HA; Charlemagne Tower to EC; EC to Henry W.
Wilkinson; Henry W. Wilkinson to EC; HA to Martha Cameron; Ronald Lindsay to
HA; HA to Ronald Lindsay; HA to Mabel La Farge; Cecil Spring-Rice to EC; EC to
Ronald Lindsay; HA to Mrs. Jack Gardner.
  Interviews: J. Burke Wilkinson, 1979, 1980.
  Books: Larz Anderson, *Letters and Journals of a Diplomat* (London: Revell,
1940).
  Newspaper: The Washington Post, 19 March 1909.

CHAPTER 17, "THE ROMAN MATRON BUSINESS" (1909-12)
  Letters: HA to John Hay; HA to EC; HA to Martha Lindsay; EC to HA; EC to
Henry Sherman; HA to Bessie Lodge; HA to Margaret Chanler; HA to Anna Cabot
Lodge; HA to Mabel La Farge; John Hay (letters and extracts from Diary); Ronald
Lindsay to HA; HA to Charles Milnes Gaskell; Martha Lindsay to HA; Edith Wharton
to EC; Henry James to EC; Charles Francis Adams to EC; Charles Francis Adams to
Anna Cabot Lodge; Mary Adams Quincy to Charles Francis Adams; Dr. Yarrow to EC;
Henry James to EC; Bernhard Berenson to EC.
  Books: Consuelo Vanderbilt Balsan, *The Glitter and the Gold* (New York:
Harper, 1952); Bernard Berenson, *Sketch for a Self-Portrait* (New York: Pantheon,
1949); Gladys Rice Brooks, *Boston and Return* (New York: Atheneum, 1962);
Kenneth Clark, *Another Part of the Wood* (New York: Harper & Row, 1974); Anita
Leslie, *The Marlborough House Set* (New York: Doubleday, 1973); R. W. B. Lewis,
Edith Wharton (New York: Harper & Row, 1975); Elizabeth Sherman Lindsay, *The
Letters, 1911-1954,* ed. by Olivia James (New York: Marchbanks Press, 1960); V.
Sackville-West, *The Edwardians* (New York: Doubleday, 1930); Edith Wharton, *The
Decoration of Houses* (New York: Scribner, 1897).

CHAPTER 18, "DEATH KNOCKS AT EVERY DOOR BUT MINE" (1912-18)
  Letters: HA to EC; HA to Charles Milnes Gaskell; HA to Mabel La Farge; HA to
Ronald Lindsay; EC to HA; EC to Cecilia Reber; EC to Henry W. Wilkinson; EC to
Harriet Sherman; EC to Edith Wharton; EC to Ralph Curtis; EC to Sherman Miles;
Aileen Tone to Mabel La Farge; Martha Lindsay to Sherman Miles; Edith Wharton to
EC; William R. Thayer to EC; Lord George Curzon to EC; Bernard Berenson to EC;
Elizabeth Adams to EC.
  Interviews: Louis Auchincloss, 1976; Laura Chanler White, 1976.
  Books: R. D. Blackmur, *Henry Adams* (New York: Harcourt Brace Jovanovich,
1980); R. D. Blackmur, *A Primer of Ignorance* (New York: Harcourt Brace, 1967);
Gladys Rice Brooks, *Boston and Return* (New York: Atheneum, 1962); Harold Dean
Cater, *Henry Adams and His Friends* (Boston: Houghton Mifflin, 1947); Leon Edel,
Henry James: The Master, 1901-1916 (Philadelphia: Lippincott, 1972); Stephen
Gwynn, *Letters and Friendships of Sir Cecil Spring-Rice* (London: Constable, 1929);
John La Farge S. J., *The Manner Is Ordinary* (New York: Harcourt Brace, 1954); Paul

Notes

C. Nagel, *Descent from Glory: Four Generations of the John Adams Family* (New York: Oxford University Press, 1983); Ernest Samuels, *Henry Adams: The Major Phase* (Cambridge, Mass.: Harvard Universtiy Press, 1964); Sir Arthur Willet, *Washington and Other Memories* (Boston: Houghton Mifflin, 1972).

Magazine: Louis Auchincloss, "Never Leave Me, Never Leave Me," *American Heritage,* February 1970.

CHAPTER 19, "A GREAT LADY" (1918-44)

Letters: EC to Cecilia Reber; Ronald Lindsay to Elizabeth Hoyt; Edith Wharton to EC; Mary Berenson to Bernard Berenson; Elizabeth Hoyt to Sherman Miles; John Singer Sargent to EC; Lord Crawford to EC; William R. Thayer to EC; HA to Henry Cabot Lodge; Julia Parsons to EC; EC to Julia Parsons; Elizabeth Hoyt to EC; EC to Nelson Miles; EC to Sherman Miles; EC to Henry W. Wilkinson; EC to Samuel Reber; EC to Worthington C. Ford; Worthington C. Ford to EC; Brooks Adams to EC; EC to Charles Bosanquet; EC to Sherman Hoyt; Ronald Lindsay to Sherman Hoyt; Mabel La Farge to Wilbur L. Cross.

Letters to author: Mary Ogden Abbott; Harriette Barnes; Alfred O. Hoyt; Clement Kennedy; Henry Cabot Lodge; Nelson Miles; Nigel Nicolson; Baroness Helena Lodge de Streel.

Interviews: Dr. John Adams Abbott; Charles and Barbara Bosanquet; Blair Clark; Wilhelmina Sellers Harris; Abigail Adams Homans; George C. Homans; Elizabeth Sherman Hughes; R. W. B. Lewis; Alice Roosevelt Longworth; Julia Reber; Bayard Schieffelin; John Sherman; Louisa Hooper Thoron; William R. Tyler.

Book: Elizabeth Hoyt Lindsay, *The Letters, 1911-1954,* ed. by Olivia James (New York: Marchbanks Press, 1960).

Newspapers: The New York Times; Philadelphia *Public Ledger.*

$\mathcal{A}$cknowledgments

$\mathcal{D}$uring the writing of any biography, an author incurs innumerable debts of gratitude which can be acknowledged only with simple thanks and in a spirit of intellectual humility.

For their continuing encouragement and helpful insights during the course of my research, my special thanks are offered to J. Burke Wilkinson, author, Washington, D.C.; William Royall Tyler, director emeritus of Dumbarton Oaks, Washington, D.C.; Ernest Samuels, author of the definitive three-volume biography *Henry Adams,* and his wife Jayne Samuels, author and researcher, of Evanston, Ill.; Charles A. Vandersee, co-editor of the three-volume *Letters of Henry Adams.* University of Virginia, Charlottesville, Va.; and the Hon. Patrick Lindsay, picture director, Christie's, London.

The Sherman family, of which Lizzie Cameron was an illustrious member, have been most generous in supplying hundreds of her unpublished letters, family photographs, and personal reminiscences. Indefatigable in their efforts were John Sherman, McLean, Va.; Elizabeth Sherman Hughes, Cleveland, Ohio; Julia Reber, Tyringham, Mass.; and the late Samuel Reber, Princeton, N.J. Also helpful were the late General Nelson Miles, Cruz Bay, St. John, U.S.V.I.; Harriette S. Barnes, Chappaqua, N.Y.: Cecilia McCallum Parker Bolin, Washington, D.C.; Cecilia Sherman Parker Geyelin, Washington, D.C.; the late Alfred O. Hoyt, Princeton, N.J.; and Sherman Hoyt, Washington, Conn.

The Adams family have offered enthusiastic support and encouragement. Deserving of particular thanks are John Adams Abbott, M.D., Lincoln, Mass.; Mary Ogden Abbott, Concord, Mass.; Professor George C. Homans, Harvard University; the late Abigail Adams Homans and the late Louisa Hooper Thoron of Boston, Mass.

The Cameron family, in the absence of any official papers of Senator J. Donald Cameron, have supplied their personal reminiscences and access to the Miles-Cameron Papers at the Library of Congress and the National Gallery of Art, Washington, D.C. Most helpful of the Cameron descendants have been Blair Clark of New York City; Montgomery Sears Bradley of Washington, D.C.; Mrs. J. Gardner Bradley of Falmouth, Mass.; J. Gardner Bradley II of West Germany; and Cameron Bradley of Winter Harbor, Maine.

Among those who shared their vivid memories of Lizzie Cameron were Barbara and Charles Bosanquet, Alnick, Northumberland, England; Paulette Howard-Johnston, Paris; the Baroness Helena Lodge de Streel, Brussels; Senator Henry Cabot Lodge, Boston, Mass.; the late Alice Roosevelt Longworth, Washington, D.C.; the Hon. Patrick Lindsay, London; Wilhelmina Sellers Harris, Quincy, Mass.; Bayard Schieffelin, Short Hills, N.J.; and Laura Chanler White, St. James, N.Y.

Acknowledgments

Scholars and writers who have been most helpful include Susan Mary Alsop, Louis Auchincloss, Edward Chalfant, Otto Friedrich, Llewellyn Howland III, Eugenia Kaledin, Anita Leslie, R. W. B. Lewis, Michael R. T. Mahoney, Abigail McCarthy, George Monteiro, Paul C. Nagel, Nigel Nicolson, Phyllis Rose, Phyllis Theroux, and Stanley Weintraub.

Special research requiring patience and resourcefulness was performed by the late Clement Kennedy, Swampscott, Mass.; John B. Black, London; Olive B. Hebert, Cleveland, Ohio; Donald B. Pritchard, Philadelphia, Pa.; and my daughter Rita E. Tehan, Washington, D.C. Additional assistance was rendered by Richard D. Moore, Jr., and Jennifer Moore, West Hartford, Conn.; Susan McLaughlin, Washington, D.C.; Cynthia Tehan, New York City; Claire Ravizza, Redondo Beach, Calif.; and James Tehan, Santa Monica, Calif.

I received courteous help and knowledgeable insights from Stephen T. Riley, director emeritus, Massachusetts Historical Society, and Celeste Walker, The Adams Papers, Massachusetts Historical Society; John C. Broderick, Manuscript Division, Library of Congress; Jerome M. Edelstein, chief librarian, National Gallery of Art, Washington, D.C.; Martin Luther King Jr. Memorial Library, Washington, D.C.; Ruth Marshall and the late Veronica LeHaine, Boston Public Library; Kathleen S. Boyd, The Library of the Boston Athenaeum; the Harvard Archives; Houghton Library at Harvard University; Beinecke Library, Yale University; New York Public Library; Bibliothèque Nationale, Paris; Freiberger Library, Case Western Reserve University, Cleveland, Ohio; Alderman Library, University of Virginia, Charlottesville, Va.; George Washington University Library, Washington, D.C.; Butler Library, Columbia University, New York City; University of Toronto Library, Toronto, Ontario. Also special thanks to Lee McCallum, Trinity College Library, Hartford, Conn.; Katherine M. Hart and Joan Andresen, West Hartford Public Library, and John W. Teahan, Wadsworth Atheneum Library, Hartford, Conn. Thanks also to Joan Romig, Historical Society of Dauphin County, Harrisburg, Pa.; the Cleveland Historical Society; Elizabeth Miller, Columbia Historical Society, Washington, D.C.; the Connecticut State Library; John O. Hamilton, The Senate Historical Office, U.S. Senate; and James L. Yarnall, National Museum of Fine Arts, Smithsonian Institution, Washington, D.C.

Index

Index

Index